Tourism Policy and

The wellspring to the future global growth in tourism is a commitment toward good policy and strategic planning. Governments, the private-sector, international organizations, academic institutions, and not-for-profit agencies must be the leaders in developing sustainable tourism policies that transcend the economic benefits and embrace environmental and cultural interests as well. *Tourism Policy and Planning: Yesterday, today, and tomorrow* (second edition) offers a comprehensive look into the policy process and how policies link to the strategic planning function as well as influence planning at the local, national and international levels.

This second edition has been fully revised and updated with important new chapters and case studies that reflect the many important developments in the travel, tourism and hospitality industry and subsequent new policies and plans needed to better understand the nuances and issues in the travel, tourism and hospitality industry. The second edition features:

- Updates to reflect recent developments and issues ranging from global economic and cultural issues to concerns for increased national and local leadership in tourism policy and strategic planning.
- Three new chapters: "Barriers and obstacles to international travel", "The international tourism policy process", and "Transformative leadership, poverty alleviation and tourism policies".
- New case studies throughout the book to illustrate practical applications of policy and planning at the international, regional, national and local levels to provide a solid foundation for a better understanding of new travel and tourism concepts and issues.
- Examination of the past, present, and future of tourism policy development and strategic planning to equip professionals, academicians, and students to better understand the global tourism marketplace.

David L. Edgell, Sr. at East Carolina University is Professor of Trade, Tourism and Economic Development in the School of Hospitality Leadership and is a Research Scholar in the Center for Sustainable Tourism, and, in addition, a Charter Member of the International Academy for the Study of Tourism.

Jason R. Swanson is Assistant Professor of Hospitality Management and Tourism at the University of Kentucky and an Adjunct professor of Strategic Tourism Planning at Assumption University in Bangkok, Thailand.

Tourism Policy and Planning

Yesterday, today, and tomorrow

2nd edition

David L. Edgell Sr. and
Jason R. Swanson

Routledge
Taylor & Francis Group

LONDON AND NEW YORK

First published 2013
by Routledge
2 Park Square, Milton Park, Abingdon, Oxon OX14 4RN

Simultaneously published in the USA and Canada
by Routledge
711 Third Avenue, New York, NY 10017

Routledge is an imprint of the Taylor & Francis Group, an informa business

British Library Cataloguing in Publication Data
A catalogue record for this book is available from the British Library

Library of Congress Cataloging in Publication Data
Tourism policy and planning: yesterday, today and tomorrow/
    David L. Edgell Sr. . . . [et al.]. – 2nd ed.
    p. cm.
    Includes bibliographical references and index.
    1. Tourism – Planning.   2. Tourism – Government policy.
    I. Edgell, Sr. David L.
    G155.A1T5924325 2013
    338.4'791 – dc23
    2012036394

ISBN: 978-0-415-53452-9 (hbk)
ISBN: 978-0-415-53453-6 (pbk)
ISBN: 978-0-203-11333-2 (ebk)

Typeset in Helvetica Neue
by Florence Production Ltd, Stoodleigh, Devon

Printed and bound in Great Britain by
TJ International Ltd, Padstow, Cornwall

DEDICATION

This book is dedicated to the men and women who work in the international travel, tourism and hospitality industry; to the destinations and local communities which make tourism possible; to the transportation and communication industries that facilitate travel; to the faculty that teach in the travel, tourism and hospitality industry; and to all those who are studying for careers in the travel, tourism and hospitality industry.

and

David L. Edgell, Sr. special dedication: To my dear friend and father-in-law, J Carl Smith and memory of his lovely wife, Gertrude Smith

Jason R. Swanson special dedication: To my dear friend and wife, Dr. Ellen R. Swanson

Contents

Illustrations

Figures

Tables

Case studies

Preface

The travel and tourism industry is the largest and fastest growing industry in today's world in spite of economic complications, turbulence, poverty, cataclysms, and conflicts taking place in our global society. Ultimately, the highest purpose of tourism policy and planning is to integrate the economic, political, cultural, intellectual, and sustainability benefits of tourism cohesively with people, destinations, and countries in order to improve the local and global quality-of-life and provide a foundation for peace and prosperity. That is what the second edition of *Tourism Policy and Planning: Yesterday, today and tomorrow* is all about.

This book has been deliberately written in a proactive style aimed at providing essential and practical guidelines in tourism policy and planning that can be understood by readers at all levels of interest in the tourism industry. The aim of this publication is to provide government policymakers, university professors, business leaders, managers, students in the tourism industry, and the general public with an introduction and examination of important policy issues in tourism. It also takes into account valuable suggestions from colleagues regarding the first edition and responds to the dynamic changes taking place in global travel and tourism policy.

The first edition of *Tourism Policy and Planning: Yesterday, today and tomorrow* set the framework for a discussion of the need for clear-cut tourism policies and strategic planning concepts for the quality growth of the travel and tourism industry. This second edition of *Tourism Policy and Planning: Yesterday, today and tomorrow* is different from the first edition, in that it has been revised, altered, and updated with new exciting chapters, the omission of a prior chapter, and includes a fresh set of case studies geared to an international constituency.

We want to take this opportunity to thank our previous co-authors Dr. Mary Virginia "Ginger" Smith and Ms. Maria DelMastro Allen for their excellent work in the first edition. As a *Professor, Chair, and Dean*, Dr. Smith, a friend and colleague of many years, has generously contributed to improving undergraduate and graduate education in the field of travel, tourism, and hospitality. Her prior work in tourism policy in the Under Secretary of Commerce's Office in Washington, D.C., her contributions as founding Dean of the International School of Tourism and Hotel Management in Puerto Rico, and as Professor and Academic Chair of Graduate and Undergraduate Studies at New York University's Preston Robert Tisch Center for Hospitality, Tourism, and Sports Management, has had positive impacts on many different aspects of tourism policy, planning, research, and administration.

In addition, and a friend and colleague of many years, Ms. Maria DelMastro Allen provided excellent research assistance, manuscript writing and administrative support in producing the first edition of *Tourism Policy and Planning*. Her strong background in business, exceptional analytic skills, and capable managerial qualities led to a better and more meaningful book. Her efforts in furthering the knowledge base of tourism policy and planning at East Carolina University led to many new and innovative approaches in this important field of study.

This second edition of *Tourism Policy and Planning: Yesterday, today and tomorrow* accounts for the dynamic changes taking place in tourism policy and planning in the global travel and tourism industry. It recognizes that more effective policies and plans need to be developed in order to address tourism's role in world economic and social development within the context of a sustainable environment. The co-authors of this book recognize that contemporary tourism policy approaches require us to "think globally and act locally" in a responsible manner. The vital importance of community involvement in the tourism development process is stressed. Equivalent attention is given to the environmental and sociocultural impacts of tourism in proper perspective to the more tangible economic benefits and costs.

The co-authors of this book have a great deal of experience in the field of tourism policy and planning. The book frequently refers to the names of the co-authors because of their strong academic and practical background in all aspects of travel and tourism, but especially with respect to tourism policy, planning, and development. A short note of explanation about the authors is included.

David L. Edgell, Sr. has more than 35 years involvement at all levels, global, national and local, in the tourism policy and planning arena. He had a distinguished tourism policy career in the U.S. Government, serving at one point as the Under Secretary of Commerce for Travel and Tourism and as the U.S. head of delegation to the United Nations World Tourism Organization, the Caribbean Tourism Organization, and tourism committees of the Organization for Economic Cooperation and Development, the Organization of American States, and the Asia-Pacific Economic Council. Later he served in the capacity as the first Commissioner of Tourism in the U.S. Virgin Islands in which he provided leadership, management and administration for tourism development, marketing, policy, planning, budgeting, legislative relations, and investment. He also worked in senior executive positions within private-sector companies involved in travel and tourism and as a private consultant. Currently, Dr. Edgell is a full time professor of travel and tourism at East Carolina University, and as a highly recognized research scholar in sustainable tourism, an author of ten books and over 100 articles on tourism, trade, and economic development, an international consultant and frequent speaker at conferences.

Jason R. Swanson likewise works in the academic world on international travel, tourism and hospitality issues. In addition to being an Assistant Professor of Hospitality and Tourism Management at the University of Kentucky, Dr. Swanson also teaches at international universities, conducts important research related to tourism policy and planning and provides international consulting services. He has contributed continuously to policy and planning interests of the Southeast Tourism Society and to additional organizations.

Tourism Policy and Planning reviews the history of tourism which has led to a better understanding of tourism issues that face the world today. Current concepts in tourism policy and planning underscore the rich foundation of literature provided by an outstanding cadre of our travel and tourism scholar predecessors and contemporaries. By exploring the future of tourism in the context of tourism policy and planning yesterday and today, we hope to offer current and future strategies for a better understanding of tomorrow's world of travel and tourism.

You may note in this second edition numerous references to the book *Tourism: Principles, Practices, Philosophies* by Charles R. Goeldner and J.R. Brent Ritchie, now in its twelfth edition. The reason for the many citations is because it is the single best textbook written about fundamental tourism issues, practical guidelines for tourism development and well-researched tourism concepts. It is used by many in the tourism industry as a key reference document in order to better understand the broad trends in travel and tourism.

In addition, this book quotes substantial material from the United Nations World Tourism Organization (UNWTO). There are many reasons for such references. UNWTO is the global forum for tourism policy issues and provides leadership and practical sources of tourism information for its many members. It is vested by the United Nations in all matters of tourism policy and is a key organization working toward poverty alleviation, and peace through sustainable tourism.

Another frequent reference in the book is to "peace through tourism". The co-authors strongly advocate that tourism can help lead to a more peaceful world. The topic of peace from a tourism perspective is covered from many different angles in this book. The old adage "When Peace Prevails, Tourism Flourishes" has a strong truthful ring to it. The book mentions the work accomplished by the International Institute for Peace Through Tourism's efforts at mobilizing the travel and tourism industry as a leading force toward a more peaceful and sustainable world.

It should also be noted that some of the important precepts in tourism are frequently repeated in some of the chapters. This is done in order to highlight certain important concepts that lead to major policy initiatives or that are significant in the planning of tourism at both the local and global levels.

In summary, *Tourism Policy and Planning: Yesterday, today and tomorrow* (second edition) provides an understanding of the many ramifications of tourism in the world's productive society, of its powerful political-economic interactions, of its immense potential as an important social force-in effect, tourism's impact on the world and the world's impact on tourism. This publication, by looking at travel and tourism within the context of world society, business, economics and politics, suggests that a world populace which understands the intricacies of tourism relationships within our society will lead to a higher quality-of-life. International tourism, through effective policies and plans, has the potential to be one of the most important stimulants for global improvement in the social, cultural, economic, political, and ecological dimensions of future lifestyles.

Introduction

The aim of this chapter is to provide introductions to the topics of tourism policy and tourism planning from a global perspective. Tourism – a set of dynamic and growing industries – involves not just people traveling, but also planning and protecting the destinations and attractions to which people travel. Tourism is composed of private, public, and not-for-profit components interested in tourism development, new products, destination marketing, economic benefits, and future sustainability. These tourism interests have broad ramifications on community life and need parameters and guidelines to help define and plan the future direction of tourism policy, ultimately providing quality tourism products and services. Tourism policy should aim to improve the quality-of-life of the local citizenry at any given destination. Good tourism policy will assist in that process.

This book identifies some of the issues and concerns that tourism policy should address in order to ensure a positive sustainable future for tourism. This chapter provides brief introductions to three central concepts – tourism, tourism policy, and tourism planning. Setting a foundation for these concepts adds to the readers' understanding of subject matter covered throughout the book. The conceptual foundations in this chapter can also be a good reference for students or tourism professionals who are new to the study of tourism-related public policy.

Understanding tourism

In this book, the term "tourism" is used synonymously with all aspects of travel and tourism, unless otherwise specified. With respect to international tourism, this text uses the following definitions as recommended by the United Nations World Tourism Organization (UNWTO):

- **Visitor**: Any person visiting a country (or community) other than that in which the person usually resides, for any reason other than following an occupation remunerated from within the country visited. This definition covers two classes of visitors: *tourist* and *excursionist*.

    - **Tourist**: A temporary visitor staying at least 24 hours in the country (or community) visited, the purpose of whose journey can be classified under one of the following headings: (a) leisure, recreation, holiday, health, study, religion, or sport; or (b) business, family, mission, or meeting.
    - **Excursionist**: A temporary visitor staying less than 24 hours in the country (or community) visited (including travelers on cruises).

- **Tourism**: In terms of balance-of-trade, accounting is defined as travel and transportation and is determined a *business service* export *from* the tourism recipient *to* the tourism generating economy.

Tourism is inherently a complex field and difficult to define, resisting comparability within itself and with other industries. As an example, consider meals served in a restaurant, which is integral to the travel experience. Depending on the restaurant's location, tables could be filled by local residents or it could be filled with visitors. In reality, customers in most restaurants come from both groups at any given time. Local residents may even be entertaining out-of-town guests at the restaurant making it even more difficult to identify how much of the restaurant demand is tourism-related and how much is derived from community members. Depending on who pays the restaurant check, the revenue generated from the meals – and subsequent economic impact – may or may not be attributable to tourism.

Despite the complexities of tourism, discussed throughout the book, simple definitions of tourism exist. Tourism is the practice of traveling and also the business of providing associated products, services, and facilities. Tourism is not a single industry but instead an amalgam of industry sectors – a demand force and supply market, a personal experience, and complicated international phenomenon. Tourism incorporates social, cultural, and environmental concerns beyond physical development and marketing. It encompasses both supply and demand, more than the sum of marketing and economic development.

Tourism has strong links to cultural and social pursuits, foreign policy initiatives, economic development, environmental goals, and sustainable planning. Tourism includes the buying, selling, and management of services and products (to tourists) that might range from buying hotel rooms to selling souvenirs or managing an airline. To accomplish these complex activities, tourism demands the most creative and innovative managers because tourism represents collections of perishable products. For example, if hotel rooms, airline seats, cruise-ship cabins, or restaurant tables are not filled daily and repeatedly, the point-of-sale moments to generate revenues from these products are gone forever. There is no opportunity to put such unsold products on sale at a later time, in storage, or in inventory. This perishability distinguishes tourism from consumer goods, such as automobiles, sunglasses, or food sales in retail markets.

Tourism is also wide-ranging in the sense that it demands products from other sectors of the economy. For example, many economies' top agricultural exports include leaf tobacco, live animals and animal products, cotton, and forestry products that supply demand throughout the world. These products are also assistance goods used by tourism. Tourism is comprised of many business components including hotels, resorts, conventions, meetings, events, entertainment venues, attractions, amusement parks, shopping malls, music venues, festivals, parks, restaurants, theaters, museums, history, heritage, culture, and nature sites and more. It is a large and highly competitive sector of the economy at all levels: local, state/province, national, and international.

The full scope of domestic and international tourism, therefore, encompasses the output of segments of many industries. The travel industries consume the output of and create a far-reaching base of wealth for feeder industries such as agriculture, fishing, food processing, brewing, construction, airports, transportation vehicles, communications equipment, and furniture to name a few. In addition, tourist activities make use of the service of other industries, such as insurance, credit cards, advertising, database and niche marketing, the internet, and e-commerce tools. In order to plan for and provide rational order to such a diverse and dynamic set of industries, it is necessary to develop policies and plans to assist decision-makers in the management of this complex phenomenon – tourism.

Since the agricultural and industrial revolutions of the nineteenth century, we have measured the wealth of nations almost entirely on the development and exportation of tangible goods (agriculture and livestock, mining and manufacturing), on the construction of infrastructure (highways and dams), and transportation (ocean vessels, railroads, airplanes, buses, automobiles, and other vehicles that transport people and assets from place to place around the world). In the twenty-first century we are deep into the services revolution that is changing the way we live and evaluate the world's wealth and economy. An ever-expanding world of innovation has already provided us with smart phones, e-commerce, digital cameras, high definition television, and satellite technology. In this bright new world, we have found another major growth service sector – tourism – sometimes referred to as an *invisible* or *intangible* activity.

According to the United States Travel and Tourism Advisory Board, the world has entered a new golden age for travel and tourism.[1] Demographic changes, increasing disposable income levels, heightened emphasis on sustainability, greater availability of leisure time, new communication tools and technology, higher levels of education, emerging tourism markets, growth in the supply of facilities and destinations and other supplementary factors are having an impact on demand for tourism. Tourism has become one of the most dynamic industries throughout the globe as it adapts to technological change, product innovations, and new markets. Tourism embraces technology in its widespread use of e-commerce tools, for its applications to new products such as space and undersea tourism and developing new methods of marketing and promotion. Managing sustainable tourism in today's world adds an important dimension to the growth of tourism. The policies we set for tourism in an ever-changing world will direct the courses of action for tourism in the future. This book is an effort to meet this challenge and to provide policy and planning solutions for the orderly growth and development of tourism and add to its sustainability.

The opportunity offered by tourism for future economic, environmental, and social benefits will depend on understanding the tourism industry of yesterday, making the best possible decisions today and addressing forward-thinking trends. We can define clear plans and policy guidelines for the future of tourism or let it happen haphazardly and hope for the best. We must define clear-cut policies and plans at this juncture in the growth of tourism before it is too late. This book provides new information and concepts to help meet the challenge of charting a favorable course for tourism's future.

Peace and tourism have interesting conceptual ties. Traveling to foreign lands increases understanding and cooperation between visitors and hosts. Tourism, also, can be hindered by the lack of peace in a destination. Thus, tourism can be seen as a generator and beneficiary of peace. Peace is an important part of the foreign policy and policy processes across nations. Because tourism is so closely related to peace, more about peace and tourism is included in Chapter 5, Chapter 9, and Chapter 11, which describe foreign policy implications of tourism and the international tourism policy process, respectively.

Importance of tourism in a global context

The twenty-first century is seeing increases in leisure time and income for millions of people. Shorter working hours in some cases, greater individual prosperity, faster and cheaper travel relative to the past, more destinations to choose from, and the impact of advanced technology have all helped to make tourism one of the fastest growing economic sectors in the world. The significance of tourism as a viable source of income and employment, and as a major factor in the balance of payments for many countries, has been attracting increasing attention on the part of governments, regional and local authorities, and others with an interest in economic development. Furthermore, sustainable tourism, concerns for the environment, social conditions, and other concepts have entered the decision-making process and will forever change the way tourism grows throughout the world. Global changes and sustainable tourism are discussed in some detail in Chapter 6.

The latest research reported by the UNWTO shows tourism's direct contribution to global gross domestic product (GDP) was US$1.97 trillion, which represented 2.8 percent of overall GDP. The direct contribution of tourism is forecasted to increase by 4.2 percent per year over the period of 2012 to 2022. Total contribution (direct, indirect, and induced contribution) of tourism was estimated at more than US$6.4 trillion in 2012. This is 9.1 percent of global GDP. Direct employment in tourism totaled roughly 100 million people in 2012, which is 3.3 percent of total employment. Considering direct employment and indirect employment, 255 million people, or 8.7 percent of the total workforce, worked in various tourism-related industries throughout the world. Total employment is expected to increase roughly 2.3 percent between 2012 and 2022. Tourism exports of US$1.2 trillion accounted for 5.3 percent of total global exports. UNWTO forecasts this figure to grow by 3.6 percent over the next decade[2] and estimated a record 1 billion international tourist arrivals in 2012.

Equally important is the fact that tourism, as an export, is of critical importance to both industrialized and developing nations. As an economic factor, tourism is growing faster than the rest of the world economy in terms of export, output, value added, capital investment, and employment. See Chapter 4 for a more complete discussion of the economics of tourism in an international context.

While tourism has been growing rapidly since World War II and will continue its dynamic growth into the future, this does not mean the sector will grow smoothly. As evidenced, there will be occasional structural, economic, political, environmental, social, and conceptual impediments in its path. An example of this was the severe decline in travel worldwide at the start of the Persian Gulf War in 1991. Mediterranean destinations, North America, and parts of Asia, far from the war zone and Middle East conflicts were all affected. A more complete analysis of the history of tourism policy is presented in Chapter 2. Coupled with this is the public's and, in some cases, governments' inadequate understanding about the economic, environmental, and social importance of tourism and the low levels of access to current information about tourism affairs. At the same time, however, the global importance of tourism is becoming better understood because, in many geographic areas, tourism is replacing other industries that have traditionally been the paramount economic drivers. This, in turn, necessitates better tourism research, policy, and planning to support this momentum.

As part of the overall growth of services, tourism's recognition as an important sector in the global economy is more frequently accepted. Key multilateral governmental policy organizations such as the United Nations (New York), the United Nations World Tourism Organization (Madrid), the Organisation for Economic Co-operation and Development (Paris), the Organization of American States (Washington, DC), the Asia-Pacific Economic Cooperation (Singapore), the Caribbean Tourism Organization (Barbados), and other international bodies provide important research reports and data to the tourism industries. One of their shared goals is to link tourism to other sectors of the international economy. The European Community, North America Free Trade Agreement, and other regional economic instruments are seeking to break down traditional barriers to providing and accessing tourism services across borders, which will ultimately aid international tourism. The World Travel and Tourism Council (London), the Pacific Asia Travel Association (Bangkok), and other groups representing mainly private interests and some public concerns are already establishing a higher level of cooperation and coalition building to tackle broad policy issues. These changes indicate increasing recognition of the impact of tourism in the twenty-first century. Refer to Chapter 5 for more information on these intergovernmental organizations.

The importance of what has happened globally in the tourism policy arena since September 11, 2001, has been manifested by the movement of the world to better understand the necessary implementation of new safety and security measures. The prognosis for the future growth of tourism is good in spite of the adjustments most nations have had to make to the threat of terrorism. This acknowledgment of forced change distinguishes much of the tourism industry today. Chapter 12 highlights similar future tourism trends that need to be addressed within policy and planning.

Economic changes taking place in China, India, United States, Indonesia, and Brazil, with more than 3.2 billion people (nearly half the world's population of more than 7 billion), will have major impacts on the global tourism markets of tomorrow. The emerging power of Brazil as a major player on the global tourism scene is illustrated by the South American nation being chosen to host major sporting events. Brazil is host to the 2014 World Cup of Soccer and the 2016 summer Olympic Games. As host, Brazil will welcome millions of visitors and gain a significant amount of international exposure.

Europe faces opportunities and challenges that cause the outlook for European tourism to be mixed. Social-cultural changes in Europe, with borderless tourism crossings and a common currency, are increasing opportunities for tourism growth. Some nations within Europe have been slow to recover from the global economic recession of the early twenty-first century. Nations such as Greece and Spain have faced significant economic crises, the outcomes of which are uncertain. However, many destinations within Europe are proximate to strong markets-of-origin, such as India and China. In forecasting tourism metrics for Europe over the next decade, the UNWTO predicts direct contribution to GDP, direct employment, visitor exports, and tourism investment to increase and total contribution to GDP and total employment to decrease.

FIGURE 1.1 Visitors from around the globe enjoy Chateau de Versailles, a major European attraction (Photo: Jason R. Swanson)

FIGURE 1.2 Gateway to the Temple of Literature in Hanoi, Vietnam (Photo: CIA)

Southeast Asia – including the countries of Brunei, Cambodia, Indonesia, Laos, Malaysia, Myanmar, Papua New Guinea, Philippines, Singapore, Thailand, and Vietnam – is experiencing growth and change in tourism. Tourism investment in these nations is expected to increase by nearly 7.9 percent per year over the next decade. Many of these Southeast Asia countries, although smaller and with fewer natural resources but a large supply of cultural resources, rely more on tourism to sustain their economy than larger countries currently do. Tourism success in such countries is based on sound tourism planning. A country similar to and nearby many countries in Southeast Asia is the island nation of the Maldives. The tourism planning efforts of the Maldives is the focus of this chapter's case study.

Economic and non-economic benefits

Tourism is an economic activity that provides local destinations, states, provinces, or countries with new sources of income and currency exchange. The impact tourism has on the economy can be tremendous as it creates jobs, reduces unemployment, fosters entrepreneurship, stimulates production of food and local handicrafts, demands effective communications, facilitates cultural exchanges, and contributes to a better understanding of the local area, state, province, country, and the world at large. These concepts are illustrated in depth in Chapter 11.

A problem area in most countries is many legislators and administrators lacking an in-depth understanding of tourism. However, tourism in many communities is increasing in political and economic importance and the positive economic impact of tourism is the best argument presented by tourism professionals to their policymakers when looking for increased funding and recognition. Logical and documented research on tourism's economic impact can help to lead to better public policy decisions. Youth sports tourism is an example of an emerging market, the development of which can be enhanced with better information. Research shows the value of the economic impact from sports tourism is tied to destination managers using the findings from economic impact research to garner support from the host community for youth sports.[3]

Destination managers' decisions often focus primarily on the economic benefits of tourism, but destinations are (and should be) increasingly expanding their analysis to include non-economic measures such as social, cultural, environmental, and other concerns. As laid out in previous decades, but still applicable to today, tourism development should be in harmony with the socio-cultural, ecological, and heritage goals, values, and aspirations of the host community.[4] It is important to consider all these concerns, not just economic gain, to assure a greater chance of increased participation from all stakeholders. For example, tourism adds many opportunities for members of the host community in the form of participation in cultural and historical attractions and events. Local artisans and tourism employees also reap the direct benefits of visitor expenditures beyond economic development, including increased pride in the local heritage, enhanced self-worth, or global recognition through bringing the world and other cultures to the destination's doorstep. Furthermore, market demand is now forcing communities to consider these other impacts as a means to stay competitive. An important example is found in coastal communities as clean beaches and a certain amount of tranquility is sought by many visitors who are willing to pay for beach quality.[5]

Economic and non-economic costs

While positive economic impacts are often more important to developers and governments, tourism managers must also recognize the negative possibilities when formulating policy and creating strategic plans. The United States provides two powerful examples. First, new tourism development in local communities (and especially in regions known as gateway or entrance communities to major tourism destinations such as national parks and man-made attractions) may drive up real estate values making the cost for housing prohibitive to community residents and the labor market servicing the needs of visitors. A second scenario deals with environmental use, or overuse, such as the recent debates regarding the permissibility of winter snowmobiling in Yosemite National Park in the US.

More research and better solutions are needed regarding the negative social, economic, and environmental impacts of tourism. This will be increasingly important as tourism becomes more widespread throughout the world. Knowing benefits-to-costs ratios enables tourism organizations to invest in attracting and developing the appropriate and optimal market segments and tourism facilities.[6] Policy should address these issues in a proactive way to achieve an optimum return for all tourism investments and assets. An inadequate capability by destination managers to address negative impacts on their attractions can lead to degradation of the tourism destination and a detrimental reputation, hampering both travelers and outside marketing agents. Affecting and influencing tourism policy based on research and policy analysis is explored in detail in Chapter 8.

Historically, understanding non-economic impacts of tourism has been low on the research agenda of major tourism offices. According to a 1994 study by the Travel Industry Association of America, only 68 percent of US state travel offices conducted research, at least periodically, on the psychological impact of tourism. More recently, an insightful article in the September 2005 issue of *American Psychologist*, highlights the need and opportunity for more psychological research on tourism.[7] The article concludes:

> Natural laboratories for the investigation of stress and coping, culture learning, and social identification are found in tourist settings in which tourists' experiences, tourist-host impressions and encounters, and changes in host communities are all novel topics for psychological inquiry. The application of psychological theories for promoting positive results for individuals, communities, and the tourist industry more broadly presents groundbreaking opportunities for health, social, community, and applied psychologists. It also promises innovative outcomes for tourism researchers and contributes to tourism that is both sustainable and beneficial to the people it affects most.

Understanding tourism policy

For tourism to be sustainable in the future, it is vital that effective policy and planning take place today. Policymakers, planning officials, and stakeholders must identify the emerging trends in tourism and orchestrate new measures that lead to orderly growth and quality products that benefit tourists and communities. Unfortunately, in the past, many governments have not given tourism the same concern given to manufacturing or other service industries. However, news of conflicts, terrorism, health concerns, natural disasters, and weather conditions in countries throughout the world often bring the tourism industry to the forefront. The severe acute respiratory syndrome (SARS) epidemic and concerns about avian influenza have taken their toll on tourism along with earthquakes, hurricanes, tsunamis, and other natural disasters. The escalation of petroleum prices, the ups and downs in the world economy, and adjustments to new technologies are affecting tourism in unprecedented ways. This book discusses many of these changes and issues as they relate to public policy, and, in some cases, suggests remedies. In addition to providing workable definitions of tourism policy, this section also presents new challenges and approaches to tourism policy.

A simple dictionary definition of policy is "A definite course or method of action selected from among alternatives and in light of given conditions to guide and determine present and future decisions."[8] The popular textbook *Tourism: Principles, Practices, Philosophies*[9] defines tourism policy as:

> . . . a set of regulations, rules, guidelines, directives, and development/promotion objectives and strategies that provide a framework within which the collective and individual decisions directly affecting long-term tourism development and the daily activities within a destination are taken.

Another useful discussion of tourism policy is contained in a book titled *Travel and Tourism: An Industry Primer*,[10] which adds an important social aspects to the definition of tourism policy by stating:

> A tourism policy defines the direction or course of action that a particular country, region, locality, or an individual destination plans to take when developing or promoting tourism. The key principle for any tourism policy is that it should ensure that the nation (region or locality) would benefit to the maximum extent possible from the economic and social contributions of tourism. The ultimate objective of tourism policy is to improve the progress of the nation (region or locality) and the lives of its citizens.

Perhaps the best approach to an initial understanding of tourism policy may also be the simplest by beginning with Thomas Dye's classic definition of public policy, which is "whatever governments choose to do or not to do" and applying it to tourism.[11] In essence, tourism policy is any government act – legislative, administrative, or judicial – that affects tourism. For purposes of the approach taken in this book, tourism policy will be more broadly defined to include marketing, planning, and sustainability. In this context, tourism policy is *a progressive course of actions, guidelines, directives, principles, and procedures set in an ethical framework that is issues-focused and best represents the intent of a community (or nation) to effectively meet its planning, development, product, service, marketing, and sustainability goals and objectives for the future growth of tourism.*

The definition acknowledges the important role marketing, product development, and hospitality services play in tourism policy. In addition, the tourism sustainability concept must support the long-term goals related to economic, environmental, and social development. More importantly, this definition recognizes that tourism policy is dynamic and flexible enough to allow adjustments and refinements as occasions arise.

Tourism policy plays an important role in many societies. Tourism policy has the potential to engage and change the economic, political, social, and ecological dimensions of future lifestyles. Edgell[12] asserts:

The highest purpose of tourism policy is to integrate the economic, political, cultural, intellectual and economic benefits of tourism cohesively with people, destinations, and countries in order to improve the global quality-of-life and provide a foundation for peace and prosperity. The political aspects of tourism are interwoven with its economic consequences. Tourism is not only a continuation of politics but an integral part of the world's political economy. In short, tourism is, or can be, a tool used not only for economic but for political means.

In the mid-1990s, Fayos-Sola[13] suggested a more balanced role in tourism policymaking between the private, public, and voluntary sectors. He stated: "The changing nature of the tourism industry with its move away from mass tourism towards greater market segmentation, use of new technologies, differentiation of the product and adoption of new management styles demands a change in the substance of governments' tourism policies." At the end of the 1990s, Edgell[14] went further, stating, "The tourism industry will be faced with some difficult challenges over the next several years. Technology, whether in communications information, new aerospace developments, or other fields, will heavily impact the tourism industry. The industry will need to develop effective policies and plans to deal with terrorism and other disruptions to the tourism market." Goeldner and Ritchie[15] have stated, "Tourism policy seeks to ensure that visitors are hosted in a way that maximizes the benefits to stakeholders while minimizing the negative effects, costs, and impacts associated with ensuring the success of the destination." This positivist outlook, set forth by Goeldner and Ritchie, is more how tourism policy should be, but not necessarily how tourism policy is actually implemented by most governments. New challenges related to creating and implementing tourism policy are presented in the next section.

New challenges

As many places in the world become better known and accessible, many governments will seek to encourage greater travel to their respective destinations. Many developed and developing countries conduct their national tourism offices under the aegis of government tourism policy covering research, strategic planning, marketing, coordination, development, and training. Often this process is in conjunction with associations of private-sector tourism interests, joint public-private consultative bodies, and international and intergovernmental organizations.

Tourism policymakers' ability to fashion policies and plans in the future will depend upon solid research to understand better and accept new concepts as they appear. Such research, conducted in a chaotic world, may hammer out innovative and creative approaches that differ from traditional guidelines for policy once held by tourism managers and scholars. The policies must be flexible and resilient enough to foster the development of new tourism products and services in a rapidly changing world. A static policy that is firmly in place can be rendered useless whenever tragic events or new global disturbances erupt, as has been the case in recent years.

The broad range of economic, political, environmental, and social implications for tourism on both the domestic and international fronts is yet to be fully realized. One way to focus attention on this need for recognition is to examine the larger role that tourism plays beyond its marketing and promotional goals. Sound tourism policy goes well beyond the marketing and promotion objectives to consider and evaluate tourism's comprehensive effect on the host community. The changing dimensions of tourism as it expands have introduced the need for a sharper focus when dissecting the economic, cultural, ecological, environmental, social, and political consequences of tourism. These issues cover the future sustainability of tourism.

With a thorough understanding of tourism's implications, policymakers, planners, and business people can better facilitate community involvement in tourism development at all levels. The more vested the local community is in the decision-making process, the more likely the future of tourism will create economic, environmental, and social improvements to the quality-of-life of the local citizenry and lead to sustainability of the area. Chapter 3 highlights several of the key tourism policy issues of today that tourism managers and policymakers must understand in many destinations throughout the world.

A new look at tourism policy

Since tourism is difficult to clearly define because of the involvement of many different economic sectors and stakeholders, it tends to foster several major policy development challenges. Fundamentally, tourism policy should present a set of guidelines which, when combined with planning goals, charts a course of action for sound decision-making. For the past decade, leading tourism thinkers have called for increased attention to the social science aspects of tourism in an effort to continue to improve quality-of-life and promote global peace through tourism policy.

Public policy is both a process and a product – the decision-making process and the product of that process. Policy should serve not only the government, but also the public interest. Policy, when properly applied, is a vehicle for a government to direct and stimulate the tourism industry, as for example through tax legislation and sponsoring tourism research. The actions of not only government, but also the public, private, and non-profit sectors are influenced by policy as well and play an important role in policy determination.

As stated earlier in this chapter, research is an important component of the tourism policy process. Only reliable and comprehensive research on tourism's impacts will lead to good decision-making and policy development. Within the last 15 years, many experts have cited the importance of research in tourism. At a minimum, a tourism office's research department should utilize a travel monitoring system to enhance marketing and promotion initiatives.[16]

One way to begin the tourism policy process is to research a tourism policy issue, such as a local hotel bed tax, and take the analysis through several of the steps outlined in Figure 1.3. Once resources, conditional factors, such as the political environment and sustainability, and goals and objectives are understood through research, then the policy can be formulated and implemented. The final stage in the policy process is evaluation, which involves more research. The importance of research as the foundation for visionary policies is being recognized as essential by local, provincial/state, regional, and national tourism planners as they prepare for the future development of tourism.

It can be argued that in the past, the bulk of tourism policy and subsequent tourism policy research has focused on the demand side of the equation or on economic and marketing issues, which leads to underestimating other important considerations that must be viewed within the supply side of tourism. Marketing a destination is sometimes complicated by the difficult supply characteristics of the industry.

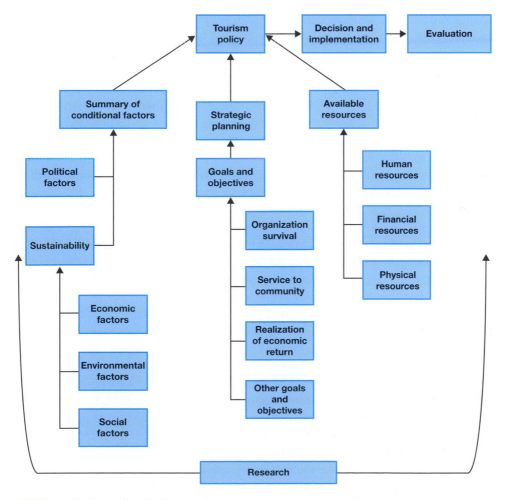

FIGURE 1.3 Tourism policy development process

A community should operate under a coordinated tourism policy so that the many suppliers and promotion organizations can work well together.[17] An applied example of this dilemma was presented in a study of London's tourism policy. The study highlighted the challenges associated with the long-term sustainability of short-term changes in the city's marketing policy and concluded that for long-term sustainability, infrastructural issues had to be dealt with first. One conclusion to be drawn from this analysis is that tourism is more than just marketing and tourism policy should reflect that.

Opponents of tourism often cite the negative impacts an influx of visitors might have on the destination and there is a need to have policy that recognizes these concerns. Positive impacts of tourism also exist of course that should be equally important to policymakers and tourism professionals. Understanding both positive and negative impacts will lead to practical sustainable tourism development. When the negative impacts on the environment are recognized, corrected, and managed well and the positive attributes are built upon, the results can be presented to stakeholders and tourism can become an important driving force in community development. The benefits derived from visitors have an impact on the economy in numerous ways including generating income, creating jobs, spawning new businesses, spurring economic development, promoting economic diversification, developing new products, and contributing to economic integration.

Tourism encompasses specialties within industry segments, not often realized as tourism demand generators by policymakers or tourism outsiders. Tourism consumers may be classified as business travelers, leisure travelers, air and auto travelers, solo travelers, or travelers with children. They engage in travel that includes social/family events, or have many other travel motivations.[18] Travelers to national parks, minority travelers, multi-generational travelers, and other niche demand groups look for specific environments and tourism supply components when planning their travels. For example, heritage tourism fulfills a specialized demand and supply. These activities are important to realize in many areas of the world where tourism is being developed to offset the decline of manufacturing industries, mining, and agriculture. A fully comprehensive tourism policy will encompass all aspects of supply and demand that can be associated with tourism.

Local, state/provincial, regional, and national governments should view tourism policy across agencies as it affects various components of the operating sectors. Tourism impacts infrastructure and planning in multiple areas simultaneously. Transportation, zoning, and water use are example areas where policy crosses functional boundaries. These types of issues are highly sensitive to local residents and have the potential to greatly impact tourism. On the other side, rather than the potential to stress a system, tourism developers could use information and research to determine the feasibility of a proposed investment in all industry-operating sectors. Included in this policy process should be a listing of the quality, quantity, and geographic distribution of the tourism superstructure and special events, such as festivals. To be meaningful, this measure should be related to demand to assess adequately the nature of tourism supply in the market.

For the wellbeing of a destination's citizenry in terms of economic, political, environmental, social, and cultural issues, the public-sector plays an active role in the development, legislation, financing, and planning of tourism. Because of fragmentation inherent among tourism stakeholders, the government must do more than just set policy – it must also assist in the implementation of policy. One method to accomplish this is by offering incentives to reach the established objectives.

Historically, coordination related to tourism policy and programs within governments among different departments within European nations, the United States, and most other countries, has been poor. Consequently, tourism has received low priority and has often been overlooked when governments distribute limited resources or when comprehensive policies are developed. A coordinated approach with a full and complementary partnership in tandem with public-sector and private-sector organizations will go a long way towards alleviating some of these past problems.

Policy issues should be extended beyond those traditionally thought of as tourism, to be inclusive of all public programs concerned with tourism, not just what is typically perceived as tourism products. For instance, water management issues usually concern local businesses and residents. However, water parks, large golf resorts, and other tourism infrastructure can consume vast quantities of water. Therefore, waterworks departments will want to consider both the tourism industry and the local residents when developing policy. This will be crucial for tourism's long-term success in a community. There must be recognition of the need to give the tourist the experience they want as well as to extend the sustainability of the experience. Resources should be earmarked to promote tourism while at the same time care is given to protect and enhance the sustainability of the destination.

Cooperation and integration

Stakeholder participation, when developing tourism policy, is important because of the diversity of organizations and interests in both the public and private sector. Stakeholders can include local citizens, business owners, public regulatory and land-use departments, public, private, and non-profit organizations – any and all constituencies involved or who ought to be involved in the decision-making process. Another important stakeholder is the destination's visitors. In the past, tourism and economic development projects and processes overlooked the important role of a wide range of stakeholders. Some recent research on *coopetition* (discussed in Chapter 4) is lending additional support for greater cooperation in tourism decision-making at all levels. The many organizations involved in promoting tourism and their different objectives make tourism policy difficult to coordinate and implement; therefore, it is important to have an integrated policy. Without a comprehensive tourism policy, tourism's economic, political, and legal implications often have unguided results, which may not lead to high-quality tourism development.

Understanding tourism planning

Tourism policy assembles the planning function and political goals for tourism into a set of guidelines to give the tourism community direction as it moves ahead. Without such guidance we might find tourism's future considerably less beneficial than the plans that have been laid out. With the information and precepts presented in this book, students, professionals, and policymakers will have a set of conceptual tools for understanding the myriad factors that make up tourism planning and help foster the industry's future growth in positive ways. Chapter 10 illustrates the important concepts of strategic tourism development planning.

This book, with some divergences, utilizes the classic tourism-planning model that includes a vision and mission statement. The vision should be a few words that describe where local or national tourism strategy wants to be, while the mission statement explains how to get there. The vision and mission statement are followed by a set of goals, objectives, strategies, and tactics, sometimes represented in the form of a *tree diagram*, as shown in Figure 1.4.

Tourism for local communities is a vital economic development tool, the economic benefits of which bear repeating: generating income, creating jobs, spawning new businesses, spurring economic development, promoting economic diversification, developing new products, and contributing to economic integration. If local and national governments are committed to broad-based tourism policies, tourism will provide its citizens with a higher quality-of-life while it generates sustained economic, environmental, and social benefits.

A look at travel and tourism within this context mandates that policymakers must understand the need for developing wide-ranging strategies and long-term plans, adjusted as conditions fluctuate or mature. Policymakers and planners as well must be knowledgeable about market trends and flexible enough to adjust strategic plans in the face of rapidly changing market forces. Tourism planning within the new tourism horizon must fully encompass the complex nature of tourism and the far-reaching mechanics of its implementation.

Tourism policy and planning will drive the appropriate management techniques and tools essential for meeting emerging trends. This transformation must take place

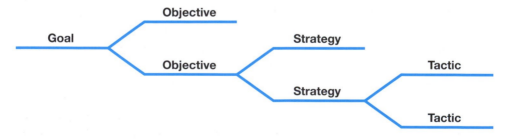

FIGURE 1.4 Tree diagram: Goal-oriented tourism planning

in a new world of globalization and competition, in which, at the same time, the world's population and economies are changing. New technology (particularly in communications and transportation), barriers to travel (described more in Chapter 7), political relations, and many other factors will impact tourism policy and planning in the future. The need to enhance the understanding and visibility of tourism being a wide and multi-sectoral phenomenon, requires a strong cooperation with a myriad of organizations, public administrations, communities, stakeholders, and the academic world. The remaining chapters in this book set out to increase the understanding of tourism, tourism policy, and tourism planning.

CHAPTER REVIEW QUESTIONS

1. What is tourism?
2. What definition of tourism policy is offered by this book?
3. Why is tourism becoming more important worldwide?
4. What kind of impact does tourism have on the economy?
5. Explain the diagram of the tourism policy development process.
6. Why do governments need to consider tourism policy across agencies?
7. Why should the host community be taken into consideration when developing tourism?
8. What are the costs, or negative aspects, of tourism development?
9. What are examples of tourism stakeholders?
10. Tourism policy should consider issues that are not traditionally associated with tourism. What are some examples of these types of issues or public programs that could impact tourism?
11. Why is tourism policy more than just a marketing policy?

CASE STUDY 1 Tourism planning in the Republic of Maldives

This case study was written by Ms. Sudarat (Toi) Sangchumnong, a doctoral student in tourism at Assumption University in Bangkok, Thailand. The work was supervised by Dr. Jason R. Swanson, co-author of *Tourism Policy and Planning: Yesterday, today, and tomorrow* (second edition). Dr. Swanson teaches an advanced strategic tourism planning course at Assumption University, using this textbook. The case study, which is an analysis of the Third Tourism Master Plan developed by the government of the Republic of Maldives, was designed around planning and policy concepts covered in the book.

*   *   *

The Republic of Maldives has placed a strong emphasis on tourism during the past 30 years. Beaches in Maldives are famous throughout the world for offering breathtaking natural scenery and scores of water activities. The nation, however, faces unique challenges concerning catastrophic global warming possibilities that could cause major problems as developers have constructed several upscale resorts and other tourism-related developments throughout the coral-like archipelago. These issues are challenging the government to be well prepared with tourism development plans. The issues also provide an excellent case study to highlight the intricacies of tourism policy and planning.

This case study is a review of the Third Tourism Master Plan (TTMP) of Maldives, which apply to the period of 2007 to 2011. The case study consists of four parts covering Maldives tourism, elements of the TTMP, outcomes of the plan, and recommendations on how to improve planning efforts in the future. Each of these areas is described in detail following a discussion of the distinctive geographic characteristics of the island nation.

FIGURE 1.5 Map of southwestern Asia showing relative position of Maldives (Image: CIA)

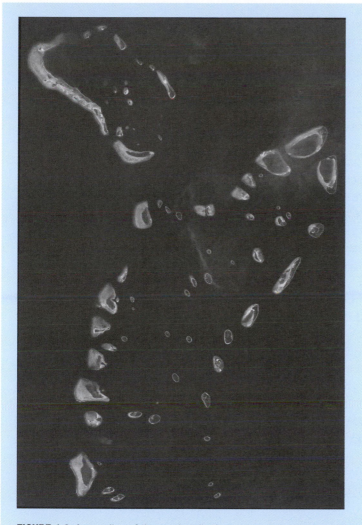

FIGURE 1.6 A sampling of the coral atolls that make up the Maldives (Photo: NASA)

Situated in the Indian Ocean, approximately 600km southwest of India, the Maldives is made up of nearly 1,200 coral islands within 26 atolls grouped in a double chain. An atoll is a set of islands made of coral that form a circle – often an incomplete circle – to create a lagoon. Only 200 of the islands are inhabited. Although officially uninhabited, 80 islands are improved with resort developments. Each atoll has approximately five to ten inhabited islands, while the number of uninhabited islands of each atoll ranges from roughly 20 to 60. Several atolls, however, consist of one large isolated island surrounded by a steep coral beach. The most notable example of this type of atoll is the large island of Fua Mulaku situated in the middle of the Equatorial Channel. Most islands in the Maldives lie less than 1.5m above mean sea level, with the highest point, on Addu Atoll, situated 2.4m above sea level.[19]

The tropical vegetation of Maldives includes groves of breadfruit trees and coconut palms towering above dense scrub, shrubs, and flowers. The composition of the soil severely limits agricultural potential. Slightly more than 10 percent of the land, or about 2,900ha, is cultivated with taro, bananas, coconuts, and other fruit. Only lush Fua Mulaku produces fruits such as oranges and pineapples partly because the terrain is higher than most other islands, leaving the groundwater less subject to seawater penetration.[20]

Freshwater floats in a lens-like layer above the seawater that permeates the limestone and coral sands of the islands. These lenses are shrinking rapidly on Malé, the national capital, and on many islands with resorts catering to foreign tourists. In recent years, mango trees have reportedly been dying on Malé because of salt penetration. Most residents of the atolls depend on groundwater or rainwater for drinking purposes.[21]

As measured by population, the Maldives is one of the smallest countries in the world. In 2011, the population was estimated at 394,451 persons and is reported to be slightly decreasing at a rate of 0.127 percent. Maldivians are scattered throughout the island chain, but the greatest concentration of residents – roughly 120,000 Maldivians – is in the capital, Malé, which enjoys a central location within the archipelago. Overall, 40 percent of the population can be found in urban areas, which is an increasing trend in recent years.[22]

In addition to tourism, which is described in detail in the next section, other major economic contributors are fishing and manufacturing. Fishing employs about 11 percent of the labor force and the fisheries industry, including fish processing, traditionally contributes about 7 percent of GDP. Fish export earnings were estimated at $80 million in 2009. More than 40 percent is exported, largely to Sri Lanka, Japan, Hong Kong, Thailand, and the European Union. The manufacturing sector, primarily in the form of boat building and handicrafts, provides less than 7 percent of GDP.[23]

Maldives tourism

Significant tourism development in the Maldives began in 1972 with 280 beds in hotels on two resort islands. Since then, tourism has grown rapidly – transforming the Maldives into a quintessential island holiday destination with global reputation and winning international acclaim and awards. The tourism capacity, as measured by number of hotel rooms, had an annualized average compound growth rate of 11.7 percent between 1972 and 2005. This rate peaked at 26.5 percent between 1972 and 1982 and dropped off to 6.7 percent between 1982 and 2003.

In recent years, Maldives has successfully marketed its natural resources for tourism – beautiful, unpolluted beaches on small coral islands, diving in blue waters abundant with tropical fish, and glorious sunsets. Tourism brings in about $600 million a year.[24] Tourism and related services contributed 34.4 percent of GDP in 2010.[25] But tourism's indirect contribution is much greater. As a result,

FIGURE 1.7 Jumhoorie Maidan (Republic Square) and the tourist boats on the Malé waterfront
(Photo: CIA)

tourism is the catalyst for economic growth. Since the first resort was established in 1972, more than 95 islands have been developed, with a total capacity of approximately 23,600 beds.[26]

More than 790,000 tourists (mainly from Europe) visited Maldives in 2010. The average annual occupancy rate is about 70 percent. Maldives had experienced capacity utilization rates of over 80 percent – reaching over 95 percent in the peak winter tourist season – prior to the new resort drive that began in 2008. The average tourist length-of-stay is eight days. The Maldives has embarked on ambitious tourism expansion plans with several new resorts developments. However, resort expansion has not been planned very well as there are several half-built resorts.

Key to the recent success of Maldivian tourism is incorporating sustainable development planning. Sustainable planning is a requisite in a fragile ecosystem, such as the Maldives. The major attraction of the nation is the tiny coral islands on which much of the tourism superstructure has been built. Damaging the nation's unique supply of natural environmental aspects would significantly reduce tourism demand. The Maldivian government has established a regulatory framework that covers environmental issues; development, operations, and quality of tourism supply components; and health and safety issues important for tourism.[27] The growth of tourism in the Maldives has progressed largely on a planned path determined by the First Tourism Master Plan (1983–1992), the Second Tourism Master Plan (1996–2005), and the Third Tourism Master Plan (2007–2011). Maldivian tourism planning is the focus of the next section.

The Maldives Third Tourism Master Plan

Prior to creating the Third Tourism Master Plan (TTMP), the nation underwent two planning processes that resulted in planning documents. The first plan laid out tactics and strategies for the years 1983 through 1992. In November 1980, the Department of Tourism and Foreign Investments (DTFI) commissioned the DANGROUP under assistance from the Kuwait Fund for Arab Economic Development to carry out a feasibility study for project preparation in the tourism sector. The outcome of this study was the First Tourism Development Plan of the Maldives, referred to as the First Tourism Master Plan (FTMP). The FTMP focused attention on preservation of the environment and centralized infrastructure, creating a legacy defined by unprecedented awareness amongst stakeholders in practicing sustainable and responsible tourism. The focus of the FTMP was environmental protection and sustainable development.

The consultation process of the Second Tourism Master Plan (STMP) began in 1994 with the assistance of the European Union, and was completed in 1996. The key theme of the plan was to establish policies that would facilitate and foster the private-sector. This impetus for enabling the private-sector was a policy shift from the control mindset of the FTMP. The Second Tourism Master Plan focused on six broad strategic directions: 1) balancing regional development; 2) facilitating private-sector investments; 3) strengthening the institutions; 4) developing human resources and cultural aspects; 5) harmonizing tourism and the environment; and 6) strengthening marketing and promotion.

The Maldives Third Tourism Master Plan (TTMP) covers the period 2007 to 2011. The policies, strategies and actions incorporated into the TTMP align with policies in the 7th National Development Plan for the Republic of Maldives. According to this plan, the vision has been designed to expand and strengthen Maldives tourism as an instrument of economic and social development in a manner that benefits all Maldivians throughout the archipelagic nation. This vision also encompassed a model of sustainable tourism development with environmentally and socially responsible tourism practices. In order to achieve the vision and goals, the Ministry of Tourism and Civil Aviation (MTCA) and others involved in the planning process set out the Action Plan as follows:

1. Facilitate sustainable growth and increase investment in the industry, while enhancing public share of economic benefits from tourism.
2. Increase employment opportunities and open up opportunities for gainful public and community participation in the tourism industry.

3. Develop and maintain supporting infrastructure required for the growth of the tourism industry.
4. Ensure environmental sustainability in development and operation of all tourism products, and strive for global excellence in environmentally-responsible tourism.
5. Continue to brand Maldives as a unique destination with innovation products and retain Maldives positioning as a top ranking destination in traditional and emerging source markets.
6. Continue to strengthen the legal and regulatory framework and the institutional capacity of the Ministry of Tourism and Civil Aviation.

The TTMP aims to develop tourism in harmony with nature, facilitating private-sector investment, developing human resources, increasing employment opportunities, diversifying market and products. More equitable distribution of tourism benefits across the archipelago is new to the third plan. Its stated vision is one of "expanding and strengthening the Maldives tourism industry as an instrument of economic and social development in a manner that benefits all Maldivians in all parts of the country."[28]

Project management

The TTMP was formulated by the MTCA, under the direction of a Project Steering Committee (PSC). The TTMP formulation process was conducted by a Technical Team appointed by MTCA, under the leadership of a Chief Technical Expert. Figure 1.8 illustrates the organization of the project's management.

The PSC consisted of representatives from 14 government ministries selected on the basis of their institutional links to tourism development and planning in the Maldives. The government agencies making up the PSC are listed in Table 1.1. The technical team consisted of Maldivian consultants with expertise in economic and finance, community-based tourism, market and product development, legal and institutional processes, human resource development, infrastructure and support services, and environmental management.

FIGURE 1.8 TTMP organization chart

TABLE 1.1 Represented ministries on the Project Steering Committee for the TTMP	
Ministry of Tourism and Civil Aviation	Ministry of Health
Ministry of Planning and National Development	Ministry of Economic Development and Trade
Ministry of Transport and Communication	Ministry of Atolls Development
Ministry of Defense and National Security	Maldives Police Service
Ministry of Finance and Treasury	Maldives Airports Company, Ltd.
Ministry of Environment, Energy and Water	Maldives College of Higher Education
Ministry of Higher Education, Employment and Social Security	Ministry of Fisheries, Agriculture and Marine Resources

TTMP Planning Process

The PSC and TTMP Technical Team agreed that a dynamic planning process should be adopted for the TTMP. This is in recognition of the dynamic tourism planning environment in the Maldives that will exist in the next five years with regard to changing product, market, and institution conditions. For this reason, the TTMP planning process shown in Figure 1.9 was developed. The process involved research, monitoring, evaluation, and revision as integral components of the process.

Situational analysis

The TTMP built on the previous planning work and included an in-depth situational analysis of the current tourism environment when the plan was developed in the years leading up to 2007. The tourism problems covered in the situational analysis focused on economic and financial status, tourism trends, human resource development, the state of the environment, community involvement, legal and institutional capacity, and infrastructure and services. The situation of these areas at the time of planning is briefly described in the following paragraphs.

Economic and financial: The Maldives recorded relatively strong economic growth over the past three decades, reaching a GDP of US$706 million in 2004 and an economic growth rate of 8.8 percent. The Maldives' GDP per capita was among the highest in the South Asian Region, with US$2,293 in 2005. While income from tourism was significant, the economic leakage from tourism was also substantial. Economic leakage from tourism occurs due to the repatriation of wages by expatriate workers, repatriation of profits by foreign corporations, tourism services (i.e., travel bookings) sold by foreign tour operators and travel agents, and dependence on foreign airlines.[29]

Arrivals, markets, and products: Opportunities existed for the Maldives to capture a higher share of the meetings, incentives, conventions, and exhibitions

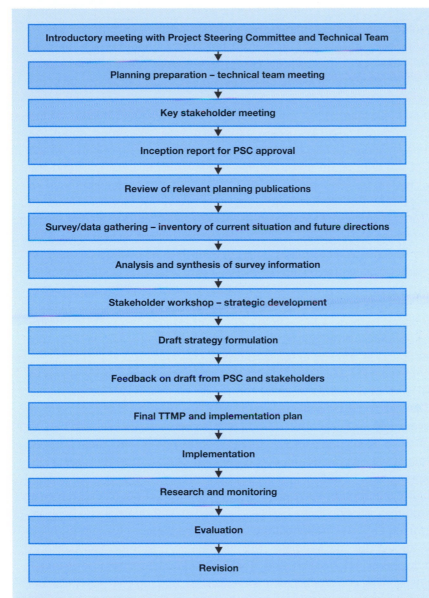

FIGURE 1.9 The TTMP planning process

(MICE) market, especially from sources closer to the destination such as Singapore, China, Hong Kong, and Japan in Asia and Dubai and Doha in the Middle East. To diversify demand, facilities at existing and proposed resorts were altered or created to support family holiday and health and wellness target markets. Additional big game fishing and dolphin watching attractions were also planned.

Human resources: An adequate supply of labor has long been a major problem of Maldives tourism. It is estimated that every year there were around 10,000 school leavers. While tourism offers employment in various fields, a key impediment to increasing Maldivian employment in tourism has been school leavers' attitude toward resort-based jobs. In recent decades, many young Maldivians have been unaware of the job opportunities offered in tourism and many perceive jobs in the industry as low grade.

Environmental: Tourism managers in Maldives have remained mindful of the fragility of the environment. Maldivian authorities were concerned about the impact of erosion and possible global warming on their low-lying country, where 80 percent of the area is 1m or less above sea level. Both the FTMP and the STMP drew the link between environmental protection and sustainable tourism development. At the time of the TTMP, the rapid growth of tourism presented further environmental challenges related to: 1) preserving natural beauty of the islands; 2) ensuring the adherence to Environmental Impact Assessment (EIA) requirements during and after resort construction; 3) conservation of reefs; 4) disposal of garbage generated by tourist resorts; and 5) discharge of effluent water.

Community-based tourism: Cultural and heritage tourism has not taken root in the Maldives despite the fact that the country is rich in culture and history. Community-based tourism, a focus in the TTMP, is expected to bring in greater economic opportunities to inhabited islands in the form of jobs and other gainful activities generated as a result of tourist demand.

Policy framework: The Maldives Tourism Act and lease agreement needed to be reviewed and amended to facilitate further development of tourism in the Maldives. The Act could be enhanced by taking into account the possibility of enacting several laws with each law dealing with separate subjects. Examples of such legislation could include an act on tourist resorts, hotels, and guest houses; an act on tourist vessels; an act on diving centers; or an act on tour operators and travel agents.

Infrastructure and support services: The government had developed ten new domestic airports in addition to the facilities planned in Alifu Dhaalu and Lhaviyani atolls. Developing airports throughout the nation helped spread tourism demand and supply throughout the Maldives. Marine-transport, storage facilities and distribution logistics, information and communications technology, disaster management planning, construction of marina facilities, and regional hospitals also presented infrastructure development opportunities.

Tourism planning outcomes

Economic expansion continues to be powered mainly by tourism, the backbone of the economy, and its spin-offs in the transportation, communication, and construction sectors. In 2011, reported tourist arrivals increased to 800,000 tourist visits annually. The total tourist arrival numbers during the TTMP period have trended higher. Tourist arrivals in 2010 rose dramatically by 20.7 percent over the previous year.[30] The Maldives Monetary Authority reported the decline

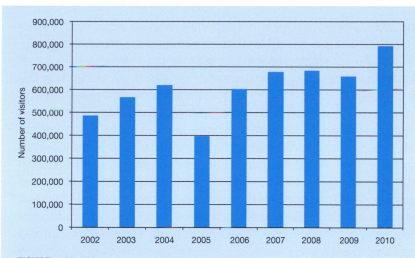

FIGURE 1.10 Historical tourist arrivals in the Maldives

in tourist arrivals in 2009, caused by the global downturn, appears to have bottomed out as indicated by the latest tourism statistics. Tourist arrivals, which have been on a downward trend since the last quarter of 2008, recorded an annual expansion for the second consecutive month and grew by 7 percent during November 2009.[31] The trend in visitation is presented in Figure 1.10.

The Indian Ocean tsunami in December 2004 destroyed many islands. The Maldivian economy made a noteworthy recovery, with a rebound in tourism and post-tsunami reconstruction that linked to the second and third tourism master plans. The negative impacts and strains of the unexpected natural event were lessened because of the planning efforts that were already in place. The tsunami interrupted the pattern and tourism losses were estimated to be US$300 million.[32] Recovery was well underway by 2006 when the international tourist number reached nearly 602,000.[33] However, after the recovery, the government still has a very difficult task in implementing TTMP strategies related to six areas: 1) facilitate sustainable growth; 2) increase employment opportunities and community participation; 3) infrastructure development; 4) environmental sustainability development; 5) Maldives' brand development; and 6) law and regulation development.

Recommendations for future planning

The Maldives has a huge economic dependence on tourism. Because of this and the severe consequences rises in sea level could have on the small island nation, the key lies in how to combine economic prosperity and biodiversity, which is part of the sustainable tourism concept.[34] Many studies have aimed to find the proper way to preserve and protect the Maldives' environment, such as Blanca de-Miguel-Molina and Rumiche-Sosa,[35] who analyzed the impact of luxury hotel development and operations on sustainability. Findings from this study show luxury resorts offer proportionately more activities and services that are not sustainable. Therefore, even if the Maldives is currently an exotic and luxury destination, it has the potential to be a luxury sustainable tourism destination, if sustainable practices were enhanced. Reaching this status will depend on the coordination of the various stakeholders involved and on the incentives given to the resorts in order to make them both sustainable and profitable.

At this point, policymakers could enhance the application of environmental policies as an incentive for resorts to be sustainable and profitable.[36] Moreover, the luxury resorts that would like to attract responsible travelers should communicate their environmental policies through their websites and other marketing avenues. The Third National Environment Action Plan of the Maldives, includes some goals which aim to reduce climate-related risks in the tourism sector and will need to be coordinated by strengthening Environmental Impact Assessments (EIAs) to ensure that all the significant impacts associated with new developments are understood and accounted for, taking stakeholder participation into consideration.[37]

The Maldives needs to be well-prepared for the next plan which must be built on lessons learned from past experience and studies showing new knowledge about tourism policy and planning. Tourism policy precepts that could be employed include localizing tourism advocacy, reaching out to atypical advocacy partners, anticipating policy needs, analyzing impacts of tourism policy, and confronting political realities.[38]

Nearly all major tourism stakeholders were involved in the tourism planning process. However, the general public was not as involved as they could have been. This is perhaps because of the unique geographic and access challenges for many of the Maldivians who are spread throughout the archipelago. In future planning efforts, this issue could be mitigated through the use of technology, such as Skype so that more citizens could participate in the planning process. The Fourth Tourism Master Plan, if one is to be developed, stands to be successful based on the positive outcomes of the previous three plans and the willingness of planners and policymakers in the Maldives to set a course for tourism development through sound tourism planning principles.

Concluding critical questions

As stated in the case study, the Maldivian tourism planning initiative is strong in several ways, but thinking critically about the plan and the concepts the plan employs could increase understanding of tourism planning using this case study. Most users of this book likely view tourism as more positive for economic and social development than negative, as this is true for many tourism planners, professionals, and some academics. Such readers may be more prepared to tackle questions that are less philosophical and more applied, but should always be willing to challenge their own perspectives on tourism development.

Philosophical questions raised by this case study abound. For example, should the Maldivian government develop tourism at all? How much does tourism development threaten the sustainability of the island nation? Is tourism development damaging to the social structure of Maldivians? Would the nation be better off with fewer international visitors?

Despite the strong philosophical debate to be had based on this case, more applied questions can also be asked, such as, other than what is mentioned in the case study, what else is missing in the tourism planning efforts? What can be done to remedy the missing pieces in future planning efforts in the Maldives or elsewhere? What could other destinations with fragile ecosystems learn from the planning efforts in the Maldives? Even destinations with ecosystems that are less fragile or with more-developed economies could learn from how Maldivian officials have planned tourism. What does the Maldives have to teach those destinations? What can the world learn from tourism development in the Maldives?

Notes

1 US Travel and Tourism Advisory Board (2006) *Restoring America's Travel Brand: National Strategy to Compete for International Visitors*. US Travel and Tourism Advisory Board, Washington, DC.

2 World Travel and Tourism Council (2012) *Travel & Tourism Economic Impact 2012 WORLD Edition*. Retrieved from www.wttc.org/site_media/uploads/downloads/world2012.pdf on July 1, 2012. London, UK.

3 Williams, W. & Riley, K. (2003) "Economic Impact Studies to Gain Support for Youth Sports from Local Businesses." *The Journal of Physical Education, Recreation & Dance, 74*(6), 49–51.

4 Ritchie, J.R.B. (1991) "Global Tourism Policy Issues: An Agenda for the 1990s." *World Travel and Tourism Review, 1*, 149–58.

5 Klein, Y.L., Osleeb, J.P., & Viola, M.R. (2004) "Tourism-Generated Earnings in the Coastal Zone: A Regional Analysis." *Journal of Coastal Research, 20*(4), 1080–8.

6 Frechtling, D. (1994) "Assessing the Impacts of Travel and Tourism – Measuring Economic Costs," in J.R.B. Ritchie and C.R. Goeldner (eds) *Travel, Tourism, and Hospitality Research: A Handbook for Managers and Researchers*, 2nd edn. New York: John Wiley and Sons, 401.

7 Berno, T. & Ward, C. (2005) "Innocence Abroad: A Pocket Guide to Psychological Research on Tourism." *American Psychologist, 60*(6), 593–600. Quote is from page 598.

8 Merriam-Webster Online Dictionary (2007).

9 Goeldner, C.R. & Ritchie, J.R.B. (2012) *Tourism: Principles, Practices, Philosophies*, 12th edn. New York: John Wiley and Sons, 326.

10 Biederman, P.S., Lai, J., Laitamaki, J.M., Messerli, H.R., Nyheim, P., & Plog, S. (2007) *Travel and Tourism: An Industry Primer*. New Jersey: Pearson Education, Inc.

11 Jenkins, J. (2001) "Editorial." *Current Issues in Tourism*, *4*(2–4), 69–77.

12 Edgell, D.L. (1990) *International Tourism Policy*. New York: Van Nostrand Reinhold, 1.

13 Fayos-Sola, E. (1996) "Tourism Policy: A Midsummer Night's Dream?" *Tourism Management*, *17*(6), 405–12.

14 Edgell, D.L. (1999) *Tourism Policy: The Next Millennium*. Champaign, IL: Sagamore.

15 Goeldner, C.R. & Ritchie, J.R.B. (2012) *Tourism: Principles, Practices, Philosophies*, 12th edn. New York: John Wiley and Sons, 327.

16 Cook, S.D. & Azucenas, V. (1994) "Research in State and Provincial Travel Offices," in J.R.B. Ritchie & C.R. Goeldner (eds) *Travel, Tourism, and Hospitality Research: A Handbook for Managers and Researchers*, 2nd edn. New York: John Wiley and Sons, 165–8.

17 Bull, P. (1997) "Tourism in London: Policy Changes and Planning Problems." *Regional Studies*, *31*(1), 82–5.

18 Travel Industry Association of America (2004) *Domestic Travel Market Report*. Washington, DC.

19 Central Intelligence Agency (2012) *World Fact Book: Maldives*. Retrieved from www.cia.gov/library/publications/the-world-factbook/geos/mv.html on July 1, 2012.

20 Metz, H.C. (ed.) (1994) *Maldives: A Country Study from Washington.* GPO for the Library of Congress, http://countrystudies.us/maldives/2.htm.

21 Ibid.

22 Central Intelligence Agency (2012).

23 Maldives Monetary Authority (2011) *Monthly Statistics May 2011*. Maldives: Maldives Monetary Authority.

24 Ministry of Finance and Treasury (2009) *Maldives Fiscal and Economic Outlook 2009–2011.* Paper presented at the Maldives Partnership Forum, Maldives.

25 Maldives Monetary Authority (2011).

26 Ministry of Finance and Treasury (2009).

27 Ministry of Tourism and Civil Aviation (2007) *Maldives Third Tourism Master Plan 2007–2011*. Maldives.

28 Ibid.

29 Ibid.

30 Maldives Monetary Authority (2011).

31 Maldives Monetary Authority (2009) *Monthly Economic Review December 2009*. Maldives: Maldives Monetary Authority.

32 Carlsen, J. (2006) "Post-tsunami tourism strategies for the Maldives." *Tourism Review International 10*, 69–79.

33 Henderson, J.C. (2008) "The Politics of Tourism: A Perspective from the Maldives." *Tourismos: An International Multidisciplinary Journal of Tourism*, *3*(1), 99–115.

34 Viner, M.A. (2005) *Climate Change and Its Impacts on Tourism*. Norwich, UK: University of East Anglia.

35 Blanca de-Miguel-Molina, M. & Rumiche-Sosa, M. (2011) "Does Luxury Indicate Sustainability? An Analysis of the Maldives." *Electronic Journal of Business Ethics and Organization Studies*, *16*(1).

36 Fotiu, S., Buhalis, D. & Vereczi, G. (2002) "Sustainable Development of Ecotourism in Small Island Developing States (SIDS) and Other Small Islands." *Tourism and Hospitality Research*, *4*(1), 79–88.

37 Zubair, S., Bowen, D. & Elwin, J. (2011) "Not Quite Paradise: Inadequacies of Environmental Impact Assessment in the Maldives." *Tourism Management*, *32*(2), 225–34.

38 Swanson, J.R. & Brothers, G.L. (2012) "Tourism policy agenda setting, interest groups and legislative capture." *International Journal of Tourism Policy*, *4*(3), 206–221.

Tourism policy issues of yesterday

To understand tourism policy in the current context and how tourism policy might change in the future, it is important to appreciate how tourism policy has developed over time. Tourism policy has progressed as travel began and evolved over the past 6,000 years. This chapter provides some historic perspectives of tourism policy and describes the beginnings of modern tourism policy in a global context.

Tourism policy in the United States is used to illustrate how tourism policy has progressed in one of the most popular global destinations, yet challenging tourism systems in terms of planning.

Historic perspectives

There is no single moment in the history of tourism to pinpoint as the sole foundation for tourism policy and planning. However, several key incidents throughout time have laid the foundation for modern tourism policy and planning. The invention of paper, innovation in shipbuilding, and mapmaking are examples of historical advancements that have influenced modern tourism policy. The following sections expand on these and other key incidents in prehistoric times, the period of antiquity, and the Middle Ages.

Prehistoric

The prehistoric period covers the time before recorded history. Archaeologists, paleontologists, and anthropologists have provided evidence that our ancestral species *Homo erectus*, about two million years ago, was the pre-human long-legged man that walked upright with long strides much as we do today. *Homo erectus* stood erect and had the ability to walk or run long distances. While *Homo erectus* had very small brains, the species was capable of building fires, organizing hunts for food, and fashioning crude tools. A next step in human evolution and in the history of travel is when *Homo erectus* began to travel beyond their normal habitats to new environments.

By about 400,000–500,000 years ago *Homo erectus* had evolved into our more advanced ancestors, the *Homo sapiens*. With larger skulls, more brain capacity and greater curiosity, *Homo sapiens* traveled much greater distances than their predecessors. The travel of this species was largely confined to moving from place to place in search of food, shelter, and safety from wild beasts and hostile tribes. Certainly, in relation to this early travel there is no way of knowing how decisions related to travel developed and progressed.

Antiquity

The period of antiquity spans from c.4000 BCE (Before the Common Era) to the fourth century CE (Common Era). Eventually, after thousands of years and many evolutionary changes, antediluvian man migrated from the Rift Valley in East Africa, eventually into the Middle East and Asia. By about 4000 BCE in the *Fertile Crescent*, referred to as "The Cradle of Civilization," part of the present day Middle East region, roughly including segments or all of the countries of Iraq, Iran, Kuwait, Turkey, Syria, Jordan, Israel, Lebanon, Palestine, and Egypt, is the area from which modern travel evolved. It was the progressive Sumerians in this time period that revolutionized the ability to travel. This society invented the plow, money, cuneiform writing, the wheel, and a concept for a tour guide. Partially as a result of the plow, agriculture production led to increased travel to trade food for goods. Having money allowed travelers a choice to either barter or pay for their travel needs. Cuneiform writing made it easier to produce travel directions, rough maps, and some form of a travel itinerary. The invention of the wheel was of major significance as crude wagons were developed for transport, travel, and commerce. These inventions led to greater business relations with such distant countries as India, a desire to visit new destinations, and a need for a travel guide. Such developments became the basis for travel *planning*, which eventually would produce rudimentary *policy* guidelines making travel easier and more organized.

By 3000 BCE the Egyptian society was building wooden boats as long as 75ft for trade and military purposes and for use in traveling the beautiful 4,000 miles of the Nile River to celebrate the changing of the seasons, good harvests, and thanking the gods for their rich life. Certainly before this time period primitive man had developed crudely constructed boats for fishing and other purposes but most of these were roughly hewn canoes or simply-assembled rafts, possibly coracles, or skin-floats. But the famed Greek historian Herodotus (c.485–425 BCE), a worldly traveler and travel writer, recorded that:

> The Egyptians have religious gatherings not just once a year but frequently, especially and most enthusiastically in the city of Bubastis in honor of Artemis

[The virgin goddess of the hunt and the moon and twin sister of Apollo] . . . This is what they do when they travel to Bubastis: men actually travel together with women, and large numbers of both travel in each boat. Some of the women have rattles, which they shake, while some men play the flute during the whole voyage. The rest of the men and women sing and clap their hands . . . When they arrive at Bubastis, they celebrate huge sacrifices and have a feast. They drink more grape wine during this feast than in all the rest of the year . . .[1]

The walls of the temple of Deir el-Bahri in Luxor, Egypt hold bas-reliefs and text describing Egyptian Queen Hatshepsut's journey to the land of Punt, c.1480 BCE. In addition, the building of the great pyramids, the Sphinx and other facilities led to travel for pleasurable pursuits. While we know the Egyptians enjoyed many of the tourism-related activities that continue to be popular in modern times, both on water and land, their principal contribution to early tourism *policy* and *planning* is founded in the organization of cruises, and the identification and *planning* of festivals and events.

Not long after 3000 BCE, innovative boat-builders began to design vessels that could sail along seacoasts and beyond. About 2000 BCE the master shipwrights and bold navigators, the Phoenicians, developed impressive sea-going vessels and mapped trade routes throughout the Mediterranean region. These highly intelligent peoples fabricated sophisticated sea-worthy merchant vessels, state-of-the-art warships, and pleasure cruise ships that could sail the open seas safely and for long distances. Their mapped trade routes increased the knowledge of waterways and coastlines. They developed travel patterns that were made easier to follow by using stars to navigate (the North Star – so named by the Greeks – was originally known as the "Phoenician Star"). They also established trading centers along the coasts of North Africa, Sicily and Spain, spreading their culture and knowledge among less-advanced peoples. There are even theories that the Phoenicians were the first to travel to America, and accounts written by Greek historian Herodotus imply that they circumnavigated Africa. In addition to seamanship, the Phoenicians excelled in literature, arts, architecture and engineering. They invented an alphabet (still in use today), teaching it to the Greeks and Mediterranean communities. Certainly their travels added important information about Mediterranean destinations. One could surmise that the Phoenicians were travel planners and possibly had developed some fundamental *policy* guidelines related to trade and tourism.[2]

The Greeks were one of the first societies to understand and write about tourism as we think of it today. Homer, writing in *The Odyssey* towards the end of the eighth century, BCE said: "A guest never forgets the host who had treated him kindly." This quotation is a precursor to the modern definition of quality tourism. In Plato's *Phaedo* (360 BCE), Socrates stated, "A great many different countries go to make up our world . . . It is an enormous place, and we, whose civilization spreads from the river Phasis to the Pillars of Hercules, occupy only a small part of it. In other places, there are other men living in countries similar to ours."

The Greeks were also the first to organize, promote, and accommodate large numbers of visitors for sporting events. The early Greek society revered the body, especially with respect to performances in sporting events. As outlets for their athletic prowess and cultural interest, and to appease the gods, they developed a series of athletic-cultural events and contests. The more popular ones became known as the Olympic Games, Pythian Games, Isthmian Games, and Nemean Games. Much like today's sporting events, these early athletic contests and activities attracted leisure visitors from near and far. The oldest and most popular of the four great Games were the Olympic Games held every four years in honor of Zeus at Olympus. The Olympic Games, first held in 776 BCE, included, in addition to athletic events, contests of dance and choral poetry. During the Games, there was also much attention to art, music, sculpture, plays, storytelling, public speaking, food, drink, and other cultural activities. The Olympics then and now truly represent tourism in all its many varieties and vagaries. Herodotus and a few other early travelers began to make suggestions of popular places to visit. By 170 CE, the Greek Pausanias published a comprehensive travel publication. His ten-volume travel guide titled *A Guide to Greece*, described the wonderful opportunities for travel throughout Greece. The Greeks certainly gave future generations some food for thought in developing tourism policies and plans.[3]

There is interesting information[4] about the contributions to tourism by the Roman society as described by the Roman Sidonius Apollinaris (c.430–489 CE). The Romans, largely for military purposes facilitated travel by means of the building of good roads (many of which were paved), rest-stops, inns, eating establishments, and recreation centers throughout their empire. There are earlier accounts of built roadways, such as the well-developed roads in India as early as 326 BCE, and in Persia, between 500 and 400 BCE but the Roman roads were the best for different kinds of travel. The principal contribution to modern tourism policy by the Romans was their emphasis on security; keeping the roads safe from terrorists, bandits, and marauding enemies and the seas clear of pirates. The Romans' efforts to meet travelers' demands for accommodations and tourist services were certainly a prelude to tourism *policy* and *planning*.

Travel by a sea-going vessel advanced at different stages and for differing reasons throughout the world. Journeys by the Vikings or the Norse explorers, warriors, merchants, and pirates – who, from about 800 CE until 1066 CE, raided, traded, explored, and settled in new lands – added significantly to the travel lore. These incredible travelers used their famed longboats to travel to the great city of Constantinople as well as into Russia. Records of their travel and explorations have largely survived by word of mouth and legend, making it difficult to fully understand their impact on the world of travel. However, it is clear they made many new discoveries but unfortunately left no written reports of where they had been and how they had traveled. Figure 2.1 shows a well-maintained relic of Viking travel.

As civilizations advanced in different parts of the world, travel became more commonplace. The Mongol empires and the reign of the Khans, rulers of China, added a completely new dimension to land travel. Lest we forget, the empire of

FIGURE 2.1 The Viking ship *Oseberg* on display at the Viking Ship Museum in Bygdøy, Norway – home of the world's best preserved collection of Viking ships (Photo: Jason R. Swanson)

the great Mongol conqueror and military traveler, Genghis Khan, was more than twice the size of the Roman Empire at its zenith. However, there appears to be no helpful records that would shed light on whether tourism policy or planning took place.

Middle Ages

We have to wait for Marco Polo (1254–1324), one of the earliest Europeans known to have crossed the continent of Asia, recording what he saw and heard, to provide a rough concept of travel policy and planning direction in tourism. Marco Polo is thought to have been born in the city-state maritime Republic of Venice, a highly advanced world trading center. Venice was a major maritime power, the epicenter of commerce and a trade leader with the Byzantine Empire and the Islamic world. Marco Polo's interest in travel developed as a result of being part of a family of aggressive commercial businessmen who had traveled and traded extensively in the Middle East and beyond for a long time. This Venetian traveler left vivid accounts of his travel, written in his book, *The Travels of Marco Polo*, which allow us to begin to understand the early, broad ramifications of tourism development and some possible policies governing tourism at that time.

We do know that travel in the world of over 700 years ago represented anything but rational order. For example, a foreign traveler was beset with strange customs, chaotic travel conditions, and, depending on the chosen destination and culture, varying degrees of hospitality. To pursue the wonders of the world at that particular moment in time, Marco Polo was willing to travel by foot, horseback, camel, carriage, and boat under some of the most difficult circumstances imaginable. This famous traveler endured enormous hardships in his quest to arrive at his destinations. However, Marco Polo brought back with him copious amounts of information revealing new inventions, different customs, interesting products and nuances of other cultures. His interactions with the great ruler Kublai Khan of China and his ability to learn and to transfer knowledge are aptly chronicled in his travel book. His book, a bestseller throughout Europe, was accepted as the *bible* for describing the social, cultural, economic, and environmental conditions of the places he had visited – Central Asia, Mongolia, China, Tibet, Burma, Siam, Ceylon, Java, India, and other destinations largely unknown in Europe.

Marco Polo's book, originally written in French, captured the imagination of Europe and was in constant demand for many years, having been translated into many different languages. Educated Europeans read Marco Polo's book, which further stimulated Europe's interest to obtain spices, silks, and other products from the East. Indirectly it was Polo's book, read many times and with notes scribbled on certain pages by Christopher Columbus that increased Columbus' interest in travel and explorations. This was also true of another explorer, Ferdinand Magellan, who (reportedly) read Marco Polo's book before and during his circumnavigation of the globe. There were many other explorers and travelers that became excited about travel to Asia as a result of reading Marco Polo's famous book.

Marco Polo, then, is the best early "cornerstone" person to provide information that made rational sense regarding travel, gave it some direction and helped us to understand how travel impacts world culture. He identified socio-cultural aspects of travel, environmental conditions at a number of locations, and the complications of traveling in sparsely populated areas. His book aroused curiosity in others, leading to greater world travel, which continues to grow to this day. Marco Polo most likely deserves partial recognition as the "father of early tourism policy."

Many great travelers followed Marco Polo, including Ibn Battuta (1304–1374), the great Muslim traveler of the Middle East. Often referred to as the "Marco Polo of the Middle East," Ibn Battuta traveled much further than Marco Polo and for a longer period of time. He was a man of enormous curiosity and energy, but the book he wrote about his travels in the Middle East (and beyond to India and China) were mainly of interest to a limited number of Muslims. The book received very little publicity and was almost forgotten. However, those who learned of Battuta's travels changed the outlook for Muslim travel and, while he added greatly to the knowledge of important destinations of that time, tourism policy was beyond his scope.

Another great traveler following Marco Polo and Ibn Battuta was Zheng He (1371–1433) of China. During the fourteenth century, the Chinese led the world in oceangoing ship construction and technology, having developed large compart-mentalized ships and effective sails. The Chinese super vessels, with six masts, had decks that could carry as many as 1,000 men. The Chinese Yongle Emperor chose Zheng He to organize a huge armada of ships to sail long distances and make announcements to the world of his great accomplishments in China. Zheng He prepared a fleet of more than 300 vessels with approximately 37,000 men as crew and support personnel. At that time, the world had never seen such an extravagant expedition nor ships as large (the largest was 444ft long). Zheng He visited nearly every inhabited land bordering the China Sea and the Indian Ocean. His voyages set the stage for future travel and explorations. While highly organized and exceedingly well planned, the "policy" was to let the world know of the great Chinese empire and not necessarily to increase travel.

The beginnings of modern tourism policy

If Marco Polo is considered as providing some aspects that might be related to early tourism policy, we have to wait almost another 700 years to reach a place in history where we can identify what leads to the beginnings of modern tourism policy. In searching for a place to begin the discussion of tourism policy, we have focused on a partial review of the background and history of the most important global tourism body, the United Nations World Tourism Organization (UNWTO). There were important tourism policies developed by individual countries prior to UNWTO but their contributions to overall tourism policy are beyond the scope and research of this book.

The UNWTO is the most widely recognized and the leading international organization in the field of travel and tourism. "It serves as a global forum for tourism policy issues, provides moral leadership for the vast international tourism sector, and is a practical source of tourism know-how for its members. Its member-ship includes 154 countries, 7 territories, and more than 400 affiliate members representing local government, tourism associations, educational institutions, and private-sector companies, including airlines, hotel groups, and tour operators."[5]

The UNWTO began in 1925 as the International Congress of Official Tourist Traffic Associations, located in The Hague, Netherlands, and was renamed the International Union of Official Tourist Publicity Organizations in 1934. After World War II, and as tourism was beginning to increase, another conversion took place in 1947 resulting in a new name: the International Union of Official Travel Organizations (IUOTO) and it relocated in 1951 to Geneva, Switzerland. In this era, a key policy was to promote trade and tourism as part of economic development strategies, especially for developing nations. By 1970, IUOTO, seeking to form a strong world organization for tourism held a Special General Assembly meeting in Mexico City and adopted statutes to form the World Tourism Organization (WTO). For the next four years discussions took place on strategies to obtain acceptance by enough countries to ratify the statutes. A key concern was developing a budget formula that potential member countries could justify to their respective leaders. The key budget decision came in 1974 in a meeting in Lusaka, Zambia, whereby no single country would pay more than 20 percent of the total WTO budget. The prescribed 51 countries ratified the statutes and IUOTO became the World Tourism Organization. The next major question was where WTO would be located. Many countries were seeking to be the headquarters for WTO but in the end Madrid, Spain, was selected. The General Assembly was held in 1975 in Madrid and in 1976 WTO became an executing agency of the United Nations Development Program. Then, in 2003, WTO became a United Nations specialized agency and today is the United Nations World Tourism Organization.

The UNWTO is vested by the United Nations with a central and decisive role in promoting the development of responsible, sustainable, and universally accessible tourism, with the aim of contributing to economic development, international understanding, peace, prosperity, and universal respect for and the observance of human rights and fundamental freedoms. In pursuing this aim, the UNWTO pays particular attention to the interests of the developing countries in the field of tourism.[6] In effect, UNWTO is the leading international organization in almost every aspect of international tourism, including tourism policy. It serves as a global forum for tourism policy issues, definitions, directives, data, research, education, human resource development, facilitation, crisis guidelines, sustainability, development and worldwide economic cooperation. Additional information with respect to the impact of the UNWTO on tourism policy appears throughout this book.

Another global organization that has impacts on tourism policy is the World Travel and Tourism Council (WTTC). WTTC is composed of the chief executives of 100 of the world's foremost travel and tourism-related companies representing all regions of the world. In the 1980s it was noted that travel and tourism was the largest sector of the world economy providing the most jobs yet few people recognized its impact. As a result, WTTC was established in 1990 to raise the awareness of the impact of travel. "Their vision of travel and tourism is that of a partnership among all stake-holders, delivering consistent results that match the needs of national economies, local and regional authorities, and local communities with those of business, based on: (1) governments recognizing travel and tourism as a top priority; (2) business balancing economics with people, culture, and the environment; and (3) a shared pursuit of long-term growth and prosperity."[7] WTTC, through its research partner, United Kingdom-based Oxford Economics, provides enormous amounts of research and data that explain the macroeconomic impact on the world from travel and tourism. This information in turn is used by governments in developing their tourism policies and plans.

A tourism policy issue that has gained recent interest and momentum is the debate regarding the impact tourism may have on peace. The Ancient Olympic Games (776 BCE), may offer early evidence for this concept. At the time of the first Olympic Games, many city-states in Greece and nearby countries were in constant conflict. The Olympic Games, the largest international event in ancient times, introduced what became known as the Olympic Truce whereby warring factions would cease all warfare and hostilities so that athletes and visitors could travel in safety to participate in or attend the Olympic Games.[8] Today, there is an organization exclusively devoted to peace through tourism, the International Institute for Peace Through Tourism (IIPT) headquartered in Stowe, Vermont, US. IIPT is a not-for-profit organization dedicated to fostering and facilitating tourism initiatives that contribute to international understanding and cooperation, a quality environment, and preservation of the history, heritage, and culture of the destination.

International tourism policy for the United States

As an example of how a single country went about developing a tourism policy, we have chosen the United States of America for discussion, because of our intimate knowledge and in some cases direct participation (by David L. Edgell, Sr.).[9] The development of a tourism policy for the United States came late in comparison with most major countries of the world. As noted earlier, by 1925 many countries were joining together to further the interests in world tourism.

The first humble efforts in developing a US tourism policy appeared in 1940 with the passage of the US Domestic Travel Act (US 76th Congress – Public Law 755). This Act charged the Secretary of the Interior, through the US National Park Service, with the responsibility for encouraging travel within the US, its territories, and possessions. In conjunction with this policy, the Act authorized the Secretary to disseminate travel information, including graphic materials, in foreign languages. Suggesting the use of foreign languages in the promotion of travel materials was a rather novel idea for the US.

The US Domestic Travel Act was superseded in 1941 by American involvement in World War II. It ceased to be an effective travel policy as the US geared up to produce war materials to ship overseas and most domestic and international leisure travel decreased substantially except such travel related to the war efforts. After the end of the war, US tourism policy was linked to helping improve economic conditions in Europe. Europe was in economic shambles resulting from the devastation, lack of money, and destruction caused by the war. US efforts were aimed toward ways and means to help rebuild Europe's economy, and tourism became a prime tool for economic development and a potential source for Europe to quickly earn badly needed foreign currency exchange. Despite widespread destruction, most of Europe's ancient historic treasures, beautiful architecture and unique structures survived the war. As part of the effort toward the restructuring of Europe's economy, the US Government encouraged American citizens to visit Europe, which resulted in a large infusion of US currency into Europe's economy at a critical point in time. Americans had the economic means to travel, and Europe was in a position to rekindle its tourism industry much faster than its industrial production base. Thus, the US development of an *ad hoc* international tourism policy was, at first, principally oriented toward helping in Europe's economic recovery.

The best place to review the development of US tourism policy is to read the White Paper *Tourism in the European Recovery Program*, June 1950, developed jointly by the US Economic Cooperation Administration and the US Department of Commerce.[10] These two administrative units of the US Government worked with various European groups, largely through the Organisation for European Economic Co-operation (a predecessor of the Organisation for Economic Co-operation and Development), to alleviate travel restrictions and barriers and to promote American travel to Europe.

The White Paper evolved from the "Travel in the Marshall Plan" of 1948–9. This was named for George C. Marshall, a general during World War II, Chief of Staff, United States Army and chief military adviser to President Franklin D. Roosevelt. As Secretary of State after the war, his name was given to the Marshall Plan for which he was awarded the Nobel Peace Prize in 1953. The Marshall Plan was comprehensive including a major segment on US travel to Europe. Under the Marshall Plan, the US Government worked to lift visas and other restrictions, and encouraged the US private-sector to promote and provide reasonable travel costs for Americans traveling to Europe. Limited statistics available during the 1950s revealed that American travel to Europe increased, greatly helping Europe's economic recovery.

By 1954, it was clear that a tourism policy that was beneficial to the United States needed to be developed. New statistics had become available making it clear that US travel abroad, particularly to Europe, had increased notably and that the early US tourism policy had been successful. The statistics clearly pointed to the fact that the international balance of trade in tourism was beginning to hurt the US balance of payments. It was determined that US Government agencies needed guidelines to follow when engaged in foreign economic policy discussions with other nations regarding tourism. On May 27, 1954, recognizing the need for a tourism policy, US President Dwight D. Eisenhower sent a memorandum to the Secretary of Commerce giving general guidelines for such a policy. The memorandum is reproduced here in its entirety:

> In my message to the Congress on the subject of foreign economic policy I emphasized the Importance of international travel both for its cultural and social advantages of the free world for its great economic significance. In my message I stated that I would instruct the appropriate agencies and departments, at home and abroad, to consider how they can facilitate international travel. I made specific note that these agencies would be requested to simplify procedures where practicable relating to customs, visas, passports, exchange or monetary restrictions, and other regulations that sometimes harass the traveler. I request that you take appropriate steps on these and related matters, consistent with your responsibilities in this field, to encourage international travel consonant with the national interest. I am sending similar requests to the Departments of Justice, State, and Treasury.

A side note to US tourism policy is that, as Supreme Allied Commander in Europe during World War II, General Dwight D. Eisenhower witnessed the horrific results of war. Memories of the devastation and suffering that took place during the war haunted him for the remainder of his life. On September 11, 1956, President Eisenhower established People to People International (PTPI)[11] to enhance international understanding and friendship through educational, cultural and humanitarian activities involving the exchange of ideas and experiences of peoples of different countries and diverse cultures. This work continues, led by Eisenhower's grand-daughter, Mary Jean Eisenhower. In 2006, PTPI was the first organization awarded the Cavaliere per la Pace (Knight of Peace Award).

Under the Mutual Security Act of 1957, President Eisenhower directed that a study of the barriers to international travel and ways of promoting such travel be undertaken. A very small Office of International Travel was created within the US Department of Commerce to assist with this effort. This study was completed on April 17, 1958, and submitted as an *International Travel Report to the President of the United States* by Clarence B. Randall, Special Assistant to President Eisenhower.[12] In his transmittal letter to the president, Randall identified some of the policy implications of international tourism:

> I hold the strong conviction that tourism has deep significance for the peoples of the modern world, and that the benefits of travel can contribute to the cause of peace through improvement not only in terms of economic advancement but also with respect to our political, cultural, and social relationships as well . . .
>
> The freedom to travel is a dramatic freedom. It is a unique instrument of the friendly, peaceful communication among the nations and the peoples of the earth . . . The United States could exercise no more powerful influence in behalf of peace than to display strong leadership in promoting through travel the interchange of friendly visits among the people of the world . . .

Randall's report, *International Travel*, stimulated the Eisenhower administration and the US Congress to action in developing legislation resulting in the International Travel Act. By the time the US Congress passed this legislation, John F. Kennedy had been elected President and he signed the International Travel Act into law in 1961.[13] President Kennedy, like President Eisenhower, had served in the military during World War II and wished to promote international travel as an economic development tool and as a means to lead toward a more peaceful world. The International Travel Act established the United States Travel Service (USTS) and mandated that USTS seek to "stimulate and encourage travel to the United States by residents of foreign countries for the purpose of study, culture, recreation, business, and other activities as a means of promoting friendly understanding and good will among people of foreign countries and the United States." A few selected provisions taken from the Act help explain the policy implications:

(b) There is established a national tourism policy to –

1) Optimize the contributions of the tourism and recreation industries to the position of the United States with respect to international competitiveness, economic prosperity, full employment, and the balance of payments;

2) Increase United States export earnings from United States tourism and transportation services traded internationally;

7) Contribute to personal growth, health, education, and intercultural appreciation of the geography, history, and ethnicity of the United States;

8) Encourage the free and welcome entry of individuals traveling to the United States, in order to enhance international understanding and goodwill . . .

As long as President Kennedy was in the White House, progress on implementing the tourism policy provisions in the Act was made. After President Kennedy's assassination in 1963, Vice-President Lyndon B. Johnson became President. His administration seemingly took very little interest in the Act, nor did that of his successor, Richard Nixon. When President Nixon resigned in 1974, Vice-President Gerald Ford became President. It was under the short term of President Ford in 1974 when significant tourism policy research began in his administration and in the US Congress. This shift toward US tourism policy will be fully explained in the next section, which details the US National Tourism Policy Act of 1981.

Momentarily returning to President Eisenhower's impact on tourism policy, it is significant to review his contribution to domestic tourism policy and his interest in establishing the US system of interstate highways. His initial interest in US highways can be directly attributed to his experiences as an army military officer in 1919. He was a participant in the US Army's first Transcontinental Motor Convoy across the United States on the historic Lincoln Highway, the first major highway across the country. He noted that as the convoy crossed the country they were greeted warmly by the people in each community and there was a sense that the population was interested in a better highway program than the poorly constructed and maintained Lincoln Highway. Eisenhower realized after this trip the desirability for a high-quality system of roadways throughout the United States for the movement of military personnel and equipment, should such a need ever arise.

His 1919 experience would be revisited during his wartime experiences of World War II. During the war he gained respect and appreciation of the speed and movement of military vehicles in the highly developed German Autobahn highway system. He noted that the US needed a highway system that could be used in moving troops and military supplies if the country were invaded. Eisenhower also envisioned the importance and benefits of uniting American communications and transportation systems that a strong interstate highway system would provide.

Once Eisenhower became President, he had the opportunity to act on developing a US interstate highway system. His administration led efforts through Congress that resulted in his signing the Federal Aid Highway Act on June 29, 1956. This Act provided the funding for the building of interstate highways throughout the nation and the actions mandated by this Act forever changed domestic tourism (and to a lesser extent international tourism) in the United States. Initially the interstate highway system was called the National Highway Defense System but it was later renamed the Dwight David Eisenhower National System of Interstate and Defense Highways.[14,15]

Importance of the US National Tourism Policy Act of 1981

From a broad spectrum, President Dwight D. Eisenhower is the most likely candidate for the title of "father of US tourism policy," however, additional efforts toward a comprehensive tourism policy commenced in the 1970s. On June 24, 1974, US Senate Resolution 347, cosponsored by 71 senators, authorized the Senate Committee on Commerce, Science, and Transportation (Committee) to undertake a National Tourism Policy Study. The purpose of the Study was ". . . to develop legislation and other recommendations to make the Federal role in tourism more effective and responsive to the national interests in tourism, and the needs of the public and private-sectors of the industry." The US Department of Commerce, representing the executive branch of government on tourism policy, served as a major resource of information and a contributor of valuable research for this Study. At the same time, US Senate staffers and the US tourism private and public sectors made their views known.

Work on the Study continued for two years and in October 1976, the Committee issued the Study's first interim report, *A Conceptual Basis for the National Tourism Policy Study*.[16] This report gave an overview of legislation that affects tourism, tentatively identified the national interests in tourism and listed problems associated with the federal role in tourism policy. It also identified research that was needed for developing a national tourism policy.

In June 1977, the Committee issued a second interim report, the *National Tourism Policy Study Ascertainment Phase*.[17] This report reviewed and analyzed input from the tourism and travel industry on the issues, problems, and needs of local, state, public, and private-sectors of the industry, both in general terms and in terms of their specific relationships to federal agencies and programs. It suggested that the Federal Government had a significant role to play in tourism, and that its programs must be developed in full partnership with other public and private entities. This report provided valuable data and analysis for a national tourism policy.

The last phase, the *National Tourism Policy Study Final Report*, was completed in April 1978.[18] The *Report* recognized that the tourism and travel industry has a significant and enduring contribution to economic growth, employment, and income in the United States as well as to the physical, social, and cultural welfare of US citizens. It added that, ". . . leisure travel and associated recreational activities are a principal means for maintaining the physical and mental well-being of the population, for contributing to personal growth and education, and for enhancing cultural understanding and appreciation of the diverse nature of the Nation's historical, cultural and natural heritage." Furthermore, from the development of a fundamental tourism policy, the report recognized that "Within the Federal Government there exists a very large number of policies and activities with impacts on tourism, travel and associated recreational activities, which are fragmented and often duplicative and conflicting." Recommendations were made in the report to resolve such conflicts.

On March 27, 1978, author David L. Edgell, Sr., discussed the need for a US Government Tourism Policy when he addressed the Eighth Annual Conference of the Society of Government Economists in Washington, DC. He suggested that "The success of the tourism sector as an economic development tool will depend heavily on the United States pragmatically exercising its responsibility in planning public policy initiatives, coordinating policy with the public and private-sectors, and explaining to the public the important role tourism plays in international (and domestic) economic policies."[19] Dr. Edgell advocated that international trade in tourism policy would bolster the US balance-of-trade and add to the country's overall economic policies. He explained that tourism could help local communities increase economic development, realize increased revenues, create new jobs, benefit from a diverse economy, add new products, generate additional income, spawn new businesses, and contribute to overall economic integration while enriching the public and private partnerships and improving the quality-of-life of the local citizenry.

By 1979 it was fully recognized by the Committee on Commerce, Science, and Transportation that, "To date no legislation has been enacted which provides tourism and tourism-related programs with policy guidance regarding the national interests in tourism or the resolution of conflicts among various interests." The Committee submitted a comprehensive piece of tourism policy legislation for consideration by the US Congress. After considerable discussion in 1979 of the results of the studies, debates in Congress and within the executive branch as well as consultations with states, cities and the private-sector, a compromise piece of legislation – Senate 1097 – titled the *National Tourism Policy Act*, was passed in 1980 by the US Congress (both the House of Representatives and the Senate). All segments of government and the private-sector appeared to fully endorse the Act. On December 24, 1980, President Jimmy Carter surprisingly vetoed the legislation. This move, which blind-sided tourism professionals and policymakers, left the US without a comprehensive tourism policy.

In January 1981, Ronald Reagan took office as US President. Part of his campaign message in 1980 was aimed at supporting tourism. Shortly after he became President, he directed his Secretary of Commerce, Malcolm Baldrige, Jr. to review the National Tourism Policy Act that had previously been passed by Congress. The legislation was reintroduced early in 1981 and was passed by Congress on October 11, 1981. Shortly thereafter it was signed into law by President Ronald Reagan on October 16, 1981 (with a retroactive date of October 1, 1981). This Act, which is reprinted as a case study for this chapter, redefined the national interest in tourism and created the United States Travel and Tourism Administration (USTTA), which replaced the US Travel Service, as the nation's national government tourism office.

The principal mission of USTTA under the Act was to implement broad tourism policy initiatives, to develop travel to the United States from abroad as a stimulus to economic stability and the growth of the US travel industry, to reduce the nation's travel deficit and to promote friendly understanding and appreciation of the United States abroad. Although the USTTA was responsible for implementation, the comprehensive nature of the 1981 Act includes various cabinets and agencies within the United States federal government: the Department of Transportation, the Department of Labor, and the Department of the Interior are examples of agencies

FIGURE 2.2 Tourists enjoy the Abraham Lincoln Home National Historic Site in Springfield, Illinois, US. The site is administered by the National Park Service, an agency of the United States Department of the Interior (Photo: Jason R. Swanson)

listed in the Act. Each of these agencies is responsible for managing or regulating important tourism supply components such as highways, employment, and recreation.

By passage and implementation of the Act, the importance of tourism policy within the US was elevated. The appointment of an Under-Secretary of Commerce for Travel and Tourism (a high-level position appointed by the President) was a major step in demonstrating to the US travel industry and the international community the importance of tourism policy to the United States. It is important simply to recognize that this Act was the most comprehensive identification of tourism policy within the US and allowed the country to be a major player in the United Nations World Tourism Organization and other international bodies interested in tourism policy.

US tourism policy after the National Tourism Policy Act of 1981

To further enhance tourism policy, the Tourism Policy and Export Promotion Act of 1992 was passed by Congress and signed into law by President George H.W. Bush. This law recognized the importance of tourism's contribution to the US economy.

The Act supported a working budget for USTTA and created the Rural Tourism Development Foundation, intended to help utilize tourism as an economic development tool for rural areas across America. The original intent was that the private-sector would fund the Foundation. In reality, the private-sector in travel and tourism saw very little reason to support the Foundation and, with a few minor exceptions, funding for rural tourism development has been ignored.

Under the National Tourism Policy Act of 1981, international tourism to the United States grew by large percentages over previous years and the US tourism profession blossomed. The United States became an important contributor to international organizations such as the United Nations World Tourism Organization (UNWTO) and regional organizations such as the Organisation for Economic Co-operation and Development, the Organization of American States, the Asia-Pacific Economic Council, and the Caribbean Tourism Organization. The image of the US abroad had greatly improved as global tourism grew. From 1981 to 1995, the US enjoyed the benefits of having a broad international tourism policy.

In 1993, Bill Clinton became President of the United States. His initial lack of interest in a tourism policy appeared early on in his administration as he delayed appointing a new Under Secretary of Commerce for Travel and Tourism. However, in 1995, he did hold the first ever White House Conference on tourism in which the private-sector and state representatives advocated a strong tourism policy. But in 1996, President Clinton and the 104th Congress purposely failed to fund the USTTA, which in effect abolished the organization. For all intents and purposes the US was left without a comprehensive tourism policy. The country resigned its membership in the prestigious UNWTO and no longer played a role in regional international tourism organizations.

George W. Bush became President in 2001. There is no information to suggest whether President Bush intended to ignore tourism policy like his predecessor or to introduce new tourism policies principally because of attacks by terrorists on the United States on September 11, 2001. The terrorist attacks transformed the President's policies into a wartime mode. Following the attacks, international travel to the US declined dramatically. President Bush formed a new cabinet-level Department of Homeland Security and the US followed a foreign policy making it difficult for international visitors to come to the country. Restrictive visa policies and onerous inspections at airports and elsewhere were instituted, further suggesting to the world the US was not that interested in international visitors. Some would say that the terrorists had won: their actions forced governments to rethink and abandon policies favorable to tourism; governments and businesses were denied the commercial and economic benefits of tourism; and many leisure travelers became fearful to travel.

While the US Government was floundering as far as tourism policy was concerned after the terrorist attacks, tourism in the US was suffering. In an August 2005 issue of *Travel Insights*, a publication of the Travel Industry Association of America (now the US Travel Association), the cover page was titled "The Challenge to Brand America: The Travel Industry Is the Answer to Reversing America's Deteriorating Image Abroad." The publication stated:

The image of the US in the international community is poor and has been slow to improve. While inbound international travel grew 12 percent from 2003 to 2004, it is still more than 5 million visitors behind 2000 levels. Travel Industry Association of America analysis shows the US market share of worldwide international travel has declined 36 percent since 1992. In this day and age of a global economy and the global village that is shrinking as more and more people have easy access to travel quickly and easily, the US is being marginalized in the new global travel market.

The article further cited additional problems and that the US Government had no firm tourism policy or budget for promoting international tourism while most of the rest of the world's governments were actively promoting tourism to their respective countries.

On May 10, 2004, President Bush's Secretary of State Colin Powell addressed the Travel Business Roundtable: "We can continue to be a welcoming country even as we take measures to secure our borders . . . Travel and tourism is one of the most vital segments of that [US] economy." Later, on November 4, 2005, as a private citizen, Powell delivered a keynote address at a dedication ceremony at the Terry Sanford Institute of Public Policy in North Carolina. He expressed concern that after the September 11, 2001, terrorist attacks, people got the impression that America was not as friendly, due in part to restrictive travel measures. He said the US had to take such steps, but after a few years, he saw that America was paying a price for it. He also stated that America needed to show the world that it had not changed, that it was still generous and open. "If we convey to the rest of the world 'you're not welcome, we don't want you here,' then the terrorists are winning."

Shortly after Powell left the office of Secretary of State on January 26, 2005, President Bush appointed Condoleezza Rice to that post. Early on she acknowledged some of the difficulties the United States was having with its negative image abroad. During an April 12, 2006, address at the Global Travel and Tourism Summit Breakfast, Secretary Rice set the stage for her remarks about the US image with several statements. She observed,[20]

> Since the attacks of September 11th [2001], our nation's commitment to openness has been tested by new and unprecedented threats from global terrorism . . . We recognize, though, that striking a balance is important. And we certainly do not want to make things more difficult for legitimate travelers. I know that some of our initial security measures after September 11 have caused delays in getting visas and even led some foreign citizens to believe that the United States is no longer welcoming to them. We've heard these legitimate concerns and we are doing everything that we can to improve our visa policy while also maintaining our security.

Unfortunately, very little was accomplished with such remarks and tourism professionals continued to be frustrated that the US had no overt policy to increase international tourism.

In 2006, the Travel Industry Association of America issued a report, *The Power of Travel 2006.*[21] It had a special section titled "America's Image Abroad." Parts of it are reproduced here to demonstrate how concerned tourism professionals were at that time:

> In recent years, the US travel and tourism industry has suffered from America's declining image abroad. Some of our policies, our economic power and aspects of our culture have obscured our positive attributes like freedom, opportunity and openness . . . The image issue is most pressing when you consider worldwide market share. The US share of international tourism declined 36 percent between 1992 and 2004 while world tourism was growing by 52 percent . . . Reversing this trend is vital to the economic health and prosperity of our nation and industry. If the US increased its market share by just 1 percent it would equal 8 million more visitors, $12 billion more in expenditures, 151,000 new jobs, $3 billion increase in payroll and $2 billion more in federal, state and local tax revenues . . . Reversing America's declining image abroad is a big job but not an impossible one. A recent Pew Institute study showed that when travelers come to America and experience the culture, history and most of all the people, their impression of America improves. And the more they visit, the more positive their opinion becomes.

Since 1997 there has not been serious momentum to reintroduce tourism policy legislation in the United States. There have been some feeble attempts to utilize the government-led Tourism Policy Council (a holdover from the National Tourism Policy Act of 1981) to address a few tourism policy questions. However, the demise of the National Tourism Policy Act of 1981 has left the United States at a distinct disadvantage in international tourism policy. While there are many individuals, organizations and tourism leaders who would like to see the US reinstitute a national tourism policy and regain some of its leadership and prestige in the international tourism arena only a few minor recent steps have been made in that direction.

Recent changes in US tourism policy

In January 2009, Barack Obama became President. Initially, President Obama simply continued the tourism policies he had inherited from his predecessor. He had campaigned on a theme of openness and the US travel industry moved aggressively to let him know their views about the lack of a US policy for the tourism industry. While he did not dismiss the views of the industry, he also did not move toward a comprehensive tourism policy. The result was more or less a compromise piece of legislation – the Travel Promotion Act that was passed on February 25, 2010, as Section 9 of HR 1299, "United States Capitol Police Administrative Technical Corrections Act of 2009" and signed into law by President Obama on March 4, 2010.[22] The fact that it was a part of another piece of legislation is somewhat indicative of its lack of importance. However, for travel and tourism professionals it was at least a step closer to a comprehensive tourism policy. The tourism policy provisions included: "The bill [legislation] establishes a non-profit Corporation for Travel Promotion governed by an 11-member board of directors appointed by the Secretary of Commerce after consultation with the Secretaries of Homeland Security and State. The Corporation shall develop and execute a plan to provide information to those interested in traveling to the United States; identify and address perceptions regarding US entry policies; promote the United States to world travelers; and identify opportunities to promote tourism to rural and urban areas equally." The legislation also established an Office of Travel Promotion within the Department of Commerce. The intent of the legislation is to increase international travel to the United States by improving the international image of the United States, thereby creating jobs and stimulating economic growth. In effect, the measure is aimed at reversing a decline in foreign visitors to the United States of nearly 10 percent over the past decade. Tourism professionals were simply pleased to at least obtain government support for international travel to the United States.

While the Travel Promotion Act is a helpful piece of legislation, it did not substantially resolve the issue of legitimate international visitors obtaining visitor visas on a timely basis. Again, tourism policy advocates brought this issue to the attention of the President and on January 19, 2012, the President issued an Executive Order "Establishing Visa and Foreign Visitor Processing Goals and the Task Force on Travel and Competitiveness."[23] This Executive Order is a strong measure to "improve visa and foreign visitor processing and travel promotion in order to create jobs and spur economic growth in the United States, while continuing to protect our national security." Responding to this policy change, the US Travel Association (formerly Travel Industry Association of America), representing tourism interests, suggested that President Obama's remarks about travel and the Executive Order "give tremendous visibility to our industry . . . provide us with a unique opportunity to establish our industry as key to our country's economic prosperity." Even though the Executive Order and resulting strategic plan are helpful, what is needed for the US is a national tourism policy similar in scope to that of the National Tourism Policy Act of 1981.

CHAPTER REVIEW QUESTIONS

1. From what area of the world did modern travel evolve and why?
2. What contributions did the Egyptians make to tourism's history?
3. The Greeks contributed a lot to tourism. Describe two examples.
4. What was the major contribution of the Romans to tourism?
5. What is the importance of Marco Polo to tourism policy?
6. Describe the UNTWO and its importance.
7. What was the first United States tourism policy legislation and describe it?

8. What was the American tourism policy after World War II?

9. How did President Eisenhower contribute to tourism policy in the US?

10. What did the United States National Tourism Policy Act of 1981 do?

11. What setbacks has the US faced in its tourism policy in the past 20 years?

12. What has President Obama done for United States tourism policy in recent years?

CASE STUDY 2: US National Tourism Policy Act of 1981

Begun and held at the City of Washington on Monday, the fifth day of January, one thousand nine hundred and eighty-one.

AN ACT

To amend the International Travel Act of 1961, to establish a national tourism policy, and for other purposes.

Be it enacted by the Senate and House of Representatives of the United States of America in Congress assembled,

SHORT TITLE

SECTION 1. This Act may be cited as the "National Tourism Policy Act."

NATIONAL TOURISM POLICY

Sec. 2. (a) The International Travel Act of 1961 (hereinafter in this Act referred to as the "Act") is amended by striking out the first section and inserting in lieu thereof the following: "That this Act may be cited as the 'International Travel Act of 1961'."

TITLE I – NATIONAL TOURISM POLICY

Sec. 101. (a) The Congress finds that

(1) the tourism and recreation industries are important to the United States, not only because of the numbers of people they serve and the vast human, financial, and physical resources they employ, but because of the great benefits tourism, recreation, and related activities confer on individuals and on society as a whole;

(2) the Federal Government for many years has encouraged tourism and recreation implicitly in its statutory commitments to the shorter work year and to the national passenger transportation system, and explicitly in a number of legislative enactments to promote tourism and support development of outdoor recreation, cultural attractions, and historic and natural heritage resources;

(3) as incomes and leisure time continue to increase, and as our economic and political systems develop more complex global relationships, tourism and recreation will become ever more important aspects of our daily lives; and

(4) the existing extensive Federal Government involvement in tourism recreation, and other related activities, needs to be better coordinated to effectively respond to the national interest in tourism and recreation and, where appropriate, to meet the needs of State and local governments and the private-sector.

(b) There is established a national tourism policy to –

(1) optimize the contribution of the tourism and recreation industries to economic prosperity, full employment, and the international balance of payments of the United States;

(2) make the opportunity for and benefits of tourism and recreation in the United States universally accessible to residents of the United States and foreign countries and insure that present and future generations are afforded adequate tourism and recreation resources;

(3) contribute to personal growth, health, education, and intercultural appreciation of the geography, history, and ethnicity of the United States;

(4) encourage the free and welcome entry of individuals traveling to the United States, in order to enhance international understanding and goodwill, consistent with immigration laws, the laws protecting the public health, and laws governing the importation of goods into the United States;

(5) eliminate unnecessary trade barriers to the United States tourism industry operating throughout the world;

(6) encourage competition in the tourism industry and maximum consumer choice through the continued viability of the retail travel agent industry and the independent tour operator industry;

(7) promote the continued development and availability of alternative personal payment mechanisms which facilitate national and international travel;

(8) promote quality, integrity, and reliability in all tourism and tourism related services offered to visitors to the United States;

(9) preserve the historical and cultural foundations of the Nation as a living part of community life and development, and insure future generations an opportunity to appreciate and enjoy the rich heritage of the Nation;

(10) insure the compatibility of tourism and recreation with other national interests in energy development and conservation, environmental protection, and the judicious use of natural resources;

(11) assist in the collection, analysis, and dissemination of data which accurately measure the economic and social impact of tourism to and within the United States, in order to facilitate planning in the public and private-sectors; and

(12) harmonize, to the maximum extent possible, all Federal activities in support of tourism and recreation with the needs of the general public and the states, territories, local governments, and the tourism and recreation industry, and to give leadership to all concerned with tourism, recreation, and national heritage preservation in the United States.

Duties

Sec. 3. (a) The following heading is inserted before section 2 of the Act:

TITLE II – DUTIES

(b) Section 2 of the Act (22 U.S.C. 2122) is amended by striking out "purpose of the Act" and inserting in lieu thereof "the national tourism policy established by section 101 (b)."

(c) Section 3(a) of the Act (22 U.S.C. 2123(a) is amended by striking out "section 2" and inserting in lieu thereof "section 201", by striking out "and" at the end of paragraph (6), by striking out the period at the end of paragraph (7) and inserting in lieu thereof a semicolon, and by adding after paragraph (7) the following new paragraphs:

(8) shall establish facilitation services at major ports-of-entry of the United States;

(9) shall consult with foreign governments on travel and tourism matters and, in accordance with applicable law, represent United States travel and tourism interests before international and intergovernmental meetings;

(10) shall develop and administer a comprehensive program relating to travel industry information, data service, training and education, and technical assistance;

(11) shall develop a program to seek and to receive information on a continuing basis from the tourism industry, including consumer and travel trade associations, regarding needs and interests which should be met by a Federal agency or program and to direct that information to the appropriate agency or program;

(12) shall encourage to the maximum extent feasible travel to and from the United States on United States carriers;

(13) shall assure coordination within the Department of Commerce so that to the extent practicable, all the resources of the Department are used to effectively and efficiently carry out the national tourism policy;

(14) may only promulgate, issue, rescind, and amend such interpretive rules, general statements of policy, and rules of agency organization, procedure, and practice as may be necessary to carry out this Act; and

(15) shall develop and submit annually to the Congress, within six weeks of transmittal to the Congress of the President's recommended budget for implementing this Act, a detailed marketing plan to stimulate and encourage travel to the United States during the fiscal year for which such budget is submitted and include in the plan the estimated funding and personnel levels required to implement the plan and alternate means of funding activities under this Act."

(d) (1) Paragraph (5) of section 3(a) of the Act is amended (A) by striking out "foreign countries." and inserting in lieu thereof "foreign countries;", (B) by striking out "this clause;" and inserting in lieu thereof "this paragraph.", (C) by inserting the last two sentences before the first sentence of subsection (c) and (D) by striking out "this clause" in such sentences and inserting in lieu thereof "paragraph (5) of subsection (a)".

(2) Paragraph (7) of section 3(a) of the Act is amended by striking out "countries. The Secretary is authorized to" and inserting in lieu thereof "countries; and the Secretary may" and by striking out "this clause" and inserting in lieu thereof "this paragraph."

(3) Section 3 of the Act is amended by striking out "clause (5)" each place it appears and inserting in lieu thereof "paragraph (5)".

(e)(1) Sections 2 and 3 of the Act are re-designated as sections 201 and 202, respectively, and section 5 is inserted after section 202 (as so re-designated) and re-designated as section 203.

(2) Section 203 of the Act (as so re-designated) is amended by striking out "semi-annually" and inserting in lieu thereof "annually".

(f) The following section is inserted after section 203 of the Act (as so re-designated):

Sec. 204. (a) The Secretary is authorized to provide, in accordance with subsections (b) and (c), financial assistance to a region of not less than two States or portions of two States to assist in the implementation of a regional tourism promotional and marketing program. Such assistance shall include

(1) technical assistance for advancing the promotion of travel to such region by foreign visitors;

(2) expert consultants; and

(3) marketing and promotional assistance.

(b) Any program carried out with assistance under subsection (a) shall serve as a demonstration project for future program development for regional tourism promotion.

(c) The Secretary may provide assistance under subsection (a) for a region if the applicant for the assistance demonstrates to the satisfaction of the Secretary that

(1) such region has in the past been an area that has attracted foreign visitors, but such visits have significantly decreased;

(2) facilities are being developed or improved to re-attract such foreign visitors;

(3) a joint venture in such region will increase the travel to such region by foreign visitors;

(4) such regional programs will contribute to the economic well-being of the region;

(5) such region is developing or has developed a regional transportation system that will enhance travel to the facilities and attractions within such region; and

(6) a correlation exists between increased tourism to such region and the lowering of the unemployment rate in such region.

Administration

Sec. 4. (a)(1) The first sentence of section 4 of the Act (22 U.S.C. 2124), is amended to read as follows: "There is established in the Department of Commerce a United States Travel and Tourism Administration which shall be headed by an Under Secretary of Commerce for Travel and Tourism who shall be appointed by the President, by and with the advice and consent of the Senate, and who shall report directly to the Secretary."

(2) The second sentence of section 4 of the Act is amended by striking out "Assistant Secretary of Commerce for Tourism" and inserting in lieu thereof "Under Secretary of Commerce for Travel and Tourism."

(3) Section 4 of the Act is amended by striking out the last sentence and inserting in lieu thereof the following: "The Secretary shall designate an Assistant Secretary of Commerce for Tourism Marketing who shall be under the supervision of the Under Secretary of Commerce for Travel and Tourism. The Secretary shall delegate to the Assistant Secretary responsibility for the development and submission of the marketing plan required by section 202(a)(15)."

(4) Section 5314 of title 5, United States Code, is amended by striking out "Under Secretary of Commerce" and inserting in lieu thereof "Under Secretary of Commerce and Under Secretary of Commerce for Travel and Tourism."

(b) Section 4 of the Act is amended by inserting "(a)" after "Sec. 4.", and by adding at the end the following:

(b) (1) The Secretary may not reduce the total number of employees of the United States Travel and Tourism Administration assigned to the offices of the Administration in foreign countries to a number which is less than the total number of employees of the United States Travel Service assigned to offices of the Service in foreign countries in fiscal year 1979.

(2) In any fiscal year the amount of funds which shall be made available from appropriations under this Act for obligation for the activities of the offices of the United States Travel and Tourism Administration in foreign countries shall not be less than the amount obligated in fiscal year 1980 for the activities of the offices of the United States Travel Service in foreign countries.

(c)(1) The following heading is inserted before section 4 of the Act:

TITLE III – ADMINISTRATION

(2) Section 4 of the Act is redesignated as section 301 and the following new sections are inserted after that section:

Sec. 302. (a) In order to assure that the national interest in tourism is fully considered in Federal decision-making, there is established an interagency coordinating council to be known as the Tourism Policy Council (hereinafter in this section referred to as the 'Council').

(b)(1) The Council shall consist of

(A) the Secretary of Commerce who shall serve as Chairman of the Council;

(B) the Under Secretary for Travel and Tourism who shall serve as the Vice Chairman of the Council and who shall act as Chairman of the Council in the absence of the Chairman;

(C) the Director of the Office of Management and Budget or the individual designated by the Director from the Office;

(D) an individual designated by the Secretary of Commerce from the International Trade Administration of the Department of Commerce;

(E) the Secretary of Energy or the individual designated by such Secretary from the Department of Energy;

(F) the Secretary of State or the individual designated by such Secretary from the Department of State;

(G) the Secretary of the Interior or the individual designated by such Secretary of the National Park Service or the Heritage Conservation and Recreation Service of the Department of the Interior;

(H) the Secretary of Labor or the individual designated by such Secretary from the Department of Labor; and

(I) the Secretary of Transportation or the individual designated by such Secretary from the Department of Transportation.

(2) Members of the Council shall serve without additional compensation but shall be reimbursed for actual and necessary expenses, including travel expenses, incurred by them in carrying out the duties of the Council.

(3) Each member of the Council, other than the Vice Chairman, may designate an alternate, who shall serve as a member of the Council whenever the regular member is unable to attend a meeting of the Council or any committee of the Council. The designation by a member of the Council of an alternate under the preceding sentence shall be made for the duration of the member's term on the Council. Any such designated alternate shall be selected from individuals who exercise significant decision-making authority in the Federal agency involved and shall be authorized to make decisions on behalf of the member for whom he or she is serving.

(c)(1) Whenever the Council, or a committee of the Council, considers matters that affect the interests of Federal agencies that are not represented on the Council or the committee, the Chairman may invite the heads of such agencies, or their alternates, to participate in the deliberations of the Council or committee.

(2) The Council shall conduct its first meeting not later than ninety days after the date of enactment of this section. Thereafter the Council shall meet not less than four times each year.

(d)(1) The Council shall coordinate policies, programs, and issues relating to tourism, recreation, or national heritage resources involving Federal departments, agencies, or other entities. Among other things, the Council shall

(A) coordinate the policies and programs of member agencies that have a significant effect on tourism, recreation, and national heritage preservation;

(B) develop areas of cooperative program activity;

(C) assist in resolving interagency program and policy conflicts; and

(D) seek and receive concerns and views of State and local governments and the Travel and Tourism Advisory Board with respect to Federal programs and policies deemed to conflict with the orderly growth and development of tourism.

(2) To enable the Council to carry out its functions

(A) the Council may request directly from any Federal department or agency such personnel, information, services, or facilities, on a compensated or uncompensated basis, as he determines necessary to carry out the functions of the Council;

(B) each Federal department or agency shall furnish the Council with such information, services, and facilities as it may request to the extent permitted by law and within the limits of available funds; and

(C) Federal agencies and departments may, in their discretion, detail to temporary duty with the Council, such personnel as the Council may request of for carrying out the functions of the Council, each such detail to be without loss of seniority, pay, or other employee status.

(3) The Administrator of the General Services Administration shall provide administrative support services for the Council on a reimbursable basis.

(e) The Council shall establish such policy committees as it considers necessary and appropriate, each of which shall be comprised of any or all of the members of the Council and representatives from Federal departments, agencies, and instrumentalities not represented on the Council. Each such Policy committee shall be designed

(1) to monitor a specific area of Federal Government activity, such as transportation, energy and natural resources, economic development, or other such activities related to tourism; and

(2) to review and evaluate the relation of the policies and activities of the Federal Government in that specific area to tourism, recreation, and national heritage conservation in the United States.

(f) The Council shall submit an annual report for the preceding fiscal year to the President for transmittal to Congress on or before the thirty-first day of December of each year. The report shall include

(1) a comprehensive and detailed report of the activities and accomplishments of the Council and its policy committees;

(2) the results of Council efforts to coordinate the policies and programs of member agencies that have a significant effect on tourism, recreation, and national heritage preservation, resolve interagency conflicts, and develop areas of cooperative program activity;

(3) an analysis of problems referred to the Council by State and local governments, the tourism industry, the Secretary of Commerce, or any of the Council's policy committees along with a detailed statement of any actions taken or anticipated to be taken to resolve such problems; and

(4) such recommendations as the Council deems appropriate.

Sec. 303. (a) There is established the Travel and Tourism Advisory Board (hereinafter in this section referred to as the 'Board') to be composed of fifteen members appointed by the Secretary. The members of the Board shall be appointed as follows:

(1) Not more than eight members of the Board shall be appointed from the same political party.

(2) The members of the Board shall be appointed from among citizens of the United States who are not regular full-time employees of the United States and shall be selected for appointment so as to provide as nearly as practicable a broad representation of different geographical regions within the United States and of the diverse and varied segments of the tourism industry.

(3) Twelve of the members shall be appointed from senior executive officers of organizations engaged in the travel and tourism industry. Of such members

(A) at least one shall be a senior representative from a labor organization representing employees of the tourism industry; and

(B) at least one shall be a representative of the States who is knowledgeable of tourism promotion.

(4) Of the remaining three members of the Board

(A) one member shall be a consumer advocate or ombudsman from the Organized public interest community;

(B) one member shall be an economist, statistician, or accountant; and

(C) one member shall be an individual from the academic community who is knowledgeable in tourism, recreation, or national heritage conservation.

The Secretary shall serve as an ex-officio member of the Board. The duration of the Board shall not be subject to the Federal Advisory Committee Act. A list of the members appointed to the Board shall be forwarded by the Secretary to the Senate Committee on Commerce, Science, and Transportation and the House Committee on Energy and Commerce.

(b) The members of the Board shall be appointed for a term of office of three years, except that of the members first appointed

(1) four members shall be appointed for terms of one year, and (2) four members shall be appointed for terms of two years, as designated by the Secretary at the time of appointment. Any member appointed to fill a vacancy occurring before the expiration of the term for which the member's predecessor was appointed shall be appointed only for the remainder of such term. A member may serve after the expiration of his term until his successor has taken office. Vacancies on the Board shall be filled in the same manner in which the original appointments were made.

No member of the Board shall be eligible to serve in excess of two consecutive terms of three years each.

(c) The Chairman and Vice Chairman and other appropriate officers of the Board shall be elected by and from members of the Board other than the Secretary.

(d) The members of the Board shall receive no compensation for their services as such, but shall be allowed such necessary travel expenses and per diem as are authorized by section 5703 of title 5, United States Code. The Secretary shall pay the reasonable and necessary expenses incurred by the Board in connection with the coordination of Board activities, announcement and reporting of meetings, and preparation of such reports as are required by subsection (f).

(e) The Board shall meet at least semi-annually and shall hold such other meetings at the call of the Chairman, the Vice Chairman, or a majority of its members.

(f) The Board shall advise the Secretary with respect to the implementation of this Act and shall advise the Assistant Secretary for Tourism Marketing with respect to the preparation of the marketing plan under section 202(a)(15). The Board shall prepare an annual report concerning its activities and include therein such recommendations as it deems appropriate with respect to the performance of the Secretary under this Act and the operation and effectiveness of programs under this Act. Each annual report shall cover a fiscal year and shall be submitted on or before the thirty-first day of December following the close of the fiscal year.

Authorizations

Sec. 5 (a) Section 6 of the Act (22 U.S.C. 2126) is re-designated as section 304 and the first sentence is amended to read as follows: "For the purpose of carrying out this Act there is authorized to be appropriated an amount not to exceed $8,600,000 for the fiscal year ending September 30, 1982."

(b) Section 7 of the Act (22 U.S.C. 2127) is re-designated as section 305 and sections 8 and 9 of the Act (22 U.S.C. 2128) are repealed.

Effective date

Sec. 6. The amendments made by this Act shall take effect October 1, 1981.

Concluding critical questions

Reading the legislative verbiage and understanding some of the background that goes into developing major policy can give tourism students and professionals a better appreciation for the complex nature of tourism policy. With this familiarity, readers can also begin to question elements of the outcome of a comprehensive tourism policy, such as the United States National Tourism Policy Act of 1981, and can also apply both the inputs and the outcomes of such legislation to policy development in their home communities.

With some thought, a variety of questions can be raised. For example, why does the United States no longer have a comprehensive national tourism policy? This leads to questioning if a comprehensive national tourism policy is needed in the US or in other developed economies. A heated discussion on the topic might lead to debates about what arguments could be used for or against a developed nation having a national tourism policy. Within the United States, and similar nations, how important is tourism relative to other policy sectors, such as education or national defense? Do these other policy sectors have more stable policies or receive greater political attention, and if so, why? What differences might exist when governments must prioritize national issues? Is tourism more politically and economically important to developing nations than to those nations that are more developed? How can tourism professionals and scholars communicate the benefits of tourism and what will help political decision-makers understand tourism? Answering these questions is a continual struggle for those involved in tourism development and provides fertile opportunity for rich discussion and research.

Notes

1   Casson, L. (1974) *Travel in the Ancient World*. Baltimore and London: The Johns Hopkins University Press.

2   Ibid.

3   Edgell, Sr., David L. (n.d.) *The Worldly Travelers* (unpublished book manuscript). Greenville, NC.

4   History of Tourism. (1966) From the Leisure Arts Ltd Series, "Discovery of Sciences," London, 9–13.

5   Goeldner, C.R. & Ritchie, J.R.B. (2012) *Tourism: Principles, Practices, Philosophies*, 12th edn. New York: John Wiley and Sons, 72.

6   Ibid.

7   Ibid, p. 75.

8   D'Amore, L.J. (2012) *An Olympic Sprint for Peace*. International Institute for Peace Through Tourism Newsletter. Retrieved July 30, 2012, from www.iipt.org/newsletter/2012/may.html.

9   The case study at the end of this chapter includes the actual legislation that defines the National Tourism Policy Act of 1981. Co-author of *Tourism Policy and Planning: Yesterday, Today and Tomorrow* (second edition) Dr. David L. Edgell, Sr., formally a policy director in the US Department of Commerce, worked on tourism policy and is intimately familiar with the *Act* and the documents that led to its development. He helped to craft many of the provisions contained in the document. At one point in his career in tourism policy he served as the Acting Under-Secretary of Commerce for Travel and Tourism with the responsibility of implementing the National Tourism Policy Act of 1981.

10 US Government (1950) *Tourism in the European Recovery Program*. Washington, DC.

11 People to People International, 2001 Annual Report: 1.

12 Randall, C.B. (1958) *International Travel*. Report to the President of the United States. Washington, DC: US Government Printing Office.

13 International Travel Act of 1961, Chapter 31, Section 2122, 158.

14 Snyder, L.T. (2006) "Broader Ribbons Across the Land." *American History*, 32–9.

15 Edgell, D.L., Allen, M.D., Smith, G., & Swanson, J.R. (2008) *Tourism Policy and Planning: Yesterday, Today, and Tomorrow*. London: Elsevier.

16 United States Committee on Commerce (1976) *A Conceptual Basis for the National Tourism Policy Study*. Washington, DC: US Government Printing Office.

17 United States Committee on Commerce (1977) *National Tourism Policy Study Ascertainment Phase*. Washington, DC: US Government Printing Office.

18 United States Committee on Commerce (1978) *National Tourism Policy Study Final Report*. Washington, DC: US Government Printing Office.

19 Edgell, D.L. & Wandner, S.A. (1978) *Role of Tourism in the International Economic Policy of the United States*. Presented at the Western Economic Association Annual Meeting, Honolulu, Hawaii, June 22, 1978.

20 United States Department of State Travel Warnings (2006) Remarks by Secretary Condoleezza Rice at The Global Travel and Tourism Summit Breakfast on April 12, 2006. Washington, DC.

21 Horsley, L. (2006) "America's Image Abroad." *The Power of Travel 2006*. Travel Industry Association of America, Washington, DC, page 8.

22 Travel Promotion Act 2010. White House, Washington, DC.

23 The White House (2012) EXECUTIVE ORDER Establishing Visa and Foreign Visitor Processing Goals and the Task Force of Travel, and Competitiveness.

Pin

Hype

MBac

A

Tourism policy issues for today

Ongoing evaluation of tourism policy issues is important because of tourism's integrative role in firing growth – for better or worse – across multiple sectors of local, state/provincial, regional, national, and international economies. The highest purpose of tourism policy can be to integrate benefits, while reducing costs for communities to improve the quality and sustainability of life for local citizens. Several frameworks have been set forth to help policymakers propose and grapple with tourism policy issues. The first, advanced by the World Tourism Organization in 1999, calls upon all individuals involved in tourism-related organizations to develop and adhere to a Code of Ethics for Tourism. More recently, the European Commission adopted a step-by-step approach to developing sustainable tourism policies.

The Global Code of Ethics for Tourism[1] adopted in October 1999, by the 13th session of the General Assembly of the World Tourism Organization outlines principles to guide tourism development and to serve as a powerful frame-of-reference for tourism stakeholders "with the objective of minimizing the negative impact of tourism on the environment and on cultural heritage while maximizing the benefits of tourism in promoting sustainable develop-ment and poverty alleviation as well as understanding among nations." The Code further states that "provided a number of principles and a certain number of rules are observed" it should be possible to reconcile tourism in its increasingly prominent role in the services industry with contending issues in international trade such that all stakeholders in tourism develop-ment – "with different albeit interdependent responsibilities . . . rights and duties" – will contribute collectively to this aim. This is envisioned through genuine partnership and cooperation between public and private stake-holders in tourism development in an "open and balanced way."

The European Commission adopted the Agenda for a Sustainable and Competitive European Tourism in October, 2007.[2] The purpose of the plan is to provide a framework for policies – within the tourism domain and in other policy arenas – to be developed in support of European tourism. The plan was based on input from a variety of sources including tourism industries, government, and the public at large. The ultimate goal was to provide added value to European tourism stakeholders.

The high-level guidelines suggested by organizations such as the UNWTO and the European Commission are a good starting point, but much more is to be understood about the intricacies of current tourism policy issues. For example, even within one segment of tourism, multiple issues exist that must be addressed by public policy and planning. For example, international airlines carry cargo and passengers making air rights and safety issues consummate. Cargo is rarely checked for bombs whereas domestic travelers' luggage is thoroughly checked. Increasing cargo inspection could lead to increased costs and added delays. Public policy in this arena collides with privacy rights and business profits versus traveler safety and security issues.

As another example of the complexities of current tourism policy issues, consider how many tourism assets are used by residents of an area and visitors to the same area. Restaurants and entertainment organizations serve local residents and tourists alike and are involved in business activities (such as special events, conferences, and meeting planning) that are demanded by both audiences. These add additional complexity to the planning for simultaneous use in areas accommodating visitors and host community needs.

Key tourism policy issues for today are vast and depend in large part on the needs of individual nations and local destinations. However, an overview of tourism policy issues can be organized around general themes within tourism development. These themes are product development, demand development, financing, and human rights. This chapter provides an overview of such important issue areas, which is followed by current tourism policy issues of various nations. Many issues, such as tourism education and training and the transformative impacts of tourism on global socio-economic progress, among others are as significant in the future as they are today. Such issues are covered in greater depth in Chapters 11 and 12.

Product development policy issues

Public policies related to product development could include a wide array of issues, ranging from public/private partnerships associated with developing convention centers and stadiums to partnering with community groups to create festivals or preserving natural areas for recreation uses. Land-use zoning and agritourism, described in the following sub-sections, are two important tourism policy issues that many communities are currently dealing with.

Zoning

Land-use zoning, which involves allocation of scarce land, public and private utility, and public support services and resources, is another example showing the complexities of public policy related to tourism. Zoning aids tourism development while mitigating the negative impacts. Officials in the Brazilian state of Minas Gerais wrestle with a potential water contamination problem as water demand rises due to tourism-related activities. With more tourism demand comes more visitors and more residents to support tourism. Zoning to protect the natural resources, which in turn protect the water, has been recommended as the means to preserve the water.

In the Colorado municipality of Routt County in the United States, zoning has been used in an effort to mediate the competing needs of the tourists and the locals. Routt County is home to the well-known ski resort of Steamboat Springs. Public lands in the county include parts of four state parks, two national parks, two national wilderness areas, and the Continental Divide National Scenic Trail. According to Parizzi,[3] "Over the past decade, county and city officials, tourism leaders, and local ranchers . . . have worked together to preserve the remaining agricultural open space." With a change in zoning laws, the county adopted regulations that encouraged clustering homes to preserve open space. Housing lot size requirements were reduced allowing developers to build more units using a smaller footprint overall. In exchange, the developers must set aside undeveloped land.

Agritourism

The significance of agriculture in social terms stems largely from a community's desire to retain agriculture's aesthetic and heritage values and their contribution to sense-of-place and charm. Consistent with the findings from US studies that indicate resident attitudes being influenced by *amenity value* rather than production value, many individuals consider agriculture very important but have very little understanding about the actual situation with agriculture in terms of economic contribution, benefits to the region, land uses, and the implications of changes in agricultural production in the future. The direct aims are to generate jobs and increase returns to farmers while the indirect aims are landscape conservation through retention of agriculture, attitudinal changes in the farming community to farming practices, and sustainable development that links the farming community to other sectors of the economy.

Many rural communities are looking to their agricultural assets to diversify their local economy through agritourism. Rules for developing agritourism vary from country to country, and regimes can be highly bureaucratic. As an example, in the Veneto region of Italy, farmers providing holidays are limited to hosting 30 overnight guests per night for a maximum of 160 days per year and must produce over 50 percent of the food they sell to tourists. In Britain, Germany, and elsewhere, stringent health and safety controls are in place, including fire regulations and rules governing contact with farm animals.[4] As a whole, agritourism is blooming worldwide and cultivating the need for tourism policy and planning in this field.

Demand development policy issues

Tourism demand is created by successfully implementing good marketing strategies. A critical component of sound tourism planning is matching tourism demand and tourism supply. Policies that facilitate this lead to a balanced approach to tourism. Three critical areas of creating tourism demand are tourism technologies and information communication, international marketing, and measurement and evaluation. These areas are discussed in the remainder of this section.

Knowledge sharing and innovation

A great majority of travel and tourism companies worldwide are small- to medium-sized businesses. The internet allows strategically-managed smaller companies to compete with larger companies for international visibility and positioning. This combination of attributes places the tourism industry in an excellent position to achieve world leadership in the movement and management of the capital and information embodied in global service industries. This can be facilitated with favorable government policies in place.

The nation of Denmark has contributed to information-based innovation that can help destinations facilitate demand. The Danish Ministry of Science, Technology and Innovation, along with the European Union and the University of Southern Denmark, have provided funds for INNOTOUR, which is a web-based platform for sharing innovative tourism development practices. The user-created content, found at www.innotour.com, began in 2009. The program encourages innovation with the hopes of leading to increased competitiveness for public and private-sector businesses. INNOTOUR was designed specifically for diffusion of innovation of tourism ideas. Diffusion of innovation involves how advances and changes are communicated and adapted into a social system.

Increased knowledge sharing can bring increased innovation and result in higher demand for tourism globally, which is especially important to combat slowing tourism growth. This is according to the Organisation for Economic Co-operation and Development (OECD) in its publication *Innovation and Growth in Tourism.*[5] In many destinations around the world, competition is the main driver of tourism innovation. Key to the dissemination of information that can lead to increased competitiveness and new demand are partnerships between the public-sector, private-sector, and educators. This collaboration should be included in policies and tourism planning efforts.

Such a sharing of information can lead to information overload, which shows the importance of information management. Knowledge needs to not only be collected but also be retrievable and in a form that tourism professionals can understand. The Tourism Intelligence Network (TIN) in Quebec is a good example of a system that has been developed by government to provide information in a form that can more easily lead to increased competitiveness for the provincial tourism sector. With support from the Tourisme Quebec and Canada Economic Development, TIN was founded in January 2004 at the School of Business Administration at the University of Quebec at Montreal. The purpose of the initiative is to gather strategic intelligence related to tourism and present it in meaningful and useful ways to tourism professionals. Part of their stated mission is to help enhance Quebec's tourism competitiveness and help tourism leaders develop informed marketing strategies.

Measurement and evaluation

Ways to measure the impacts of tourism policies are especially important because of tourism's ability to employ workers with lower skills and its contribution to poverty alleviation in developing and developed economies. More than just collecting data for planning efforts, research can also be used to evaluate the effectiveness of tourism policies and programs. For example, to evaluate the effectiveness of Spain's 2011 €100 million marketing campaign targeting India, tourism managers in Spain can use in-bound tourism data on Indian visitors such as length of stay, expenditures, and propensity to make a return visit, among other variables.

Much work remains to create reliable tools to measure tourism impacts. Recently, many nations and tourism communities have developed tourism satellite account (TSA) systems to measure the economic impact of tourism across the broad spectrum of tourism-related industries. The TSA system has been criticized for being too static and not being able to measure how changes in tourism demand may affect key parameters, such as gross value added and employment.[6] Another generation of tourism measurement tools is being implemented based on computable general equilibrium (CGE) models. CGE models use historical economic data to gauge economic reactions to policy changes or fluctuations in other external factors. Scotland and Australia have employed successful CGEs. While these models are being tested, the most reliable tool to measure the effectiveness of tourism policies and programs are cost-benefit analyses or public workshops to collect qualitative feedback on how effective policies are believed to be in the minds of community members.

Another important evaluation is the impact of a policy or program on the local community. For example, the vehicular traffic a new theme park development may create could unexpectedly increase the time community residents spend commuting home after work so that time with their family is negatively affected. This decrease in family time could lead to social problems with community teenagers as they have less interaction with their parents. Much of this analysis cannot be determined using quantitative methods. For example, a survey questionnaire using Likert scaled questions may not detect the severity of the social implications of tourism development on families. Thus, qualitative methods, such as personal interviews, focus groups, or observations are needed to determine many social and community impacts.

International marketing

A primary objective of tourism development is to increase exports and the balance-of-trade for nations. In doing this, a destination brings money from the outside into the community, as when residents of Brazil travel to Peru, for example. Creating demand, so that exports are increased, is done through international marketing and promotion. Examples of international tourism marketing policies can be found in almost every nation. The West African nation of Ghana, for example, established a strategy to position tourism as the nation's leading economic sector and attract one million tourists by 2012. Ghanaian tourism officials budgeted GH¢15 million (approximately US$7.75 million) to attend international sales fairs, enhance links with tour operators, establish tourist information offices in Ghana and other key markets-of-origin, and use guerrilla marketing techniques, such as having Ghanaian football players in European clubs wear clothing with messages promoting visits to Ghana.[7]

Ireland, a more mature destination, implemented a similar campaign in the hope of attracting 7.8 million visitors in 2012. Irish tourism officials noticed an increase in interest and tried to turn that interest into actual visitation by marketing to 60 million consumers via television in Great Britain, France, and Germany; print in the United States, Spain, and Italy; and outdoor advertising in Great Britain. Two interesting parts of the Irish marketing campaign is targeting the Irish Diaspora in North America and going after Indian, Chinese, and Middle East travelers as part of the new Irish visa-waiver program.[8]

With the crowded international tourism marketing landscape, maintaining and increasing competitiveness is crucial for successful destinations. Maintaining competitiveness means keeping the position relative to other destinations in terms of price and quality, profitability, sustainability, and meeting visitors' needs. Remaining competitive involves creating new supply and refreshing existing supply while still maintaining sustainability. For destinations to improve their competitive positions, policies and programs integrated across all policy sectors are needed. Improving tourism competitiveness depends on coordination among several agencies, such as transportation, cultural resources, public lands, finance, and others. Enhancing communities' competitive positioning involves more than just marketing.

Finance policy issues

A common theme among tourism professionals is a lament over the lack of funding for tourism promotion and development. For government tourism offices, the organization's budget is a direct result of legislative or administrative policy. One way to work to increase the tourism office's budget is to show the effectiveness of the government expense in tourism through cost-benefit analysis or other methods of policy analysis described in Chapter 8. Other means can be used to provide tourism development agencies with more money. Some of these means, as described in this section, include tax legislation, international development aid, loans and bonds, and grants.

Tax legislation

Tourism and taxes have brought the industry to the forefront of travelers' concern. While seeking the benefits of tourism, travelers often do not want to support the infrastructure. Taxing residents to support tourism is as unpopular as other taxes; therefore, government officials often tax the visitors through hotel occupancy taxes, which are paid by anyone (not just visitors) purchasing a hotel room stay in communities with an occupancy tax. Such a tax is popular with politicians who see it as a way to increase tax revenues without burdening local voters. Tourism businesses may not always favor a new use tax on their customers, but are often sated by a portion of the occupancy tax revenue being used for tourism promotion. However, tourism managers and politicians must be conscious of how an increase in overall costs for their visitors could negatively affect competitiveness in the destination. This is a point often overlooked by tourism planners unfamiliar with, or unwilling to undertake, in-depth policy analysis.

Another example of how tourism taxes are used emanates from the city of Richmond in the US state of Virginia: "[T]he additional tax shall be designated and spent for the development and improvement of the Virginia Performing Arts Foundation's facilities in Richmond, for promoting the use of the Richmond Centre, and for promoting tourism, travel or business that generates tourism and travel in the Richmond metropolitan area."[9] Other Virginia localities such as Williamsburg levy a flat $2 fee for marketing the historic triangle of Williamsburg, James City County, and Yorktown. Although popular with many politicians and tourism professionals, tax issues are divisive. On the one hand, they are necessary for generating revenue to finance the tourism industry. On the other hand, travelers are growing weary of the added expense to the trip. In some places, auto rental taxes can be as much as 40 percent of the bill.

International development aid

Finance for tourism development often requires an international commitment. The World Bank is heavily involved with committing monetary resources to sustainable tourism projects. Through the International Development Association (IDA), the World Bank grants long-term interest-free loans and grants for the purpose of supporting economic growth, reducing poverty, and improving living conditions: "IDA's long-term no-interest loans pay for programs that build the policies, institutions, infrastructure, and human capital needed for equitable and environmentally sustainable development. IDA's grants go to poor countries already vulnerable to debt or confronting the ravages of HIV/AIDS or natural disasters."[10]

Three factors determine eligibility for assistance:

- Relative poverty, defined as Gross National Product (income) per person below an established threshold, currently US$965 per year.
- Lack of creditworthiness to borrow on market terms and therefore a need for concessional resources to finance the country's development program.

- Good policy performance, defined as the implementation of economic and social policies that promote growth and poverty reduction.

Two examples of World Bank/IDA-supported projects are Mozambique's initiatives in conservation and tourism development. The first initiative resulted in support with an "IDA credit of US$20 million to support the conservation of biodiversity and natural ecosystems as well as promote economic growth and development based on the sustainable use of natural resources by local communities in Mozambique."[11] This demonstrates the interconnectedness of tourism and other municipal functions – and, therefore, requires policies which cross departmental boundaries. IDA has also supported a project emphasizing ecological and commercially sustainable solid waste collection and disposal services in Montenegro coastal municipalities, which are needed to maintain a clean, environmentally attractive coastal area: "The project will also help develop the sector's institutional, policy and regulatory framework."[12] Additionally, it is hoped the project will benefit tourism prospects by eliminating the current solid waste collection and disposal problems impacting environmentally sensitive tourist areas on the coast.

Loans and bonds

Alternative sources for financing include bands and bonds. Often poor nations turn to these sources when they have exhausted the IDA backing. Loans are an excellent source and developing nations often turn to wealthy countries for support. There are direct loans – where the bank backs the money and bonds which are floated and then used as collateral for the loans. The Japan Bank for International Cooperation has agreed on an IDA loan totaling ¥5.732 billion (US$52.874 million) with Egypt, for the Borg El Arab International Airport Modernization Project. The development consists of the construction of an air terminal with a capacity of one million passengers and 4,000 tons of cargo annually, as well as improvements in related facilities at the airport, 40km southwest of Alexandria.[13]

Guam, a US territory in the Pacific Ocean, can issue bonds that are exempt from federal, state, and local income taxes. Infrastructure improvements financed by military construction funds will not address all of Guam's critical infrastructure, essential services, and economic development needs. Guam cannot attract enough working capital for its projects, nor does it have a sufficient debt ceiling to underwrite the loans required for infrastructure improvements. Proceeds from bonds sales would be reissued in the form of loans to finance reconstruction projects. The concept of a bond bank was discussed in April 2006, at a meeting of the Interagency Group on Insular Areas, which coordinates federal policy towards Guam, American Samoa, the US Virgin Islands and the Northern Mariana Islands.[14]

Grants

Grants are a more preferred method of obtaining money because no repayment is required; however, one condition often set forth is that matching amounts of money must be raised to receive the grants. Other stipulations may include partnerships or other support mechanisms. Mozambique's project, which received IDA money, received grants also. The Global Environment Facility (GEF) Board approved the credit for the project, which was also financed by a US$3.7 million grant from the Japanese Policy and Human Resources Development Fund.[15]

Human rights policy issues

Human rights are privileges believed by many to be fundamental to all humans. Examples of human rights include freedom of religion, freedom to organization, and freedom from discrimination. Human rights can be an important consideration to many travelers as they select their travel destinations. The following sub-sections relate tourism policy to the important human rights issues of labor rights and sex tourism.

Labor issues

Since tourism is a labor-intensive set of industries, often employing members of lower economic strata, the workers in various businesses are integral and management of human resources in tourism creates unique challenges related to fair treatment and human rights. Fair treatment of tourism workers is also important because of the inseparability of services and those who provide services. Without hospitable, knowledgeable, and happy workers, the visitors' experiences will be less than optimal. More than just managing, tourism managers and planners must develop human resources in tourism. According to the OECD, countries are increasingly having difficulties staffing professionals with certain skills, such as management skills, and recommend that long-term policies and plans include provisions for education and training programs.[16] Such training programs should include not only management training at the university level, but also should include training on crafts important to the culture of local communities and hospitable customer service.

Some countries have had to implement creative policies in efforts to recruit and develop their tourism workforce. For example, Scotland implemented a program known as the Fresh Talent Initiative in 2004 to combat a population that was declining. The immigration policy allowed international students who graduate from Scottish universities to work in the country for two years after graduation. The policy is structured to give Scottish universities a competitive advantage in recruiting students and tourism businesses a competitive advantage in staffing qualified and skilled workers. The innovative program was short-lived and was overtaken by the UK Border Agency and phased into the United Kingdom's point-based system to identify various tiers of immigrants based on their expected contribution to the UK society and economy. While this program did not last long in Scotland, for political reasons, the program could be easily copied by more independent states and create a quick competitive advantage in terms of human resources in tourism.

An important aspect of human resources in any industry is labor relations, which often involves working with labor unions. The European Federation of Trade Unions in the Food, Agriculture, and Tourism sectors represents more than 100 trade unions, with more than 2.5 million members, related to food and tourism in 35 countries. The business structure of multi-national hospitality companies is complicated and since multi-national hospitality companies can be structured in several ways – such as for example as leaseholds, management contracts, or franchises – regulating the working conditions of the labor force can be quite difficult. For example, a hotel in a particular country may be branded as a Hilton, but owned by a group from another country who has hired a management company headquartered in a third country to hire local employees to staff the hotel.[17] The ownership and operation of cruise ships can be even more complicated. This ownership ambiguity can lead to serious issues for workers and dealing with labor relations is an important policy arena for most nations. The case study for this chapter illuminates some of the challenges that tourism currently faces regarding labor issues by showing examples of labor strife that has affected tourism in past years.

Sex tourism

Policy as created by elected officials can demonstrate which path to take on ethical issues in tourism. Some countries garner a significant portion of their tourism demand from sex tourism. Sex tourism involves travel that leads to sexual activity, particularly involving children. "In 1998, the International Labour Organization reported its calculations that 2–14% of the gross domestic product of Indonesia, Malaysia, the Philippines, and Thailand derives from sex tourism. In addition, while Asian countries, including Thailand, India, and the Philippines, have long been prime destinations for child-sex tourists, in recent years, tourists have increasingly traveled to Mexico and Central America for their sexual exploits as well."[18] Countries that are starved for hard foreign currency often look the other way as the cash flows in. Western governments, including that of the United States, are now enacting laws that allow prosecution for sex tourism and the tourists despite the crimes taking place on foreign soil. Existing laws make it illegal to travel with the intent to have sex with a minor, and proposals for new laws that would make it illegal to have sex with a child in another country are now being pursued. Policy creation and implementation is complex and frustrating as the activities are international in scope, with victims and perpetuators coming from different countries. Further complicating this situation is the fact that each country, in many cases, has jurisdiction over only part of the criminal activity. A few countries, including the United States, have pursued legislation that will provide stricter punishment for citizens engaging in sex tourism abroad and for sex tour operators working internationally.[19]

Further efforts to eliminate child sex tourism are being pursued by the tourism industry itself.

- European airlines are showing videos on their long-haul flights that inform travelers of the laws against child sex tourism. The World Tourism Organization (WTO) established a Child Prostitution and Tourism Watch Task Force, whose goals are to "prevent, uncover, isolate and eradicate" the exploitation of children in the sex trade.

- The International Federation of Women's Travel Organizations (IFWTO) holds seminars across the US and globally, which educate their members about the problems of child sex tourism and what they can do to help.

- In 1994, the Universal Federation of Travel Agents' Association (UFTAA) was the first tourism industry organization to adopt the Child and Travel Agents' Charter. In 1996, the members of the International Air Transport Association (IATA) unanimously passed a resolution condemning the commercial sexual exploitation of children.

- A "No Child Sex Tourism" logo has been adopted worldwide by industry organizations that are actively working to prevent and eliminate child prostitution. These sticker-logos can be obtained from the IFWTO.

- In 1996, the International Hotel and Restaurant Association passed a resolution against the sexual exploitation of children and published a leaflet urging its members to help stop child sex tourism.

- In Europe, tour operators have adopted codes of conduct for agents to combat sex tourism.[20]

While these efforts do not use the force of law, the approaches do include moral suasion for both the industry and the consumer. Various approaches to implementing policy goals are being used to fight sex tourism.

Nation-specific tourism policy examples

A review of the tourism-related public policies from countries around the globe completed by the OECD[21] shows many current tourism policies related to competitiveness and sustainability issues. The following paragraphs include tourism policy examples from a small sampling of countries including New Zealand, Belgium, Norway, and Greece.

As part of the 2015 Tourism Strategy for New Zealand, the tourism sector is charged with taking a leading role in protecting and enhancing the natural environment while sustaining the viability of private-sector businesses as they work to deliver on the 100% Pure New Zealand brand promise. Part of this strategy is for operators of tourism businesses to achieve accreditation in the Qualmark program, which is a way to measure and communicate quality tourism businesses. The New Zealand government has developed a program to mentor operators of Maori cultural tourism businesses. The Maori are the Polynesian people indigenous to New Zealand. The Maori cultural tourism business development program assigns a qualified business mentor to Maori business owners who provides one-on-one support and helps the business owner create a business plan and identify opportunities for the business to take part in international marketing campaigns.

Through its Centre for Travel Participation, Belgium has established a program called "Tourism for All," which creates opportunities for Belgians with a limited income to travel. Travel opportunities can be day-trips, overnight expeditions, group travel, or individual trips. The program has strong support from the industry as the government program creates not only a steady stream of demand, but also has the potential to create potential future customers for unsubsidized travel. This program supports Belgium's policy foundations that tourism is an important contributor to socio-economic development.

In addition to the requisite attention paid in tourism strategic plans to stake-holder collaboration, recent policy statements in Norway focus on stabilizing tourism in rural communities by creating year-round demand that would lead to year-round employment. The government further extends the normal scope of sustainable tourism development by including aspects related to social responsibility, such as product innovation, service quality, protecting the cultural environment, and creating wealth.

Although Greece has experienced significant economic turmoil in the twenty-first century's second decade, the Mediterranean nation has made a commitment to tourism development by creating innovative tourism policies based on the nation's rich cultural heritage. Greece is a well-rounded destination that is working to mitigate elements of seasonality with its diverse product offerings of recreation and culture. Recent policy initiatives include: a presidential decree on camping site specifications; skill requirements for hotel workers; an Ecolabel Certification program for small- and medium-sized tourism businesses, and decreased taxes for tourism businesses.

Conclusion

By looking at public policy issues from global destinations, it is easy to see the conflicting needs that call for effective actions and evaluation. Tourism policy provides direction on what action is appropriate. This is particularly relevant for developing countries and other regions of the world addressing economic, socio-cultural, and environmental sustainability issues, such as air and water pollution, crowding, degradation and resource depletion. Tourism policy and planning evolves as demand grows generating new requirements for communities such as in commerce activity, telecommunications, sustainability, and land use.

How contending issues central to today's tourism policy development and implementation affect future populations is central to the study of tourism policy and planning. Adoption of tourism policy issues sustaining the natural, physical, human, and man-made tourism environments will be policymakers' greatest contribution to the future of tourism.

CHAPTER REVIEW QUESTIONS

1. What does the Global Code of Ethics for Tourism do?

2. Why are tourism policy issues so complex? Give an example.

3. What are some of the current issues in tourism policy?

4. Why is sex tourism such a problematic issue and what is being done to fight it?

5. Why is international development aid important and what organizations distribute aid?

6. What has Belgium done to promote tourism and travel?

7. Compare and contrast the tourism policies of two of the countries listed in this chapter.

8. Why is evaluating tourism policies important?

9. Why is tax legislation so divisive in tourism communities?

CASE STUDY 3 Three strikes when tourism was out – labor and tourism interruptions

This case study, written by Dr. Jason R. Swanson, co-author of *Tourism Policy and Planning: Yesterday, Today, and Tomorrow* (first and second editions), was inspired by personal observations during travel.

* * *

As stated earlier in this chapter, labor is an important tourism policy and planning concern today. While some tourism policy issues are clearly focused on travel and tourism, other issues have a primary focus not directly related to tourism. For example, issues such as funding international governmental tourism marketing campaigns and providing tax subsidies for developing hotels are clearly focused on tourism. On the other hand, border regulations are examples of a policy issue that is in place first to make the homeland safe and secure from outside threats. Border-crossing regulations will have an impact on travel and tourism, but the regulations have been put into place for reasons that do not involve tourism development.

Issues of labor relations, or managing unionized employment, can lead to interesting conflicts to study, as management wants wages as low as possible and workers want to make as much money as possible. This conflict occurs as professionally-trained managers and competent workers are two pivotal pieces in the tourism development puzzle. The debate between labor and management is ongoing, with many positive results from the labor movement throughout the world. For example, the Polish Solidarity movement in the early 1980s, which was the first trade union not controlled by the Communist Party within the communist nations of Eastern Europe, contributed to the fall of communism in the Soviet Union and inspired the Arab Spring of the early 2010s. Some credit the labor movement with assisting the rise of the middle class in many countries, as wealthy employers became less able to force the lower-class into harsh working conditions and sub-standard pay.

Labor issues affecting travel and tourism for the consumer do not always directly involve travel and tourism businesses. As we know, many industries such as manufacturing and real estate contribute inputs to the tourism system. When the people who work in these supporting industries exercise their collective action options, severe disruptions to travel can be the result. This case study illustrates how labor strikes in industries peripheral to tourism can have a severe impact on travel. The immediate impacts are often negative, but over the long term, effects of labor strikes on tourism can be beneficial. These effects are illustrated and tied together by examples from the national coal strike of 1912 in the United Kingdom, the public workers' strike in summer 2012 in Norway, and the labor strike of construction workers in Dubai in 2007. The case study concludes with some critical questions that can be used to stimulate discussion.

United Kingdom national coal strike of 1912

Nearly everyone familiar with the sinking of the *RMS Titanic* in April 1912 would say the ship sank because it collided with an iceberg off the Canadian coast. An iceberg is what caused the gash in the ship's hull, and the water let in by the gash that filled the hull is what led the ship to its ultimate resting place 12,415 feet below the surface of the Atlantic and 715 miles east of Halifax, Nova Scotia. More than 1,500 people died, due in large part, to inadequate management practices and government policies regarding how emergencies – such as a hole in the hull – were handled. The *Titanic* inquiry pointed out the iceberg was only part of the problem, as the speed at which the ship hit the iceberg was more important than the iceberg itself.[22] Why would the largest ship of its day cruise at more than 21 knots (39km/h or 24mph), near full-speed, in the dark in waters known to be dotted with icebergs? The ship was, after all, built for luxury not speed. Reports at the time[23] claim this to be standard practice as no one could have imagined that the state-of-the-art in shipbuilding would allow nature to dominate the human presence on the open seas. However, the official inquiry into the disaster found the speed to be excessive given the ice conditions. The inquiry also revealed a fire within the ship's coal storage bunkers that was ignited the day before the ship's departure[24] and some believe the fire burned until the ship sank.[25]

A labor strike was in progress at the time of the ship's maiden voyage that some believe led to the ship's sinking. From February 26, 1912, until April 11, 1912 (the day after the departure of the *Titanic*), coal miners in the UK were striking as they demanded a standard minimum wage as opposed to variable wages based on output. With nearly one million workers taking part in the strike, shipping and train operations were severely disrupted. The strike was ultimately settled and new legislation, the Coal Mines Minimum Wage Act of 1912, was the result.

One of the impacts of the coal miner's strike was a concern that there would not be enough coal to power *Titanic* across the ocean, which would take at least 650 tons of coal per day. Owners of the ship decided to transfer coal from other ships to the cruise liner. Moving coal around can cause it to catch fire and it is believed some of the coal combusted as it was loaded into the storage bunkers on the *Titanic*. During loading, other coal was placed on top of the hotspot, which made it difficult to extinguish. The fire was only completely extinguished once the ship was submerged into the Atlantic.

Speed in steam engines, such as those on the *Titanic*, is regulated by the amount of fuel burned to make steam. For the *Titanic*, that fuel was coal. More coal brings hotter fires, added steam, and greater speed. To control the fire, a crew shoveled coal continuously into the ship's boilers. This caused the ship to flow through the waters at top speeds. Coal on the *Titanic* was stored in bunkers below the water line. The coal fire in the bunker would have heated the steel, which would have caused it to weaken and lessen the integrity of the ship's hull. The iceberg hit in the same area where the fire was reported.

The tragic events of the *Titanic* caused many changes in cruise ship travel. Recommendations of the British Wreck Commissioner's Inquiry: Report on the Loss of the *Titanic*, included mandating the appropriate number of lifeboats, properly orchestrated lifeboat drills for passengers, and a 24-hour watch of all communications systems on seagoing vessels.[26] The International Ice Patrol was established to assess safe passage of ships through the North Atlantic. Other public policy, in the form of the International Convention for the Safety of Life at Sea, was established to make guidelines consistent across ships sailing under flags and in waters of a plethora of nations.

I learned about the connection of the national coal strike to the *Titanic* while traveling in Halifax, Nova Scotia, on the night of the 100th anniversary of the sinking of the ship. Halifax was the port from which many rescue ships were deployed and where many of the recovered victims' remains lie in rest. The news reports, including the one I saw about the strike, made me think about my upcoming honeymoon cruise through the Baltic Sea. I thought I had nothing to worry about, I didn't think a labor strike would have any impact on my vacation 100 years later.

Norwegian public worker strike of 2012

Once everyone was onboard our cruise ship, which sailed through the Baltic Sea in June 2012, we were informed by the captain on the public address system that it was time for our compulsory muster. The captain explained how this was required by the International Convention for the Safety of Life at Sea. As stated in the previous paragraphs, the requirement in these regulations was an outcome of the investigation into the sinking of the *Titanic*. While standing on deck and thinking about all the tragedies that could happen at sea, I remembered what I learned while in Halifax about the national coal strike in the United Kingdom. And then I realized our cruise voyage would have more in common with the *Titanic* than I had originally hoped.

At the start of that day, before we boarded our ship, I snuck in a quick check of emails as I lay awake adjusting to the time changes. We were supposed to leave the Oslo harbor at 5pm and head through the Oslo fjord on our way to the Baltic Sea. The late afternoon passage through the fjord was expected to be a highlight of our journey as three days of our seven-day cruise would be spent at sea and we would not get much scenery beyond an expanse of sea water, wind turbines in the distance, and cheesy lounge singers aboard the ship. Looking at the fiords from our stateroom balcony would be a nice way to begin this leg of our journey.

But my email was telling me instead of a cruise through the glacial valley, we would be treated to an afternoon bus ride along the multi-lane highway connecting Oslo and Gothenburg, Sweden. Our ship had docked in Gothenburg that morning instead of reaching its intended destination of Oslo where this morning's passengers were to disembark and the new passengers, including us, were supposed to board. The cause of this change of plans was a labor strike.

A week before our arrival in Norway, public workers – numbering roughly 30,000 – went on strike with the hopes of having their pay increased to be more in line with the private-sector. Local and national government workers took part in the strike.[27] What started with workers in schools, daycare centers, and nursing homes, quickly spread and ultimately included harbor pilots.

Harbor pilots board large ships and are responsible for guiding the vessel from the open seas into the harbor and docking the ship. The pilot also takes ships from port to the sea. The pilot has an in-depth local knowledge of the port and is required by law in most major seaports. The pilot does not work for the commercial ship owner, but instead is in place to protect the public interest. Without harbor pilots, cruise ships and other large vessels could not enter or depart the Oslo port. The harbor pilots' inclusion in the strike was particularly important because the cruise season was just getting started. The threat of several thousand stranded and probably angry tourists and the international attention such a scene might garner through social and traditional media, gave new power to the strikers.

The strike not only disrupted departures and arrivals of cruise ship voyages, but also eliminated the ability of cruise ships to deposit their passengers and their money on the Norwegian shores for temporary port-of-calls. Without the sudden influx of visitors; retail shops, restaurants, museums, tour companies, and other tourism businesses, as well as tourism workers, would lose significant revenue each day of the strike. Princess Cruises' *Emerald Princess* was unable to make a scheduled stop in Oslo, but instead was forced to provide passengers with a scenic cruise of the Oslo fiords[28] without giving them a chance to leave any money behind in Norway. In this case, the striking workers pushing for increased wages for public-sector employees were using the high-visibility and economic contribution of tourism to help them accomplish their goals.

Beyond harbor pilots, passport control and immigration officers were also on strike. Even the rental lockers at the train station were closed because of the striking workers, which meant cruise passengers and others with several spare hours in Oslo would not be able store their bags and easily traverse the downtown area while waiting for an evening flight. Many were forced to sit in the train station with their bags and miss out on the true Oslo scene. Effects were felt beyond tourism as well as cargo ships and petroleum tankers were unable to reach ports within Norway. This was expected to drive up prices on consumer goods and fuel.

The time we were to arrive at the Oslo terminal remained the same. We could originally board the ship anytime between 12pm and 4pm. We had always intended to arrive at noon so we could get settled in to our floating temporary home. News of the strike did not change our morning plans and before our noon arrival to the dock, we fluttered around downtown Oslo and the surrounding neighborhoods. Our first stop after breakfast was the Tourist Information Centre. There we were told the cruise was cancelled, a labor strike was on and ships couldn't get in or out of the harbor. This would have been our first news of the situation – although incorrect – if not for my email sneak earlier in the morning. We informed the tourism information officer of the change in plans and that the cruise was still on. Another stop in the morning was the Deichmanske Bibliotek, where a friendly security guard we engaged in conversation let us know that Gothenburg was about a four-hour drive from Oslo. This was our first real notice that our debut day at sea would not be quite as pleasant as we had originally hoped. We eventually found ourselves at the dock a few minutes after noon.

As far as we could tell, the check-in process was the same as if the ship was there. But the ship was not there. The only hint of something out of the ordinary was a group of temporary baggage handlers who looked like they were learning to swim by being thrown into the deep end of a pool filled with oversized pullman suitcases and duffle bags. And the stream of bags led not to a ship's gangway but instead to the back of waiting cargo trucks.

As we were herded through the baggage drop-off area and through the check-in experience we were handed a boxed lunch and wished *bon voyage* as we walked outside the terminal. Our bus awaited, along with a fleet of 40 buses for those passengers who followed us. Figure 3.1 captures the moment of what should have been our grand entrance onto the luxury ocean liner. The passengers we replaced, boarded buses at six o'clock in the morning in Gothenberg for the final leg of their cruise to the strike-affected Oslo. The same Swedish buses that carried those passengers, waited for the return trip with the new batch of 2,000 passengers. We sat on the bus, not knowing exactly where we were going or how long it would take. It didn't matter too much to us – we were on our honeymoon! But other passengers were older or had small children. One family with a two-year-old son boarded the bus after loading their stroller, toys, and other baby necessities in the cargo hold of the bus. They didn't think they would need them, but they also didn't know it would be a four-hour ride to reach the ship.

The lack of information as we were bused to our boat made us feel like navy recruits rather than vacationers. We did eventually reach the ship and had dinner while the passengers who straggled behind us finally made their way

FIGURE 3.1 Portion of the fleet of buses that served as a cruise ship substitute
(Photo: Jason R. Swanson)

to the ship. But before we could go anywhere, we had to participate in the *Titanic*-influenced compulsory muster. By talking with crew members on the ship, we learned throughout the week of other impacts the strike had on operations, including a depletion of inventory in the retail shops and the restaurant pantries.

Dubai construction worker strike of 2007

Cruise ships are staffed with people from all over the world. A primary reason for this is the amount of money a stateroom attendant or waiter on a cruise ship could earn is likely much greater than what they could earn in their home country. Such was the case with a cocktail server on our cruise we struck up a conversation with. He was from India and we chatted about the strike that affected our departure from Oslo. He told us about another strike he was once a part of – a construction worker strike in Dubai.

Dubai is the largest of the seven emirates by population within the United Arab Emirates (UAE), which is an oil-rich nation located on the southeastern shores of the Persian Gulf. Dubai and much of the rest of the UAE experienced a tremendous amount of development in the early part of the twenty-first century as oil prices rose sharply. This led in part to a boom in construction projects as Dubai worked to establish itself as a major player in international commerce. Significant construction projects included the Burj Khalifa (the world's tallest building, which includes a hotel), Dubai World Central International Airport (the world's most expensive airport), the tourism creation known as Palms Islands (the world's largest artificial islands), and the Dubai Mall (the world's largest shopping mall).

Much of the development was fueled by lower-paid construction laborers from India, Sri Lanka, Bangladesh, and Pakistan, who were working for as little as $300 per month. As many as 700,000 Asians were employed in construction during the development boom. Just like on a cruise ship, workers left their home country to work where they could make more money relative to the jobs they could find in their home country. Many with college degrees who might be employed as bankers or computer technicians in their homeland would find it more beneficial to temporarily leave their families so that they could better support them with jobs that required less skill but paid much better.

Despite the higher pay they could receive, the foreign workers still wanted to be treated with dignity. In March 2006, workers building the Burj Khalifa walked off the job in protest trying to get improved medical care and better treatment from foremen. Although there was some violence, the work stoppage didn't last long and construction resumed as the government threatened to deport any striking worker since strikes and labor unions are illegal in the UAE. However, the unrest was not settled yet.

In October of the following year, rioting resurfaced.[29] When the government threatened deportation of rioters, the workers organized a work stoppage. They would show up to the worksite but would refuse to pick up tools. It was a more peaceful demonstration that seemed to catch the attention of government officials. Three other things were also different with this labor uprising that may have had an impact on the way the government reacted. First, the value of the UAE dirham was falling. This meant foreign workers could not send as much money back home as they were before. Second, India was beginning to experience its own economic boom. This meant more comparable options were available for Indian workers to return home and make a viable living, which was beginning to cause a labor shortage in Dubai. Third, Human Rights Watch, an independent organization focused on protecting human rights that had been observing the situation since the initial uprisings in March 2006, was calling for the UAE government to put a halt to the unfair labor practices.

Realizing outside forces leading to the work stoppage could have a significant influence on the completion of the buildings, and how the stoppage could have a negative impact on tourism development and other sectors, the government started to make concessions. In November 2007, the strike was resolved. Improved working conditions were ordered by Sheikh Mohammed bin Rashid Al Maktoum, Dubai's political leader. The police were also charged with prosecuting employers who did not meet minimum health and safety standards.[30]

According to Human Rights Watch, labor condition concerns remain in the UAE, where more than 88.5 percent of residents are foreign workers. Suicide among Indian laborers is high, with at least 26 suicide deaths reported in 2011. Most suicide victims appear to be distraught over treatment and not being able to return home at will. The UAE government reported 34 worker protests – associated with delayed payments, no overtime, or low pay – in the first three months of 2011, which is less than half of the number of protests during the first quarter of 2010. In Dubai's neighboring emirate of Abu Dhabi, the largest developer is the Tourism Development and Investment Company (TDIC). In May 2011, the TDIC contracted with PwC, an international auditing firm to monitor working conditions on Saadiyat Island, a major tourist construction project.[31] While work still remains to improve the working conditions in Dubai and throughout the tourism centers of the UAE, progress is being made as tourism developers see the impact that work stoppages can have on the burgeoning tourism sector.

Concluding critical questions

As shown in this case study, work stoppages can have a significant impact on tourism in the short term, such as in the Norwegian strike, or in the long-term such as in the construction workers strike in Dubai. Labor strikes can also indirectly affect, but still significantly affect tourism, as was the case in the UK national coal strike of 1912. The coal strike, which is connected to the sinking of *Titanic*, continues to have indirect affects on the way we travel today, such as with compulsory musters and other life-saving procedures in place on cruise ships and other passenger vessels.

In 2011, in the United States alone, work stoppages and strikes involving 1,000 or more workers totaled 19 and involved 113,000 workers and more than one million lost workdays.[32] Many strikes throughout the world directly or indirectly involve workers in some aspect of travel and tourism. Clearly, labor relations are a current tourism policy and planning issue. These issues will likely remain current as the struggles between equity and profit endure. A rich discussion can ensue by considering the examples in this case study and other examples that students and teachers might come up with on their own.

Viewing labor issues through a tourism lens can lead to several thought-provoking questions centered on policy, planning, and the power of tourism as a public relations tool. Regarding policy, how are labor and management conflicts part of the public policy spectrum? Should the government set policy that concerns labor relations and if so should the government's policies be more pro-worker or more pro-management? Answers to these questions will depend on the perspectives of those involved in the discussion, which will be affected by the political and social systems of the destination. Related to planning, how can tourism managers and government officials plan for workforce issues when proposing marketing or product development programs? Could a new tourism program lead to a work stoppage?

Public relations activities involve maintaining a favorable public image and are important tools of tourism development. For example, hosting media in the destination for familiarization tours or touting the tax breaks tourism provides host communities to local residents are common public relations tactics. Not only can public relations be a tourism tool, but tourism can also be a public relations tool. In our cruise experience during the Norway strike, how could the tourism information officials have handled the situation better? What happens when misinformation is provided by government tourism officials or private-sector businesses, such as the cruise line? In the examples provided or in other examples, how has tourism been used to advance the agendas of labor groups? How much do human rights conflicts affect tourism demand? What are the pros and cons of the support (or lack of support) by tourism policy advocates of issues relating to organized labor in tourism industries? How can tourism be used as a tool for both sides in a strike negotiation? When human rights organizations encourage people to avoid traveling to an area because of inhumane conditions of workers in the country, tourism is the tool they are using to persuade government leaders to make changes.

Notes

1   http://dtxtq4w60xqpw.cloudfront.net/sites/all/files/docpdf/gcetbrochureglobalcodeen.pdf.

2   http://www.econ-pol.unisi.it/opts/DOC%5B1%5D.%20Agenda%2021%20-%2026%20Set%20bozza%20communication.pdf.

3   Parizzi, M., Velasquez, L., Uhlein, A., Aranha, P., & Goncolves, J. (2001) "Environment, Tourism and Land-Use Planning – Riachinho Basin, Brazil." *Environmental Management and Health*, *(12)*1: 57.

4   Gumbel, R. (2004). Making a Living Off the Land Vacationers Are Increasingly Turning to the Pastoral Pleasures of Rural Holidays – and Europe's Farmers are Reaping the Benefits. *Time International* (Atlantic ed.), *(164)*6: 70.

5   www.oecd.org/cfe/tourism/innovationandgrowthintourism.htm

6   Organisation for Economic Co-operation and Development (2010) *Tourism Trends and Policies.*

7   www.ghanahero.com/Ghana_Hero_Docs/Tourism_Ghana/Ghana_National_Tourism_Marketing_Strategy-MAPS.pdf

8   www.tourismireland.com/CMSPages/GetFile.aspx?guid=9ca1193b-6c7d-4ac4-8a15-92875e54f32b

9   Virginia Tax Code, § 58.1-3823.

10   WorldBank.org

11   M2Presswire, 12/2/05

12   M2 Press wire, 9/12/03

13   Anonymous (2005) "JBIC Supports Airport Modernization in Egypt." *The Middle East*, May: 49.

14   McConnell, A. (2006) "Gueam Representative Urges Pooled Bond Bank for Territories." *Bond Buyer*, March 3: 6.

15   M2 Presswire, 2005

16   OECD's regular publication, *Education at a Glance*

17   www.effat.eu/files/19935469b716b5bba90480c124e048a9_1328626213.pdf

18   Nair, S. (2006) "Child Sex Tourism." www.justice.gov/criminal/ceos/sextour.html, retrieved March 10, 2006.

19   equalitynow.com, 2006

20   ECPAT, 2006

21   Organisation for Economic Co-operation and Development (2010).

22   www.titanicinquiry.org/BOTInq/BOTReport/BOTRepSpeed.php

23   Mowbray, Jay Henry (1912) *Sinking of the* Titanic. Harrisburg, PA: The Minter Company

24   www.titanicinquiry.org/BOTInq/BOTInq04Barrett02.php.

25   www.youtube.com/watch?v=Ny3s3iK0Mv0.

26   www.titanicinquiry.org/BOTInq/BOTReport/BOTRepRec.php.

27   http://www.bbc.co.uk/news/world-europe-18188917

28   www.travelweekly.com/print.aspx?id=239469

29   www.nytimes.com/2007/10/28/business/worldbusiness/28iht-labor.4.8084022.html.

30   news.bbc.co.uk/2/hi/business/7074917.stm.

31   Human Rights Watch (2012) *World Report – Events of 2012*.

32   www.bls.gov/news.release/wkstp.nr0.htm.

CHAPTER 4

International tourism as a commercial and economic activity

Expenditures by international tourists – traveling for recreational, leisure, or business purposes – contribute in a major way to individual country foreign exchange earnings and their balance of payments. The post-World War II years have seen a global increase in leisure time, rising incomes and a strong desire to travel for millions of people in both the developed and developing countries. Indeed, shorter working hours, greater individual prosperity, faster and cheaper travel, and the impact of advanced technology have all helped to make tourism one of the fastest-growing commercial and economic activities in the world.

Today, tourism is indeed an activity of considerable economic importance in most countries. This growing significance of tourism as a source of income and employment, and as a major factor in the balance of payments for many countries, has been attracting increased attention from governments, regional and local authorities, and others with an interest in economic development. Such an awareness of the economic benefits of tourism has been slow in coming and, even today, has not, for the most part, captured the attention of many economic policymakers. Furthermore, because the economic benefits of international tourism permeate throughout a nation's economy and on a global basis, such expenditures benefit rich nations and poor; large and small; developing and developed. International tourism can have a powerful transformative impact toward global socio-economic progress.

In learning about the commercial and economic aspects of international tourism, it is important to understand tourism's global importance, how tourism is an economic development tool, key economic concepts applied to tourism, and how competitive tourism actors can cooperate in pursuit of common goals. These areas are described throughout this chapter. The chapter is followed by a case study using Antarctica to illustrate examples of the commercial and economic activities of tourism in a setting like no other place on Earth.

Tourism as an economic development tool

Chapter 2 noted that international tourist's receipts bolster a country's balance of trade and adds to the country's overall economic policies. In effect, tourism helps local communities increase their economic development, realize increased revenues, create new jobs, benefit from a diverse economy, add new products, generate additional income, spawn new businesses, and contribute to overall economic integration while enriching the public and private partnerships and improving the quality-of-life of the local citizenry. Figure 4.1 illustrates the commercial and economic activities of tourism that lead to stakeholder benefits.

Tourism brings in large amounts of capital from the payments for goods and services by visitors, contributing an estimated 9 percent to the worldwide gross domestic product (GDP).[1] Tourism creates additional opportunities for employment in the service industries associated with tourism such as airlines, cruise ships, rental cars, and taxicabs; hospitality services; accommodations, including hotels, bed and breakfasts and resorts; entertainment activities, such as amusement parks, sports programs, casinos, music venues, theaters; food and beverage establishments; and shopping malls. Figure 4.2 illustrates the plethora of tourism supply components such as stadiums, cruise ship docks, hotels, nature trails, and other entertainment options that can be found in a very concentrated area. Tourism is also a major contributor to manufacturing and construction as for example the need for building of airplanes, airports, cruise ships, cruise ports, entertainment centers and other

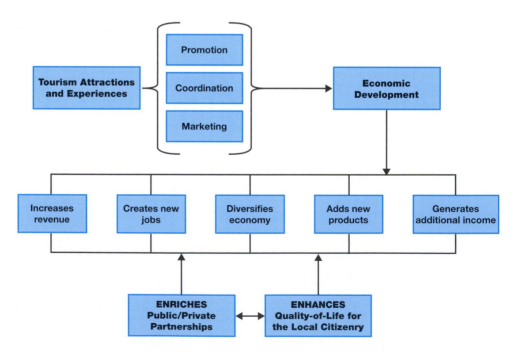

FIGURE 4.1 Schema of tourism as a commercial and economic activity

FIGURE 4.2 A wide variety of tourism supply components is shown in the area surrounding the Cape Town Harbor in South Africa (Photo: Brian Bulla)

facilities necessary to meet the expectations of international visitors. Tourism supports industries such as agriculture and fishing, which produce the food for visitors.

Tourism is an important source of income for most of the countries of the world. When strategically well-planned and executed, tourism provides an economic stream both into and throughout a local area or country and is an incentive to preserve the best things the destination has to offer – from its scenic coastlines, majestic mountains, open spaces, beautiful communities, rural towns, wildlife habitats, historic structures, local heritage and culture. Properly integrated as part of an overall local economic strategy, tourism can provide a local community with economic development, environmental sustainability, and social benefits. Utilizing tourism as an economic development tool to benefit a community requires a carefully designed tourism policy and a sound strategic plan in order to mitigate potential negative impacts of tourism. Such a balanced approach to tourism development appropriately addressed by the destination's tourism leaders, governments, businesses, communities, educational institutions, and not-for-profit entities can help individual destinations garner a larger percentage of the international tourism market. Ultimately, this increases the opportunity for utilizing international tourism's contribution to the commercial and economic benefits of the community.

Some of the broader aspects of utilizing tourism as an economic development tool were noted in 1990 by co-author David L. Edgell in his book *International Tourism*

Policy.[2] He explained that the tourism industry plays an important role in the economic and technological development of nations. Tourism:

  a) Stimulates the development of basic infrastructure (such as airports, harbors, roads, sewers and electrical power);
  b) Contributes to the growth of domestic industries that supply the tourism industry (e.g., transportation, agriculture, food processing, commercial fishing, lumbering and construction);
  c) Attracts foreign investment (especially in hotels); and,
  d) Facilitates the transfer of technology and technical know-how.

While the economic conditions in the world have changed over the years, the notes above still relate to most areas interested in economic development through tourism. Both developed and developing countries are recognizing the need and the benefits of committing resources to improving tourism facilities within their respective countries. For example, technological advances in the construction of airports were necessary to provide the appropriate facilities to handle newly designed aircraft. This has resulted in raising the level of training of skilled workers in the construction industry, utilizing newly developed building materials, a need for better-trained personnel to pilot the aircraft and to man the control towers and an understanding of new computer technology required to effectively and efficiently schedule and route the flights of both new and old airplanes and related operations. The need for highly trained personnel in industries related to tourism will continue.

The global economic contribution of tourism, the economic development of tourism in developing nations, and in rural areas are aspects to consider when developing an understanding of tourism as an economic development tool. Each of these areas are discussed in the remainder of this section.

Global economic contribution of tourism

Today, tourism is indeed an activity of considerable economic importance throughout the world. Recent studies support the hypothesis that as the world economy expands (or contracts), so does tourism. This was particularly highlighted when the world economy took a downturn in 2008 and 2009 resulting in a decrease in international tourism arrivals in 2009, the first such decline since the negative impact that took place in 2001 after the terrorist attacks in the US. The United Nations World Tourism Organization (UNWTO) has displayed the impact that international tourism has worldwide in terms of international tourist arrivals and international tourism receipts,[3] as shown in Table 4.1 and Table 4.2.

Economic development of tourism in developing nations

Possibly the newest movement in tourism as an economic development tool is happening in lesser-developed nations. Because tourism can promote economic development more quickly than is true in many other industries, it can attract much-needed financial capital, increase awareness of a country's potential as a tourism destination, improve infrastructure and provide new job opportunities. A developing country can best benefit from increased tourism based on the impact of the multiplier effect of tourism. That is, if the country can meet the demands of visitors for a quality tourism experience, then many exports of the country's local and national economy will be improved. Collaboration, whether among destinations or within governmental agencies, referred to as *coopetition* (discussed in greater detail later in this chapter), serves to enhance tourism's economic impact. An important point to remember is virtually every country and community in the world has something that tourists would be interested in, whether it is a scenic waterfall, a majestic mountain, unusual flora and fauna, built structures, or unique cultural celebrations. Visitors to a place collectively have wide interests from bird-watching to hiking, from visiting historic sites and interesting small communities, or possibly participating in a special event or festival.

An interesting example of a change of governmental policy toward using tourism as an economic development driver is that of the country of Gabon in Africa. In 2002 the President of Gabon, recognizing that the country was too dependent on petroleum production and needing to find alternative products to replace its dependence on oil, set aside 10 percent of its land for a national park system. Part of the

TABLE 4.1 Trends in international tourist arrivals

	International Tourist Arrivals (million)							Market share (%)	Change (%)		Average annual growth (%)
	1990	1995	2000	2005	2009	2010	2011*	2011*	10/09	11*/10	'05–'11*
World	435	528	674	799	883	940	983	100	6.4	4.6	3.5
Advanced economies	296	334	417	455	475	499	523	53.2	4.9	4.9	2.4
Emerging economies	139	193	256	344	408	441	460	46.8	8.2	4.3	5.0
By UNTWO regions											
Europe	261.5	304	385	440.7	461.7	474.8	504	51.3	2.8	6.2	2.3
Northern Europe	28.6	35.8	43.4	56.1	56	56.1	59.3	6.0	0.2	5.6	0.9
Western Europe	108.6	112.2	139.7	141.7	148.5	153.8	159	16.2	3.6	3.4	1.9
Central/Eastern Europe	33.9	58.1	69.3	90.4	92.6	95.7	103.5	10.5	3.3	8.1	2.3
Southern/Mediter. Eu.	90.3	98	132.6	152.5	164.5	169.1	182.2	18.5	2.8	7.7	3.0
– of which EU-27	230.1	265.9	323.7	352.4	356.8	364.9	385	39.2	2.3	5.5	1.5
Asia and the Pacific	55.8	82	110.1	153.6	181.1	204.4	217	22.1	12.9	6.1	5.9
North-East Asia	26.4	41.3	58.3	85.9	98	111.5	115.8	11.8	13.8	3.8	5.1
South-East Asia	21.2	28.4	36.1	48.5	62.1	69.9	77.2	7.8	12.5	10.4	8.0
Oceania	5.2	8.1	9.6	11	10.9	11.6	11.7	1.2	6.1	0.9	1.0
South Asia	3.1	4.2	6.1	8.1	10.1	11.5	12.4	1.3	13.6	8	7.2
Americas	92.8	109	128.2	133.3	141.7	150.7	156.6	15.9	6.4	3.9	2.7
North America	71.7	80.7	91.5	89.9	93	99.2	101.7	10.3	6.6	2.5	2.1
Caribbean	11.4	14	17.1	18.8	19.6	20	20.8	2.1	2.2	3.9	1.7
Central America	1.9	2.6	4.3	6.3	7.6	7.9	8.3	0.8	3.9	4.8	4.7
South America	7.7	11.7	15.3	18.3	21.4	23.6	25.8	2.6	10	9.4	5.8
Africa	14.8	18.8	26.2	34.8	45.9	49.7	50.2	5.1	8.5	0.9	6.3
North Africa	8.4	7.3	10.2	13.9	17.6	18.8	17.1	1.7	6.7	–9.1	3.5
Subsaharan Africa	6.4	11.5	16	20.9	28.3	31	33.1	3.4	9.6	6.9	7.9
Middle East	9.6	13.7	24.1	36.3	52.8	60.3	55.4	5.6	14.2	–8	7.3

* provisional data

Source: United Nations World Tourism Organization

TABLE 4.2 Trends in international tourism receipts

	Local currencies, constant prices change (%)				Market share (%)	US$ Receipts (billion)		per arrival	US$ Receipts (billion)		per arrival
	08/07	09/08	10/09	11*/10	2011*	2010	2011*	2011*	2010	2011*	2011*
World	1.6	−5.6	5.4	3.9	100	927	1030	1050	699	740	750
Advanced economies	1.7	−6.4	5.7	4.8	64.5	589	664	1270	444	477	910
Emerging economies	1.4	−3.9	4.9	2.2	35.5	338	366	800	255	263	570
By UNWTO regions											
Europe	−0.9	−6.5	0	5.2	45	409.3	463.4	920	308.8	332.9	660
Northern Europe	−2.5	−4.1	2.7	5	6.8	61.4	70.3	1190	46.3	50.5	850
Western Europe	−2.2	−6.6	1.1	3.7	15.6	142.2	160.4	1010	107.2	115.2	720
Central/Eastern Europe	4.3	−8	−2.9	7.9	5.4	48.1	56.1	540	36.3	40.3	390
Southern/Mediter. Eu.	−0.6	−6.9	−1	5.7	17.1	157.6	176.7	970	118.9	126.9	700
– of which EU-27	−2.7	−7	0.7	4.3	36.6	335	377.5	980	252.7	271.2	700
Asia and the Pacific	4.6	−0.6	15.5	4.4	28.1	255.3	289.4	1330	192.5	207.9	960
North-East Asia	8.2	1.9	21.4	3.8	13.9	128.6	143.1	1240	97	102.8	890
South-East Asia	−0.8	−7	15.1	9.3	7.9	68.6	81.9	1060	51.7	58.8	760
Oceania	3	5.2	−1.9	−7.3	4	39.2	41.6	3560	29.5	29.9	2560
South Asia	7.7	−4.6	16.5	14.6	2.2	18.9	23	1850	14.3	16.5	1330
Americas	4.8	−10	4.2	5.7	19.3	180.7	199.1	1270	136.3	143	910
North America	6.9	−12.2	6	6.6	14.1	131.2	145.1	1430	99	104.2	1020
Caribbean	−4.1	−6.4	−0.1	1.3	2.3	22.7	23.9	1150	17.1	17.2	830
Central America	0.3	−5.4	4.8	0.9	0.7	6.7	7.2	860	5	5.2	620
South America	3.1	0	−2.1	6.5	2.2	20.1	22.9	890	15.1	16.5	640
Africa	−2.5	−5.8	1.7	2.2	3.2	30.4	32.6	650	22.9	23.4	470
North Africa	−3.9	−4.7	0.2	−6.7	0.9	9.7	9.5	560	7.3	6.8	400
Subsaharan Africa	−1.7	−6.4	2.6	6.3	2.2	20.7	23.1	700	15.6	16.6	500
Middle East	5.5	1.2	17.2	−14.4	4.5	51.7	45.9	830	39	33	590

* provisional data

Source: United Nations World Tourism Organization

concept for this change of strategies was that Gabon hoped to become Africa's successful ecotourism destination having been aware of the success of countries such as Costa Rica in Central America. These new parks are presumably looking toward the development of sustainable tourism (including ecotourism) as an economic alternative to exploiting Gabon's forests for lumber and based on the likelihood of an eventual decline in petroleum production. To date, Gabon has not been particularly successful, possibly because of a lack of commitment to develop and implement a good tourism policy and strategic plan.

The small country of Dominica, a beautiful Caribbean island nation, fits the category of a developing country having a largely rural environment with many tourism development opportunities. Dominica has lush mountainous rainforests, is home to many rare plants and bird species, a scenic coastline, and friendly people. In the past, the nation depended mostly on agriculture production. While agriculture continues to be important, the country needs foreign exchange earnings and is now fully engaged in seeking tourism as an economic development tool to provide jobs and income. Dominica's tourist industry is in its infancy compared to other Caribbean nations, but has gained the reputation as the "Nature Island." From a tourism policy and economic development perspective, Dominica is finding that its special niche is ecotourism. It has a rich culture and heritage, provides hiking and adventure opportunities, and seeks to preserve and protect the natural environment (mainstays of ecotourism). Dominica is discussed further as a case study in Chapter 11.

Another developing nation utilizing tourism as a prime economic development tool is the country of Belize. This Central American country is making giant strides in expanding its tourism sector. The country is endowed with a beautiful seacoast, which includes a natural tourism destination with respect to the Island of Ambergris near to the world's second largest barrier reef, behind Australia's reef. Belize also has a fascinating jungle area full of exotic flora and fauna, and is host to possibly the largest number of Mayan ruins in the four countries of Mexico, Guatemala, Honduras, and Belize that are a part of "La Ruta Maya." Belize has recently launched a sustainable tourism policy as the country develops its tourism strategy.[4] Tourism, for Belize, provides the country with many job opportunities for its people and adds to the foreign exchange earnings to bolster its international trade. If Belize is to prosper in the future, tourism as an economic development sector will likely be a major factor in its progress.

Costa Rica is a good example of following through on a tourism policy and plan aimed at gaining export revenue by concentrating on ecotourism that attracts international visitors. This country of farms and ranches began developing eco-tourism many years ago and has found that international visitors are an important source of international receipts and a sustainable resource that adds substantially to the country's balance-of-trade. Kenya and Tanzania are notable examples of taking advantage of their natural beauty (as shown in Figure 4.3), wildlife, culture,

FIGURE 4.3 Candelabra trees in the Kenyan savannah (Photo: Junghee 'Michelle' Han)

and geography, especially through the popularity of their wildlife safaris, to increase tourism to rural areas that had principally relied in the past on the raising of cattle. There are many other examples of rural areas utilizing tourism to increase foreign exchange earnings as a result of international visitor expenditures.

Economic development of tourism in rural areas

Tourism as an economic development tool, especially international tourism, is often overlooked by rural communities throughout the world. Yet, many rural areas offer the most diversity in beauty, experience, culture, heritage, and service. Oftentimes the success of international tourism in rural areas depends substantially on the ability of a region to recognize its capacity for tourism, to effectively plan and manage its tourism economy, and to maximize its ability to capture tourist expenditures. A major problem in utilizing tourism as an economic development tool in rural environments is that such areas often lack the critical mass of human, financial, and technical resources.

Rural communities today are seeking alternatives to economic development other than the once-dominant industries of farming, ranching, timber production, and mining. Many areas are looking toward more sustainable resources as a development tool. Tourism can be just the right industry for rural areas that plan well for the development of new tourism-related products.

Possibly the most difficult problem in rural areas is for local residents to recognize their potential of using tourism as an economic development tool. The next key task is teaching rural residents the skills needed in the tourism industry. One advantage of tourism as an economic development tool is that its implementation relies on an area's cultural, historic, ethnic, geographic, and natural uniqueness. These resources are found in most rural areas, are renewable, and can create local pride in wanting to show off their community to both domestic and international visitors.

Key economic concepts

As an important contributor to the production, distribution, and consumption of wealth in global society, tourism can be easily viewed through the lens of economics. Viewing tourism from an economics perspective is important because the gains from visitors and their money crossing international boundaries affect nations' balances-of-trade, have implications relating to tariffs and other fiscal policy, and can affect exchange rates. This is particularly important in developing countries. Key economic concepts and variables – including supply and demand, comparative advantage, employment, income, multipliers, and exports – as they relate to tourism are discussed in the following sections.

Demand side of tourism

The demand for tourism determines how many people are interested in the product, service and location at a given price. It includes the potential interests and motivations of tourists. Added to this, in the demand analysis, are the marketing elements of product, price, place, and promotion. If the destination has a product of interest to tourists, located in a desirable environment and promoted through the most effective marketing media, then what remains is how much a visitor is willing to spend to enjoy the experience.

A special area of interest with respect to the demand for a tourism product is the effect of seasonality. The destination may have an excellent product, be located in the right place, be priced to meet the visitors' budgets, and be promoted using the best communication and marketing tools and still not be successful because the tourism season is too short to make a reasonable profit and to keep its workers employed for a long enough period of time. Seasonality in tourism is one of the major challenges in developing tourism policies and strategic plans to increase economic development. Tourism seasonality causes underemployment, underutilization of facilities, and in turn, lowered productivity. For many countries, tourists with children take their vacations in the warmer weather of the summer when their children are not in school. The concern is how to motivate other travelers to visit a destination during the other three-quarters of the year. Some destinations have extended their seasons by offering unique festivals and events or through pricing policies with heavy discounts during the off-season.

Another tourism policy concern is the demand by visitors for pristine environments. Increasingly, educated travelers are actively seeking unspoiled locations as holiday destinations. Many of the popular destinations of the world already suffer from a multitude of pollutions associated with air, water, noise, and other harmful impurities. This has become of such major concern in tourism policy that a complete chapter of this book – Chapter 6, "Managing Sustainable Tourism" – is devoted to the interest in sustainability.

Projecting or forecasting demand, and the implications for policy perspectives based on the future of tourism, is of major interest. Models and tools for forecasting travel and tourism have been around for a long time. Early projections of tourism appeared in an article "Use of Modified Scenario Research in Forecasting of Tourism in the United States."[5] Later, in the book *International Tourism Policy*,[6] projections of tourism were presented based on using special assumptions and basic determinants found in tourism at that time. Today, there are sophisticated forecasting models for making projections of tourism arrivals and receipts. Simple methodologies also exist, such as trend analysis, that when combined with executive judgments, yield reasonable forecasts. Many factors impact forecasting tourism such as the state of the economy, political situations, fuel issues, changes in tastes, and many others. The Delphi method, which is used to identify consensus among a group of experts, adds an important dimension to the forecasting methodology. Goeldner and Ritchie[7] laud the Delphi method by stating: "For estimating tourism demand, then, a combination of various mathematical statistical methods and the Delphi method is believed to produce the most reliable demand estimates in any given situation."

One of the biggest impacts on tourism demand today is the ease of the use of e-commerce tools. The internet is now used by most people as they plan their travel.

It affords the traveler more power of choice through greater access to information and has a powerful influence on which destinations a tourist chooses for their vacation. It also allows the potential traveler to preview the destination and the local amenities. In addition, the design of an effective website has a heavy influence on choices made by travelers in choosing their destination. Because the cost of a website is relatively low, it helps balance the demand for tourism in that it gives small destinations and properties an opportunity to compete with the larger tourism entities. However, this has created a very crowded internet landscape for tourism destinations, as well as most other purchase options.

With so much information available at their fingertips, sophisticated travelers can weigh their options and seek destinations affordable within their respective budgets. Many travelers today seek variety and flexibility in their choice of a destination. This is just as true for the mature traveler (those travelers over 60 years old) as it is for younger generations. Mature travelers today look for choices in their activities and options in their travel scheduling. For the most part, this generation of travelers has more time, money and interest in traveling. They can also travel during the off-season, which makes them an important market for those destinations heavily impacted by peaks and valleys of demand. This phenomenon puts even more pressure for competitive pricing for many destinations. As mentioned earlier, visitors are also seeking sustainable destinations that offer a clean and pristine environment.

Supply side of tourism

The question or cliché sometimes raised in tourism is "If we build it, they (tourists) will come." Is it logical to wait for visitors to fulfill the *demand* before the destination *supplies* them with the necessary facilities to meet their needs at the destination, or does the destination provide the supply components in advance to help stimulate the demand? Obviously, the best scenario is a balance of demand and supply. It is also necessary to pay attention to quality and quantity. If a destination does not provide the right supply components it is likely that a competitor will and the initial destination will lose market share.

Some of the elements of supply are more difficult to define. For example, in some settings the supply might be the natural scenic beauty, culture, favorable climate, fauna, or coastline that attracts visitors. But such a destination must also offer infrastructure, facilities, and visitor services. There must be transportation access to the destination. If it is a drive-to destination, good roads and appropriate signage for locating the community are necessary. If it is an outdoor location, the area must have parking, drinking water, trash disposal, restrooms and many other facilities. In other situations, tourism supply may include an airport, railroad depot, marinas and dock facilities – an almost endless list of supply components that tourists have come to expect. Transportation facilities, accommodations, eateries, attractions, and other needs must be readily available. Less easy to identify are the quality of services provided. Are the employees friendly and courteous? Are cultural activities or outdoor recreation opportunities available?

Without providing an ample amount of quality resources to visitors at a destination, and thus not meeting visitors' expectations, repeat business will decline. Usually visitors have certain expectations of supply when they visit a destination. If they go to Europe, for example, many visitors look for a special dining experience. Many international visitors find the US an interesting place to shop. Historic sites provide additional appeal to destinations throughout the Middle East. Some areas are known for their sports – skiing in the Alps, backpacking through Central America, climbing mountains in Asia.

Prices of supply components such as airlines, accommodations, and food establishments become extremely important. Prices during the busy season may deter many visitors but may be offset during the low season with bargain prices. Tourists utilize the internet or use travel agents to help them find the best transportation and accommodations at the lowest cost. Having the right tourism supply elements to meet anticipated demand is a considerable challenge for management at any destination. In addition, seasonality, as discussed earlier, is a major concern for the supply side. Providing the best facilities for the visitor without desecrating the natural environment can be very difficult in some locations if the demand is too heavy during certain times of the year. Like demand, supply has many unknowns that must be fulfilled for a visitor to have a quality tourism experience.

Detractors from tourism supply components may exist when destinations fail to recognize the importance of several variables. These elements include:

A. Pricing

- The affordability of traveling to the destination
- An unfavorable exchange rate between one currency to another
- A drop in the traveler's discretionary income

B. Quality

- Pleasant accommodations
- Substantial variety of activities
- Excellent service

C. Knowledge of location

- Good local transportation
- Security/safety of place
- Availability of visitor information

Another important factor to consider when addressing tourism supply detractions is leakage. Leakage occurs when tourism revenue generated in one destination is spent in other communities that produce goods or services not purchased in the original destination. For example, a visitor orders fish for lunch at a local seafood restaurant in coastal Spain. If the fish was not caught and processed locally, then the money the restaurateur pays to a non-local purveyor supplying the fish is an example of tourism revenue leakage. On a larger scale, leakage can also occur if a hotel's ownership group is not from the local community. In this case, the profits from hotel operations are taken outside the local economy. Leakages also arise when tourism businesses hire non-local employees who send or spend their money in their home area instead of locally in the destination where the money was earned.

Travelers want to experience the flavor of a new environment but often expect foreign or imported goods to be available at destinations they visit. In many cases, today's travelers still desire what they are used to and what makes them comfortable, expecting the destination to provide "all the comforts of home." This limited scope can adversely affect the economy and resources of the local area. In order to accommodate such international visitors, the destination must go outside the local area to find the special products expected by the visitor and thus *leaks* local profits to outside sources. Leakage tends to be a major problem in tourism within developing nations. However, comparative advantage, as described in the next section, may in many cases justify some economic leakage.

Comparative advantage

The idea of comparative advantage in tourism is not new. More new, however, may be viewing tourism as a comparative advantage from the supply side rather than demand side. When formally introduced in 1817 by the classical economist David Ricardo, the economic theory of comparative advantage in its basic interpretation stated that countries will specialize in producing and exporting those goods in which they have an advantage, relative to competitors, in terms of land, labor, and capital. In summation, according to David Ricardo:[8]

> . . . the gains from trade follow from allowing an economy to specialize. If a country is *relatively better* at making wine than wool, it makes sense to put more resources into wine, and to export some of the wine to pay for imports of wool. This is even true if that country is the world's best wool producer, since the country will have more of both wool and wine than it would have without trade. A country does not have to be best at anything to gain from trade. The gains follow from specializing in those activities, which, at world prices, the country is *relatively* better at, even though it may not have an absolute advantage in them. Because it's relative advantage that matters, it is meaningless to say a country has a comparative advantage in nothing . . .

In other words, a country that has petroleum, iron ore, fishing waters, or similar resources would concentrate on the development, production, investment and management of these supply resources to produce and export in those areas. In the past, this was based on the demand for the product or good. However, comparative advantage can also be applied to the *services* category of international trade, which includes tourism.

Countries that have a comparative advantage in tourism resources, services and facilities and have a good tourism policy that provides guidelines to support tourism will generally enjoy economic benefits from tourism. Beautiful beaches, scenic mountains, historic monuments, progressive transportation systems and other supply-side attributes have potential as tourism products and are as important to a country as is, for example, the production and export of more tangible products such as wood and steel.

In fact, in some respects, tourism is a superior export product because much of the *productive capacity* is less exhaustible and usually causes less disruption and pollution of the environment. Particularly, as travelers use the internet more often, the savvy traveler looking at what is supplied at the destination from their home computer will decide which destinations to visit. Such a visitor can determine before they make their trip whether the destination supplies the tourism products they may be interested in and view the available accommodations and other facilities at the specific location.

Tourism may express a comparative advantage where the environment may not be conducive to industrial businesses but be favorable for tourism development. Often, the destination may have natural beauty and some of the basic provisions to facilitate tourism development but may not understand how to organize and present the area as an attractive tourism destination. For example, developing nations may have a comparative advantage in natural surroundings but fall short in meeting some of the desired amenities wanted by visitors. Today's traveler is better educated, more sophisticated, and travels more often; therefore, the destination needs to recognize what the traveler wants (demands) and find a way to meet the travelers' needs in order to obtain economic benefits from tourism development. A comparative advantage sometimes can help developing nations earn foreign exchange more rapidly and with less difficulty than they might with other products. For example, take most of the Caribbean nations where about 70 percent of their foreign exchange earnings come from international visitors. Many such countries are blessed with an abundance of natural resources with tremendous tourism potential such as wonderful beaches, lush vegetation, beautiful plants and flowers, exotic trees, and bountiful recreation opportunities. These supply components are comparative advantages relative to other nations. To be successful, such locations must also meet the non-natural amenities sought by the visitor, such as commercial attractions and entertainment.

The US is richly endowed with natural and built resources needed for a major tourism program but has lacked the will to engage in governmental strategies to support its tourism industry. Even without a national tourism policy (see Chapter 2), the US garners a fair share of the international tourism market. But the US has an opportunity to better utilize tourism as an economic development strategy, especially with respect to producing new jobs and improving its image abroad. The US has a strong comparative advantage with respect to tourism and needs a tourism policy and strategic plan that stresses tourism as important to its economic development. Recently the US took small steps to begin developing a national travel and tourism strategy, which can help enhance the nation's comparative advantage over time.

Employment

One of the reasons tourism is so important from an economic perspective is that it tends to be more labor intensive than is true of many other industries. Tourism employment is concentrated mainly in the services sector rather than in the goods-producing sector and the services sector has more people-to-people contacts and thus creates more jobs. As stated in Chapter 1, global tourism employment accounts for about 255 million jobs, based on estimates made by the World Travel and Tourism Council (WTTC).

Travel and tourism play a key role in providing employment opportunities for young adults, minorities, women, youths, and immigrants who often, in some countries, encounter the greatest difficulty in finding jobs. It also is beneficial in developing countries that need a variety of new jobs to offset some of the traditional industry-type jobs in agriculture, lumber production, and mining. Tourism is a particularly good potential source of jobs because it is both labor intensive and growing; this means that for each additional dollar expended on the growing tourism sector, more jobs will be created than in most other areas of the economy.

While it demands large numbers of workers and well-trained and educated managers, tourism has the further advantage of also providing employment in the hard-to-employ, lower-skilled occupations. Oftentimes, it is these occupations that have the highest unemployment rates and that are the most resistant to broad fiscal and monetary policy aimed at lower unemployment. On the other hand, tourism is made up of many different segments that include transportation, accommodations, food service, travel arrangements, communications, entertainment, and many other components. These many different elements require innovative and creative managers that are well-educated and can adjust to changing conditions in the tourism marketplace.

In addition, because it is growing, and is so diversified, the demands placed on tourism are varied, and the job market opportunities are broad. A few examples will suffice to demonstrate the dynamic careers in the tourism industry. Technology is demanding managers who understand the need to provide tourist information through a variety of outlets whether it is the mobile phone, internet applications, smartphone apps, or navigation systems such as the Global Positioning System (GPS). Cruising as well as festivals and events are fast-growing tourism segments providing large numbers of jobs needing creativity and innovation by its employees. Sustainable tourism is changing the way some tourism segments are developing and new types of jobs in sustainable tourism are emerging. As space tourism develops in the future, a completely new area will open up employment opportunities never thought of before.

Tourism depends on quality service, and more than most other industries needs highly-trained hospitality workers. In the ultimate analysis, the success of travel and tourism in the global environment will depend on its degree of professionalism. Tourism education and training programs will need to be strengthened if a more professional tourism work force is to emerge. In question is the quality and direction of such academic programs. There are many excellent programs throughout the world meeting differing levels of needs. Since 1979, the Executive Development Institute for Tourism (EDIT) at the University of Hawaii has been conducting an excellent program for educating travel and tourism professionals to increase their knowledge and skills to work more effectively in an environment of change and innovation. The EDIT program has a segment in their course structure on international tourism policy. It focuses on the interdependence of policy issues and the need for working collaboratively towards the development of integrated policy initiatives, many of which are addressed throughout this book. The precepts covered in the EDIT program include:

- Gaining an understanding of policy coordination.
- Learning how policies emerge from within organizations.
- Developing an understanding of the potential gains from integrated policy development.
- Drawing on the creativity and expertise of departmental inputs.
- Developing policy with stakeholder and community input.

Income

Tourism is an important source of income for most of the countries of the world. As noted earlier, international receipts from tourist expenditures continue to grow. The income generated creates new employment opportunities. While creating jobs, international tourism also is an important generator of national income as well. International visitors make large expenditures on a wide variety of goods and services, and these yield a substantial increase in income. Tourists are interested in shopping for both high-quality goods and locally-made products, good dining, general sightseeing and cultural activities, which in turn represent a significant source of foreign exchange receipts.

In its broadest sense, tourism encompasses all expenditures for goods and services made by travelers. It may include purchase of travelers' checks, transportation, lodging, attractions, meals, beverages, entertainment, souvenirs, sightseeing tours, and personal grooming services. These purchases also cover the output produced in various segments of industries supportive of tourism, such as insurance, banking, credit cards, auto clubs, taxis, bus transportation, cameras and film, reservation systems, computers, televisions and telephones. Not to be forgotten is that international tourist expenditures also support airlines, cruise lines, railroads, and car rentals.

The primary advantage of wanting to attract the international visitor over the domestic tourist is that international visitors typically spend considerably more money on tourism goods and services than do domestic tourists. Their expenditures add an important influx of foreign exchange into a country's economy as new export revenue. This source of foreign exchange is of particular importance to developing countries in that tourist expenditures have a more rapid impact on improving the country's economic conditions than is true of many manufactured goods. Tourism has a rippling effect on an area's economy through the *multiplier effect*, described in detail in the next section, which leads the overall impact on the economy to be even greater than the actual expenditures for goods and services.

While explaining the importance of foreign exchange earnings in adding to a country's total income, the wages as income earned by workers in the tourism industry have a major impact on the host country's economy. As tourism grows, the income stream through employee earnings increases and the local economy improves. In addition, workers pay taxes and purchase a mix of products that may be different from those of the international visitor. Such expenditures contribute to the overall economic impact of both the local area and the nation as a whole. It also helps to create new businesses, especially small businesses that support the tourism industry and indirectly businesses that cater to the local community. Thus, local communities and their nation's economy improve.

Multiplier effect

The income multiplier effect on tourism is measured by adding up all the expenditures of travelers at a given destination and multiplying that figure by a factor, known as the multiplier, to arrive at the amount of additional income that is generated by these expenditures. Consider the following scenario as an example of the multiplier effect. Monsieur A stays at the hotel of Ms. B one night and pays her $100. Ms. B uses part of the $100 to pay Ms. C, a hotel worker. Ms. C uses part of her wages to pay Mr. D, the butcher, who then buys bread from Ms. E. the baker, and the money originally spent by Monsieur A keeps moving through the economy generating a good deal more economic activity than the $100 he spent on the hotel room. There are varying estimates of the magnitude of the tourism multiplier, and it will vary from country to country and within a country as well. However, a factor ranging from 1.5 to 1.7 is used most often to estimate the direct and indirect effects. In other words, for every dollar, yuan, rupee, yen, euro, or peso, the effect generated in the economy is multiplied by a factor of 1.6, for example. The economy of an area may be stronger or weaker and thus affect the analysis' measurement, but the multiplier will rarely be less than 1.4 or greater than 1.8.

An important point to bear in mind with respect to the income multiplier is that a nation's economic wellbeing is usually measured in terms of national income, which is the sum total of the flow of all incomes. The income multiplier is also used with respect to export earnings. International tourism receipts represent an infusion of fresh money from outside the economy and have the same impact as any other export in improving a nation's overall economy. International tourism is subjected to the *given moment* exchange rate of the currency of one country in relation to another country. The international traveler planning a pleasure trip may be influenced by the exchange rate, and tour operators must *hedge* on purchasing fares. For example, if the euro is strong, then destinations in the European Union may be more expensive for non-European travelers.

While the income multiplier is looked at as a part of the macroeconomic policy measurement, it may fluctuate for many different reasons. Economists tell us that the multiplier is a double-edged sword. When economic conditions are good and the multiplier effect is positive, a country's economy would normally improve. But, a sudden drop in investment, export earnings or tourism receipts reduces national income by a multiplied amount. A decline of $1 million in a nation's tourism earnings can result in a decline of more than $1 million in that nation's national income. That decline affects not only sales, profits and employment in tourism but also the fortunes of feeder industries that supply tourism. Another detriment to full utilization of the multiplier is that it often takes time to gather the information and figures necessary to determine the final amounts, thereby rendering the results outdated which may sway the economic decisions made by the leaders of the country.

Tourism exports

Tourism is highly diverse as it is part public, part private and composed of many industries and many firms. There are easily recognized large corporations that own hotel chains, airlines, cruise ship lines, rental car agencies, theme parks and airport catering operations. At the same time there are many more small operations vying for the tourism dollar that might include family-owned bed and breakfast properties, restaurants, gift shops, and other amenities. These differing firms are interested in tourism as an export, because international visitors spend more than domestic tourists. However, in some circles, tourism is sometimes thought to be a lesser product than a manufactured product. Yet in terms of the balance-of-trade, tourism as a service export is equal to, for example, a merchandise product.

As mentioned in Chapter 1, tourism as an export is sometimes considered to be fragile, an export in reverse, invisible, and marketed upside-down. It is fragile in that its shelf life is very short. When a manufactured good is not sold today, it can be saved in inventory and sold later. Because of service perishability, an airline seat, a restaurant table, or a hotel room cannot be put in inventory. It is either sold that day or it is lost forever. In that respect, tourism products are fragile and must be sold immediately.

Tourism as an export in reverse is sometimes confusing if compared to a manufactured good. The manufactured good is considered an export once it is sold and shipped to the buyer located in another country. For tourism, the export is in reverse. The international visitor's expenditures are not counted as an export until the tourist arrives in the destination country. The easiest way to understand tourism's export characteristics is to think about how the money flows in an export situation. For example, a Japanese-made Nissan car is an export for Japan when purchased by a resident of Spain. In this case, the money flows from Spain to Japan. Likewise, when a Spaniard visits Japan, the money flows from Spain to Japan. In this case, tourism is also an export for Japan, although nothing (such as a car) was shipped to Spain. In both instances, the money flowed from Spain to Japan, which makes the Nissan car and the Spaniard's Japanese tourism experience exports for Japan.

Tourism is sometimes referred to as an "invisible" product. Tourism is invisible in the sense that, as an export product, it is not produced, packaged, shipped or received like physical consumer goods. In tourism, consumers bring themselves to the point-of-sale, pay for the product (i.e., service or experience), and at some point in the future or almost immediately, receive the services. Furthermore, even though tourism may be sold abroad, it is consumed within the selling country, thus generating additional opportunities for selling other goods and services.

Another aspect of tourism that is contrary to the export of goods is the way it is marketed. For example, at an export trade show most manufactured products will be available for display and to feel and touch, whereas the tourism product being sold is neither tangible nor visible. At a tourism trade show, an agent who represents the tourism destination markets the area through visual aids, such as brochures, posters, internet, PowerPoint presentations, websites or videos.

Coopetition

Coopetition sometimes spelled *co-opetition* is a portmanteau word that combines the words cooperation and competition. Ray Noorda, founder of the networking software company Novell, is credited as the first person to use the term in the business world. Coopetition occurs when companies, destinations, or other groups interact with partial congruence of interests to benefit both groups. David Edgell was the first person to introduce *coopetition* as an important means to facilitate economic and competitive growth in tourism.[9] The definition of the word in the tourism industry is the need for *coop*eration among tourism destinations in order to better market the tourism product effectively and meet the com*petition* at the regional or global level. In other words, tourism entities cooperate with each other to reach a higher value of competitive advantage in the marketplace. By working together, such entities can share knowledge and research and outsmart competitors in a market they could not reach as a single entity. Figure 4.4 and Figure 4.5 juxtaposes two differing entities combining their resources through coopetition. Figure 4.4 diagrams larger entities' intertwinement while Figure 4.5 shows its adaptability for smaller units such as two destinations. This model can be adapted for use by any number of entities and/or by any combination, and that in the case of small communities, even by two or more sites within one area seeking to boost their economy.

A 1996 book titled *Co-opetition*, authored by Adam M. Brandenburger (Harvard University) and Barry J. Nalebuff (Yale University), advanced the concept by stating: "When a business strategy is so new in design, a new word must be coined to capture its value. Such is the case with *co-opetition*, a method that goes beyond the old rules of competition and cooperation to combine the advantages of both. Co-opetition is a pioneering, high-profit means of leveraging business relationships."[10]

Goeldner and Ritchie focus on *partnerships* in their book, *Tourism*:[11] "This [partnership] highlights the high degree of interdependency among all destination stakeholders, as well as the need for alliances and working relationships that build

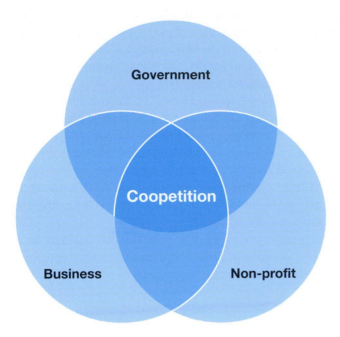

FIGURE 4.4 Venn diagram of government, business and non-profit coopetition

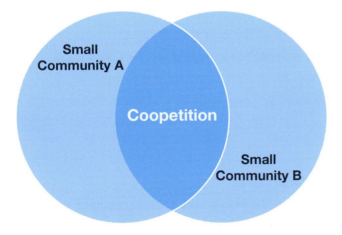

FIGURE 4.5 Venn diagram of two small communities practicing coopetition

cooperation – sometimes with competitors as well as colleagues. Edgell's concept of coopetition . . . captures the value of partnership in a unique way." Edgell first applied the concept of coopetition when working on a number of rural tourism projects. He was able to convince a number of rural tourism destinations that were competing against each other to form partnerships or alliances to better market their tourism products and to increase the number of visitors from further distances.

The formation of partnerships is the more important factor in the idea of coopetition. For example, when booking a flight, the airline representative or website will often ask if they can assist in the reservation of a rental car or a hotel room. The book *Co-opetition* included an airline example: "American Airlines, Delta . . . competitor and complement or . . . compete for passengers, landing slots, and gates, but complement each other when commissioning Boeing to build a new plane." Tourism enterprises, destinations and communities working cohesively can improve policies that will lead to enhancement and enrichment of the traveler's experience while advancing the economic vitality of the combined destinations. Coopetition has proven to be an effective tool for increasing tourism to areas that are not often represented in the tourism mainstream. Partnership formations assist in the transition of competition into a healthy, profitable environment of cooperation. Coopetition is a win-win situation for all the entities involved.

This chapter discussed the broad ramifications of international tourism as a commercial and economic activity. In addition to the examples described throughout the chapter, Case Study 4 presents a comprehensive analysis of policy challenges of tourism as a commercial activity in Antarctica.

CHAPTER REVIEW QUESTIONS

1. Why is tourism an important source of income for most countries?
2. Why could tourism be a good economic development tool for rural communities?
3. What roles does tourism play in the economic development of nations?
4. What are some examples of countries using tourism as an economic development tool?
5. How does seasonality affect tourism?
6. What are some elements of tourism supply?
7. What is tourism "leakage"? Give an example.
8. How can tourism be a comparative advantage in some countries relative to manufacturing industries?
9. Explain the multiplier effect.
10. Why is tourism sometimes a fragile export?
11. Explain coopetition, and explain the use of partnerships within the concept of coopetition.

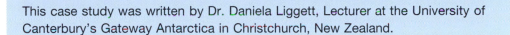

CASE STUDY 4 Policy challenges of tourism as a commercial activity in Antarctica

This case study was written by Dr. Daniela Liggett, Lecturer at the University of Canterbury's Gateway Antarctica in Christchurch, New Zealand.

* * *

Assessing the commercial and economic activity of tourism in Antarctica reveals unique tourism policy and planning challenges. Aside from the utilization of the Antarctic landmass for bioprospecting (i.e., searching for new organic compounds to be used in new medicines), tourism is the only commercial pursuit on the Antarctic continent itself. Other activities such as fishing derive financial gains primarily from the Southern Ocean. Whereas commercial fishing operations have been closely linked to the history of Antarctic exploration, Antarctic tourism is a late starter. As a regular activity with purely commercial purposes, tourism to the Antarctic gained a foothold only in the mid-1960s and then developed quietly for a couple of decades in conjunction with, but largely outside, the governmental framework of the Antarctic Treaty System (ATS), which will be described in a detail in a later section. Antarctic tourism differs from tourism to most other places in the world by being conducted in an area that is beyond the sovereign jurisdiction of any one country.

Only since the late 1980s has Antarctic tourism received increasing political and media attention, owing largely to its unprecedented exponential growth and diversification in the 1990s and early twenty-first century. The rapid increase of tourists visiting Antarctica has significant consequences for the regulation and management of Antarctic tourism. Increasingly, the laissez-faire attitude that dominated the regulation of tourism through the ATS for most of the second half of the last century is being replaced by a range of regulatory mechanisms that focus on Antarctic tourism operations. However, questions remain about the success of tourism regulation by the Antarctic Treaty Consultative Parties, who have been criticized for taking an inconsistent and non-strategic approach to regulating tourism operations in the Antarctic Treaty area. This case study explores some of these questions after introducing the main characteristics of Antarctic tourism, its brief history, and some impacts that can arise from conducting tourism in the Antarctic.

Characteristics of Antarctic tourism

When discussing Antarctic tourism, definitional clarity is important. For practical reasons, we use the same geopolitical boundary of 60°S Lat. for demarcating Antarctic tourism that the ATS utilizes to define the extent of Antarctic governance. In the early years of Antarctic tourism research in the 1990s, Antarctic tourism was defined loosely as "all existing human activities other than those directly involved in scientific research and the normal operation of government bases."[12] However, complications arise when we are asked to distinguish between recreational activities of base personnel, such as skiing or hiking, and similar activities undertaken by visitors to the continent who are not stationed there. We recognize the need for investigating the recreational activities of base personnel, especially with regard to their potential environmental impacts and management implications. Nonetheless, for regulatory purposes, a narrower definition for more conventional Antarctic tourism is necessary. The commercial aspect inherent in most Antarctic tourism ventures needs to be reflected in any definition of Antarctic tourism – be it from the perspective of those who supply the product (i.e. who make money from it) or those who constitute demand (i.e. who pay money for it). With this in mind, Antarctic tourism can be defined as "all human activities either mainly pursuing recreational and/or educational activities in the Antarctic Treaty areas south of 60°S Lat."[13]

Seasonality is a differentiator of Antarctic tourism. Antarctic tourism typically takes place between November and March, when the sea ice extent is at its minimum, when temperatures are milder and when many of the wildlife species are breeding. Recent years have seen an expansion of the tourist season, with some operators offering visits to the Antarctic in October and April. This expansion of the season has been attributed to increased demand but

FIGURE 4.6 Cruise passengers touring a scientific research station (Photo: CIA)

also to the effects of climate change, which result in decreased sea ice cover especially in the Antarctic Peninsula region and consequently enlarge the window of opportunity for tourism operators to organize commercial expeditions to the Antarctic.[14]

One of the most distinguishing characteristics of Antarctic tourism is its strong reliance on ships as the main mode of transport. The vast majority of Antarctic tourists visit the continent by ship. Fewer people visit the Antarctic as land-based and airborne tourists, but from a regulatory and management perspective these visits are no less important. Nonetheless, most attention is paid to ship-based tourism, which is the sector of Antarctic tourism that experienced an unparalleled exponential growth over the last two decades. Figure 4.7 illustrates the increases in Antarctic visitation over the last half-century. It is evident that, aside from the growth in the expedition cruise sector, cruise-only tourism was firmly established as part of the Antarctic tourism spectrum in the 1990s. Land-based tourism and airborne tourism do not report significant increases in numbers of tourists; rather the opposite seems to be the case. A peculiarity in Figure 4.7 is a sudden collapse of the overflight market in the late 1970s, and a complete absence of overflights until 1994. This development was entirely supply-driven and will be explored in greater detail in the subsection on airborne tourism.

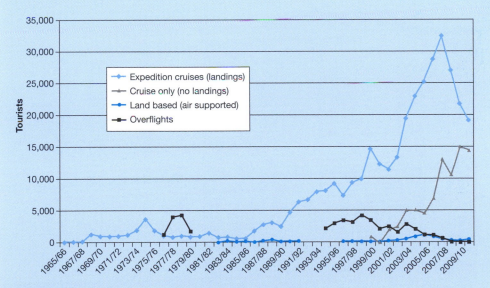

FIGURE 4.7 Estimated numbers of Antarctic tourists 1965–2009[15]

Ship-based tourism

Antarctic ship-based tourism represents the oldest segment of Antarctic cruise tourism, dating back to the late nineteenth or early twentieth century, with the first tourist-only Antarctic cruises beginning in the 1950s. At present, for a typical Antarctic tourist, the cruise begins in one of the five gateway ports (Ushuaia, Argentina; Punta Arenas, Chile; Hobart, Australia; Christchurch/Lyttelton, New Zealand; Cape Town, South Africa). From there, tourists venture across the Southern Ocean to explore sub-Antarctic islands and coastal areas of the Antarctic continent.

Roughly 90 percent of Antarctic ship-borne tourism passes through South American gateway ports and takes passengers to the Antarctic Peninsula.[16] The Antarctic Peninsula is a much sought-after destination for tourists, because of its proximity to South America and its diverse and attractive landscapes and fauna. Gentoo, Chinstrap and Adélie penguin rookeries, elephant and fur seals on rocky beaches, numerous seabird colonies, and jagged ice-covered mountains looming in the background represent important drawing cards for tourism operators.

FIGURE 4.8 A Chinstrap penguin observes a cruise ship before its passengers land ashore (Photo: CIA)

Additional attractions on the Peninsula are the numerous historic monuments and huts and the presence of more than 50 percent of all Antarctic stations.[17] Many Antarctic stations welcome visits by tourists and expeditioners because these visits showcase the research supported through the stations and are also ways to generate additional funds through the sale of souvenirs.

From 2009 onwards, roughly 10 percent of all known commercial vessels operating in Antarctica were capable of carrying more than 500 passengers. Despite comprising only a tenth of Antarctic ship-based tourism, in terms of numbers of ships, these large vessels were carrying approximately one-third of all Antarctic cruise tourists in 2009 through 2011. Indeed, over the past decade, cruise-only tourism, using vessels with a capacity of more than 500 passengers, has significantly grown and now constitutes a considerable share of the Antarctic tourism market (Figure 4.7). Cruise-only tourism operations have been reason for concern due to the difficulties of search-and-rescue operations for a large number of passengers and crew in a remote location and the potential environmental destruction should incidents occur.

Airborne tourism

Airborne tourism made a sporadic appearance in the 1960s, when the Richard E. Byrd Polar Center in Boston, US, negotiated access to the US airstrip near McMurdo Station to organize a non-commercial sightseeing flight for 75 passengers.[18] Between 1968 and 1987, flights with fixed-wing aircraft that included landings were mostly short-distance flights at the periphery of the Antarctic, but a few commercial flights ventured further south and landed at the American McMurdo Station in the Ross Sea or the Argentinean Marambio Station in the Antarctic Peninsula region.[19] The first known fly-cruise operation, which took tourists across the Drake Passage on a plane to allow them to board a cruise ship on King George Island, was organized by Fuerza Aérea de Chile (FACH, the Chilean Air Force) in January 1982.[20] Soon, fixed-wing aircraft started opening up the Antarctic to land-based adventure tourists.

From 1987 onwards, airborne tourism supported land-based adventure tourism, primarily facilitated through Adventure Network International (ANI) and its parent company Antarctic Logistics & Expeditions (ALE). The pioneering effort of landing wheeled aircraft, rather than the less economic and less fuel-efficient ski-equipped aircraft, on blue ice runways by ANI pilots in 1987 broadened the scope and reduced the cost of aircraft-support tourism that pushed further into Antarctica's interior.[21]

In the late 1970s, overflights gained popularity, and a series of flights carrying approximately 10,000 passengers were organized by Qantas and Air New Zealand.[22] These flights explored the Ross Sea region, Adélie coast and Victoria Land.[23] Overflights came to an abrupt end when an Air New Zealand DC-10 crashed into Mount Erebus in November 1979, resulting in the death of all 237 passengers and 20 crew.[24] This accident caused Air New Zealand and Qantas to discontinue Antarctic overflights, and it took more than a decade before Qantas resumed its Antarctic overflights in 1994. Despite the serious implications of the Air New Zealand crash, the Chilean airline LADECO has been conducting very occasional overflights from South America since 1980.[25]

Land-based tourism

Even though expedition cruise tourism includes a range of land-based experiences, from short strolls along the beach to overnight camping, its primary mode of transport and method of accommodations is ship-based and most of the tourists' time will be spent on board a vessel. By contrast, Antarctic land-based tourism concentrates on experiences and activities on land and uses air or ship support only to transport tourists, expedition staff and equipment across the Southern Ocean. Often, Antarctic land-based tourism involves adventure activities (i.e. undertakings that entail risks and uncertainty).[26]

In 1983, the Chilean Teniente Rodolfo Marsh Station on King George Island opened its airways to commercial and private aircraft[27] and encouraged land-based tourism operating out of Marsh Station, where accommodation for paying visitors was provided in the government-operated Hotel Estrella Polar (the Polar Star Hotel). In 1987, a semi-permanent camp was established by ANI in the Patriot Hills to facilitate a wide range of active and adventure tourism operations in Antarctica. ANI, the largest provider in the Antarctic adventure tourism market, offers activities that ANI grades from "safe" private flights, photo safaris and skiing expeditions to more challenging mountaineering and climbing expeditions.[28] Marathon running in the Antarctic is another land-based tourism activity[29] that is currently offered not only in the Antarctic Peninsula region but also further inland at the foot of the Ellsworth Mountains at 80°S Lat.[30]

Impacts of Antarctic tourism

Tourism in all destinations can have varying degrees of positive and negative impacts on the environment and host community. With such a delicate ecosystem and lack of indigenous population, the impacts of tourism in Antarctica are unlike any other destination in that the potential negative consequences can greatly outweigh the positive benefits if tourism is not carefully planned and managed. The most tangible benefits of Antarctic tourism might be the financial gains it brings to gateway cities in Argentina, Chile, Australia, New Zealand, and South Africa that have many tourists and ship crews moving through every summer. Research stations in the Antarctic can also benefit financially from the sale of souvenirs[31] or from receiving logistics support from Antarctic tourism operators. Antarctic tourism operators occasionally provide free passage to scientists on the way from or to Antarctica, assist in emergency situations or supply some Antarctic stations with much-needed freshwater. Less tangible benefits of Antarctic tourism include the contested notion of turning tourists into ambassadors for the

Antarctic,[32] the donations tourists and operators make towards environmental and heritage conservation[33] and the sometimes questionable political benefits that some Antarctic Treaty states gain from supporting tourism.[34]

The potential negative impacts of Antarctic tourism are more obvious. Antarctica is a remote and potentially dangerous destination, which is characterized by slow growth rates of native flora and lengthy breakdown rates of waste or sewage. As a result, it is important to carefully assess any potential impacts human activities may have on the Antarctic environment and to eliminate or minimize these impacts to the greatest possible extent. Below are lists of potential negative environmental, social, and cultural impacts of tourism in Antarctica.[35]

Environmental impacts can include:

- The disturbance of wildlife resulting in modifications of their behavior or diminishing numbers of breeding bird colonies.
- Littering or waste disposal (accidental or intentional).
- The trampling of flora and fauna.
- The development of footpaths, soil erosion and compaction.
- The introduction of diseases or non-native species (e.g. through ballast water of ships or through seeds or spores unintentionally carried in the backpacks or clothing of visitors).
- Marine pollution (e.g. fuel or oil spills).
- Air pollution through aircraft, ship and small-boat operations.
- Noise pollution, which is generally a temporary impact.

Social impacts can include:

- The disruption of research activities, including the social costs incurred by base personnel when having to provide support to expeditioners in distress.
- The potential harm to unmarked sites of scientific interest.
- Negative effects of crowding at a limited number of landing sites on visitors' perception of the Antarctic environment.
- Broadly speaking, any interference with the activities of other stakeholders.

Cultural impacts can include:

- The detrimental effects of changes in the internal climate of buildings due to visitation.
- Damage to or appropriation of historical artifacts.
- The transportation of material on boots (snow/ice/rocks) into historic huts.
- Adverse effects of visitation and human activity on Antarctic wilderness values.

Economic costs can include those incurred by National Antarctic Programmes if they have to participate in search and rescue operations for members of private expeditions or commercial tourism operations.[36] Political impacts relate to the discordance of positions among Antarctic Treaty Consultative Parties (i.e. the ultimate political decision-makers for the Antarctic) with regard to Antarctic tourism regulation. As a result, Antarctic tourism could contribute to opening new avenues for international dispute that might pose a threat to the stability of the Antarctic Treaty System and that might re-animate questions of sovereignty and territorial claims.[37]

Linking negative impacts to maritime incidents and accidents

Land-based activities such as skiing, hiking, climbing or mountaineering, that venture deeper into the Antarctic hinterland have been viewed as having greater adverse impacts on the Antarctic environment than ship-based operations[38] because they spend more time on the continent itself and because they move further inland than the more traditional ship-based tourism operations. However, it has to be considered that most land-based activities occur further away from the more sensitive coastal areas, which are breeding sites for the marine mega fauna.

Marine accidents and incidents involving Antarctic tourism vessels, such as groundings, collisions with whales or icebergs, could result in serious environmental disasters, such as the significant oil spill resulting from the grounding and sinking of the *Bahia Paraiso* in 1989 or the rescue efforts required to save all the passengers aboard the *Explorer* that sank in Bransfield Strait in 2007. At least 24 incidents and accidents involving ships carrying tourists occurred between 1968 and early 2011, which is a testament to the riskiness of operating tourist ships in the Southern Ocean. On average, one ship ran aground or sunk every two years, sometimes causing fuel leaks and loss of life. Since 2010, at least four incidents have been reported, which may indicate an increasing trend as demand has increased. Many of the incidents are caused by human error or an inadequate understanding of the waters. Rescuers are often sent out from the scientific stations to deal with tourist ship accidents.[39]

A critical look at impacts and their assessment

Relatively few studies have focused on quantifying and validating the environmental impacts of Antarctic tourism. Two of the reasons for a lack of such research are their costly nature and the long-term commitment that is required to measure human impacts, especially cumulative impacts. Due to the extremes of the Antarctic weather, and the resulting low regeneration rates of the Antarctic flora, the consideration of cumulative impacts arising from Antarctic tourism is of great importance.

As Antarctic tourism is not officially endorsed by the 1959 Antarctic Treaty, which devotes the Antarctic continent to science and peace, Antarctic policymakers can easily justify taking a critical, and in many cases unfavorable, approach to Antarctic tourism regulation. It must not be forgotten that any form of human activity can have a significant impact on the Antarctic environment, and the impacts of science and scientific support activities will have to be scrutinized in the same way as Antarctic tourism operations. Although tourists outnumber scientists and their support staff in the summer months by far, the overall person-days spent by tourists on the Antarctic continent are estimated to be only about 5 percent of the person-days spent there by scientists and support staff.[40] National Antarctic Programmes operate more than 50 stations in the Antarctic, whereas there are no permanent tourism facilities on the continent. This makes us pause and think about the relative footprints of scientific activities as compared to tourism. This aspect and other considerations touched on in the aforementioned paragraphs are elegantly summarized by Jabour:[41]

> All humans have an impact, of this there is no doubt, and being a scientist with a 'legitimate' reason for being there does not legitim[ize] the impact. But, neither does being a tourist visiting by the good grace of some Antarctic Treaty Parties make the impact worse. If anything, national operators could take a leaf from the book they have written for the tourism industry and adopt for their stations site-specific guidelines with environmental codes of conduct, long-term monitoring programs, agreed terminology, fine-scale maps and the input of organizations like SCAR (Scientific Committee on Antarctic Research) to help with calibrations on the sensitivity of the receiving environment.

Regulation and management of Antarctic tourism

Antarctic tourism regulation and management is primarily undertaken by two different groups – the International Association of Antarctica Tour Operators (IAATO) and the Antarctic Treaty Consultative Parties (ATCPs). There is some overlap between the self-regulatory system the tour operators have developed and governmental regulation through the ATCPs, but significant synergies exist as well.[42] Whereas the ATCPs are primarily concerned with high-level regulation of all human activities in the Antarctic, IAATO focuses on tourism operations in particular and assumes considerable management functions in the field. Finally, indirect regulation of Antarctic tourism is achieved through, for instance, shipping codes imposed by the International Maritime Organization, or other guidelines such as the World Tourism Organization's Global Code of Ethics for Tourism.

The industry approach to tourism regulation

To a large extent, Antarctic tourism regulation draws on the self-organization and motivation of Antarctic tourism operators. In 1991, seven Antarctic tourism operators formed the International Association of Antarctica Tour Operators (IAATO), which has developed a range of guidelines for responsible tourism to the Antarctic. Over the past two decades, IAATO has grown from a small organization of owner-operators to a diverse international group of more than 100 members comprising ship-based operators, land-based operators, operators of overflights, travel organizers, ship and travel agents, and non-governmental organizations concerned about Antarctic heritage and conservation. IAATO subscribes to what has been referred to as "environmental stewardship" with the intention to "advocate, promote and practice safe and environmentally responsible private-sector travel to the Antarctic."[43] As such, IAATO embraces a proactive approach to managing its members' activities, which is aided by IAATO's commitment to develop and adopt best-practice operational guidelines. IAATO also represents its member organizations' interests within the framework of Antarctic governance.

The host of guidelines developed and adopted by IAATO includes procedures on "numbers ashore, wildlife watching, small boat and helicopter operations, activity reporting, passenger, crew and staff briefings; contingency and emergency medical evacuation plans; and communication procedures to coordinate site visits."[44] The coordination of site visits is facilitated through a web-based ship scheduling system. This system allows the individual operators to log their itineraries with IAATO and to "book" landing sites at certain times, when no other operator will be allowed to land there. The "Guidance for Visitors to the Antarctic," which was developed by IAATO in the 1990s has been translated into eight languages (aside from English) and made widely available online and in hardcopy (e.g. it is handed out to passengers on cruise vessels). In 1994, this guidance was adopted by the Antarctic Treaty Consultative Parties as Recommendation XVIII-1.

Aside from these generic visitor guidelines, IAATO members are to adhere to strict decontamination protocols. Among other responsibilities, these protocols require tour operators to ensure that visitors do not carry any diseases or alien species onto land in the Antarctic. Operators are asked to have the boots of everyone leaving the ship and landing in the Antarctic washed and disinfected, usually prior to any landings as well as after boarding the vessel again after landings.

In general, the scope of any form of self-regulation is limited to those who subject themselves to it by belonging to a certain group or professional body. As such, IAATO self-regulation only applies to those operators who are members of IAATO. IAATO membership is not compulsory and comes with certain costs (e.g. membership fees) and obligations (e.g. compliance with the Bylaws and other rules and guidelines; participation in Annual General Meetings and decision-making). The benefits of being an IAATO member include having a forum for representation, rights to participate in decision-making, positive advertising and a boost to the image of the company, and a range of operational benefits. Despite the significant benefits that operators receive from being IAATO members, not all commercial tour operators may want to join IAATO. The mere fact of voluntary membership and incomprehensive coverage of the Antarctic tourism sector weakens the regulatory power and influence of IAATO's self-regulation. Currently, the vast majority of commercial Antarctica tour operators are IAATO members, but this could change in the future.

The strength of self-regulation through IAATO rests within the organization's capacity to react swiftly, creatively and knowledgably to changing situations by drawing the combined experience and expertise of IAATO members. In addition, low levels of hierarchy and majority decision-making processes in IAATO also facilitate quick responses to emerging issues, incidents, or changing requirements. Finally, it is in the operators' interest to maintain the relatively pristine character of the Antarctic environment they "sell" to the tourists, and they monitor each other's activities as well as keep an eye out for each other.

Tourism regulation through the Antarctic Treaty System

Within the framework of the Antarctic Treaty System (ATS), tourism regulation occurs at two main levels, through (a) the Protocol of Environmental Protection to the Antarctic Treaty, which regulates all human activities in the Antarctic, and (b) a range of recommendations, resolutions, decisions and measures adopted during annual Antarctic Treaty Consultative Meetings (ATCMs). Between 1966 and 2011, 33 regulatory mechanisms directly focused on tourism have been adopted by the ATCPs, out of which only eight mechanisms were adopted prior to 1991, and only 13 of them before the turn of the century. Such a steep increase in the number of tourism mechanisms indicates the growing concern and urgency ATCPs sense with regard to tourism. Most of the mechanisms adopted by the ATCPs are recommendations or resolutions, both of which have a largely hortatory character and can be best described as "guidelines" that tourism operators are encouraged to take into account. Only two binding mechanisms on tourism have been adopted by 2011:

1. Measure 4 (2004) on insurance and contingency planning
2. Measure 15 (2009) on landing operations

Neither of these two binding measures is effective yet. Measure 15 (2009) builds on IAATO practice and provides a framework for landing operations in the Antarctic. This measure stipulates the following:

- Only one vessel can land at any one site at any one time.
- No more than 100 passengers can land at one time.
- The guide-to-passenger ratio on land has to be 1:20 (or less).
- Vessels carrying more than 500 passengers are not permitted to land.

With IAATO's support, the ATCPs also developed site-specific guidelines, which are now available for 27 frequently visited sites primarily in the Antarctic Peninsula region. These site guidelines provide a site map, outline the key characteristics of a site, detail specific landing requirements, and make operators and tourists aware of closed areas, potential impacts and precautions that have to be taken. All of these site guidelines contain visitor codes of conduct.

The ATCPs are recognized as the ultimate decision-makers and authority with regard to Antarctic governance. Consequently, Antarctic tourism regulation by ATCPs can have regulatory teeth and can be substantiated and strengthened through national legislative acts. However, tourism regulation by ATCPs is hampered by their consensus decision-making system, and it takes a long time for the ATCPs to react to tourism developments, agree on and adopt regulatory mechanisms and ratify them so that they enter into effect. Furthermore, the extent to which tourism operations are monitored and regulation is enforced varies among ATCPs and is generally impeded by the lack of resources and lack of Antarctic tourism experience.

Concluding critical questions

The commercial and economic aspects of tourism in Antarctica provide an interesting case in policy and regulations. Antarctic tourism has grown rapidly and diversified considerably since the 1990s. Its future development will depend on the global economic situation, but market shifts, including a further opening up of the Asian market, are to be anticipated. Along with shifts in demand, shifts in the structure of supply have to be considered. The role of National Antarctic Programmes in supporting and facilitating Antarctic tourism by opening their runways to tourism operators, or by providing tourism services themselves, will affect how tourism is perceived and operated in the Antarctic. An increasing blurring of the boundaries between science and tourism can have significant geopolitical repercussions and might widen the gap between ATCPs.

Private and independent expeditions and tourism operations out of states that have not signed the Antarctic Treaty might test the limits of tourism regulation through ATCPs and IAATO. With regard to private expeditions, matters of operational safety and risk management are of primary concern. Are National Antarctic Programmes obliged to come to the rescue of private expeditioners in distress, especially if they have not heeded any advice or warning? How can the behavior and impact of operators that fall through the cracks of tourism regulation through ATCPs or IAATO, both of which are only binding to member states or member operators, be controlled?

The consumer also plays a significant role. What experience do visitors expect, what do they want to see, and how far are they going to go to encounter what has been heralded as one of the world's last wildernesses? Finally, with increasing consumer demand, what might happen if competing tour operators no longer want to cooperate because they believe their economic gain would outweigh the environmental consequences that might result from not cooperating?

Notes

1   World Travel & Tourism Council (2012) Presentation by David Scowsill, President and CEO of the World Travel & Tourism Council Global Summit in Tokyo.

2   Edgell, Sr., David L. (1990) *International Tourism Policy*. New York: Van Nostrand Reinhold.

3   UNWTO (2012) *Tourism Highlights*. Madrid: United Nations World Tourism Organization.

4   Belize Tourism Board (2009) "Sustainable Tourism Program (2060/OC-BL) Initial Baseline Report," July 2, 2009, Belize City: Belize Tourism Board.

5   Edgell, Sr., David L., et al (1979) "Use of Modified Scenario Research in Forecasting of Tourism in the United States." *Travel Research Journal*, 1st Quarter.

6   Edgell (1990).

7   Goeldner, Charles A. & Ritchie, J.R. Brent (2012) *Tourism: Principles, Practices, Philosophies*, 12th edn. Hoboken, NJ: Wiley, 295.

8   Samuelson, Paul A. (1983) *Economics: An Introductory Analysis.* Cambridge, MA: Harvard University Press.

9   Edgell, Sr., David L. & Haenisch, R. Todd (1995). *Coopetition: Global Tourism Beyond the Millennium.* Kansas City, MO: International Policy Publishing.

10 Brandenburger, Adam M. & Nalebuff, Barry J. (1996) *Co-opetition.* New York: Doubleday.

11 Goeldner and Ritchie (2009), p. 419.

12 Hall, C.M. (1992) "Tourism in Antarctica: Activities, Impacts, and Management." *Journal of Travel Research*, Spring 1992, 2–9. Quote taken from page 4.

13 Liggett, D.H. (2009) *Tourism in the Antarctic: Modi Operandi and Regulatory Effectiveness*. Saarbrücken: VDM Verlag, 48.

14 Lamers, M., Haase, D., & Amelung, B. (2008) "Facing the Elements: Analysing Trends in Antarctic Tourism." *Tourism Review*, *63*(1), 15–27.

15 Based on historical records published by Enzenbacher, D.J. (1993) "Tourists in Antarctica: numbers and trends." *Tourism Management*, *14*(2), 143–6; Headland, R.K. (2005) *Chronological List of Antarctic Expeditions and Related Historical Events*. Cambridge: Cambridge University Press; Reich, R.J. (1980) "The Development of Antarctic Tourism." *Polar Record*, *20*(126), 203–14; as well as annual reports by the International Association of Antarctica Tour Operators (IAATO)

16 Liggett (2009); Mason, P.A. & Legg, S.J. (2000) "The Growth of Tourism in Antarctica." *Geography*, *85*(4), 358–62.

17 Cessford, G. (1997) "Antarctic Tourism: A Frontier for Wilderness Management." *International Journal of Wilderness*, *3*(3), 7–11; Mason & Legg (2000).

18 Stonehouse, B. & Snyder, J. (2010) *Polar Tourism: An Environmental Perspective*. Bristol, UK: Channel View Publications.

19 Swithinbank, C. (1993) "Airborne Tourism in the Antarctic." *Polar Record*, *29*(169), 103–10.

20 Ibid.

21 Ibid.

22 Bauer, T. (2007) "Antarctic Scenic Overflights." In J. Snyder & B. Stonehouse (eds), *Prospects for Polar Tourism*. Wallingford: CABI, 188–97.

23 Stonehouse & Snyder (2010).

24 Bauer (2007).

25 Swithinbank (1993).

26 Lamers, M. & Amelung, B. (2007) "Adventure Tourism and Private Expeditions in Antarctica: Framing the Issue and Conceptualising the Risk." In J. Snyder & B. Stonehouse (eds), *Prospects for Polar Tourism*. London: CABI, 170–87.

27 Swithinbank (1993).

28 Murray, C. & Jabour, J. (2004) "Independent Expeditions and Antarctic Tourism Policy." *Polar Record*, *40*(215), 309–17.

29 Mortimer, G. & Prior, E. (2009) "Antarctic Tourism: An Operator's Perspective." In K.R. Kerry & M.J. Riddle (eds), *Health of Antarctic Wildlife: A Challenge for Science and Policy*. Dordrecht, Heidelberg, London, New York: Springer, 231–40.

30 Donovan, R. (2011) "Antarctic Ice Marathon." Retrieved October 31, 2011, from Document1www.icemarathon.com.

31 Snyder, J. (2007) *Tourism in the Polar Regions: The Sustainability Challenge*. Paris: UNEP.

32 Powell, R.B., Kellert, S.R., & Ham, S.H. (2008) "Antarctic Tourists: Ambassadors or Consumers?" *Polar Record*, *44*(230), 233–41.

33 Snyder (2007).

34 Enzenbacher, D.J. (2007) "Antarctic Tourism Policy-Making: Current Challenges and Future Prospects." In G. Triggs & A. Riddell (eds), *Antarctica: Legal and Environmental Challenges for the Future*. London: The British Institute of International and Comparative Law, 155–89.

35 Liggett (2009).

36 Snyder (2007).

37 Enzenbacher (2007).

38 Kriwoken, L.K. & Rootes, D. (2000) "Tourism on Ice: Environmental Impact Assessment of Antarctic Tourism." *Impact Assessment and Project Appraisal*, *18*(2), 138–50.

39 Liggett, D. (2011) "From Frozen Continent to Tourism Hotspot? Five Decades of Antarctic Tourism Development and Management, and a Glimpse into the Future." *Tourism Management*, *32*, 357–66.

40 Jabour, J. (2009) "National Antarctic Programs and their Impact on the Environment." In K.R. Kerry & M.J. Riddle (eds), *Health of Antarctic Wildlife: A Challenge for Science and Policy*. Dordrecht, Heidelberg, London, New York: Springer, 211–29.

41 Ibid, page 228.

42 Scully, T. (2008) *Chairman's Report from the Miami Meeting (March 17–19, 2008) on Antarctic Tourism*. Kiev, Ukraine: Information paper (IP) 19, XXXI Antarctic Treaty Consultative Meeting (ATCM).

43 IAATO (2011) "Home – International Association of Antarctica Tour Operators." Retrieved October 27, 2011, from http://iaato.org/home.

44 Mortimer & Prior (2009), page 235.

5

Political and foreign policy implications of tourism

The political aspects of tourism are interwoven with its economic consequences. Thus, tourism is not only a continuation of politics but also an integral part of the world's political economy. In short, tourism is, or can be, a tool used not only for economic but also for political means. For obvious economic reasons, most countries seek to generate a large volume of inbound tourism. As we learned in Chapter 4, expenditures by foreign visitors add to national income and employment and are a valuable source of foreign exchange earnings. Various measures are taken by governments to encourage foreigners to visit their respective territories. Promotion offices have been established in most key tourism receiving countries and are bolstered by extensive advertising campaigns to attract tourists. It is commonplace to find tourism offices located in practically every locale, be it local, provincial/state, region, or nation.

Tourism facilitation

In the aftermath of various terrorist attacks and actions across the globe during the past decades, governments are re-addressing their visa regulations and entry requirements. The question of safety and security has become a high priority. In many countries, an integrated biometric chip in passports is required to ensure proper identification of travelers. The biometric identifiers most commonly used for identification are face imagery or electronic fingerprint impressions. The accuracy of identification registers above 90 percent verification when both are used.

The US Visa Waiver Program (VWP) allows nationals from 37 countries to travel to the United States visa-free for stays up to 90 days. In addition to the United Kingdom, France, Japan, and similar large countries, other nations included in the US VWP include smaller countries such as Andorra, Brunei, Liechtenstein, and Monaco. This program began in 1986 to promote better relations between the US and the participating countries when the principal purpose of the stay in the US is related to tourism or business. Such travel accounts for more than two-thirds of all overseas travel into the US and the successful transition to using biometrics is imperative. The United States requires the governments of VWP nations to issue their citizens who intend to travel to the United States without a visa, machine-readable passports with a digital photograph and biochip. Transportation carriers could be fined up to $3,300 per violation for transporting any visitor traveling under the VWP to the United States who does not meet these requirements.

In a similar measure to facilitate travel while maintaining security, the US Department of Homeland Security has also implemented a Registered Traveler Program (RTP). The RTP allows selected frequent airline travelers to have priority in airport security lines in exchange for providing more personal information. The program began with several thousand frequent travelers hand-picked by the airline companies and was implemented at six airports. Following an evaluation by the Transportation Security Administration (TSA), the program was expanded because of the strong support from the travel industry, major airports, and the traveling public.

Currently there is considerable discussion arising about the determination of security measures. The question that is uppermost in the tourism industry's debate is determining the most effective and efficient methods of security inspections without overly disrupting travel. As shown by the examples of the VWP and RTP programs, careful consideration and cooperation must be concurrent with all participatory countries if desired policy outcomes are to occur. Added to this, governments are also seeking ways to stimulate the construction of needed tourist infrastructure, access roads, communications, airport facilities, and the many other supply-side requirements for supporting tourism. Efforts are being devoted to conserving areas of natural beauty and developing and maintaining resort areas and sightseeing attractions. Local and national governments often encourage special festivals, sports-related events, entertainment, and cultural activities to entice tourists to the area. As a result of increased visitation, other services performed by governments, such as police protection and crime control, maintenance of good health and sanitary conditions, and good communications are also necessary to support tourism. Taken in tandem, governments must work in a cohesive manner to ensure the best practice is used to provide these services for the traveler.

A number of political, economic, and social factors influence the government actions and regulations that affect tourism. Travel bans are imposed from time to time for political reasons. It is not unusual, for example, for governments to prohibit travel of their citizens to war zones or to territories of hostile nations where the government has no means of protecting the life and property of their citizens. Nations issue travel warning and consular information sheets, which are travel advisories to warn citizens considering going abroad about adverse conditions in specific countries or territories.

Special precautions must also be taken when episodes of contagious diseases occur as evidenced by the outbreaks of SARS (severe acute respiratory syndrome) and West Nile Virus or other potential outbreaks such as Avian Influenza A, also denoted as "H5N1." On April 3, 2006, the World Health Organization reported an outbreak of H5N1 affecting humans in Egypt: "Egypt is the ninth country to report laboratory-confirmed human cases in the current outbreak, which began in Vietnam in December 2003. Four of these countries reported their first human cases this year, including Turkey, Iraq, Azerbaijan, and Egypt."[1] Another precautionary factor is food handling and preparation to reduce intestinal illnesses and/or exposure to life-threatening epidemics. Information can be found on the websites of international travel organizations addressing warnings and advisories. While these measures may result in discouraging or inconveniencing tourists, they are necessary to ensure not only an enjoyable tourism experience at the destination, but also to decrease the chance of global epidemic spread as visitors traverse the globe.

The airline industry has experienced the most noticeable burdensome practices (exhaustive inspections of luggage, restrictions on items in carry-on bags and on person) as it has become the norm for passenger safety and security globally. Many travelers may avoid travel altogether as they see this as a hardship that they choose not to endure, or they may alter their destination choice and stay closer to home, which allows the selection of alternate modes of travel, such as trains, buses, or private car. Others do not let these security measures deter them and see them as part of the adventure. This, of course, depends on the motivations of individual travelers.

A continuing concern of many governments is immigration control. Nearly all countries strictly control the entrance of immigrants and enforce laws against illegal entrants. Of particular concern are the social pressures created by the need to care for jobless immigrants and the opposition expressed by the local labor force when jobs are scarce. Also, governments are forced to address the accuracy of the immigrant's paperwork to safeguard their homelands. To admit foreign visitors and to facilitate their travel within a nation's borders is a political action; therefore, the method in which a nation's international tourism is approached becomes an aspect of its foreign policy, as well as a part of its economic and commercial policy, setting the stage for careful planning.

Examples of the political and foreign policy implications of tourism are endless. The history of travel contains numerous references to tourism with political overtones. These range from Marco Polo's vivid descriptions of the political events in the Orient to the uncertainty, lack of knowledge, and myths associated with the "dark continent" of Africa prior to its exploration by the Europeans.

Increased contacts between persons of different cultures can lead to increased knowledge and understanding, contributing to a relaxation of tensions between nations. As mentioned in Chapter 2, the adage "When peace prevails, tourism flourishes" is important enough to repeat. International organizations, such as People to People International and Rotary International, recognize this truth and support an exchange of people and culture. The implementation of Glasnost in the 1980s led to the doors being opened in Russia in the 1990s, thereby increasing travel into the country. And furthermore, the dramatic occurrence in 1989 of the demise of the Berlin Wall had profound effects upon East-West travel and continues to do so. The result is a deeper understanding among people of the world, increased commerce, and a greater step toward international cooperation. Today, a different climate prevails in which Russian relations with the rest of the world are shifting back to more centrist governmental functions. One further positive effect of this is evidenced in the field of education. East Carolina University in the United States for example, has recognized the contributions of Russian scholars and has supported hiring faculty and promoting visits by its faculty members to Russia as well as hosting Russian visitation on its campus.

Tourism and foreign policy

The prospective economic benefits of tourism frequently influence the internal policies of governments. In some corners of our globe, inbound tourism is used to showcase the accomplishments of the government or party in power and to increase understanding abroad of the government's policies. Sometimes this approach is successful; sometimes not. The point is that tourism expands the horizon of the tourist and presents the host government or community with a unique opportunity to influence visitors from abroad, and vice versa. Alternatively, countries, including the United States, sponsor numerous exchanges, cultural programs, lecture services, and other events to make people of the world aware of a country's customs and standards of living.

At the same time, a country must be made safe for tourism. Civil strife and disorders, such as those occurring in Northern Ireland and England, have had a detrimental impact on tourism. The 1999 military discord in the former Republic of Yugoslavia, a country that used to welcome more than 10 million visitors a year, has brought tourism to a virtual standstill. The current political problems in Venezuela and other parts of the world discourage tourism. Using Sri Lanka as an example, the effects of war on tourism are described in detail later in this chapter.

In addition, the constant threat of terrorism weighs heavily on international tourism in the United States. The impact of the terrorism in New York, Pennsylvania, and Washington, DC, in 2001 significantly affected international arrivals to the US, as evidenced by declines in international tourism in 2002 and 2003. Fortunately, the trends have changed since 2004, with current trends showing increasing numbers of international tourists to the US. In 2007, international visitor arrivals to the United States surpassed levels before the terrorist attacks of 2001.

Jean-Maurice Thurot, noted for his research in tourism advertising, suggests that tourists create an economic dependence by the host country on tourist-generating countries. This dependence can influence the foreign policy of the host country toward the generating country. This is especially true in nations needing foreign exchange, or hard currency, for economic development. Nations in the process of economic development need to buy key items, especially capital equipment and technology, from the industrial nations in order to speed their own growth. They, in turn, can sell these tourism products to the developed nations. International tourism can be an engine of economic growth by providing an important source of foreign exchange. Most of the former socialist countries and less-developed nations need tourist revenues, especially "hard" financially-stable Western currencies, for economic growth. These governments are continually seeking avenues to entice the traveler to their destinations and are implementing policy changes to accommodate tourism.

Tourism as a policy for peace

Traveling contributes to "interchange between citizens which helps to achieve understanding and cooperation," according to Ronald Reagan, a leading historical international peacemaker.[2] But can tourism be a generator of peace in today's society? Or is tourism simply a beneficiary of peace? Using democratic peace theory as a foundation in light of recent world conflicts and non-peace events, the answer to both queries could be yes.

The democratic peace theory is founded upon the premise that democracies rarely enter into war or militarized disputes with one another because of their common values. Although there are several examples of disputed cases, the claim that democracies do not engage each other is generally accepted as empirical fact by democratic peace theorists.[3] However, that has not stopped the debate on the legitimacy of the theory. The American Revolution; World War II with Great Britain and the United States pitting against, among other nations, Finland; and the Border War in 1995 in which Peru fought Ecuador, are just three examples of nearly two dozen commonly debatable democratic wars, which date back to the Greek Wars of the fifth and fourth centuries BCE.[4]

Since democracies do not engage each other, then democratic states are motivated to spread global democracy because it will enhance national security and promote world peace – true even though it may involve engaging in war to create sustainable peace. This is a distinguishing characteristic of the democratic peace theory.

The democratic peace theory is based on the principles Immanuel Kant laid out in his essay entitled *Project for Perpetual Peace* in 1795.[5] In the essay, he proposed that the three definitive articles for perpetual peace are:

1. The civil constitution of every state should be republican.
2. The law of nations shall be founded on a federation of free states.
3. The law of world citizenship shall be limited to conditions of universal hospitality.

A republican civil constitution ensures representation and requires citizen consent for the declaration of war. As citizens are the bearer of the financial and human burdens of war, they are less likely to support the declaration of unnecessary wars. Democratic leaders will typically not engage in a conflict that is unpopular among constituents for fear of being removed from office. Through a federation of free states, nations would be under a set of parameters that would transcend the laws of any one nation. If that set of laws ruled out war, then countries would be legally bound to settle disputes in peaceful ways. As the federation is extended, so too would be the principles of peace. Universal hospitality implies the right of a visitor in a foreign land to be treated hospitably – not as an enemy. Because of the finite size of the Earth, its inhabitants must peacefully coexist for humanity to be sustainable.

As the theory has evolved since Kant's original work more than two centuries ago, the following are the three generally acceptable reasons that could lead democracies to engage in war: 1) self-defense in protection of the homeland; 2) prevention of blatant human rights violations in other states; and 3) to bring about conditions in which democratic values can take root abroad.[6] The theory also provides at least two reasons why democracies do not compromise peace with other democratic states. They are norm externalization and mutual trust and respect. This foundation of democratic peace is illustrated in Figure 5.1.

Under the assumption that peace can be achieved through the spreading of democratic ideals, and if two countries share similar democratic norms and values, then there are no norms that must be externalized upon other nations. Therefore nations with similar values will not fight with each other. Mutual trust and respect connotes that when conflict arises between democracies they will be inclined to accommodate each other or refrain from engaging in hard-line policies. Democracies trust the judgment of nations that believe similarly.

The expansion of democracy in the former Soviet states lent credence to Kant's theory of democratic states seeking pacific relations with one another. In other words, once democratic, the Soviet Union (or its remnants) was no longer the enemy of the United States.

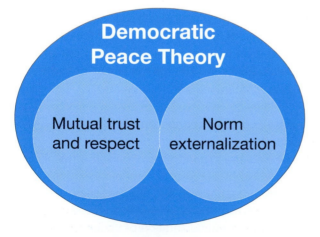

FIGURE 5.1 Components of the Democratic Peace Theory

A reason to maintain peace

International tourism is vital to global trade. Tourism growth is also positively correlated to growth in global GDP growth. As the global economies grow, disposable income typically also rises. The growth of international tourism arrivals generally outpaces GDP. However, because of the elasticity of demand for travel, if the economic situation tightens spending on tourism will also typically decline.[7]

The costs of war disrupt international trade and investment. The absence of peace disrupts global trade. And when global trade is disrupted, travel declines, which compounds the decline in global GDP. Therefore, tourism benefits from peace and the global economy benefits from tourism development.

Political stability, safety, and tourism

When safety and security is endangered by expansionist policies of others, it is an occasion for democracies to jeopardize peace.[8] The democratic peace theory implies democracy will bring about political stability. Political stability leads to safety and security in democratic nations. When safety and security is threatened, war will be engaged upon to ensure future safety and security.

Kant explicitly states the visitor to a foreign land has the right "not to be treated as an enemy when he arrives in the land of another."[9] As noted earlier, the visitor must not be treated with hostility, as long as the visitor acts peacefully within the destination. Unfortunately, the tourist of today may find this not to be the case as, globally, many countries have experienced terrorist attacks upon their lands, thereby heightening concerns held by government officials not only for the local citizenry but also for the country on the whole.

Travelers rank safety and security as key factors in planning a vacation or convention, 63 percent of international travelers to the United States report a destination's safety and security as extremely important. Without safety and security in the destination, both business and leisure travel will be negatively affected. "Safety and Security" occupies the number two position in *The Ten Important World Tourism Issues for 2012*.[10] Once again, tourism benefits from peace.

The absence of peace can often, if not always, have detrimental effects on travel and tourism. These effects are not felt only in the destination where the conflict lies, but can also affect global travel. Sri Lanka provides an excellent example of the effects of war on a nation's tourism industry. Sri Lanka was involved in a civil war from 1983 to 2003. The conflict stemmed from the desire of the Liberation Tigers of Tamil Eelam to create an independent state in the northeast region of the island. While the clash officially ended in 2003, the August 2005 assassination of the Lankan foreign minister threatened to revive it. In addition to the foreign minister, the war resulted in fatalities estimated at 60,000 people.

During the years leading up to the war, the island nation had played host to a steadily increasing number of international visitors. As represented in Figure 5.2, international visitor arrivals decreased by 17.1 percent in 1983 – the first year

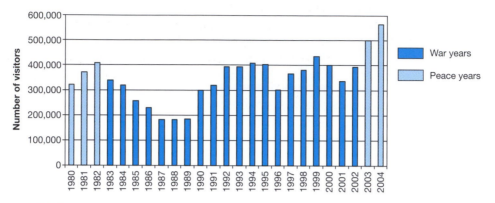

FIGURE 5.2 International visitor arrivals to Sri Lanka

of the conflict. During the 20-year war, international visitation averaged 326,064 persons, ranging from 182,620 in 1987 to 436,440 in 1999. Only once in 20 years did visitation surpass pre-war numbers. After the end of the war in 2003 and 2004, international visitation made significant gains, increasing 27.3 percent the first year and 13.1 percent the second year.[11] Civil war in Sri Lanka stifled tourism for 20 years.

Tourism-created mutual trust and respect among cultures

Tourism is often promoted by industry organizations as a vehicle for cultural understanding. The United Nations World Tourism Organization states its position on the matter as: "Intercultural awareness and personal friendships fostered through tourism are a powerful force for improving international understanding and contributing to peace among all the nations of the world."[12] Indeed, an entire subset of tourism has developed around the concept of promoting peace through travel. The International Institute for Peace Through Tourism was founded in 1986 to foster and facilitate tourism initiatives that create a peaceful and sustainable world through travel.

In addition to tourism industry organizations endorsing tourism's awareness-creating abilities, world leaders throughout modern history have also realized the benefits of tourism. Mahatma Gandhi once said, "I have watched the cultures of all lands blow around my house and other winds have blown the seeds of peace, for travel is the language of peace."[13] In 1963, John F. Kennedy stated, "Travel has become one of the greatest forces for peace and understanding in our time. . . . we are building a level of international understanding which can sharply improve the atmosphere for world peace."[14]

In April 2006, US Secretary of State Condoleezza Rice, speaking to attendees at the "Global Travel and Tourism Summit Breakfast" celebrated the power of tourism by stating, "Travel fosters understanding. It builds respect. The knowledge and experience that citizens gain in their private travels is vital to the cause of diplomacy and international understanding in the twenty-first century."

Tourism cannot flourish without political stability and safety, which are restricted when peace is absent. Without peace, tourism is diminished; therefore, tourism is a beneficiary of peace. Through creating cultural awareness, tourism can be a stimulus for peace, assuming peace can be incremental. However, tourism through intercultural awareness can either promote peace or can be used by the opposition to impart violence, or any other ideal closely held by either the traveler or host country.

As indicated in Figure 5.3, peace can lead to political stability, which can lead to safety and security in the destination, which facilitates tourism. Depending upon the motivation of the traveler and the structure of the destination, tourism can create cultural understanding. Understanding of the people of other nations is a key ingredient leading to norm externalization and mutual trust and respect – critical components of the democratic peace theory, as previously discussed in this chapter.

Tourism development – demand creation through marketing and supply expansion through investment – can be part of a strategy for geopolitical stability that includes the promotion of peace, economic development, and cultural awareness. Undoubtedly, a sound governmental strategy for peace must be based on more than just tourism.

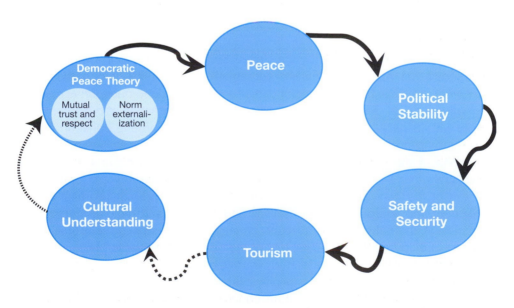

FIGURE 5.3 The relationship of tourism and peace

Tourism agreements

In the past 30 years, the United States has negotiated tourism agreements with many countries. While the concept behind a tourism agreement is for the promotion of trade in tourism, these agreements also serve additional national policy objectives, such as encouraging international understanding, friendly relations, and goodwill. The tourism agreements entered into by the US Government focus on the following specific criteria:

- Aim to increase two-way tourism.
- Support efforts by the National Tourism Organization travel promotion office(s).
- Improve tourism facilitation.
- Encourage reciprocal investments in the nations' tourism industries.
- Promote the sharing of research, statistics, and information.
- Recognize the importance of the safety and security of tourists.
- Suggest mutual cooperation on policy issues in international tourism.
- Provide for regular consultations on tourism matters.
- Acknowledge benefits from education and training in tourism.
- Enhance mutual understanding and goodwill.

Two prominent examples of international tourism agreements involving the United States and its trading partners are those with the United Mexican States and with the Republic of Venezuela. Both agreements accredit tourism officials as members of a diplomatic or consular post and facilitate the exchange of tourism statistics and information among the two nations involved in the agreement. Interestingly, these and other agreements state the US will participate in the World Tourism Organization; however, as stated in the following section, the United States is not a member of that august organization.

The agreement entered into by the United States and Mexico in October 1989 superseded the April 1983 tourism agreement between the two parties. The agreement assists in facilitating motor carrier and other ground transport across the international border and calls for the parties to share information about automobile liability with its neighbor. Understanding policies involving ground transportation is critical for visitors in this case as many cross the border in private vehicles. Other provisions of the agreement include developing bi-national cultural events that would strengthen ties and promote tourism, waiving applicable visa fees for the entry and exit of teachers and experts in the field of tourism, promoting travel to and developing and improving tourist facilities and attractions in regions that contain examples of the native culture of each country, and conducting joint marketing activities in third countries. The full text of the 1989 United States/Mexico tourism agreement is included in the case study for this chapter.

The US-Mexican agreement explicitly states that the nations "will endeavor to facilitate travel of tourists into both countries by simplifying and eliminating, as appropriate, procedural and documentary requirements." This eliminates the documentary requirement of all who enter the United States including US citizens who have a valid passport. This is of course, in response to acts of terrorism in the United States, and is a good example of how tourism strategy and policy must be fluid so that it is not only reactive but also proactive as market conditions and foreign policy change.

Venezuela and the United States entered into a tourism agreement on September 7, 1989. An interesting aspect of this agreement calls for complementary agencies in the two countries to enter into agreements with each other. For example, the National Park Service in the United States and the Instituto Nacional de Parques in Venezuela are encouraged to pursue cooperative policies related to tourism development and facilitation. The agreement is specific about exchanges and mutual assistance, including efforts to identify tourism experts for short-term exchange assignments and identifying volunteer private-sector executives and professors of tourism who are eligible for sabbatical leave. This not only promotes cross-cultural understanding, but also serves to increase the body of knowledge in the field of international tourism development.

Intergovernmental organizations

There are several intergovernmental organizations designed specifically to handle international tourism policy issues. Two organizations at the world level are the United Nations World Tourism Organization (UNWTO) and the World Travel and Tourism Council (WTTC). Regional organizations include, for example, the Organisation for Economic Co-operation and Development (OECD), the Organization of American States (OAS), the Asia-Pacific Economic Cooperation (APEC), and the Caribbean Tourism Organization (CTO). While there are many other organizations that cannot be described here due to space limitations, these groups are examples of proactive organizations working to advance tourism in their jurisdictions.

United Nations World Tourism Organization

The UNWTO, as part of the United Nations, is the leading international organization in the field of travel and tourism and is headquartered in Madrid, Spain. Originally established as the International Congress of Official Tourist Traffic Associations in 1925, it was renamed the International Union of Official Travel Organizations after World War II, before restructuring occurred in 1967. In 1974 in Lusaka, Zambia, a UNWTO budget formula and statutes were adopted allowing for the UNWTO to become an official organization the following year. Its first General Assembly was held in Madrid in May 1975 and the intervening years have seen its emergence as the key world organization for tourism.

In 2003, the UNWTO achieved status as a UN specialized agency. Its current mission statement summarizes its primary responsibility as providing "a central and decisive role in promoting the development of responsible, sustainable and universally accessible tourism, with the aim of contributing to economic development, international understanding, peace, prosperity and universal respect for, and observance of, human rights and fundamental freedoms." UNWTO offers national tourism administrations and organizations the machinery as a clearinghouse for the collection, analysis, and dissemination of technical tourism information, developing partnerships between the private and public sectors, and supports the Global Code of Ethics for Tourism. Activities include facilitating international dialogue and implementation of worldwide conferences, seminars, and other means for focusing on important tourism development issues and policies. The official languages of the UNWTO are English, Spanish, French, Russian, and Arabic.

Membership includes roughly 155 member countries, seven associate members, and about 400 affiliate members composed of private-sector companies, educational institutions, tourism associations, and local tourism organizations and authorities. One country that is not a member of UNWTO is the United States. As part of the downgrading of the US national tourism office in 1996, its membership in UNWTO was canceled; however, there is current interest in having the US rejoin the UNWTO.

The structure of the UNWTO is multipartite. At its core is the General Assembly, which meets every two years to discuss its budget, programs, and policy. The Executive Council, governing board for the UNWTO, is composed of 27 members as elected by the General Assembly and meets biannually. The Secretariat, located in Madrid, is made up of officials who are entrusted with implementing UNWTO's programs and responding to members' needs. There are six regional commissions (Africa, the Americas, East Asia and the Pacific, Europe, the Middle East, and South Asia) who meet annually. Nine committees of UNWTO members advise on management and program content. These are the Programme Committee, the Committee on Budget and Finance, the Committee on Statistics and Macroeconomic Analysis of Tourism, the Committee on Market Intelligence and Promotion, the Sustainable Development of Tourism Committee, the Quality Support Committee, the UNWTO Education Council, the UNWTO Business Council, and the World Committee on Tourism Ethics.[15]

World Travel and Tourism Council

The World Travel and Tourism Council (WTTC) is unique in its structure as it is the only organization representing the private-sector in the global context of the travel and tourism industry. It is comprised of business leaders from around the world who are presidents, chairs, and CEOs of 100 of the world's foremost travel and tourism companies representing almost all sectors of the industry. According to WTTC, their mission "is to raise the awareness of the full economic impact of the world's largest generator of wealth and jobs – travel and tourism." WTTC was established by a group of chief executives from major companies within the industry to convince governments of travel and tourism's strategic importance. For more than two decades, WTTC has worked with governments to increase understanding of the industry's economic benefits and to persuade them to re-evaluate the role of travel and tourism in their overall policy priorities. An Executive Committee resides in WTTC's headquarters in London, England, and hosts the administration of its programs.

In July 2003, WTTC revealed its *Blueprint for New Tourism*, "which issues a call to action for both government and the industry to make several long-term commitments to ensure the prosperity of travel and tourism – one of the world's largest industries, responsible for over 200 million jobs and over 10 percent of global GDP (Gross Domestic Product)." The reasoning for this action stems from recovery measures necessitated by setbacks experienced in the industry as a result of terrorism, war, economic slowdown, and pandemics. The president of WTTC, speaking at the 2003 Global Travel and Tourism Summit, stated, "There is now a new consciousness amongst governments that they cannot leave the growth of travel and tourism to chance. What is needed is a new vision and strategy involving a partnership between all stakeholders – public and private to turn future challenges into opportunities. The *Blueprint for New Tourism* spells out how that can be achieved." The guiding principles of "New Tourism" recognize global consciousness of the importance of tourism, takes a fresh look at the opportunities and partnerships it produces, and the delivery of commercially successful products that provide benefits for everyone – not just for the traveler but also the local people and communities with respect to the natural, social, and cultural environments.

In response to acts of terrorism and to prepare for the possibility of future attacks, the WTTC formed a Crisis Committee. The Crisis Committee has been charged with producing an immediate forecast of the impact of such events on travel and tourism so that industry and government leaders can make informed planning decisions. A model was developed based on the real effects of catastrophic events including the Gulf War (1991), Croatia Peace (1996), Luxor Attack (1997), Hurricane George (1998), September 11th USA (2001), September 11th World (2001), Bali Bombing (2002) and Hong Kong SARS (2003). The London Underground bombing on July 7, 2005, allowed the global tourism industry to showcase its new proactive preparedness. The WTTC Crisis Committee was convened within 24 hours to forecast impact and propose strategies. In this case, historical non-peace has made the tourism industry more proactive.[16]

Organisation for Economic Co-operation and Development

The Organisation for Economic Co-operation and Development (OECD) located in Paris, France, is bipartite in its structure. It serves as a forum in which governments work together to focus effectively on the challenges of interdependence and globalization through economic, social, and environmental segments. In its efforts to "underpin multilateral cooperation," OECD produces global research data, analyses, and forecasts to enable economic growth and stability, strengthen trading systems, expand financial services and cross-border investments, and promote best practices on the international forefront. It was started after the Second World War as the Organisation for European Economic Co-operation to coordinate the Marshall

Plan and, in 1961, adopted its current name in order to address transatlantic and, ultimately, its global reach. There are 34 member countries and more than 70 developing and transition economies working in partnership with OECD who share a "commitment to democratic government and the market economy."

The mission of OECD is as follows:

- to achieve sustainable economic growth and employment and rising standards of living in member countries while maintaining financial stability, hence contributing to the development of the world economy;
- to assist sound economic expansion in member countries and other countries in the process of economic development; and
- to contribute to growth in world trade on a multilateral, non-discriminatory basis.

The OECD's Tourism Committee, headed by an executive-level Bureau, has taken a leadership role in identifying and working toward the reduction of barriers to travel in its member countries. In view of the major importance of tourism among the principal service industries, the OECD Trade Committee in 1979, 1981, and again in 1983 addressed updating and revising the Code of Liberalization of Current Invisible Operations by carrying out a survey of obstacles to international tourism and reporting its findings in a comprehensive report to the OECD Council.

In 1985, a milestone was achieved in efforts to reduce impediments to travel with the approval of a new instrument on International Tourism Policy, which reaffirmed the importance of tourism to the political, social, and economic wellbeing of the member countries and agreed to set up formal procedures to identify travel impediments and to take cooperative steps to eliminate them. The OECD tourism instrument recommended minimum amounts for the import and export of national currency, for travel allowances, and for duty-free allowances for returning residents and for non-residents. It also made recommendations concerning travel documents and other formalities that strive towards facilitation of tourism. A finding then was that the most numerous and highly rated concerns among the countries responding were those impediments related to market access and the right of establishment. This reflects the importance of reaching customers in the country of residence in order to attract tourist and travel business. Without a local branch or subsidiary, travel agents, tour operators, airlines, and other tourist companies are unable to market their services adequately, thus placing them at a competitive disadvantage. Today, the OECD is involving itself with emerging issues dealing with sustainable tourism and new directions in rural tourism.[17]

Organization of American States

The Organization of American States (OAS), headquartered in Washington, DC, is currently composed of the following countries: Antigua and Barbuda, Argentina, the Bahamas, Barbados, Belize, Bolivia, Brazil, Canada, Chile, Colombia, Costa Rica,

Cuba (by resolution in 1952, the current Government of Cuba is excluded from participation in the OAS), Dominica, the Dominican Republic, Ecuador, El Salvador, Grenada, Guatemala, Guyana, Haiti, Honduras, Jamaica, Mexico, Nicaragua, Panama, Paraguay, Peru, Saint Kitts, and Nevis, Saint Lucia, Saint Vincent and the Grenadines, Suriname, Trinidad and Tobago, United States of America, Uruguay, and Venezuela.

This organization actually had its beginnings in the 1820s, stemming from Simón Bolivar's vision of a region "united in heart." In 1890, the nations of the inter-American region formed the Commercial Bureau of American Republics, which later evolved into the Pan American Union, and finally became the OAS. In 1948 it expanded into the English-speaking nations of the Caribbean and Canada, encompassing the hemisphere.

The OAS is committed to democracy for the people (all people have a right to democracy) and governments (government has an obligation to promote and defend democracy) in the member countries of the Western Hemisphere. "Building on this foundation, the OAS works to promote good governance, strengthen human rights, foster peace and security, expand trade, and address the complex problems caused by poverty, drugs, and corruption. Through decisions made by its political bodies and programs carried out by its General Secretariat, the OAS promotes greater inter-American cooperation and understanding."[18] The OAS promotes "Peace, Justice, and Solidarity in the Americas" as titled in their organizational heading. Sustainable tourism is of major concern to the OAS.

The Inter-American Travel Congress (IATC), which was established in 1939, develops travel and projects in the Americas by conducting studies that maintain dialogue between governments and the private-sector and provides support (technical and research) for tourism development initiatives. Today, this focus still prevails. The purposes and functions of the IATC are to:

- Aid and promote, by all means at their disposal, the development and progress of tourist travel in the Americas.
- Organize and encourage regular meetings of technicians and experts for the study of special problems related to tourist travel.
- Foster the harmonization of laws and regulations concerning tourist travel.
- Take advantage of the cooperation offered by private enterprise through world and regional organizations concerned with tourist travel which hold consultative status with the United Nations or maintain relations of cooperation with the OAS.
- Promote cooperative relations with similar world or regional organizations, either governmental or private, and to invite them to participate as observers at the meetings of the Congresses.
- Serve as advisory body of the organization and its organs in all matters related to tourism in the hemisphere.

Within this organization is the Inter-Sectoral Unit for Tourism. This branch promotes sustainable tourism practices and the importance of tourism as an economic development tool, in recognition of tourism's role as the world's number one growth industry. Recent activities have "focused on tourism development programs and projects aimed at encouraging cooperative and operational ties at the internal, regional, and international levels." It utilizes the internet and websites to promote its findings.

Asia-Pacific Economic Cooperation

Convening its activities in 1989, the Asia-Pacific Economic Cooperation (APEC), headquartered in Singapore, was formed as the "premier forum for facilitating economic growth, trade, and investment in the Asia-Pacific region." The general philosophy is that strong, vital economies cannot be supported by governments alone, thus the need for melding governments and the key stakeholders in the business sector, academia, industry, policy and research institutions, and interest groups within the community. APEC is consistent in its approach to ensure open dialogue and equal respect among its 21 member economies, which are Australia, Brunei Darussalam, Canada, Chile, People's Republic of China, Hong Kong, Indonesia, Japan, Republic of Korea, Malaysia, Mexico, New Zealand, Papua New Guinea, Peru, Philippines, Russian Federation, Singapore, Chinese Taipei, Thailand, United States of America, and Vietnam. These member economies account for more than 2.5 billion people and 46 percent of world trade. Its uniqueness is that it is "the only multilateral grouping in the world committed to reducing trade barriers and increasing investment without requiring its members to enter into legally binding obligations."

Within this umbrella, there are 14 working groups focusing on agricultural technical cooperation, anti-corruption and transparency, emergency preparedness, energy, health, oceans and fisheries, human resources development, illegal logging, industrial science and technology, policy partnership on women and the economy, small and medium enterprises, telecommunications and information, tourism, and transportation. The Tourism Working Group (TWG) has set four policy goals to support its function of creating jobs, promoting investment and development, and improving the tourism industry across the region. These policy goals are:

1. Removal of impediments to tourism business and investment.
2. Increase mobility of visitors and demand for tourism goods and services.
3. Sustainable management of tourism outcomes and impacts.
4. Enhance recognition and understanding of tourism as a vehicle for economic and social development.

The focus for the APEC TWG is on public and private partnership for facilitating tourism investments in the APEC member economies and exploring best practices of e-commerce application to the small and medium tourism enterprises in the APEC region.[19]

Caribbean Tourism Organization

In 1989, the Caribbean Tourism Organization (CTO) emerged from its predecessors, the Caribbean Tourism Association, founded in 1951, and the Caribbean Tourism Research and Development Center, founded in 1974. The CTO, headquartered in Barbados, is an international development agency and the official body for promoting and developing tourism throughout the Caribbean. This organization provides information and assistance to its member countries and non-governmental members in order to achieve sustainable development. According to the CTO, the organization and its members work together to encourage sustainable tourism that "is sensitive to the economic, social and cultural interests of the Caribbean people, preserves the natural environment of the Caribbean people, and provides the highest quality of service to Caribbean visitors."[20]

CTO also has offices in the United States, Canada, the United Kingdom, and Barbados with smaller chapters in France, Germany, Holland, across the United States, and in the Caribbean. Its composition is not only destination countries, but also private companies including airlines, hotels, cruise operators, and travel agencies. Membership is open to all Caribbean countries and currently consists of English, French, Spanish, and Dutch speaking nations and territories including the following member countries: Anguilla, Antigua and Barbuda, Aruba, Bahamas, Barbados, Belize, Bermuda, Bonaire, British Virgin Islands, Cayman Islands, Cuba, Curaçao, Dominica, Grenada, Guadeloupe/St. Barts/St. Martin, Guyana, Haiti, Jamaica, Martinique, Montserrat, Puerto Rico, St. Eustatius, St. Kitts and Nevis, St. Lucia, St. Maarten, St. Vincent and the Grenadines, Suriname, Trinidad and Tobago, Turks and Caicos Islands, US Virgin Islands, and Venezuela.

The central thrust of the CTO is to promote the Caribbean as a vacation destination. Over time, the CTO has produced high quality websites that, in turn, address the travelers' quests to make better decisions regarding destination choices. The CTO has successfully and efficiently utilized database marketing as a promotion tool. The organization supports sustainable tourism practices, development of tourism education and awareness programs, financial guidelines, and technical assistance to its members.[21]

Pacific Asia Travel Association

The Pacific Asia Travel Association (PATA) is the foremost authority on tourism and travel in the Pacific Asia region. The non-profit organization was founded in 1951 under the name, Pacific Interim Travel Association. In 1953 the name was changed to Pacific Area Travel Association. The name was changed again in 1986 to its current name to reflect the importance of Asia on the world stage. PATA exists to "enhance the sustainable growth, value and quality of travel and tourism to-from-and-within, the region." The organization has more than 1,000 member organizations including government tourism bodies, airline companies, airports, and travel industry companies. PATA also has 39 chapters across the world. PATA created the PATA Foundation in 1984 to protect and encourage the cultural heritage and has since been expanded to include environmental protection, educational support, and sustainable development of tourism. For the past 60 years, PATA has strived to develop responsible travel and tourism to and from Pacific Asia. The most recent goals for PATA include: building the business for members, providing valuable insights, forecasts and analysis to help members make better business decisions, and taking a lead position on travel industry issues that need to be addressed.

Middle East and North Africa Travel Alliance

The Middle East and North Africa Travel Alliance (MENATA) is a UK-based travel association that advocates tourism in the Arab region. This region includes Algeria, Bahrain, Egypt, Iraq, Kuwait, Jordan, Lebanon, Libya, Mauritania, Morocco, Oman, Palestine, Qatar, Saudi Arabia, Syria, Tunisia, United Arab Emirates, and Yemen, as well as Cyprus, Iran, and Turkey. Their objectives as stated from their website are:

- Raising the profile of the Middle East and North Africa as one of the world's most exciting, distinctive and rewarding tourism regions.
- Bringing together travel industry representatives with a shared interest in driving tourism to the Middle East and North Africa region and expanding the market.
- Helping to foster greater understanding of the Middle East and North Africa region; its peoples and cultures.

MENATA supplies the initial contact for travel trade professionals searching for information about the Middle East and North Africa region. MENATA also provides an annual schedule of events for its members and promotes support between members.[22]

World Heritage Alliance for Sustainable Tourism

The World Heritage Alliance (WHA) is an initiative of the United Nations Foundation. This organization, with 50 members from the travel industry and governments, has preserved 20 world heritage sites in seven countries. The WHA aims to:

- Promote environmentally and economically sustainable business practices around UNESCO World Heritage sites.
- Educate travelers about traveling responsibly.
- Support the development of local communities around these special sites.[23]

Conclusion

In terms of foreign policy, the response by governments to the impact of terrorism on tourism surpasses any prior attentions to security. The global tourism industry has been generally unprepared to deal with increasingly sophisticated acts of violence that use elements of the industry as weapons or targets. Elements of the industry used as weapons or targets include attacks against passengers on trains in Madrid in March 2004, the October 2002 nightclub bombings in Bali, and commercial airliners used as missiles in New York, Pennsylvania, and Washington, DC, in September 2001. As security becomes more important, organizations such as the WTTC have measures in place to proactively handle crises as they happen.

Private-sector groups have conducted training sessions to deal with potential terrorism in light of recent attacks. The aftermath of such devastation has raised the awareness of service organizations, the medical community, and the individual. Such efforts help, but for many pleasure travelers the worry, strain, and inconvenience exact too much of a toll. It will take a strongly concerted effort of global cooperation, through policy, if the terrorism of the past three decades and its effects on travel and tourism are to be avoided in the future. This will facilitate international trade and development and contribute to efforts to foster peace and understanding. One means to facilitate this cooperation is through the work of intergovernmental tourism organizations such as those described and many other proactive and productive groups throughout the world.

CHAPTER REVIEW QUESTIONS

1. What is the US Visa Waiver Program?
2. Why is immigration control a concern for many governments?
3. How is the safety of a country an issue to tourism? Give examples.
4. What is democratic peace theory?
5. What would lead democratic states to war?
6. How did the civil war in Sri Lanka affect tourism?
7. Why is peace important for tourism?
8. What are some of the criteria the US Government looks for when entering into tourism agreements?
9. Describe the WTTC and explain why it is unique.
10. Elaborate on the uniqueness of Asia-Pacific Economic Cooperation.

CASE STUDY 5 Bilateral Tourism Agreement between the United States and Mexico

This full text of the 1989 agreement between Mexico and the United States is included to illustrate the complexities involved in written agreements related to tourism among nations. As with all the case studies in this book, the section concludes with critical questions to stimulate thought and discussion.

* * *

Agreement between the United States of America and the United Mexican States on the development and facilitation of tourism

CONSIDERING that the United States of America and the United Mexican States share an extended border and have developed close neighborly and commercial relations;

RECOGNIZING that international cooperation and economic exchange should serve to foster man's development, to enhance mutual respect for human dignity, and to promote common welfare;

ACKNOWLEDGING that the promotion of tourism is considered a legitimate diplomatic and consular function;

CONVINCED that tourism, because of its socio-cultural and economic dynamics, is an excellent instrument for promoting economic development, understanding, goodwill, and close relations between peoples;

NOTING that a valuable structure for tourism, already existing between both countries, stands ready for further development;

The Governments of the United States of America and the United Mexican States (the Parties) agree to conclude a Tourism Agreement which, within their respective legal frameworks, will promote the objectives stated in the following provisions;

ARTICLE I
Government Tourism Offices and Personnel

1) In conformance with the laws, regulations, polities and procedures of the host Party, each Party:

   (a) May establish and operate official travel promotion offices in the territory of the other Party, and,

   (b) Agrees to accredit as members of a diplomatic or consular post tourism officials of the other Party.

2) Such tourism personnel shall perform traditional diplomatic or consular functions (e.g., the officials do not perform commercial transactions, including making airline or other travel arrangements or performing other similar services normally provided by travel agencies).

ARTICLE II
Development of the Tourism Industry and Infrastructure

1) The Parties, subject to their laws, will facilitate and encourage the activities of tourism service providers such as travel agents, tour wholesalers and operators, hotel chains, airlines, railroads, motor coach operators, and steamship companies generating two-way tourism between their countries.

2) Each Party will,

(a) Permit air, sea and surface carriers of the other Party, whether public or private, to open sales agencies and to appoint representatives in its territory in order to market their services;

(b) In accordance with the bilateral Air Transport Agreement, encourage the carriers of the other Party to develop and promote, through designated and authorized sales outlets in its territory, departures from their own territories with special or excursion fares designed to encourage reciprocal tourist travel;

(c) Permit the sale of promotional transportation tickets for use in the territory of one Party by carriers of the other Party through authorized outlets in its territory;

(d) Expedite, to the extent possible, the award to carriers of new air routes established under the bilateral Air Transport Agreement signed by both countries; and

(e) In accordance with overall discussions and negotiations between the two countries, initiate substantive dialogue on motor carrier issues which impact on tourism.

3) To the extent that either Party is subject to statutes imposing duty on the entrance of ticket stock or sales materials of the carriers or tourism enterprises of the other, that Party shall review those statutes with the objective of providing for the eventual duty-free entry of such materials on a reciprocal basis.

ARTICLE III
Facilitation and Documentation

1) The Parties will endeavor to facilitate travel of tourists into both countries by simplifying and eliminating, as appropriate, procedural and documentary requirements.

2) Each Party shall facilitate, to the extent permitted by its laws, the entry of performers and artists who:

(a) Are nationals of the other Party; and

(b) Have been invited to participate in international cultural events to be held in its territory.

3) Each Party shall take all necessary facilitative measures to encourage binational cultural events which would strengthen ties and promote tourism.

4) The Parties will consult on the opening of additional border crossing points and on the designation of such points as high priority based on the needs of touristic development of each area.

5) The Parties will encourage the training of personnel at ports of entry and elsewhere within their respective territories so that tourists' rights are

respected and tourists of both countries are extended all appropriate courtesies.

6) The Parties shall consider, on the basis of reciprocity, and on official request, waiving applicable visa fees for the entry and exit of teachers and experts in the field of tourism.

7) Aware of the importance of automobile collision and liability coverage to automobile tourism between the two countries, the Parties shall publicize in the territory of the other, in accordance with applicable regulations in each country, the respective automobile insurance requirements, either by distributing information through their respective national tourist offices or by other appropriate means.

8) Both Parties recognize the necessity of promoting, within their respective facilities and administrative capabilities, the health and safety of tourists from the other country, whether traveling by automobile or any other means of transportation, and will either provide information about available medical services or encourage government and non-government organizations or agencies to do so as needed.

9) Both Parties recognize the need for promoting and facilitating, where possible, investment by American and Mexican investors in their tourism sectors.

10) The Parties shall consult with each other, as appropriate, in their multilateral efforts to reduce or eliminate barriers to international tourism.

ARTICLE IV
Cultural and Tourism Programs

1) The Parties regard it appropriate to encourage tourist and cultural activities designed to strengthen the ties between the peoples and to improve the overall quality-of-life of the inhabitants of both countries and will consider exchange programs which are consistent with the cultural heritage of each country.

2) The Parties will consider it a priority to promote travel to developing regions which contain examples of the native culture of each country, and to develop and improve tourist facilities and attractions in those areas.

3) The Parties will encourage the balanced and objective presentation of their respective historic and socio-cultural heritage and promote respect for human dignity and conservation of cultural, archaeological, and ecological resources.

4) The Parties will exchange information concerning the use of facilities for shows and exhibitions in their countries.

ARTICLE V
Tourism Training

1) The Parties consider it desirable to encourage their respective experts to exchange technical information and/or documents in the following fields:

(a) Systems and methods to prepare teachers and instructors in technical matters, particularly with respect to procedures for facilitation, hotel operation and administration;

(b) Scholarships for teachers, instructors, and students;

(c) Curricula and study programs to train personnel who provide tourism services; and

(d) Curricula and study programs for hotel schools.

2) Each Party will encourage their respective students and professors of tourism to take advantage of fellowships offered by colleges, universities, and training centers of the other.

ARTICLE VI
Tourism Statistics

1) Both Parties will do what is possible to improve the reliability and compatibility of statistics on tourism between the two countries, in both the border and interior regions.

2) The Parties agree to establish a technical committee on tourism statistics in which the appropriate agencies of both countries shall participate.

(a) The committee shall address itself to the exchange and reconciliation of statistical data measuring tourism between the two countries and to the improvement of collecting such data.

(b) The committee will consider the conduct of joint research studies.

(c) The committee shall meet alternately in the United States and Mexico at least twice a year.

3) The Parties consider it desirable to exchange information on the size and characteristics of the actual and potential tourism markets in their two countries.

4) The Parties agree that the guidelines on the collection and presentation of domestic and international tourism statistics established by the World Tourism Organization shall constitute the requirements for such a data base.

ARTICLE VII
Joint Marketing of Tourism

1) Subject to budgetary limitations, the Parties shall consider the conduct of joint marketing activities in third countries.

2) Activities which shall receive consideration include joint operation of inspection trips for tour wholesalers and operators, and journalists from third countries, film festivals, travel trade shows and travel missions.

ARTICLE VIII
World Tourism Organization

1) The Parties shall work within the World Tourism Organization to develop, and encourage the adoption of, uniform standards and recommended practices which, if applied by governments, would facilitate tourism.
2) The Parties shall assist one another in matters of cooperation and effective participation in the World Tourism Organization.

ARTICLE IX
Consultations

1) The Parties agree that tourism and tourism matters shall be discussed, as appropriate, in bilateral consultations attended by representatives of their official tourism organizations. These meetings shall be held alternately in the United States and Mexico at least once a year.
2) Whenever possible these consultations will be held in conjunction with other meetings of the United States of America and the United Mexican States. Both Parties will consider the possibility of establishing working groups to consider specific issues or articles of the Agreement.
3) The consultations to be undertaken under this Agreement constitute a part of the efforts to improve bilateral cooperation in the framework of the U.S.-Mexico Binational Commission. Therefore, both Parties shall report periodically to the Binational Commission on their programs, results and recommendations.
4) The United Mexican States designates the Tourism Secretariat as its agency with primary responsibility for implementing this Agreement for Mexico.
5) The United States of America designates the U.S. Department of Commerce as its agency with primary responsibility for implementing this Agreement for the United States.

ARTICLE X
Protocols

1) The Parties may implement this Agreement through protocols. Protocols may cover subjects such as cooperative activities to facilitate tourism, tourism training, joint marketing, development of tourism statistics, funding, procedures to be followed in such joint projects, and other appropriate matters.
2) The cost of all activities under this article shall be mutually agreed upon. These expenses for such activities will be borne subject to all applicable laws and regulations and to the availability of human and financial resources.

ARTICLE XI
Tourism Agreement of 1983 Superseded

This Agreement shall supersede and replace the Tourism Agreement between the Parties, signed April 18, 1983.

ARTICLE XII
Period of Effectiveness

1) Each Party shall inform the other by way of diplomatic note of the completion of necessary legal requirements in its country for entry into force of the present Agreement. The Agreement shall enter into force upon receipt of such notification by the second Party.
2) Upon entry into force, this Agreement shall be valid for a period of five years and will be renewed automatically for additional periods of five years unless either Party expresses objection in writing, through diplomatic channels three months prior to the expiration date.
3) This Agreement shall be terminated ninety days after either Party transmits written notice of its intention to terminate to the other Party.

ARTICLE XIII
Notification

After entry into force, both Parties agree to notify the Secretariat General of the World Tourism Organization of this Agreement and any subsequent amendments.

DONE at Washington, DC this third day of October, 1989 in two originals in the English and Spanish languages, both texts being equally authentic.

Concluding Critical Questions

After reading the case study and relating it to the concepts and other examples presented in this chapter on the political and foreign policy implications of tourism, several questions can be raised to stimulate discussion and thought about the underlying theories involved in engaging in international tourism agreements. Other questions can be used to analyze the applicability and practical implementation of multi-national tourism agreements in today's political and economic landscape.

Rich discussion questions include the following. How can one nation justify cooperating with another nation if it might mean sacrificing tourism demand in its own country? Tourism coopetition benefits local communities but how effective can it be across international borders? Could free-rider problems arise when two nations enter into such agreements and how can those problems be resolved or avoided?

Who might settle such disputes if conflicts arose among the parties in an international tourism agreement? Finally, how could this particular example of a bilateral tourism agreement be strengthened? Is anything missing in the agreement or is anything that is included not needed?

Notes

1   www.cdc.gov, 05/01/2006.

2   Reagan, R. (1985) Correspondence to 25th Session of the Executive Council of the World Tourism Organization, The White House, Washington, DC, April 18.

3   Rosato, S. (2003) "The Flawed Logic of Democratic Peace Theory." *American Political Science Review*, 97: 585–602.

4   White, M. (2000) *Democracies Do Not Make War on One Another . . . Or Do They?* Retrieved October 22, 2012, from http://users.erols.com/mwhite28/demowar.htm.

5   Kant, I. (1795) *Project for Perpetual Peace*. Retrieved October 22, 2012, from www.mtholyoke.edu/acad/intrel/kant/kant1.htm.

6   Rosato (2003).

7   WTTC (2005) *World Travel & Tourism Economic Research*. Retrieved November 20, 2005, from www.wttc.org/2005tsa/pdf/World.pdf.

8   Rawls, J. (1999) *A Theory of Justice*. Oxford: Oxford University Press.

9   Kant (1795).

10 Edgell, D. (2012) *The Ten Important World Tourism Issues for 2012*.

11 Sri Lanka Tourist Board (2004) *Annual Statistical Report of Sri Lanka Tourism*. Colombo, Sri Lanka: SLTB.

12 Cited in Strausberg, M. (2012). *Religion and Tourism: Crossroads, Destinations and Encounters*. New York: Routledge, p. 5.

13 Cited in Theobald, W. (ed.) (1994) *Global Tourism, the Next Generation*. Oxford: Butterworth-Heinemann, p. 44.

14 Kennedy, J.F. (1963) *The Saturday Review*, January 5.

15 Part of the reference for this section was obtained from www.world-tourism.org/aboutwto.

16 Part of the reference for this section was obtained from www.wttc.org.

17 Part of the reference for this section was obtained from www.oecd.org.

18 www.oas.org.

19 Part of the reference for this section was obtained from www.apec.org/about.

20 www.doitcaribbean.com/info/index.html.en-US.

21 Part of the reference for this section was obtained from www.onecaribbean.org.

22 Part of this section was taken from www.menata.org/about-menata.

23 Part of this section was taken from www.unfoundation.org/what-we-do/campaigns-and-initiatives/world-heritage-alliance.

6

Managing sustainable tourism

As in times past, one of the strongest motivations for travel today is interest in the natural environment and in the heritage, arts, history, language, customs, and cultures of people locally and in other lands. The opportunity to observe how others live, think, and interact socially and within their environment exerts a powerful attraction for many visitors. Travelers may seek to experience examples of a locale's arts, sculpture, architecture, celebrations, and festivals, or cultural interests in food, drink, music, or some other special activity of travel and tourism hospitality. The attraction may be a built environment with significant historic buildings or unique museums, or the natural environment with a beautiful landscape, pleasant seashore, a magnificent mountain, a lovely forest, the flora and fauna of the area, or simply the social interactions of human beings in their local surroundings. It is this aspect of the environment – natural habitats, built structures, culture, heritage, history, and social interactions – that, with effective policies and good management, will sustain tourism into the future.

It is essential to conserve and maintain these sustaining resources for future generations to enjoy.[1] "Responsibly managed tourism enhances and enriches natural, heritage, and cultural values and embraces the need to preserve them so that the community and visitor have a quality tourism experience now and in the future . . . Sustainable tourism, properly managed, can become a major vehicle for the realization of humankind's highest aspirations in the quest to achieve economic prosperity while maintaining social, cultural, and environmental integrity."[2]

Today, tourism is recognized as one of the fastest growing industries in the world. Within contemporary tourism, growth in sustainable tourism is moving to the forefront of interest in tourism policy and planning. Such rapid changes and its concurrent development practices have put particular pressure on sustainable tourism planning, policy, and management. The tenet with respect to sustainable tourism is to understand that tourism experiences may be positive, or in some circumstances negative, and to recognize when there is a need for planning and policy guidance to ensure that the continued growth of tourism will allow for a balanced and positive tourism experience. Comprehensive planning decisions and implementation are requisite to policy decision-making. (The relationship of planning to policy is more fully discussed later in this book.) In effect, sustainable tourism is a part of an overall shift that recognizes that orderly economic growth combined with concerns for the environment and quality-of-life social values offers the best future for the tourism industry.

Sustainable tourism – its essence

Managing sustainable tourism depends on forward-looking policies and sound management philosophies that include building a harmonious relationship among local communities, the private-sector, and governments regarding developmental practices that protect the natural and built environments while being compatible with economic growth. As stated earlier, sustainable tourism practices can be a viable means of providing a community or destination with an improved quality-of-life. There is only a limited environment to work with, and much of that environment is already under siege from the many different industrial, technological, and unplanned tourism developments underway. To preserve environmental resources, to have a positive impact on the social values of the community, and to add to the quality-of-life of local citizens worldwide and, at the same time, elicit favorable economic benefits for tourism is indeed, a major challenge.

Pleasant climates, scenic wonders, beautiful coastlines and beaches, majestic mountains and valleys, rugged woods interspersed with rolling plains, magnificent natural vistas, and the rhythmic sounds of the sea are all components of the natural environmental attractions that cause large movements of travelers worldwide, as illustrated in Figure 6.1. Built structures whether lodging, museums, art galleries or historic buildings are a major part of the built tourism environment. Least understood, but an important part of sustainable tourism products is the enjoyment of different cultures, traditions, and heritages within local communities.

It has been argued that sustainable tourism "incorporates two complimentary tacks: the 'natural environment' (ecotourism, geotourism, adventure tourism, agritourism, and rural tourism) and the 'built environment' (history, heritage, culture, arts, and unique structures). There is an expected overlap in this confluence – both within the basic concept of sustainable tourism and a cross-over in the various elements of the definition."[3] Recent research "stresses that positive sustainable tourism development is dependent on futuristic policies and new management philosophies which seek to include a harmonious relationship among local communities, the private-sector, not-for-profit organizations, academic institutions, and governments at all levels in developmental practices that protect natural, built, and cultural environments compatible with economic growth."[4]

A common misperception about sustainable tourism is that it is "consumed" by the visitor but then is instantaneously renewed. The key to renewable sustainable tourism

FIGURE 6.1 Scenic landscape surrounding Lake Manyara in Tanzania's Ngorongoro Conservation Area, a UNESCO World Heritage Site (Photo: Sam Peterson)

is to balance the equation of conserving the natural, built, and social environments on the one hand and adding economic value on the other with a well-planned and well-managed sustainable tourism program. Simply put, sustainable tourism means achieving quality growth in a manner that does not deplete the natural and built environments and preserves the culture, history and heritage of the local community in order to improve the quality-of-life for the local citizens. Sustainable tourism references the natural surroundings plus the built environment, which consists of a montage of influences from history, heritage and culture to new and modern structures.

Defining and understanding sustainable tourism

In this book, the co-authors have adopted, for the most part, the East Carolina University's Center for Sustainable Tourism's working definition of sustainable tourism: "Sustainable tourism contributes to a balanced and healthy economy by generating tourism-related jobs, revenues, and taxes while protecting and enhancing the destination's social, cultural, historical, natural, and built resources for the enjoyment and well-being of both residents and visitors."[5] Other useful definitions will come to the forefront later in the book, especially the acceptance of the United Nations World Tourism Organization (UNWTO) concept that sustainable tourism is tourism that leads to the management of all resources in such a way that the economic, social, and aesthetic needs can be fulfilled while maintaining cultural integrity, essential ecological processes, biological diversity, and contribute to poverty alleviation.

With orderly economic growth as part of the goal of sustainable tourism, the key is to balance the number of visitors with the *carrying capacity* of the given environment (whether natural or built) in a manner that allows for the greatest interaction and enjoyment with the least destruction. This must be accomplished in the milieu of interdependency of the tourism industry with many other industries locally and globally. There are many opinions on how this can best be attained; however, there is general agreement that establishing a workable sustainable tourism policy is a beginning point. In its most straightforward definition, *carrying capacity* is simply being able to accommodate the largest number of people a destination can effectively and efficiently manage within its given environ and management capabilities. When too many people convene at a location and the area cannot handle this influx, the *carrying capacity* of the place is compromised, which, in turn, harms the environment of the destination, has a negative impact on its local citizenry and the economy eventually declines. To meet this concern, effective planning steps must be taken in conjunction within overall policy guidelines.

One might argue that no other industry shares a cause-and-effect relationship with so many different industries as does the tourism industry. It is this interdependency that sets the stage for the multidisciplinary nature of tourism. Current concerns in the petroleum industry (availability and pricing of gasoline for autos) for example, have a major impact in determining a traveler's decision to take a vacation. The airline industry is also affected by the petroleum industry, as well as by evolving safety and security procedures at an airport at any given time. The production of food products is another area whereby the tourism industry depends on other sectors of the economy such as agriculture, fishing, and beverages.

Many countries have adopted, in one form or another, special sustainable tourism policies. For example, the Kenya Wildlife Service (KWS), established in 1990 has a strong legislated conservation code for protecting the wildlife in its parks. KWS acknowledges responsibility for wildlife conservation and management practices, both within protected confines and in outlying, unprotected lands. KWS's Community Wildlife Services division collaborates with stakeholders on adjacent lands aimed toward positive conservation and land-management practices. This management practice supporting the concept of sustainable tourism is summed up in the stated goal of KWS: "To work with others to conserve, protect and sustainably manage wildlife resources outside protected areas for the benefit of the people. The community wildlife program of KWS in collaboration with others encourages biodiversity conservation by communities living on land essential to wildlife, such as wildlife corridors and dispersal lands outside parks and reserves. The premise is that 'if people benefit from wildlife and other natural resources, then they will take care of these resources, using them sustainably'."

Early background and trends in sustainable tourism

Concerns with respect to identifying and recognizing environmental issues and in understanding cultural heritage have a long history. The Greek society, for example, had interest in naturalism. The great Greek traveler and travel writer Herodotus included numerous examples in his book about the differing cultures and heritages he encountered in his travels, while Marco Polo's book describes the natural areas he visited and, in addition, contains many stories of the peoples, cultures, and lifestyles he came into contact with. In 1709, English explorer, traveler, and travel writer John Lawson wrote and included drawings in his book about North American Indian tribes along with unique descriptions of the flora and fauna he noted as he walked through uncharted wilderness areas. Later, naturalists like Baron Alexander von Humboldt and Charles Darwin studied nature and provided future generations with a better understanding of the bounties of the Earth. By early in the twentieth century, local and national park systems throughout the world recognized visitor interest in the natural and built environment and developed conservation programs to protect such resources.

The red flag for modern-day concern for the environment was first raised in the book *Silent Spring* by Rachel Carson in 1962. Her arguments that the detrimental effects of pesticides was impacting on the sustainability of life itself got the world's attention with respect to environmental concerns. Then in 1972 the global think tank group the "Club of Rome" produced a report *The Limits to Growth* that analyzed crucial problems facing humanity including concerns for the environment. The report sold more than 12 million copies and caused high-level politicians, scientists, economists, and others to take notice of the concerns for the wellbeing of society in the future. Most researchers in the tourism industry usually cite the 1987 Brundtland Report that emanated from the meeting of the United Nations' World Commission on Environment and Development as a beginning point for discussing sustainable tourism. The Report gave direction for the discussion of issues on sustainability that helped stimulate the tourism industry to take action.[6] However, the impetus for many of the more recent initiatives in sustainable tourism stem from a report developed at the United Nations Conference on Environment and Development in Rio de Janeiro, Brazil in 1992 referred to as *Agenda 21*. Three basic themes of sustainable tourism developed from *Agenda 21*: first, the need for partnerships (see earlier discussion on coopetition) between the public and private-sectors; second, maintain quality-of-life without compromising the future wellbeing of the people or the planet; and, third, emphasis on preserving environmental sustainability.

In 1995, the tourism industry endorsed the principles described above and added additional guidelines to *Agenda 21*. The World Travel and Tourism Council (WTTC), the United Nations World Tourism Organization (UNWTO), and the Earth Council jointly launched an initiative titled *Agenda 21 for the Travel and Tourism Industry: Towards Environmentally Sustainable Development*, which offered a strategic plan for action. It was this report that energized the global travel and tourism entities to move ahead on sustainable tourism initiatives.

The above actions were further reinforced at the 7th Session of the United Nations Commission on Sustainable Development in 1999, which placed increased emphasis on the economic and social aspects of sustainable development, especially in relation to poverty reduction. The Commission urged governments to "maximize the potential for tourism for eradicating poverty by developing appropriate strategies in cooperation with all major groups, indigenous and local communities." The UNWTO and the WTTC became primary organizations to account for the global travel and tourism industry with respect to the Commission initiative.

At about the same time (and in some cases even earlier), regional organizations were leading or mimicking what was taking place on the world stage with respect to sustainable tourism. The Organisation for Economic Co-operation and Development (OECD) discussed several initiatives, including a special emphasis on sustainable tourism in rural areas. The Caribbean Tourism Organization organized a number of conferences resulting in the recognition that the Caribbean was particularly vulnerable to negative environmental impacts on their islands and therefore there is a strong need for sustainable tourism policies. The Tourism Committee (initially chaired by co-author of this book David Edgell) of the Asia-Pacific Economic Cooperation (APEC) worked on sustainable tourism issues and in 1996 the APEC Secretariat issued a comprehensive sustainable tourism study titled *Environmentally Sustainable Tourism in APEC Member Economies*. In 1995 Edgell prepared the report *The Organization of American States Sustainable Tourism Development Policy and Planning Guide* for the Department of Regional Development and Environment, Executive Secretariat for Economic and Social Affairs, Organization of American States (OAS). This report provided practical guidelines for the 35 member states of the OAS with respect to sustainable tourism development. There are many additional organizations both regional, national, not-for-profit, university programs, and private-sector entities devoted to discussing and implementing sustainable tourism policies and programs.[7] On a global basis, it is the work on sustainable tourism being accomplished by the UNWTO that has received considerable attention. The 2004 UNWTO "sustainable development of tourism conceptual definition" states that:

> Sustainable tourism development guidelines and management practices are applicable to all forms of tourism in all types of destinations, including mass tourism and the various niche tourism segments. Sustainability principles refer to the environmental, economic, and socio-cultural aspects of tourism development, and a suitable balance must be established between these three dimensions to guarantee its long-term sustainability. Thus sustainability tourism should:
>
> 1. Make optimal use of environmental resources that constitute a key element in tourism development, maintaining essential ecological processes, and helping to conserve natural heritage and biodiversity.
> 2. Respect the socio-cultural authenticity of host communities, conserve their built and living cultural heritage and traditional values, and contribute to inter-cultural understanding and tolerance.
> 3. Ensure viable, long-term economic operations, providing socioeconomic benefits to all stakeholders that are fairly distributed, including stable employment and income-earning opportunities and social services to host communities, and contributing to poverty alleviation . . .

Sustainable tourism development requires the informed participation of all relevant stakeholders, as well as strong political leadership to ensure wide participation and consensus building. Achieving sustainable tourism is a continuous process and it requires constant monitoring of impacts, introducing the necessary preventive and/or corrective measures whenever necessary . . .

Sustainable tourism should also maintain a high level of tourist satisfaction and ensure meaningful experience to the tourists, raising their awareness about sustainability and promoting sustainable tourism practices amongst them.[8]

In addition, the WTTC, representing the private-sector, is recognized as a partner with governments to raise the awareness of the economic and social importance of the tourism industry across the world. With respect to sustainable tourism, WTTC initially launched *Green Globe* to highlight concerns for the environment and was a partner in *Agenda 21* mentioned earlier in this section. In 2003, at the Global Travel and Tourism Summit, WTTC introduced a *Blueprint for New Tourism* report, which noted the importance of partnerships in sustainable tourism development. The *Blueprint* promoted a vision for travel and tourism that went well beyond short-term interests and focused on benefits not only for those who travel, but for people in the communities they visit, and their respective natural, social, and cultural environments. It recognized the need for strong alliances between the private and public sectors, matching the needs of economies, local and regional authorities, and local communities with those of business in all aspects of tourism including sustainable tourism. One of the top priorities of the *Blueprint* is "Business balancing economics with people, culture and environment."[9]

There are many non-governmental organizations devoted to issues in sustainable tourism. It would take an entire book to mention all such groups. However, a comment about a few of these entities should suffice to suggest their contributions toward promoting the principles of sustainable tourism. The first one that comes to mind is *National Geographic*'s Center for Sustainable Destinations (Center) that was established in 2003. This Center has developed a set of measurement criteria for evaluating destinations throughout the world. In conjunction with Leeds Metropolitan University (University) in the United Kingdom, the Center and University have developed a panel of experts in a variety of fields – ecology, sustainable tourism, geography, planning, travel writing and photography, historic preservation, cultural anthropology, archaeology, and related disciplines to evaluate the sustainability of destinations throughout the world. This sustainable tourism team effort and the Center's criteria for evaluating the sustainability of a destination will be more fully explored later in this chapter under the section "A Global Perspective."

Guidelines for sustainable tourism

This chapter would indeed be remiss if it failed to mention the popular "The Ten Commandments of Ecotourism" as delineated by the American Society of Travel Agents (ASTA), an organization that is international in the scope of its activities:

1. Respect the frailty of the earth. Realize that unless we are all willing to help in its preservation, unique and beautiful destinations may not be here for future generations to enjoy.
2. Leave only footprints – take only photographs. No graffiti! No litter! Do not take away "souvenirs" from historical sites and natural sites.
3. To make your travels more meaningful, educate yourself about the geography, customs, manners and cultures of the regions you visit. Take time to listen to the people. Encourage local conservation efforts.
4. Respect the privacy and dignity of others. Inquire before photographing people.
5. Do not buy products made from endangered plants or animals, such as ivory, tortoise shell, animal skin and feathers. Read "Know Before You Go," the US Customs list of products that cannot be imported.
6. Always follow designated trails. Do not disturb animals, plants or their natural habitats.
7. Learn about and support conservation-oriented programs and organizations working to preserve the environment.
8. Whenever possible, walk or utilize environmentally sound methods of transportation. Encourage drivers of public vehicles to stop engines when parked.
9. Patronize hotels, airlines, resorts, cruise lines, tour operators, and suppliers that advance energy and environmental conservation; water and air quality; recycling; safe management of waste and toxic materials; noise abatement; community involvement; and that provide experienced, well-trained staff dedicated to strong principles of conservation.
10. Ask your ASTA travel agent to identify organizations that subscribe to Environmental Guidelines for air, land and sea travel. ASTA has recommended that these organizations adopt their own environmental codes to cover special sites and ecosystems.

An important organization, initially founded in 2005 as a Tourism Institute (by co-author Edgell) to work on economic development through tourism and sustainable tourism issues at the local, state, national, and international levels, evolved into what is now East Carolina University's Center for Sustainable Tourism (Center). This Center has matured under excellent leadership (Dr. Patrick Long is the Center's director) to produce numerous documents on a wide variety of sustainable tourism interests, having significance not only at the local level, but internationally as well. The Center established the first "Master of Science Degree in Sustainable Tourism" in the United States in 2010. For information on the Center's research, programs, and activities, see www.sustainabletourism.org.

In 2012, the Center for Sustainable Tourism, in conjunction with Milesmedia, issued the document *Pledge to Travel Green* with "10 Ways to Care," which included:

1. **Learn About Your Destination –** Enjoy a rewarding experience by learning more about the natural environment, culture and history that makes every destination unique.
2. **Don't Leave Your Good Habits at Home –** While traveling, continue to recycle, use water wisely, and turn off lights as you would at home.

3. **Be a Fuel-efficient Traveler** – Book direct flights, rent smaller cars and keep your own vehicle operating at maximum efficiency. Once in your destination, walk or bike where possible.
4. **Make Informed Decisions** – Seek out destinations or companies that engage in energy efficiency or recycling programs and that take actions to preserve their communities and the natural environment.
5. **Be a Good Guest** – Remember that you are a guest in your destination. Engage with locals but respect their privacy, traditions and local community.
6. **Support Locals** – As a visitor, the money you spend on your trip can help support the local artisans, farmers and business owners whose livelihood depends on tourism.
7. **Dispose of Your Waste Property** – Leave a beautiful place for others to enjoy – recycle where possible and always dispose of your waste with care.
8. **Protect Your Natural Surroundings** – Be mindful of the plants, animals and ecosystems that you impact. Avoid feeding wildlife, stay on designated trails and strictly follow all fire restrictions.
9. **Make Your Travel Zero Emissions** – As an additional step, consider the option of purchasing carbon credits to fully offset your travel's impact on climate change.
10. **Bring Your Experiences Home** – Continue practicing your sustainable habits at home and encourage friends and family to travel with the same care.

Many additional tourism organizations have developed important information on sustainable tourism. Several country tourism authorities have been developing principles of sustainable tourism for many years. For example, Canada has a Code of Ethics and Guidelines for Sustainable Tourism:

1. Enjoy our diverse natural and cultural heritage and help us to protect and preserve it.
2. Assist us in our conservation efforts through the efficient use of resources including energy and water.
3. Experience the friendliness of our people and the welcoming spirit of our communities. Help us to preserve these attributes by respecting our traditions, customs and local regulations.
4. Avoid activities which threaten wildlife or plant population, or which may be potentially damaging to our natural environment.
5. Select tourism products and services which demonstrate social, cultural and environmental sensitivity.

Benefits of sustainability

Tourist destinations that encompass sustainability in their tourism products add a special dimension to economic growth and quality-of-life benefits for the community. Unspoiled natural ecosystems, well-maintained historic sites, and cultural heritage events lead to satisfied visitors. The concern in some quarters of interest in sustainable tourism is whether governments, private-sector entities, local communities, not-for-profit organizations, and others are ready to accept, plan, participate in, lobby for, and manage tourism programs that support sustainable tourism principles and practices. To ensure that sustainable tourism as an economic development strategy flourishes in the future, there must be efforts to inspire businesses and people to accept good practices whether they choose to enhance the natural scenic beauty as it intermingles with flora and fauna or enrich the built environment. In that respect, a major challenge is to provide best practices to help guide the management process and provide future generations with the opportunity to enjoy and benefit from sustainable tourism.

There are also regions and countries of the world that have for years been taking steps toward the marketing and promotion of destination environmental quality. One of the oldest and most successful programs is referred to as the "Blue Flag Campaign" initially developed and implemented in Europe under the Foundation for Environment Education in Europe (FEEE). Later FEEE was expanded to include not only European nations but such countries as South Africa, Morocco, Tunisia, New Zealand, Brazil, Canada, and countries in the Caribbean. The program was initiated in France in 1985, where concerns had been raised regarding water quality and sewage disposal at beach destinations. When the program was expanded under FEEE it added environmental quality criteria, and the program spread across Europe and beyond. With the expansion to non-European countries the program was renamed as the Foundation for Environmental Education (FEE). The FEE has basically four main criteria dealing with: 1) environmental education and information; 2) water quality; 3) environmental management; and, 4) safety and services. Each of these criteria has detailed requirements that must be met for a country to qualify to be included in the Blue Flag program. If a requesting destination is from one of the participating countries and meets the criteria, it is eligible to fly, in front of their property, an FEE Blue Flag that, in effect, tells the traveler that the destination is certified as environmentally sound.

A global perspective

As mentioned earlier, there are now numerous organizations engaged in one form or another in sustainable tourism issues and concerns. The tourism industry today is much better informed about the interests of visitors wanting a quality tourism experience in a clean and healthy natural environment and a social milieu that protects and conserves historic structures and preserves the heritage and culture of the destination. The question that remains is how best to get the sustainable tourism message to a broader audience. Certainly the use of e-commerce tools are important, the travel, nature, and history channels on our televisions are significant as well as *National Geographic Traveler* (the most-read international travel magazine), which places a special focus on quality tourism destinations. This section explains the approach taken by *National Geographic*'s Center for Sustainable Destinations (Center) efforts to publicize the positive and negative destinations as far as sustainability is concerned.

As was previously noted, the Center was established in 2003 and partnered with a team from Leeds Metropolitan University to conduct global surveys in order to rate destinations as to their sustainability. The Center developed six criteria for use in their rating system:

1. Environmental and ecological quality.
2. Social and cultural integrity.
3. Condition of any historic building and archaeological sites.
4. Aesthetic appeal.
5. Quality of tourism management.
6. The outlook for the future.

Also explained at the beginning of the discussion, a panel of experts, with backgrounds qualifying them to measure the sustainability of destinations, was assembled. Most were seasoned travelers and generally had good evaluation skills. Each year, beginning with 2004, the Center developed a list of global destinations to be rated by the experts. The experts only rated those destinations with respect to their sustainability in which they had visited within the last five years. Once the ratings were complete *National Geographic Traveler* magazine published the results. To better publicize the ratings, the magazine would prepare a special cover highlighting the ratings. Examples of some of the words on the cover in large print and bolded in different colors included: March 2004, "Destination Scorecard, 115 Places Rated;" July/August 2005, "55 Places Rated;" November/December 2006, "94 Places Rated;" November/December 2007, "Places Rated – The World's Best Islands;" November/December 2009, "World's Great Places: 133 Destinations Rated;" November/December 2010, "99 Destinations Rated – The World's Great Islands, Beaches & Coastlines." The ratings within the pages of the magazine had headings such as "The Good," "Not So Bad," and "Getting Ugly." A destination certainly did not want to be in the last category but if it were, the destination usually sought to improve its sustainability.

Climate change and sustainable tourism

Sustainable tourism management has a number of major policy and planning challenges and none is more important than addressing the effects of climate change. "Compelling evidence indicates that global climate has changed compared to the pre-industrial era – and that it is anticipated to continue to change over the 21st century and beyond ... With its close connections to the environment and climate itself, tourism is considered to be a *highly climate-sensitive economic sector* similar to agriculture, insurance, energy, and transportation. The regional manifestations of climate change will be highly relevant for tourism destinations and tourists alike, requiring adaptation by all major tourism stakeholders."[10] Especially vulnerable to the impact of climate change with respect to tourism are the world's coastal areas and islands. The case study in Chapter 1 regarding the Republic of Maldives is a good example of a series of beautiful islands that could disappear if global warming takes place. A case study at the end of this chapter will address one coastal area concerned with climate change, which may serve as a representative example of similar areas in other parts of the world. Some of the information in the following discussion appeared first in the case study that follows, but in the opinion of the co-authors of this book is worth repeating.

"The tourism industry has identified climate change as a key [issue] to future strategic planning. United Nations World Tourism Organization's [former] Secretary General, Francesco Frangialli, addressing climate change said: 'We [tourism industry] are part of the problem [global warming] and we will be part of the solution'. Social scientists recognize the need to create innovative responses to projected impacts of climate change on tourism." For the future growth and sustainability of tourism throughout the world, policy responses to climate change are critical.

Becken and Hay state: "Climate change will not only impact on tourism directly by changes in temperature, extreme weather events and other climatic factors, but also indirectly as it will transform the natural environment that attracts tourists in the first place – for example, by accelerating coastal erosion, damaging coral reefs, and other sensitive ecosystems and by reducing snowfall and snow cover in mountainous regions. It will also affect the basic services that are so critical for tourism, such as water supplies, especially during periods of peak demand."[11] Dr. Patrick Long, director at the Center for Sustainable Tourism at East Carolina University suggests that "we need to further our knowledge about climate trends . . . impacts of variability and seasonality . . . and the development of policies and strategies to adapt to and mitigate effects of climate change".[12]

Weather conditions and the climate of a tourism place often dictate why people travel, where they travel, how they travel, and when they travel, and for how long visitors stay at the destination. Generally visitors to beach areas are looking for sunshine and warm waters. Skiers and snowmobilers pray for good snow falls. Sightseers and outdoor recreationists hope for clear weather and moderate temperatures. Many tourism businesses have failed simply because of weather conditions. "[U]ntil we adequately address the issue of climate change, tourism managers will have to develop a comprehensive destination policy, strategy, and management framework that adapts to and accommodates the reality of long-term . . . climate change."[13]

Variances in weather patterns due to climate change may have immediate repercussions on visitors. Forest fires destroy the flora and fauna of areas of interest to tourists. Hurricanes and tsunamis change coastlines and often wreak havoc on resort homes, destinations, and tourism services. Floods and droughts can decimate an area once dependent on tourism. These phenomena have an impact on the sustainability of tourism for the future.

Until global leaders aggressively address issues with respect to climate altercations the tourism industry is left to its own devices to mitigate or adapt to consequences of such changes. Edgell and McCormick in a 2008 paper mentioned that, "Tourism administrators must undertake a paradigm shift away from overuse of natural resources toward environmental stewardship . . . Additionally, as global warming comes to the forefront in environmental concerns, tourism managers will need to stay attuned to forecast changes."[14] Individual regions of the world must address the impact of climate change on their specific tourism destinations. If nothing is done, the future growth and sustainability of tourism will be at risk. If tourism stakeholders do not define clear-cut policies and plans at this juncture in the growth of tourism, there may never be another opportunity.

Action with respect to climate change and sustainable tourism must take place now. "It is essential to emphasize that regardless of the nature and magnitude of climate change impacts, *all tourism business and destinations will need to adapt to climate change* in order to minimize associated risks and capitalize on new opportunities, in an economically, socially and environmentally sustainable manner . . . The unmistakable conclusion of studies in the field have shown that the significance of climate change to tourism is not in some distant and remote future. Climate change is already influencing decision-making within the tourism sector, including that of tourists, forward-looking tourism businesses and investors, and international tourism organizations."[15]

Best practices for managing sustainable tourism

In this chapter, a review of many different concepts and ideas about sustainable tourism has been explored. What is left lacking, to complete the intent of the chapter, is a concrete example of an actual destination that typifies the best practices of developing and managing a highly successful sustainable property. In a global search of available information in terms of sustainable destinations, Maho Bay Resorts on the island of St. John, US Virgin Islands, appeared at the top of many lists. This property has won countless global awards, more than any other property researched for this chapter, in exemplifying the highest principles of developing and managing a sustainable tourism destination.

In an article "Making Paradise Last: Maho Bay Resorts" in the book *Sustainable Tourism: A Global Perspective*, authors Christina Symko and Rob Harris carefully analyzed Maho Bay Resorts in terms of its sustainable features. The developer of Maho Bay Resorts, an early pioneer in sustainable ecotourism is Stanley Selengut. In their introduction, they have this to say:

> Developing appropriate tourism facilities and accommodations in fragile environments requires inspiration, innovation and technical ingenuity. Ecolodge developers contend both with the challenge of finding ways to build in harmony with nature and the need to engage visitors in nature-based experiences so that

they have an enhanced understanding of the environment around them. This case study details how one Ecolodge Maho Bay Resorts (MBR) in the US Virgin Islands, has sought to address these challenges. In so doing MBR has sought to encompass the philosophy of sustainability in its broadest sense, extending beyond the environmental dimension to embrace economic and social goals linked to surrounding communities . . . Market demand for the various MBR products has been strong with occupancy levels approaching 100 per cent in the high season (mid-December to mid-April), while off-season occupancy rates are significantly above the norm for the Caribbean as a whole.[16]

After analyzing Maho Bay Resorts, the article concludes that, in effect, this destination more than meets the standards of development of sustainable resort practices.

A 1996 Yale University Bulletin Series on "The Ecotourism Equation: Measuring the Impacts" included an article by developer Stanley Selengut titled "Maho Bay, Harmony, Estate Concordia, and the Concordia Eco-Tents, St. John, US Virgin Islands." In the article Selengut tells his personal story on the development of the sustainable tourism property, Maho Bay. As mentioned earlier in this chapter, most authors discussing sustainable tourism start with the Brundtland Report from the 1987 meeting of the United Nations' World Commission on Environment and Development. It is interesting to note that Selengut began developing his *environmentally* sound resort destination in 1975, 12 years earlier.

The Yale Series explains the process of developing an ecotourism property in Selengut's words:

> I designed a light inexpensive "tent-cottage" which could be built within the existing trees and plants. The walkways [elevated] were built first, on hand-dug footings. Construction materials were wheeled along the walks and carried into place. Pipes and electrical cables were hidden under the walks rather than buried in trenches. The finished walkways flow naturally through the trees and foliage . . . We started small with only eighteen units and a modest cash investment. The campground [resort] won the 1978 Environmental Protection Award, was featured in the *New York Times* travel section, and attracted more customers than we could handle. We used the profits to add units a few at a time. Now, with 114 units, Maho Bay is one of the most profitable and highly occupied resorts in the Caribbean . . . The floor decking is made from 100 per cent recycled newspaper. The floor is composed of . . . 100 percent recycled newspapers. The siding is made from a composite of cement and recycled cardboard . . . The bathroom tiles and furniture tops are made from 73 percent post-consumer glass bottles.

The Maho Bay property used recycled materials, wind energy, solar panels or whatever saving-the-environment technologies were available. The flora and fauna are fully protected. Asked about the reasons for such a concern for the environment and using recycled building materials and Selengut will tell you that it is "because, it is much more profitable! What makes sense from an environmental and conservation point of view also saves money."[17]

With respect to scenic beauty, magnificent white sand beaches, and luscious flora, the area of Maho Bay, St. John, US Virgin Islands, is certainly one of the best such destinations in the world. Selengut could not have picked a more suitable site in 1975 to begin building his ecotourism facilities. One advantage of building a sustainable property on St. John is that two-thirds of the island is a US National Park that protects the area's natural habitats.

Important precepts

It is important to recognize that sustainable tourism policies should combine the interests of the present benefits of sustainability for a destination as well as in protecting its future opportunities. It is imperative adults ensure that children tomorrow have the same opportunity to enjoy a quality destination as many of us did yesterday and do today. In addition, sustainable tourism development should benefit the local population as well as the visitor. In many countries of the world it is their national parks that have led the way with respect to sustainability. Many national parks today face pressures inside and outside of their borders; efforts to maintain pristine environments in view of large numbers of visitors is a real challenge; and, in some circumstances getting governments to budget the money needed to support the sustainability of the park is often the toughest job. However, most stewards of the parks are proponents of maintaining quality environments for flora and fauna and in seeking to be on good terms with local populations and we hope future policies and plans will support such stewardship.

Canada has an excellent sustainability policy for maintaining and managing its parks. Canada's National Parks Act of 1930 states: "The Parks are dedicated to the people of Canada for their benefit, education, and enjoyment . . . such parks shall be maintained and made use of so as to leave them unimpaired for the enjoyment of future generations." The first amendments to this impressive act, in 1988, emphasized ecological integrity and the protection of "intact ecosystems," and include public participation in management. In 1994, additional enhancements were made to the "Guiding Principles and Operational Policies" to further protect the environment on the basis "that park management must reflect Canada's national identity and its international responsibilities." One of the parks striving, with some difficulty, to uphold these park precepts is Banff National Park.

While Canada's oldest and most popular park, Banff National Park is faced with some real challenges, it continues to provide a great outdoors experience for visitors and the local population that lives within the park. It may be Canada's most studied park in the sense of its ability to accommodate large numbers of visitors and still maintain its sustainability. As a United Nations World Heritage Site, the park must meet high standards of environmental management. An interesting aspect of Banff National Park is that a small community of about 7,600 people lives within the bounds of the park, carrying on normal everyday activities. With millions of visitors each year, the park must continually evaluate its carrying capacity for so many tourists. Constant efforts are made to strengthen the ecological integrity of the park and achieve a balance between conservation and use. In the *Banff National Park Management Plan Summary*, the Minister of Canadian Heritage describes the park as "a place where nature will always be the integral part of everyone's visit, responsibility and lives . . . and it is a place for nature, visitors, community, heritage tourism, open management and environmental stewardship." This management plan is about as good a description of a positive sustainable tourism policy as can be found anywhere in the world.

CHAPTER REVIEW QUESTIONS

1. What is the definition of sustainable tourism?
2. Define carrying capacity.
3. Why does carrying capacity have such an effect on a destination?
4. What are the themes of sustainable tourism?
5. What should sustainable tourism do according to the UNWTO?
6. What are some of the commandments of ecotourism?
7. What are the benefits of sustainable tourism?
8. What does the Foundation for Environmental Education (FEE) do?
9. What criteria do the Center for Sustainable Destinations use in their rating system?
10. Why is Maho Bay Resorts an excellent example of sustainable tourism?

CASE STUDY 6 Climate change and impacts on tourism – Outer Banks of North Carolina

This case study was written by David Edgell and Carolyn McCormick, who first met in 2006 and their mutual interest in researching sustainable tourism with respect to the Outer Banks began. After visiting the communities along the 115-mile stretch of coastline of the Outer Banks area by vehicle and later in an airplane, it became clear that the sustainability of the Outer Banks was in jeopardy. Edgell and McCormick decided to conduct some limited research to determine possible opportunities to mitigate some of the damage being perpetrated on the Outer Banks. The result was a paper titled "Climate Change and Tourism: The Case for the Coastline of the Outer Banks, North Carolina" presented at *The Coastal Society's 21st Biennial Conference*. The work continued after the conference, much of which is contained in this case study.[18]

* * *

The early work on this case study began in 2004. Carolyn E. McCormick, then managing director at the Outer Banks Visitors Bureau, had already noted a need for a better understanding of climate change. In 2006 she was appointed to the Climate Action Planning Advisory Group by the North Carolina Department of Environment and Natural Resources. An initial article "Climate and the Coast" by McCormick appeared in the September 2007 issue of *The Island Breeze*, a local newspaper. She stated: "It's important to understand that we [Outer Banks] are part of a national and international argument about climate change. We can't let others make the decisions without us." Later, on February 11, 2009, McCormick testified at the Oversight Hearing "Perspectives on the Outer Continental Shelf" in the US House of Representatives in which she stated the need for the preservation and protection of North Carolina's Outer Banks.

In 2003, Dr. David L. Edgell, Sr., Professor of tourism at East Carolina University, participated as a member of *National Geographic*'s Center for Sustainable Destinations panel of experts to rate 115 world destinations with respect to their sustainability. The results were published in the March 2004 issue of *National Geographic Traveler* magazine and the Outer Banks fell into the category called "Getting Ugly," which meant the destination had problems with respect to its sustainability but also that there was hope it could be corrected for the future. In 2005, Edgell received a National Oceanic and Atmospheric Administration North Carolina Sea Grant Award and produced a study, "Sustainable Tourism as an Economic Development Strategy for the Waterways and Coastline of North Carolina." By 2006, Edgell wrote a book, *Managing Sustainable Tourism: A Legacy for the Future*, which presented some policy prescriptions for orderly sustainable growth and development.

Characteristics of the North Carolina Outer Banks

The continued growth of international tourism over the past 60 years and increased dependence of national economies on tourism-generated revenues elevate the relevance – across all sectors of governance – of concerted policy analysis of tourism's complex interdependence with global climate change. With timely intervention, it is increasingly understood that sustainable tourism development can have an important role in the mitigation of climate change. Annually, one billion

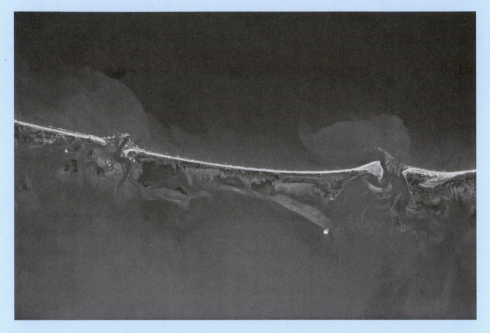

FIGURE 6.2 The fragile coastal landscape of Ocracoke Inlet in North Carolina's Outer Banks
(Photo: Image Science and Analysis Laboratory, NASA-Johnson Space Center,
"The Gateway to Astronaut Photography of Earth")

people travel internationally. Travel thrives on favorable conditions including health, safety, security . . . and weather. The impacts of climate change are rapidly becoming important factors in sustainable tourism. Regardless of whether climate change is human induced or a part of a natural cyclical trend, or for some other reason, social scientists in sustainable tourism need to act proactively and lead in creating innovative responses regarding projected changes in climate.

The changing global climate will pose profound policy challenges and demand strategic decisions from world leaders in coming decades. Climate variability has multiple dimensional impacts depending on the severity of the changes and the vulnerability of the area in question. Few sectors are more dependent on the outcome of changes in climate than tourism. For the future growth and sustainability of tourism in the United States and elsewhere in the world, policy responses to climate change are critical. This case study is geared to the impacts of climate change on tourism in the dynamic barrier islands known as the Outer Banks of North Carolina.

The Outer Banks is a tourism-based economy, hosting more than five million visitors a year, from more than 50 different countries – a leading sector in employment generation for the area. In the last decade, the Outer Banks has seen hundreds of ocean-front rental and second-home properties, and hospitality and tourism facilities fall victim to the sea; "nor'easters" (major storms), hurricanes, and sea-level rise, partly due to poor construction and location and partly due to over construction during the economic boom in the late 1990s, all contributed to a significant number of losses. For example just recently, in south Nags Head, North Carolina alone, some 40 vacation beach homes sit in peril of possible intense storms and rising sea levels; and, as a result, some are condemned for habitation and removed from revenue generating tax levies. This same phenomenon, but under differing conditions, is happening for similar coastal tourism destinations throughout the world. Thus, it is hoped that the research and analysis contained herein will shed some light on climate change that will be useful across a broad spectrum of countries, especially the Caribbean Islands, which have characteristics alike and analogous concerns as included in this case study.

Issues

"Largely as the result of growing concern about carbon emissions and resulting climate change, concern for the environment now occupies center stage in tourism."[19] Becken and Hay[20] state: "Climate change will not only impact on tourism directly by changes in temperature, extreme weather events and other climatic factors, but also indirectly as it will transform the natural environment that attracts tourists in the first place – for example, by accelerating coastal erosion, damaging coral reefs and other sensitive ecosystems and by reducing snowfall and snow cover in mountainous regions. It will also affect the basic services that are so critical for tourism, such as water supplies, especially during periods of peak demand." Dr. Patrick Long, director at the Center for Sustainable Tourism at East Carolina University suggests that "we need to further our knowledge about climate trends. . . . impacts of variability and seasonality . . . and the development of policies and strategies to adapt to and mitigate effects of climate change".[21] Former UNWTO Secretary General, Francesco Frangialli said in 2007, that those involved in the tourism industry "are part of the problem [global warming] and we will be part of the solution."

Until recently, limited research existed on the potential impact of climate change on specific tourism destinations in the United States. On January 17, 2011, the Associated Press article titled "Rising Sea Waters Threaten State's Delicate Coastline" stated, "A North Carolina science panel is predicting the sea level will raise by 1 meter by 2100." This report provided an up-to-date review of known facts about climate change relevant to the high-density tourist zone of the Outer Banks. It suggested the need for discussion of policy issues at the core of climate change decision-making with respect to the tourism industry. It also advocated research to help provide a policy agenda for climate change mitigation through sustainable tourism development and management in the United States and possibly elsewhere in the world.

Weather conditions and the climate of a tourism area often dictate why people travel, where they travel, how they travel, when they travel, and for how long visitors stay at the destination. What tourists want in their tourism products and destinations vary considerably. Generally visitors to beach areas are looking for sunshine and warm waters. Skiers and snowmobilers pray for good snow falls. Sightseers and outdoor recreationists hope for clear weather and moderate temperatures. The livelihoods of providers of visitor services at destinations are often dependent on a certain number of good weather days during the tourism season. Many tourism businesses have failed simply because of negative weather conditions. For many global destinations, now is the critical time to fashion a comprehensive tourism policy and strategic plan that looks to the future with respect to climate change. This case study regarding the Outer Banks falls into that category as well as, for example, the case study in Chapter 1 regarding the Republic of Maldives.

Variances in weather patterns due to climate change may have immediate repercussions on visitors. Forest fires destroy the flora and fauna of areas of interest to tourists. Hurricanes and tsunamis change coastlines and often wreak havoc on resort homes, destinations, and tourism services. Floods/droughts can decimate an area once dependent on tourism. All these concerns will determine the sustainability of tourism for the future.

Researcher Bill Birkemeier, Hydraulic Engineer at the US Army Corps of Engineers Field Engineer Research and Development Center on the Outer Banks said:

> Over the past twenty years there has been a slight rise in both sea temperatures and sea levels due to climate change. Because the Outer Banks are dynamic and ever changing, and since sea-level rise is at present small and gradual, relative to twice-daily tidal variation and surges caused by frequent storms, it is difficult to determine what changes on the coastline are due directly to sea-level rise. A more immediate concern would be whether climate change may increase the number or severity of storms on the coast as storms have a major impact on coastlines.[22]

It is time that global leaders aggressively address issues with respect to climate altercations on the tourism industry; otherwise the industry is left to its own devices to mitigate or adapt to the consequences of such changes. Edgell, Allen, Smith, and Swanson[23] state: "Tourism administrators must undertake a paradigm shift away from overuse of natural resources toward environmental stewardship. . . . Additionally, as global warming comes to the forefront in environmental concerns, tourism managers will need to stay attuned to forecast changes." Individual regions must address the impact of climate change on their specific tourism destinations. If nothing is done, the future growth and sustainability of tourism will be at risk. If tourism stakeholders, including governments and destination managers, do not define clear-cut policies and plans at this juncture in the growth of tourism, there may never be another chance.

The Outer Banks is home to the third largest estuary system in the world, the highest sand dunes on the East Coast of the United States, numerous beaches, wildlife preserves, and historical sites. Damage sustained by powerful storms erodes the beaches enjoyed by vacationers, as well as the land on which residences and hotels are built. Understanding effects of climate change on tourism in the Outer Banks is critical to travel decision-making, environmental stewardship, social evolution, and the economic viability of its travel and tourism industry. Government at all levels and the travel and tourism industry are now more cognizant of the need to address efforts to sustain natural and built resources under changing climate conditions. Given the complexity and breadth of the current science of climate change on the tourism industry increases the need for research to effectively develop action plans in coastal areas. This study addresses a limited range of climate change issues with respect to the Outer Banks tourism industry. However, this research may be useful in providing valuable information applicable to similar tourism destinations throughout the world.

Frameworks and ideas

While climate change is increasingly becoming an area of interest in academic research and industry applicability, it still remains a relatively new phenomenon within the mainstream of tourism.[24] According to the Intergovernmental Panel on Climate Change (a scientific body that, on a volunteer non-paid basis, contributes valuable research) there is agreement that a majority of scientists maintain that the world's climate is warming. What factors are causing this movement toward the changes in climate is an issue where there is considerable debate. Is it cyclical; is it caused by the actions of humans; is it endemic to the universe? Whatever the answer(s), climate change is proceeding at a rate in which there will be unavoidable impacts on the tourism industry. The economic impact alone from climate change on "beach recreation and tourism" is enormous on coastlines like that of the Outer Banks. The current understanding of how visitors and destinations respond to climate variability has not been adequately researched. In the meantime, until we have better data and research, the question remains of just how the tourism industries will address the issues raised in dealing with climate change in a rational matter. Mitigation policies or adaptation strategies and management actions will be an important part of any plan to reduce the impacts of climate change on the tourism industry.

The Outer Banks in jeopardy

The Outer Banks community must better understand that climate is changing and is having a serious impact on their coastal tourism and recreation economy. Local businesses and management authorities need to recognize the changes and make plans to adapt.[25] The rich complexity of the Outer Banks, a dynamic group of barrier islands and coastline, provides a strong platform for discussion of mitigating impacts of climate change. The Outer Banks tourism industry is particularly sensitive to climate, which can make or break the tourism businesses.[26] A comprehensive research study reporting on the impacts of climate change on fish and wildlife in North Carolina (an important contributor to the tourism experience), says, "Coastal wetlands are also highly vulnerable to sea level rise, and loss of this habitat has the potential to adversely affect a number of priority species" along the Outer Banks.[27] As properties in the barrier islands begin to disappear into the ocean, solutions become critical.

An article in *The Associated Press* (reproduced in *The Daily Reflector*, September 24, 2009) titled "Officials Cite Climate Change Threats in South" said that the US Fish and Wildlife Service (Service) "will try to save barrier islands, fight invasive species and work with companies to restore wildlife habitat as they confront the risks posed by climate change." Sam Hamilton, director of the US Fish and Wildlife Service said the Service "is on the forefront of climate change threats and that coastal wildlife refuges from North Carolina . . . are endangered. We're seeing sea level rise issues, coastal erosion issues; we're seeing a lot of the sea turtle nesting beaches are stressed and absolutely disappearing." Since unique floral and faunal diversity are reasons why many visitors vacation in the Outer Banks, federal, state, and local agencies are concerned about the critical nature of climate change. Several universities throughout North Carolina, and elsewhere across the country, are investigating the impact of weather and other factors of the *mise en scène* of the Outer Banks. One leader in this effort is the Center for Sustainable Tourism at East Carolina University. This Center has sponsored numerous events and conducted studies to investigate climate change in the Outer Banks.

New directions and opportunities

Studying climate change with respect to the Outer Banks is a connatural composite topic that is both controversial and often misunderstood. This lack of understanding, particularly with respect to many local residents, is largely due to limited information available. This exploratory, qualitative study has utilized a modified Delphi approach as the principal instrument of investigation. The reasoning for using this research method is that an analysis of the combined experiences of tourism executives, experts from the North Carolina Climate Action Plan Advisory Group, sustainable tourism advocates from the Center, climate scientists, renewable energy experts, and marine conservationists presents ample data and comments to evaluate and better understand the impact of climate change on the Outer Banks tourism industry.

In the application of a modified Delphi approach by the co-authors of this case study facts and opinions were obtained from a wide variety of persons and groups who have studied and confronted the climate change issues or were otherwise interested in climate change impacts on the Outer Banks. Some of the members represent scientific and technical fields and others include business persons in the travel and tourism industry. It takes into account scientific work conducted by the Outer Banks Field Research Facility, US Army Corps of Engineers, considered one of the finest national centers for measurements of coastal waters and climate change, as well as other research entities studying the Outer Banks coastal sustainability.

A first step in understanding the impact of climate change on tourism in the Outer Banks was to analyze the barrier islands and coastline. These dynamic coastal areas both retreat and accrete, with long-term consequences. They act as buffers to protect the interior of the coast. The co-authors of this study have a long association with the Outer Banks business and technical community and have had full access to the published research regarding climate change impacts on tourism in the Outer Banks. In addition, they made an aerial reconnaissance to review and better understand the dynamics of the coastal changes. They also walked or traveled by car along 115 miles of the 200-mile stretch of the Outer Banks, including the barrier islands, stopping along the way to gather additional personal comments and data from Outer Banks residents and visitors. Through discussions, interviews, meetings, and by other means, the authors accumulated a large amount of published and unpublished facts and intelligence sources used throughout this research study. It also includes data and information available from North Carolina's Climate Action Planning Advisory Group (see Appendix for membership). This research, combined with studies not necessarily directed toward the Outer Banks tourism, along with comments from knowledgeable tourism executives, was included in the study.

Once the information was gathered, synthesized, and prioritized, further discussions took place with stakeholders, researchers, academics and others to obtain a general consensus of the perceived results of climate change on the Outer Banks. One science panel predicted that the sea level will rise by 1m by 2100. For the Outer Banks that could mean more than 2,000 square miles and adjacent environs would be at considerable risk. Because this area contains some of the most expensive real estate in North Carolina, there could be a $7 billion shock to the residents. The Center for Sustainable Tourism and many other research entities are continuing to conduct additional surveys, gathering new information, and seeking to add additional dimensions to the study of climate change impacts on tourism in the Outer Banks.

Economic impacts and implications

Some visitors to this unique set of barrier islands represent generations of parents, children, and grandchildren over a long period of time. The beautiful environmental coastline is a major reason why five million visitors from more than 50 countries visit the Outer Banks each year. More than half of the leisure travelers to the Outer

Banks participate predominately in beach activities. However, the importance of natural settings, the history and heritage of the area, and wildlife experiences are becoming increasingly important in family vacations to the Outer Banks.

In North Carolina tourism is an $18 billion industry with employment at 200,000, and North Carolina's Outer Banks accounts for expenditures of more than $1 billion and 20,000 jobs. The visitors to the Outer Banks environs are most interested in the natural, cultural and historic resources; primarily the long stretch of beaches of the Outer Banks. The Outer Banks are truly "America's Beach;" free and open access chains of barrier islands off the northeastern coast of North Carolina. It is clear to those individuals who have studied and observed changes in the Outer Banks over a period of years that the sea is rising and shifts in these dynamic islands continue.

Near to the Outer Banks are many attractions such as the Fort Raleigh National Historic Site, birthplace of English-speaking America in 1587; Wright Brothers National Memorial, home of man's first powered flight in 1903; Cape Hatteras National Seashore, the nation's first national seashore established in 1937; Pea Island National Wildlife Refuge; and Alligator River National Wildlife Refuge; all are integral parts of visitor interest in the Outer Banks. Seventy percent of the dynamic barrier islands are owned by the people of the United States and managed by the United States Department of the Interior.

Climate change presents a special challenge to the Atlantic Ocean coastline of the Outer Banks. Weather and climate fluctuations in the Outer Banks region have tremendous impacts on the economic vitality of the area. Tourism is the most important economic activity for the Outer Banks, increasing economic development, realizing increased revenues, creating new jobs, benefiting from a diverse economy, adding new products, generating additional income, spawning new businesses, and contributing to overall economic integration. Economic success in tourism on the Outer Banks is measured by the ability to attract visitors' year around, not just during the more traditional tourist season. While climate change plays a major role in this industry, just the *perception* of weather conditions as presented by the media impacts heavily on the tourism decisions by visitors.

Vulnerabilities and new directions

As discussed previously in this case study, the Outer Banks are dynamic. The coastal zone of today is not permanent and will continue to change as it has in the past. It is the fragile fixed human infrastructure that can easily be destroyed by natural processes and climate change. This is a principal reason our coasts are in crisis. In addition, it is important to understand that the Outer Banks area is incredibly varied, with rivers, swamps, estuaries, marshes, barrier islands, inlets, beaches, and offshore shoals and rock. If the warming climate spawns more frequent and intense hurricanes and other storms, the future will see coastal erosion and associated loss of urban infrastructure, wetlands, and wildlife habitats. Despite the growing knowledge about and interest in climate change by a wide variety of interested parties, there appears to be a continuance of a "business as usual" attitude by many coastal destination managers. The question remains as to the best methods for communicating the impact of climate change with the local businesses and communities. Communication through emails, FAQ sheets, blogs, internet, university programs, governmental data, and community meetings are, in addition to research, ways in which scientists, both physical and social, can help the general public better understand climate change on tourism.

The negative effects of climate change on the Outer Banks have recently been exacerbated by the fact that so many new residents are moving into the area. Such a phenomenon means the area is being inundated by enormous amounts of infrastructure. This wreaks havoc on the natural environment and sets the stage for an even greater crisis as the climate changes. As the climate gets warmer and more frequent and intense storms take place, it becomes more difficult to evacuate tourists and residents during such crises. Since the barrier islands called the Outer Banks change and physically move as a result of the storms, what might have seemed possible to alleviate negative impacts one day may not work in the future. The implications from changes resulting from climate change can be mind-boggling. These concerns are a wake-up call for action. Citizens, businesspeople, and political leaders in the community must develop plans of action. Our children and grandchildren are dependent on community action today so they will be able to enjoy the beautiful Outer Banks tomorrow.

It is clear that climate change is a serious threat to humans, fish, and wildlife in the Outer Banks. In response to this threat, efforts to sustain natural resources under changing climate conditions must be forthcoming before it is too late. Otherwise the negative effects of climate change will decrease the quality-of-life for all concerned. Climate change is a complex set of situations and can be challenging to understand, but good communications, management, planning, and policies can move the community in a positive direction and alleviate some of the pressure on future climate change in the Outer Banks. This study confirms an urgency to develop policy guidelines and promote long-term planning to offset negative effects of climate change and move forward to conserve and protect resources for the future.

Consequences of climate change

As noted throughout this study, few industries are more dependent on an understanding of climate change than tourism. Tourists have many choices with respect to locations and activities and climate plays an important role. Today, travelers visit the internet to view the destination they are interested in and the weather reports for the area and then make a decision on where they want to spend their holiday.

Paradoxically, global climate change may not be totally negative to beach tourism; certain coastlines may be able to extend their seasons due to higher water and air temperatures. Regardless, the tourism industry must better understand the interactions of climate change and tourism and respond with responsible plans and policies. In the meantime, mitigation policies and actions to reduce greenhouse gas emissions that contribute to global warming must continue if the long-term impacts of climate change are to be manageable.

The Outer Banks of North Carolina, particularly the barrier islands, is disproportionately affected with respect to the climate change impacts on tourism and beachfront real estate. Beach erosion near vacation homes and businesses is already critical with, for example, more than 100 properties recently lost and 40 currently in peril along a few miles stretch of the beach. Loss of wildlife habitat (due to erosion and the increasingly close link between the land and near shore waters causing decreased water quality) is already at a critical stage. Climate changes affect the quality of the environment, the experience of tourists, wildlife, and the very sustainability of these barrier islands. The potential economic and social consequences could be devastating.

Policy strategies for the future

A key to resolving some of the issues with respect to climate change and tourism in the Outer Banks will be through positive tourism policies and careful planning for the long-term management of tourism resources. It is well-known that favorable weather conditions along the Outer Banks are a principal draw for tourists to choose the Outer Banks instead of many other destinations. Tourists have many choices with respect to locations and activities and climate plays an important role.

In the long-term, successful mitigation policies may stem the tide with respect to global warming and climate change. With respect to the present, we no longer have the luxury of debate. The impact of climate change on the Outer Banks is now and it is necessary to work toward immediate climate change adaptation strategies. Based on the research contained in this report, and after participating in many different meetings and planning sessions with stakeholders along the Outer Banks, the co-authors concluded that at the very least, a coordinated strategic plan to adapt to climate change should include the following guidelines:

- Assure maintenance of a safe and secure recreational environment
- Examine the need for beach restoration
- Study the need for hardened structures such as jetties, groins, and seawalls along coastlines
- Work toward sound policies for wildlife and habitat conservation
- Protect the history, heritage, and culture of the area

- Develop educational/awareness programs to explain climate change impacts
- Keep abreast of new research on climate trends
- Advocate good waterway and coastal management practices
- Regularly check the health of ecosystems
- Provide developers and agencies with risk assessments to guide development
- Encourage communications and coordination amongst all interested parties
- Review opportunities for resource savings with respect to energy
- Improve data collection and share results with local, state, and national offices
- Be willing to help develop, monitor, and test climate change models

While discussions and controversy about climate change may arise over how best to utilize these guidelines or to make other changes, businesses, developers, tourists, local communities, state and federal agencies, not-for-profit entities, and educational institutions all have a stake in working together toward a healthy, safe, and well-managed coastal environment. If it is not understood now, the stakeholders and community will lose in the future. The Outer Banks waterways and coastline is an excellent but fragile laboratory to study climate change and to convince those engaged in coastline activity that now is the critical time for action. It is clear from the research in this report that climate change and rising water levels could have a tremendous and devastating impact on tourism in the Outer Banks. Researchers, businesses, and government agencies in the Outer Banks are only recently cooperating more and developing strategies and new ideas to respond to climate change and storm severity. Tourism stakeholders are beginning to understand the need for long-term management of resources and to seek solutions in order to cope with the impact of climate change on tourism in the future.

In summary, the issue of climate change, and its impact on tourism, is being researched as a potential local security threat to the beautiful Outer Banks area that welcomes millions of visitors each year. These visitors arrive by carbon-spewing automobiles. They use up energy resources and trample about on natural environments. They don't always understand that their actions have a major bearing on the future sustainability of the area. The question is how to find the right balance such that the visitor has a positive experience and, at the same time, the area is not desecrated and the local community is able to maintain a quality lifestyle for its citizens. One hope is that lessons being learned about climate change are implemented by knowledgeable professionals – through sustainable tourism policies and strategic planning – to provide leadership and management for making a difference for the future.[28] The ultimate goal is to preserve the Outer Banks such that future generations of visitors can enjoy their vacation, local residents will have better quality-of-life, and natural resources and wildlife will be conserved and protected.

Concluding critical questions

The debate about climate change need not focus on whether climate is changing, but rather how to prepare the communities in sensitive environments for the future. How will native plant and animal species be protected? How will the community's way of life, with close ties to the natural environment, be protected? If the environment declines and fewer travelers visit the area, how will the economy suffer? If the heat becomes more intense, how will public health be at risk, especially that of children and the elderly? These are all issues for discussion.

While this case study shows some of the direct negative effects of climate change, some may wish to take alternative approaches to thinking about the issue. What sort of opportunities might climate change present for destinations? If the beaches were to erode, what might tourism look like in the future? How might that change demand for inland destinations? Much of the concern about protecting the beaches in coastal communities has more to do with protecting the built assets. How much of the debate is about protecting the natural resources versus the built environment? If the natural versus the built environment are two sides of the climate change debate, which side is better prepared with fact-based information to make a stronger argument to policymakers?

Appendix to Chapter 6 case study

North Carolina Climate Action Planning Advisory Group – members

Stan Adams, *NC DENR, Division of Forestry Resources (now retired, but active)*
Dan Besse, *Winston-Salem City Council*
Ryan Boyles, *State Climatologist, NC Climate Office*
Thomas F. Cecich, *Environmental Management Commission*
Caroline Choi, *Progress Energy*
Jerry Coker, *Weyerhaeuser*
Marion Deerhake, *Environmental Management Commission*
Dolores M. Eggers, *Professor, UNC Asheville*
Roy Ericson, *NC Utilities Commission*
George Everett, *Duke Energy*
George Givens, *Principal Legislative Analyst, Attorney at Law, General Assembly of North Carolina, Council to the Environmental Review Commission of the General Assembly of North Carolina and the Legislative Commission on Global Climate Change*
Dennis Grady, *Appalachian State University*
Steve Halstead, *NC Council of Churches*
Bob Hazel, *Senior Citizens' Interest*
Dennis Hazel, *NCSU, Forestry Extension*

Alex Hobbs, *NCSU Solar Center*

Bill Holman, *Clean Water Management Trust Fund, Duke University, Nicholas Institute for Environmental Policy Solutions*

Preston Howard, *Manufacturer Chemical Industry Council*

Gary Hunt, *NC DENR Division of Pollution Prevention and Sustainability*

Robert Jackson, *Duke University, Nicholas School of the Environment and Earth Sciences*

Robert Koger, *Advanced Energy*

Carolyn E. McCormick, *former CEO Outer Banks Visitors Bureau*

Steven McNulty, *USDA Forest Service, Southern Global Change Program*

Maximilian Merrill, *NC Department of Agriculture and Consumer Services*

Marily Nixon, *Southern Environmental Law Center*

Chuck Pickering, *Biltmore Estate*

Simon Rich, *Energy Industry & Duke University*

Lisa Riegel, *NC Natural Heritage Trust Fund*

Roger Sheats, *Global Warming Initiatives*

Paul Sherman, *NC Farm Bureau (replaced Mitch Peele)*

Larry Shirley, *State Energy Office, NC Department of Administration*

Michael Shore, *Environmental Defense*

Bob Slocum, *North Carolina Forestry Association*

Libby Smith, *NC Department of Commerce*

Stephen Smith, *Southern Alliance for Clean Energy*

Jim Stephenson, *NC Coastal Federation*

Nina S. Szlosberg, *NC Board of Transportation*

Tim Toben, *Carolina Green Energy*

Ivan Urlaub, *NC Sustainable Energy Association*

Kraig Westerbeek, *Murphy-Brown Farms*

Stephen Whitfield, *NC Woodlands*

Jim Witkowski, *International Paper (replaced Edward Kruel)*

Skip Yeakel, *Volvo Trucks North America*

Notes

1 Edgell, Sr., David L., Swanson, Jason R., DelMastro Allen, Maria, & Smith, Ginger (2008) *Tourism Policy and Planning: Yesterday, Today and Tomorrow.* Oxford: Elsevier, 1.

2 Edgell, Sr. David L. (2006) *Managing Sustainable Tourism: A Legacy for the Future.* New York: The Haworth Hospitality Press.

3 Edgell, Sr., David L. (2005) "Sustainable Tourism as an Economic Development Strategy Along Coastlines." A North Carolina Sea Grant Study, Greenville, NC, September 30, 2005.

4 Edgell (2006) p.4.

5 *Center for Sustainable Tourism* (2011) East Carolina University, Greenville, North Carolina, page 2.

6   McCool, Stephen F. & Moisey, Neil (eds) (2008) *Tourism, Recreation and Sustainability*, 2nd edn. Cambridge, MA: CABI International.

7   Edgell, Sr., David L. (1995) "The Organization of American States Sustainable Tourism Development Policy and Planning Guide." Department of Regional Development and Environment, Organization of American States, Washington, DC.

8   United Nations World Tourism Organization (2005).

9   World Travel and Tourism Council (2003) *Blueprint for New Tourism.* Oxford: WTTC.

10 Goeldner, Charles R. & Ritchie, J.R. Brent (2012) *Tourism: Principles, Practices, Philosophies*, 12th edn. Hoboken, NJ: John Wiley & Sons, Inc., p. 382.

11 Becken, Susanne & Hay, John E. (2007) *Tourism and Climate Change: Risks and Opportunities.* Clevedon, UK: Channel View Publications, page xvii.

12 Personal interview, 2012.

13 Goeldner, Charles R. & Ritchie, J. R. Brent (2009) *Tourism: Principles, Practices, Philosophies*, 11th edn. Hoboken, NJ: John Wiley & Sons, Inc.

14 Edgell, Sr., David L. & McCormick, Carolyn E. (2008) "Climate Change and Tourism: The Case for the Coastline of the Outer Banks, North Carolina" included in *The Coastal Society 2008 Conference* document, Redondo Beach, California.

15 Goeldner & Ritchie (2012), p. 382.

16 Symko, Christina and Harris, Rob (2002) "Making Paradise Last: Maho Bay Resorts." In Rob Harris, Tony Griffin and Peter Williams (eds) *Sustainable Tourism: A Global Perspective.* New York: Butterworth-Heinemann.

17 Miller, Joseph A. (ed.) (1996) "The Ecotourism Equation: Measuring the Impacts." Yale University Bulletin Series Number 99, New Haven, CT.

18 For readers interested in a technical discussion of the North Carolina barrier islands, aside from the tourism issues, read *The Battle for North Carolina's Coast* by Stanley R. Riggs, Dorothea V. Ames, Stephen J. Culver, & David J. Mallinson, The University of North Carolina Press, Chapel Hill, North Carolina, 2011.

19 Goeldner & Ritchie (2009).

20 Becken & Hay (2007), page xvii.

21 Edgell & McCormick (2008).

22 Edgell et al (2008), page 351.

23 Becken, Susanne & Viner, David (2003) "Climate Change Mitigation Policies and the Global Tourism Industry." *Climate Change Management*, December 12.

24 Riggs, S.R., Culver, S.J., Ames, D.V., Mallison, D.J., Corbett, D.R., & Walsh, J.P. (October 2008) "North Carolina's Coasts in Crisis: A Vision for the Future", East Carolina University, Greenville, North Carolina.

25 Curtis, Scott, Arrigo, Jennifer, Long, Patrick, & Covington, Ryan (2009) "Climate, Weather and Tourism: Bridging Science and Practice." Center for Sustainable Tourism, Greenville, North Carolina.

26 DeWan, Amielle, Dubois, Natalie, Theoharides, Kathleen, & Boshoven, Judith (2010) *Understanding the Impacts of Climate Change on Fish and Wildlife in North Carolina.* Washington, DC: Defenders of Wildlife.

27 Edgell & McCormick (2008).

CHAPTER

7

Barriers and obstacles to international travel

Countries and communities establish tourism policies, such as hotel occupancy tax legislation and tourism sustainability regulations, to create programs that entice visitors and to protect tourism resources. However, policymakers must be aware of the negative effects when establishing laws and regulations that might also impede travel to the destination. The negative effects of public policies on tourism are easily illustrated with an example from Egypt's tourism policies in the previous decade. Despite Egypt's relatively high position in global tourism market share, as presented in the 2007 World Travel and Tourism Council (WTTC) Economic Research, the nation ranked 66th in the *2008 Travel and Tourism Competitiveness Report* published by the World Economic Forum. The gap in competitiveness was attributed to environmental policies, infrastructure developments, and investments in human resources.[1] Many of the current border control policies in the United States have also created barriers to international outbound and inbound travel.

Policies that are barriers and obstacles to international travel often have a primary focus on areas other than tourism. International tourist visa requirements and regulations to lower carbon emissions are examples of policies that are primarily focused on border control and climate change, respectively, but can have a negative effect on tourism. In these instances, the consequences on tourism are not the primary concern and many policymakers may not consider the ramifications on international visitation until several years after policies are established. Implementing tourism policy analysis programs, as described in Chapter 8, could highlight the potential negative consequences that some policies may have on tourism.

This chapter describes important impediments to international travel common to many countries. Barriers and obstacles to international travel affect not only the consumer, but also businesses looking to expand their service offerings in foreign countries. Common impediments include visa and passport requirements, travel allowance restrictions, duty-free allowances, travel delays and inconveniences, use of credit cards abroad, increasing travel costs, foreign currency exchange, and other barriers and obstacles. The chapter concludes with a presentation of tactics to remove international travel impediments. Removing barriers and obstacles to international travel will facilitate continued growth in global travel and tourism. Those nations and local communities that confront international travel impediments with the intent to mitigate barriers and obstacles should enjoy more competitive success in the global travel arena.

Visa and passport requirements

Nations require their citizens and visitors to have proper documentation, in the form of passports and visas, to travel across borders. A passport is issued by the traveler's national government and provides a standard form to identify the traveler by name, age, gender, nationality, place of birth, photograph, and in more and more instances, biometric data. The passport itself does not allow the holder to enter a foreign land. Clearance to enter into another country for a specified period of time and to specific geographic locations is granted in the form of a visa. Applying for a visa in advance of the traveler's arrival allows time for the host country to scrutinize the traveler's circumstances related to their financial security, health, and propensity to return to their homeland. Some countries require its visitors to deposit relatively large sums of money in non-interest-bearing escrow accounts before travel begins. This will entice visitors to return to their home country and not settle in the host country illegally.

A 2011 survey conducted by Henley & Partners, a global law firm specializing in international residence and citizenship planning, ranked nations by the visa-free access its citizens have to other countries.[2] Citizens of Denmark, Germany, the United Kingdom, Belgium, Japan, the United States, Austria, Switzerland, Singapore, South Korea, and Malaysia enjoy visa-free access to more than 150 countries. At the opposite end of the spectrum, residents of Iran, Nepal, Lebanon, Pakistan, and Afghanistan can travel visa-free to less than 40 countries and territories.

Some countries maintain stricter border control policies than others. Malaysia, for example, requires foreign travelers to present a passport when traveling between the states of Sabah and Sarawak in the eastern part of the country. International travelers going from Macau or Hong Kong to Mainland China also must present a passport at immigration control points within the country. On the other extreme, nations within the area covered by the Schengen Agreement have open border arrangements with each other. The Schengen Agreement is a 1985 treaty among some of the nations of the European Community that created a borderless zone currently consisting of 22 European Union countries, as well as Iceland, Norway, and Switzerland. Ireland and the United Kingdom have chosen not to abide by the Schengen Agreement and control their borders.

Some countries may require its citizens to obtain an exit visa when traveling from their homeland. Nepal requires citizens to present a labor permit if they are leaving the country to work in another country. Similarly, the Cuban government issues a "white card" to its citizens hoping to travel internationally. While not exactly, an exit visa, citizens of the United States traveling to Cuba must obtain a special license from the US Department of Treasury's Office of Foreign Assets Control, which authorizes travelers to visit the Caribbean nation and allows them to spend money there. Much of the time, exit visas are a means for a nation to control its own citizens and requirements for exit visas can change over time as the political situations of nations change. For example, in the years after World War I and leading up to the end of World War II, the governments of Italy and Nazi Germany required visas for anyone leaving the countries.

Most nations offer the citizens of some countries the opportunity to visit the country for tourism purposes without obtaining a visa. Entrance visas, exit visas, and passport controls can be a tremendous obstacle of international travel, even if only perceived as a barrier by the traveler. Visitation data shown in Chapter 4 indicate that countries with higher rates of visitation are also those with more liberalized visa and passport requirements for its citizens and visitors. To compare and contrast policies in various nations, the following list briefly summarizes the visa requirements for seven nations from various major global regions. To remain current on the latest visa and passport requirements, readers should consult the proper foreign affairs agency of each country or use the database featured by the International Air Transport Association at www.iatatravelcentre.com.

Australia

Australia requires visas for all visitors; however, the process to obtain a visa is relatively easy for citizens of most countries. For stays of less than 30 days, most travelers can obtain a visa online. The visa is electronically tied to the traveler's passport and is accessible by travel agents, airline agents, and border agents. Australia also provides Working Holiday Maker visas for travelers who are 18 to 30 years old, staying in the country for up to 12 years, and who want to find casual employment.

Brazil

Visas, if required, are valid for 90 days. Brazil offers reciprocity to citizens of countries that do not require a visa for its nationals. For example, most European Union countries allow Brazilian citizens to enter their borders without a visa and thus, Brazil offers the same courtesy to citizens of those EU nations. The fee for Brazilian visas is also reciprocal and charges the United States, as an example, a $100 visa fee because that is what the United States charges Brazilian nationals to obtain a US visa. An exit card is also required for travelers to Brazil, the loss of which results in a fine and delays.

Czech Republic

Citizens of European Economic Area countries and European Union countries are not required to have a visa to visit the Czech Republic. Visas must be obtained in advance by nationals of all countries except citizens of the United States, Switzerland, New Zealand, Japan, Israel, Canada, and Australia, who can stay in the country for up to 90 days without a visa.

Egypt

Only passport holders from Macau, Hong Kong, and Guinea can enter Egypt without a visa. Citizens of all Arab countries, Australia, New Zealand, Japan, South Korea, the United Kingdom, and the United States can obtain a visa upon arrival at an airport. All other nationalities must obtain a visa prior to arrival. Israelis must be guaranteed by an Egyptian Travel Agency if trying to attain a visa at the border or else get a visa at the Egyptian embassy in Israel prior to arrival.

Israel

Entering Israel is generally possible with only a passport as visas are issued for most travelers at the border. Exceptions exist for individuals from most African countries, Central American nations, and some of the former Soviet republics who are required to have a visa prior to arrival. Israeli tourism authorities recommend if a traveler is visiting Israel and then going to an Arab country that the Israeli stamp should not be put in the passport.

Italy

Italy requires a tourist visa for residents of countries in the Middle East, but citizens of most other countries can enter with only a passport. The country offers many types of visas including student, business, medical treatment, and adoption.

Poland

For up to three months, visitors to Poland do not need a visa, as possession of a passport is the only requirement to enter the country. Some countries in the European Union are freely allowed to enter Poland without a passport.

Duty-free allowances

Duty is a tax associated with customs. When goods are imported into a country, the importer – be it an individual traveler or an import/export company – must pay duty on those goods. Individuals traveling as tourists are typically offered an exemption and are allowed to import some gifts and goods for personal consumption duty-free. However, most countries place a limit on the value travelers may import without having to pay duty. For example, international visitors to South Africa can import goods worth no more than R5,000 (approximately US$600) without paying import duties on the goods they bring into the country.

There is a wide variance and lack of uniformity in duty-free allowances among nations. The World Customs Organization is an intergovernmental organization based in Brussels that strives to help nations develop policies by offering best-practice advice and consultation. The organization has set standards to help countries facilitate travel by normalizing duty-free allowances. However, several countries set duty-free allowances lower than the standards set by the World Customs Organization. The duty-free allowance can be an obstacle to international travel because a low allowance may increase the costs for travelers and lower the competitiveness of the nation relative to other nations that may offer a lower travel alternative.

Travel delays and inconveniences

Inconveniences leading to travel delays can come in many forms. For some travelers, the mere processes of traveling – transferring to the airport or rail station, dealing with long waits, planning travel, or traveling with small children or elderly relatives – may be the most cumbersome aspects of international travel. However, government policies can lead to significant travel delays and inconveniences. Government policies can also work to alleviate some of the delays caused by inconvenient travel situations. While travel delays and inconveniences can result from myriad causes, three leading travel delays and inconveniences related to international travel are obtaining visas, flight delays, and security processing.

One of the major inconveniences and causes of delays when traveling inter-nationally is obtaining the necessary visas. As described earlier in this chapter, most nations require at least some of their visitors (depending on the visitor's nationality) to acquire a visa to enter the country. Obtaining the visas can be a source of frustration for many travelers and can lead to competitive disadvantages for host nations. Visas are typically obtained at the destination country's embassy within the home country of the person who is traveling. For example, a Brazilian living in Macapá, a city in the north, who wishes to travel to the United States, must travel from her home city to the capital city of Brasília to visit the embassy and begin the formal visa application process. The process can take weeks and may not be successful. During visa processing, travelers may not be able to purchase airfare or make other travel arrangements.

Increasing travel costs

Perhaps the most obvious barrier and obstacle to international travel for most travelers may be the recent rise in cost to travel to international destinations. The rising price of oil, the global economic downturn, and the depreciation of the

American dollar are partial causes of increasing travel costs. As the price of oil has risen, so has the cost of travel.

In what may be a downward spiral, some of the increases in international travel prices may be attributable to the downward slide of the global economy. According to the OECD, the global economy has caused, in part, a decline in countries being able to offer aid to other countries and may be adding to the slow pace of economic recovery. To combat this decrease in demand, some travel suppliers have reduced their services. For example, to control variable costs, most international airlines have limited in-flight food services or eliminated blankets, pillows, and other amenities that add weight to aircraft and increase fuel usage. Because businesses such as airlines and hotels have low variable costs relative to their fixed costs, prices may have to be increased to cover the high fixed costs of long-term assets, such as hotels and airplanes.

Some of the increase in costs is because of the depreciation of the American dollar. However, that is good for those looking to purchase American dollars – international visitors to the United States but bad for Americans wishing to travel abroad. With higher costs to travel internationally, more travelers are staying closer to home, thus leading to an increase in domestic travel for many nations.

Other barriers and obstacles

International travelers may confront other policy issues that create obstacles to their tourism experiences abroad. Other obstacles could include destinations giving preference to business travelers over leisure travelers, as business travel may be seen as more necessary than leisure travel. Requiring an exit visa could be another burdensome policy. In some countries, taxes on foreign travel (e.g. exit visas) are designed to encourage citizens to travel domestically rather than internationally. This increase in travel costs can rob some travelers of rich international cultural exchanges. As another example, some nations give foreign tourists a preferential exchange rate or discounted prices at attractions or hotels, which can lead to increased prices for community residents and a wider tourist/local divide.

Impediments to businesses providing travel services

The bulk of the discussion to this point in the chapter has described the barriers to travel for individual consumers. As noted in Chapter 1, several types of firms, many of them small businesses, make up the travel landscape. A variety of policies govern these businesses in each country in which these companies do business. Travel impediments should also be considered from the viewpoint of private-sector businesses that serve travelers across borders, such as tour operators, travel agents, and transportation companies.

Many countries require travel-related companies to be licensed. Licensing and other requirements for travel-related businesses vary among countries and types of businesses. To be registered as a travel agent in Singapore, for example, business owners must register their agency with the Accounting & Corporate Regulatory Authority, maintain a cash reserve of at least S$100,000 (approximately US$80,000), nominate a key executive of the agency to be approved by the Singapore Tourism Board, and maintain a physical office used solely for the travel agent business. Tour operators running tours in Belize must submit letters of recommendation from members of the tourism community, two photographs of the physical place of the business, police record of the owner, statement of financial solvency, names and nationalities of all employees, a brochure of the firm's services, and the company's emergency plan as part of the application. Regulations covering the licensing of taxi operators in the Port of Mombasa are governed by the Kenya Ports Authority and require the applicant to submit two reference letters, proof of insurance and vehicle registration, and a fee of roughly KSh12,300 (approximately US$140). Regulations for taxis operating outside of the port differ.

The purpose of most regulations such as these examples is consumer protection as government licenses are designed to ensure travel companies deliver services as promised in a customer-oriented, safe, and financially-responsible way. However, protecting the consumer can, at times, slow down or limit travel for the consumer. As Cartwright[3] states:

> [W]e need to consider the relationship between consumer protection and the market economy. It is sometimes argued that the state, through the law, should play only a restricted role in protecting consumers, because consumer protection is most effectively achieved by the operation of free and open markets. Law should be used to ensure that the markets function as freely as possible. Where markets do not work perfectly, the law should intervene to address this failure, provided this can be done cost effectively.

The license process in many countries may be slow and cause undue delays that lead to limited competition or disruptions in service. Because tourism is international commerce, objective standards across nations should be created to regulate the services of private-sector firms involved in travel services. Companies doing business in a foreign country may face additional barriers as governments put policies in place to protect domestic companies. For example, some countries do not allow foreign private-sector companies to operate a local office, thereby restricting competition with the nation's tourism promotion agency.

Obstacles to air travel

Air transportation, particularly related to long-haul or trans-ocean travel, is critical for international visitation. Other than the increasing costs of travel, as previously described, and the myriad of government policies that affect air transportation, aspects of air travel itself and its associated policy should be discussed in the same light as barriers to travel resulting from the policies of governments. Impediments to air travel found throughout the globe include flight delays, overcrowding at the airport, air traffic congestion, and slow security lines. Governments, consumers, and the airline industry must work together to find inventive solutions to mitigate the barriers to international air travel. Some nations are working to reduce barriers in air travel.

Tactics to remove barriers and obstacles to international travel

Obstacles to international travel often arise because of a problem among two or more nations. Therefore, international tourism agreements, as described in Chapter 2 and Chapter 5, are critical to remove barriers. Often, the challenges that complicate international tourism involve many nations and can take delicate diplomatic measures and multi-lateral policy. The intergovernmental bodies, such as the UNWTO, OECD, and others described throughout this book, work tirelessly to combat obstacles that impede international travel. The key to managing barriers to travel lies in governments' understanding of the positive contributions of tourism on their local communities and the complex nature of the global tourism system.

CHAPTER REVIEW QUESTIONS

1. What are some barriers to international travel?
2. What did the Schengen Agreement do?
3. Provide some examples of countries and their visa and passport policies.
4. Explain duty free allowances.
5. What sort of issues cause travel delays or inconveniences?
6. What are some reasons behind increasing travel costs?
7. What are some impediments to businesses providing travel services? Why do these impediments exist?
8. How have barriers to international travel been dealt with?

CASE STUDY 7 Similarities and differences among nations' travel advisories

This case study was written by Dr. Jason Swanson as a simple illustration of how governments can be directly involved with mitigating some barriers and obstacles to international travel. While the case study focuses on activities of the governments of Australia, Canada, and the United Kingdom; the examples in the case study would be similar to those from other countries as well.

* * *

Governments issue travel advisories to their citizens when unstable or unsafe conditions in another nation warrant the recommendation to avoid travel to the unstable area. Unsafe conditions can include not only threats to personal safety because of war or crime, but could also result from sickness and disease epidemics or natural disasters present in the destination country. Another example of when a government may issue a travel warning is when the home nation's ability to assist its citizens abroad is limited by, for example, the closing of an embassy or consulate in a particular area. For most countries, the travel advisory is just that – a recommendation. It is up to the individual to make an informed decision about their personal safety while traveling abroad.

In Australia, the Department of Foreign Affairs and Trade is responsible for issuing travel advisories. In the United Kingdom, the agency charged with issuing travel advisories is known as the Foreign and Commonwealth Office. The government of Canada offers an extremely user-friendly website that provides not only travel advisories but advice for those traveling while pregnant, real-time waiting times at border crossings, and helpful tips about packing carry-on bags, among other useful information. This helpful interface is not surprising considering the proactive nature in which the Canadian government approaches all aspects of tourism policy. These three countries – Australia, Canada, and the United Kingdom – are the subject of this case study that compares and contrasts policies related to travel advisories.

Travel advisories can be a major obstacle to travel for many travelers. For example, consider an Australian family with December holiday plans to visit the beautiful beaches of Phuket in southern Thailand. In November 2012, the Australian government issued new warnings urging its citizens to exercise a high-degree of caution when traveling to Thailand due to the threat of a terrorist attack. The threat was particularly strong in the Yala, Pattani, Narathiwat, and Songkhla provinces, which are roughly 150 miles (240 km) southeast of Phuket. While not an outright recommendation to avoid all travel to the area, the family must decide if carrying out the vacation they have planned and partially paid for is worth the risk. They must also consider the risks of being within fairly close proximity to potential threats. Will 150 miles be far enough to keep them out of harm's way if an attack was to occur in the Narathiwat province? Or if an attack was to occur anywhere in the country, how would their vacation travel be affected even in safer areas of Phuket or Bangkok?

One way to mitigate this risk is through travel insurance, although in most cases, travel insurance carriers are not obliged to make refunds based on travel advisories. Of course, it is not the travel advisory itself that is a nuisance. The real nuisance is what leads to the travel advisory, which is the threat of terrorism. However, the Australian family must weigh that threat against the images of the destination put forth in official travel marketing, as well as in the positive experiences they may hear from others about the friendly and hospitable people in Thailand, as shown in Figure 7.1.

Looking at a few of the travel advisories from Australia, Canada, and the United Kingdom can reveal some of the similarities and differences among tourism policies across nations. Table 7.1 summarizes the travel advisories from these countries covering selected international destinations.

As shown in Table 7.1, some global destinations are saddled with strong warnings against travel to the country. For example, Libya, Niger, and Afghanistan are listed as places that are recommended for Australian, Canadian, and British

FIGURE 7.1 Peacefulness and hospitality is often exhibited by people in Thailand (Photo: Jason R. Swanson)

TABLE 7.1 Example Travel Advisories (as of January 2013)

Destination	Australia Advisory	Canada Advisory	United Kingdom Advisory
Afghanistan	Do not travel	Avoid all travel	Advise against all travel to parts
Algeria	Reconsider your need to travel	Exercise a high degree of caution	Advise against all but essential travel to parts
Angola	Exercise a high degree of caution	Exercise a high degree of caution	Advise against all but essential travel to parts
Armenia	Exercise normal safety precautions	Exercise a high degree of caution	Advise against all but essential travel to parts
Azerbaijan	Exercise normal safety precautions	Exercise a high degree of caution	Advise against all travel to parts
Bangladesh	Exercise a high degree of caution	Exercise a high degree of caution	Advise against all but essential travel to parts
Burkina Faso	Reconsider your need to travel	Exercise a high degree of caution	Advise against all travel to parts
Burundi	Reconsider your need to travel	Avoid non-essential travel	Advise against all travel to parts
Cambodia	Exercise normal safety precautions	Exercise a high degree of caution	Advise against all travel to parts
Central African Rep.	Do not travel	Avoid all travel	Advise against all travel to parts
Chad	Do not travel	Avoid all travel	Advise against all travel to parts
Côte d'Ivoire	Reconsider your need to travel	Exercise a high degree of caution	Advise against all but essential travel to parts
Eritrea	Reconsider your need to travel	Avoid non-essential travel	Advise against all travel to parts
Haiti	Reconsider your need to travel	Exercise a high degree of caution	Advise against all travel to parts
India	Exercise a high degree of caution	Exercise a high degree of caution	Advise against all travel to parts
Iran	Reconsider your need to travel	Avoid all travel	Advise against all travel
Iraq	Do not travel	Avoid all travel	Advise against all but essential travel to parts
Israel	Exercise a high degree of caution	Exercise a high degree of caution	Advise against all travel to parts
Japan	Exercise normal safety precautions	Exercise normal security precautions	Advise against all travel to parts

continued . . .

TABLE 7.1 . . . *continued*

Destination	Australia Advisory	Canada Advisory	United Kingdom Advisory
Lebanon	Reconsider your need to travel	Avoid non-essential travel	Advise against all travel to parts
Liberia	Reconsider your need to travel	Exercise a high degree of caution	Advise against all but essential travel to parts
Libya	Do not travel	Avoid non-essential travel	Advise against all travel to parts
Mali	Do not travel	Avoid all travel	Advise against all travel
Mauritania	Reconsider your need to travel	Avoid non-essential travel	Advise against all travel to parts
Mexico	Exercise a high degree of caution	Exercise a high degree of caution	Advise against all but essential travel to parts
Niger	Do not travel	Avoid all travel	Advise against all travel to parts
Nigeria	Reconsider your need to travel	Avoid non-essential travel	Advise against all travel to parts
Pakistan	Reconsider your need to travel	Avoid non-essential travel	Advise against all travel to parts
Rwanda	Exercise a high degree of caution	Exercise a high degree of caution	Advise against all but essential travel to parts
South Sudan	Do not travel	Avoid all travel	Advise against all travel to parts
Turkey	Exercise a high degree of caution	Exercise a high degree of caution	Advise against all but essential travel to parts
Uganda	Exercise a high degree of caution	Exercise a high degree of caution	Advise against all travel to parts
Uzbekistan	Exercise a high degree of caution	Exercise a high degree of caution	Advise against all but essential travel to parts
Venezuela	Exercise a high degree of caution	Exercise a high degree of caution	Advise against all travel to parts

Sources: http://www.smartraveller.gov.au/z1/4v-cgi/view/Advice/Index (Australia);
http://travel.gc.ca/travelling/advisories (Canada);
http://www.fco.gov.uk/en/travel-and-living-abroad/travel-advice-by-country/(United Kingdom)

citizens to avoid – if not avoiding the whole of the country then at least some parts of the countries. As of the beginning of 2013, the West African, landlocked nation of Mali was the only country to which travel to all parts should be avoided. This warning resulted from a state-of-emergency declared by the Mali government following rising tensions among various ethnic groups. Not only are citizens asked to avoid traveling to Mali, but they are also being advised to travel from Mali, or leave, for their own safety.

At times the travel advisories issued by one nation may not correspond with advisories issued by other nations. The travel advisories for Azerbaijan issued by Australia, Canada, and the United Kingdom are examples of such differences. Australia has advised its citizens to "exercise normal safety precautions" when traveling to Azerbaijan. Canadians are warned to "exercise a high degree of caution", while British citizens are encouraged to avoid all travel to parts of Azerbaijan. Looking deeper into the lighter Canadian and Australian warnings would uncover stronger advice on which parts of the country to avoid and when traveling in the major cities to act with normal vigilance to avoid the attacks on foreigners, such as pickpocketing and muggings, that typically occur.

Japan offers another example of the difference in the sternness of travel warnings. While British citizens are advised to not travel to certain parts of the country, Canadians and Australians are encouraged to exercise normal safety precautions. The British government is concerned with the aftermath of the earthquake and tsunami from March 2011 and the potential catastrophic impact on the Fukushima Daiichi Nuclear Power Plant. In this case, these threats are viewed as being less serious by the governments of Canada and Australia. The British advisory about Japan continues on to mention other reasons why citizens should avoid travel to certain parts of the country. Additional reasons include the launching of a satellite by North Korea that could lead to reactionary measures by neighboring countries, occasional pro-nationalist and anti-western demonstrations, the regular typhoon season, and a low threat of terrorism.

Although differences among issuing nations exist, travel warnings are set with some consistency among the sample of nations included in this case study. In Canada, the Consular Services' Travel Information Program team is responsible for collecting reports on security issues from around the globe and from a variety of sources. Sources can include nationals living abroad, diplomatic staff reporting from embassies and consulates, and other military or civilian intelligence gathering services. Nations such as Australia, Canada, the United Kingdom, and others may also share and coordinate data about possible threats to safety. While ultimately working to protect the general public, providing the most reliable travel advisories help minimize barriers and obstacles to international travel.

Concluding critical questions

As stated in the case study, the advisory itself is not the root cause of the barrier to travel associated with a travel warning. However, if not issued with the primary goal of protecting the people of a nation, a travel advisory may create undue stress for international travel. This leads to the questions: Can travel advisories be used by nations as a political weapon against another country? What could be some of the consequences on international travel if travel advisories were used as a political weapon? A larger research question could involve determining the impact that travel advisories have on travel to and tourism demand in destinations that have had travel advisories issued against them. A similar research question could involve a survey of a nation's citizens to determine how much importance they place on their home country's international travel advisories when planning international travel.

With the two examples of Azerbaijan and Japan showing differences in travel advisories among the three nations, is it possible that some countries, such as the United Kingdom in this case, are more conservative when issuing travel advisories? If so, what might cause one nation to be more cautious than other nations when issuing travel advisories? Finally, how responsible must citizens be to heed the warnings of their government regarding travel to foreign lands? And how much responsibility do governments have to rescue its citizens when they have knowingly placed themselves in harm's way while traveling abroad?

Notes

1   OECD (2010) *OECD Tourism Trends and Policies 2010*. Paris: OECD.

2   www.henleyglobal.com/citizenship/visa-restrictions. Accessed May 11, 2012.

3   Cartwright, P. (2004) *Consumer Protection and Criminal Law: Law, Theory and Policy in the UK*. Cambridge: Cambridge University Press, p.1.

8

Affecting and influencing tourism policy

Previous chapters of this book have clearly laid out various types of tourism policy, how tourism policy has developed, the importance of tourism, and the foreign policy implications of tourism. This chapter presents practical approaches to affecting public policy and tourism legislation and how to choose between policy alternatives. Enhanced decision-making regarding policy, based on research and analysis instead of intuition and feeling, is currently a critical need in the global tourism industry. This chapter aligns well with the practical nature of Chapter 10, which describes the mechanics of strategic tourism planning.

Two things can be provided to elected officials to affect public policy decision-making – money and information. This chapter provides an understanding of the political decision-making process, presents techniques for developing analytical information to be provided to political decision-makers, and analyzes the contributions made by members of tourism-related industries.

Loews Hotel Chairman Jonathan Tisch has called for the hospitality industry to become more active players in shaping public policy in the United States. Tisch cited the importance of public policy issues involving immigration and international marketing. He stated: "We need to have a free flow of commerce and to help diminish the view of fortress America."[1] This comment also speaks to the perception or image of the United States held by people around the globe.

Tisch also pointed out, as has been previously mentioned throughout this book, that the United States government spends far less on tourism than does other countries. In fact, national tourism spending is a diminutive amount of the overall federal budget in the United States.

Tisch noted that important government leaders are listening to the hospitality industry as progress has been made in recent years in getting the attention of political decision-makers. Much of this progress has been the result of the tireless efforts of many of the industry trade associations who have governmental affairs arms, including those previously described in this text.

In recent years, the industry has become better organized, which is beginning to catch the attention of political decision-makers. Another factor that has contributed to the increased attention is the decline of many traditional industries in most communities, such as mining, manufacturing, and agriculture. In many areas, these traditional industries are being replaced with tourism, as civic leaders look for ways to sustain their communities. The increasing economic importance of tourism has given the industry more political power.

Working in advocacy coalitions

Advocacy groups with similar viewpoints on public policy issues can at times achieve greater success if they work together toward their common goals in a coalition. Theoretical frameworks, most prominently the Advocacy Coalition Framework (ACF), underpin the inner workings of advocacy coalitions.[2] The ACF as a theoretical construct emerged subsequent to a search for alternatives to the Stages Heuristic, which theorizes that public policy is developed along a linear process in various steps and the thought that technical information should play a more prominent role in understanding the policy process. A basic premise of policy implementation that makes up part of the foundation of the Advocacy Coalition Framework is conceptualization of public policies is similar to how belief systems are conceptualized.

Like most theoretical frameworks, important terms are associated with the ACF that must be understood. These terms are policy domain, policy subsystem, advocacy coalition, deep core beliefs, policy core beliefs, secondary beliefs, and policy preferences. A *policy domain* is the general category of related issues. For example, sales tax issues and property tax issues fall under the policy domain of taxes. A *policy subsystem* is the collection of actors who attempt to influence policy on a regular basis. These actors come from different organizations, but are interested in policy issues within common policy domains. For example, organizations interested in changing sales tax legislation would fall within the same policy subsystem. Policy subsystems are made up of *advocacy coalitions*. Members of an advocacy coalition can include agency officials, interest groups, legislators, policy analysts, researchers, and journalists who share a common belief system and show significant coordinated efforts over time. For example, organizations opposed to sales tax increases would be in one advocacy coalition and organizations supporting sales tax increases would be in another advocacy coalition.

Members of an advocacy coalition have four different types of beliefs – deep core beliefs, policy core beliefs, secondary beliefs, and policy preferences. *Deep core beliefs* are foundational values that can be found in essentially all policy domains. Basic examples include life, liberty, and the pursuit of happiness. The basic freedom to travel is also an example. *Policy core beliefs*, on the other hand, are those principles that are common among organizations within a coalition. For example, one advocacy coalition's policy core beliefs may be pro-economic development, while another coalition is concerned with advancing social justice. Organizations with differing policy core beliefs may or may not interact within the same policy subsystem and would likely not be in the same coalition.

Stances on specific issues may vary among members of a coalition. For example, in a coalition seeking to affect legislation that would encourage people to travel, airline advocates may not be concerned with legislation affecting public land use. Likewise, park managers may not be concerned with issues related to the Transportation Safety Administration. These issues are referred to as *secondary beliefs*. Policy actors may also have *policy preferences*, which involve beliefs on particular policy proposals within a policy subsystem. Differences in policy preferences may lead actors that typically work together in coalitions to oppose each other at times, depending on the issue. Policy preferences are indicated by the stances on the issues, or types of issues, taken by a policy actor.

In addition to addressing beliefs and preferences, the ACF also explains benefits gained by organizations that form partnerships. There are three conditions regarding benefits under which coalitions are likely to persist. The conditions are (a) clear identification of coalition beneficiaries, (b) benefits received are related to costs of coalition members, and (c) the mutual monitoring of coalition members' activities, which relates to trust. If coalition members have little to offer the coalition, then the costs will be too great for members who have more to offer.

The benefits of organizations aligning with each other extend beyond advocacy. Partnerships and coalitions provide organizations with the potential to offer more with less. Such relationships can reduce duplication in service delivery and common overhead expenses. Coalitions can also increase exposure to funding opportunities as organizations within the coalition may be introduced to the philanthropic communities of other coalition members. Some of the benefits that can be realized by forming a coalition cannot be defined at the beginning of the collaborative relationship, but become apparent as the relationship matures.

Organizations originally formed for purposes other than advocacy such as a private-sector business or trade association, are more efficient policy advocates than groups formed solely to provide collective benefits, according to the by-product theory of large interest groups. For example, compared to groups formed solely to provide collective benefits, businesses and large associations are able to be more selective of the issues and their positions because of the resources they are able to employ. Typically weaker ideological groups seek out businesses or trade associations with similar policy stances when looking to form advocacy coalitions, although they may be strange bedfellows at times. As a hypothetical example, a local environmental conservation group may align with a nationwide firearms association on the issue of banning the use of snowmobiles on public lands. The conservationists would be concerned with the negative environmental impact snowmobile use may have, while gun owners might be concerned with the impact that snowmobiles may have on hunters and their experience while hunting. However, outside of the snowmobiling issue, the two groups would likely oppose each other regarding hunting access on the same public lands.

Advocacy Coalition Framework and tourism

The ACF was used as the guiding theoretical framework in a study of the National Economic Council (NEC) and processes associated with its international and domestic economic policy. The NEC is a group of economic advisors responsible for vetting the policy proposals from nearly 30 federal agencies involved in economic policy, some of which include tourism. The NEC was established by President Clinton and continued by President G.W. Bush. The ACF is useful to evaluate the policy processes of the NEC and suggested that the framework can be applied to other areas of policy studies, including homeland security and domestic policy. The Tourism Policy Council, a group similar to the NEC, is coordinated by the Office of Travel and Tourism Industries in the United States Department of Commerce. The Tourism Policy Council consists of leaders from nine federal agencies and is responsible for coordinating policy relating to international travel and tourism.

Other research has shown how actors that have similar beliefs or policy preferences can also work in opposing advocacy coalitions on occasion. A case study on the land-use struggles between the National Park Service and the Bureau of Reclamation provides an example. The Bureau of Reclamation wanted to build a dam in a National Park unit as part of a larger water resources management plan. In opposition, the National Park Service wanted to protect the land in accordance with its mission of conserving the natural state of public lands for the enjoyment of future generations. The Advocacy Coalition Framework was able to explain the struggle between the two organizations, showing groups that were typically part of the same coalitions were at times in opposition because they were competing for the same resources.

In a separate forest policy study, wildlife groups such as Friends of the Earth and the Sierra Club formed *amenity coalitions* with recreation and tourism-related groups and others who also wanted to use the environmentally-stable forests for activities such as hiking, off-road motorized vehicle riding, or other trail uses. While the wildlife groups typically want to save the forest from timber harvesting to protect wildlife, they also realize that human use can have a significant negative impact on wildlife. However, with the help of recreation and tourism-related partners, wildlife groups gained a stronger voice opposing those who wanted to harvest the timber, which would negatively impact wildlife and human enjoyment. Using the unusual groupings of coalition members (i.e., amenity coalitions), research related to this example examined the relationship of a coalition's policy core beliefs and secondary beliefs, finding that actors may shift on their policy core beliefs to advance secondary beliefs.

In 2001, Tyler and Dinan described the relationship between tourism-related interest groups and the government in the emerging tourism policy network in England. The study highlighted the methods used by the policy network to affect policy development, including trust, resource-based power arrangements, and communications management. Trust involves creating understanding and relationships among trade groups, government agencies, and the private-sector. In terms of resource-based power arrangements, groups with more available resources such as money, staff time, and political clout were at an advantage over organizations with fewer resources. Regarding communications management, groups must clearly formulate and elucidate arguments based on facts that support the policy position and identify and communicate how that position aligns with objectives of political decision-makers. Those groups able to communicate reliable, fact-based information to legislators enjoyed more power.

In a separate study but also in 2001, Tyler and Dinan analyzed tourism policy coalitions operating within the framework of umbrella organizations. An umbrella organization, or peak association, is a group of groups. They usually have greater financial resources afforded by a wide array of members. One advantage was umbrella organizations were typically better able to carry out research initiatives because of financial resources and organizational capabilities.

Challenges of advocacy coalitions

Advocacy coalitions and similar partnerships are not without criticism and challenges. Some contend that coalitions may transfer power from elected officials to non-elected, self-selected groups and individuals. However, even operating within the guise that advocacy coalitions are good for democracy, inherent challenges still exist. These challenges include managing coalitions and competing for scarce resources.

From an operational standpoint, several challenges exist to forming and managing advocacy coalitions. For example, including or excluding organizations when a coalition is formed and determining how power and responsibilities are distributed within the coalition, are questions that must be addressed by coalition participants. The central challenge for a coalition lies in selecting and managing the appropriate mode of governance (i.e. network, market, or hierarchy) throughout the lifecycle stages of pre-partnership, partnership creation, partnership program delivery, and partnership termination.

Another challenge organizations face within a coalition is competing for scarce resources, including government and philanthropic money. Organizations will also try to gain control over resources that increase the reliance of other organizations on themselves. Pursuit of these goals affects the power of organizations within a coalition. Gaining control over resources is exemplified by the realities of resource-strapped nonprofits competing for limited resources. For example, organizations funded by philanthropic and government sources are competing for grant moneys, while many of the grants stipulate that applicants should collaborate. Thus, nonprofits, and other organizations, must be adept at maneuvering within the constraints of coalitions.

Coalition resources

Sabatier and Weible[3] developed a typology of resources that can be used by groups trying to influence public policy. The resources are: (a) formal legal authority to make policy decisions, (b) public opinion, (c) information, (d) mobilizable troops, (e) skillful leadership, and (f) financial resources. Having members with more formal legal authority, such as elected and appointed government officials, than other coalitions is a resource of dominant coalitions. Support from the electorate (i.e., public opinion) for a policy position is another important resource for a coalition. The resource of information includes communicating the importance of the policy problem and the costs and benefits of various policy alternatives. Mobilizable troops, or grassroots resources, enable an advocacy coalition to demonstrate broader support while investing fewer financial resources. Skillful coalition leaders are required to produce policy change. Financial resources permit the purchase of other resources.

Understanding the public decision-making process

In order to influence those making political decisions, it is important to understand how political decisions are made. Public choice theory provides a framework for this understanding. While politicians may claim to represent the will of their constituency, in reality this is often not the case as the decisions they make are often in their own self-interests. This is a basis for public choice theory.

Although this concept might sound trite, this theory was first introduced by James Buchanan and Gordon Tullock in their seminal work published in 1962 entitled *The Calculus of Consent*. Public choice theory applies economic principles to the decision-making process of political leaders. Public choice teaches how politics actually functions from a positive standpoint rather than how it should function, which is the normative viewpoint. The theory developed over the following three decades resulted in a Nobel Prize in economics for Buchanan in 1986.[4]

The thrust behind public choice shattered the common viewpoint that majority decisions are inherently fair. Under this assumption, it would be believed that a decision in the public interest would be unanimously supported by all voters. Instead, political decisions are made in the best interest of those making the decisions not in the interest of the voters because the interest of all voters cannot be served with a single decision. Moreover, the electorate masses do not have enough information about all of the issues to have a concerned opinion.

Among other areas, public choice observes and scrutinizes the activities of legislators. Although politicians might intend to efficiently spend taxpayer money, they are not necessarily inclined to do so because most of their decisions will not affect their own money. In other words, a more efficient use of tax money will not result in any proportion of the public wealth saved being given to the politician.

Under this theory, when faced with the choice of deciding between powerful interest groups and an uninformed electorate, the group with the most influence will always win. In almost all cases, this is the special interest groups. The theory states that there are too many issues about which the voting public can be informed. And thus, the incentives are weak for sound management in the public interest. Interest groups, on the other hand, consist of individuals who stand to gain significantly from governmental action. In order to influence political decision-makers, they donate money and volunteer time in exchange for increased access to the politician with the aim of influencing the politician to support their issues.[5]

Logrolling, or vote trading, is a technique closely watched by public choice economists, and is illustrated by the following example: Separate cost-benefit analyses are done on different issues for a state legislature. One study looks at providing free high-speed internet access to parks in mountain communities and another study reviews the net present value of beach renourishment along a 24-mile stretch of beach. Both projects are shown in the analysis to be inefficient and should therefore not be supported by a rational decision-maker. In order to gain support for her internet access bill, a legislator from the mountain area agrees to vote for the beach renourishment legislation so that the representative from the beach will support the mountain internet access program. Through logrolling, both legislators get what they want. And while both projects consume resources inefficiently, according to the analysis, local uninformed voters see that their representative has done something for their area. The constituents hold this view because they do not know that their tax money is supporting multiple inefficient projects because of logrolling.

Capture theory, similar to public choice theory, also claims government decision-makers do not always act in the best interest of the public but instead they may be captured by special interest groups, such as trade associations. This happens because the decision-makers want to pursue their own self-interests, such as garnering support (votes and money) for re-election or to otherwise supplement their power. Capture happens when the politician supports an issue that would not be supported by an informed constituency. The objective of the captured politician is to advance his or her own agenda, despite the public interest. Public interest is the opposite of capture. Despite the societal costs of legislative capture, it is the environment in which the political systems in most democracies currently operate. Thus, interest groups seek ways to optimize their advocacy impact. Interest groups representing a large constituency, such as retired people or gun owners, are better suited for capturing vote-seeking politicians than are more fragmented groups such as tourism-related interest groups.[6]

When attempting to affect political decisions, the relationship of bureaucrats and special interest groups is also important to understand. As opposed to professionals operating in the private-sector, bureaucrats do not have profit as a goal, but instead are motivated by achieving the mission of their agency. While relying on the legislature for agency funding, bureaucrats will informally rely on special interest groups to influence the legislature on their behalf so that they can accomplish their objectives. This leads to the potential for bureaucrats to be captured by special interest groups that are trying to advance their own agendas. This is not to imply that the relationships between bureaucrats and special interest groups are negative, but presented here to give an understanding of how decisions can be made within bureaucracy.

As principles of economics are basic tenets of public choice, competition is one way in which theorists propose to solve some of the conflicts that arise from government inefficiencies. An applied example of using competition to regulate tourism policy is for the Forest Service to charge hikers more than just a nominal fee so that the attention paid to hikers is more in line with those with a higher economic impact on the forest, such as timber harvesters. This should serve to increase the economic importance of hikers relative to other forest users and should reduce logging in popular recreation areas.[7] However, it is unclear what this might do to hiking demand. And undoubtedly, outdoor enthusiasts will cite the public benefits of nature-based outdoor recreation in their opposition to the fee.[8] Conducting a cost-benefit analysis of this problem, a technique described in the following section, is a perfect application of public choice theory in a tourism setting.

This theory has yet to be widely applied to the practice of tourism. For the purposes of this text, it is important to realize that politicians are unable to represent the will of the electorate as a whole. And it will be those interest groups who provide the most persuasive information and support for the decision-maker that stand a higher chance of influencing public policy. Research-based policy analysis, the focus of the next section, is one way to garner attention and influence policy.

Influencing political decisions with information

Cost-benefit analysis is a technique to aid in making decisions among public policy alternatives by analyzing a policy or program's total expected costs versus its expected benefits. The technique has been used to determine the value of public expenditures ranging from education programs to water resource projects and pollution control to health and nutrition policies. Cost-benefit analysis is used not only by government agencies but by those organizations wishing to persuade the opinions of public officials. Those groups who can provide information that is more meaningful to individual political decision-makers stand higher chances of achieving their policy objectives.

Cost-benefit analysis was first adopted by the US Government during the 1930s and gained prominence in Great Britain and other Western countries in the 1960s as a means to assess select public project expenditure decisions. Within the tourism industry in the United States, decisions influenced by cost-benefit analysis can be traced to the 1960s. During this time, the technique was used in transportation to establish methodology on valuing benefits such as the time savings to travelers. Other tourism-related areas that contributed to the advancement of monetizing techniques were environmental quality and natural resources.

Cost-benefit analysis has helped shape public policy in recent decades and assisted in the evolution of environmental management, which is critical to sustainable tourism. For example, the US Clean Air Act of 1970 and amendments to the Act in 1977 established air quality standards with no mention of benefits or costs. However, legislation passed in the late 1980s and 1990s included economic concerns enabling cost-benefit analysis. In the case of the 1990 US Clean Air Act Amendments, market incentives were introduced, through emission trading between polluting plants that encouraged cost-effective pollution reduction. This further encouraged research and development of pollution-reducing technologies.

In the next round of national tourism policy in any nation at the national and local levels, economic measures and cost-benefit analysis should be included so that the industry can provide more informative analysis relative to other industries in competition for scarce resources.

Environmental groups regularly utilize economic analysis in support of their environmental policies. This is important for the environmental groups because to some political decision-makers, economics are more meaningful than the environment. These leaders may not appreciate the position from an environmental argument, but may be fully persuadable with the right economic information. Providing the right kind of information to individual politicians increases the power of the environmental groups, which can result in a greater impact upon the decision-making process, as prescribed by public choice theory.

There has been a significant amount of attention paid to cost-benefit analysis by United States presidents since the mid-1970s. President Ford initiated the use of assessing benefits as part of federal regulations. President Carter set forth Executive Order (E.O.) 12044 on March 23, 1978, which stipulated that agencies had "to perform an economic analysis weighing the potential regularity costs with the potential benefits for all proposed 'major' regulations."[9]

During the Clinton administration several bills were introduced concerning cost-benefit requirements. The Risk Assessment and Cost-Benefit Analysis Act of 1995 (HR 1022) was perhaps the most prominent and controversial during this period. Although this bill passed the house, it did not garner the necessary votes in the Senate to become law. The merits of HR 1022 were widely contested with critics believing the measure would have increased bureaucracy as new staff members would be necessary to perform analysis as well as the limitations of the technique and available data. One reason why it failed was because there were significant questions about the reliability and validity of insufficiently-developed techniques and because data are too difficult or costly to collect. There is still opportunity for more effective measurements, particularly in tourism and related fields. As Fuguitt and Wilcox (1999) state, "Cost-benefit analysis offers the most comprehensive and informative systematic technique to assess decision choices inclining output or services not priced in markets."[10]

The field of health care frequently uses cost-benefit analysis to aid in decision-making when very tough choices are involved. For example, a particular policy choice may involve the saving or loss of a human life. As described in the next section, cost-benefit involves monetizing costs and benefits so that a net benefit can be calculated. In this example, human lives are valued in terms of the expected contributions the individual will make to national income through labor productivity.

Although tourism is serious business, tourism development rarely involves the end of human lives. This means two things: 1) public policies affecting tourism are often less controversial than many other types of public policies; and 2) because other industries have to consider serious issues, such as the loss of human life, they are more inclined to provide thorough analysis of their policies and programs. When trying to affect public decisions for the allocation of scarce resources, absent of politics, the case with the best information stands a better chance of prevailing. Because tourism may deal with less serious issues does not mean the analysis provided by the industry should be any less sophisticated.

Conflict and compromise

There are more than two sides to every issue and often times, different members of the tourism industry may be on opposing sides. Consider the analysis undertaken during the early 1970s regarding a third airport in London. Although it was approached from an environmental analysis perspective, the policy has a direct connection to tourism and travel. Recommendations made by the Roskill Commission regarding the location of the airport placed the new facility in a controversial inland site rather than on the coast, which was more politically acceptable. This recommendation was based on a cost-benefit analysis, which showed the noise and nuisance costs of the inland location near a significant resident base, were far outweighed by the benefits of reduced travel time by those using the airport. While some may prefer less noise to less travel time, others may take the opposite stance. Although, politics and other pressures of power may sway opinion, cost-benefit analysis is one tool that should be part of the decision spectrum in these cases.

Other examples of issues that might find members of tourism advocacy groups on different sides include hurricane forecasting and evacuation policy, economic development incentives, and funding allocations. In reality it is unlikely that any policy issue will gain the full support of the various components of the tourism industry.

How should industry advocates decide between issues when they may pit industry members against each other? In the absence of politics, the most objective measure is cost-benefit analysis. Moreover, policy analysis may be able to effectively persuade those with the opposite opinions who may be less informed. Policy analysis also provides measures of accountability for programs. In terms of international aid, for example, donor country citizens want to know that the investments their government makes on their behalf are producing positive returns.

With tourism's global reach, opportunities abound for professionals with intimate knowledge of developing economies so that national policies and international investments can be analyzed. However, monetizing costs and benefits are more complicated in developing nations. For example, market prices in developing economies may be highly skewed for various reasons, which may make it difficult to determine social value. Some of these difficulties have been mitigated by manuals detailing cost-benefit techniques produced by OECD,[11] the United Nations Industrial Development Organization,[12] and the World Bank.[13] Once again, with tourism competing with other industries for international investment, it is vital for decision-makers to be presented with persuasive information. These principles need to be applied to tourism just as they are to other economic and social sectors.

Cost-benefit analysis can also support the effort of the private-sector. During the 1970s many private-sector businesses were grappling with what they felt were burdens of government regulations. These firms used cost-benefit analysis as a way to persuade legislators that regulations needed to be curbed so that benefits to the business, government, and society could be greater. Many states require cost-benefit analysis when considering the offer of economic incentive packages to entice new businesses to their state.[14]

In another private-sector example, DuPont and other major corporations are analyzing the alternative environmental investments they might pursue. This is in response to increased environmental regulations and the need to monetize what may typically not be considered in economic terms, such as air and water pollution.[15]

Cost-benefit enables a private firm to analyze not only the expected financial risks and rewards, but also the social impacts on customers and the larger community. Smart companies can use this tool to identify long-term social issues that might outweigh short-term economic gain for the company. These principles could be utilized by land developers when considering tourism investment projects, such as condominiums, hotels, or other attractions in areas of environmental sensitivity but that are desirable and popular with consumers and travelers. In this case, most developers are unlikely to perform such non-economic analysis when faced with burgeoning consumer demand, however, a responsible developer will do it and a good government will require it.

Cost-benefit analysis has developed reactively to the need for practical decision-making tools. Particularly, to the need to prioritize policy alternatives' costs and benefits that cannot be purchased in the market place (i.e. noise pollution, improved quality-of-life, travel costs, human lives). It is still up to the decision-maker to exercise care in interpreting the findings of any cost-benefit analysis.

Techniques of cost-benefit analysis

The purpose of cost-benefit analysis is to compare benefits and costs of a project to determine the project's feasibility and to compare the project with other projects in order to determine priorities. The steps involved in this undertaking are:

1. Defining the project and alternatives.
2. Identifying, measuring, and valuing costs and benefits of each alternative.
3. Calculating cost-benefit values.
4. Reporting the results.

Step 1: Defining the project and alternatives

Answers to the following questions will help the analyst frame the project and make key assumptions. These assumptions may change throughout the project, but with a solid foundation at the beginning of the analysis, the process will be made more efficient throughout the project:

- What is the problem the project addresses?
- What are the intended benefits of the project?
- What will the project do and how will it be done?
- Who will do it and when?
- What is the purpose of the analysis? Feasibility, prioritization, or selection of projects?
- What's the appropriate level of effort that should be invested in the analysis considering the expected payoff of the project?
- Who will receive the benefits?
- Who will bear the direct and indirect costs?
- What will happen if the project does not happen?
- How else could the expected benefits be achieved?
- When will costs be incurred?
- When will benefits be realized?
- What type of analysis should be used? Cost-benefit ratio, net present value, internal rate of return, other basis?
- What geographic areas will be affected by the project and its alternatives?
- What is the time horizon for the project?

Step 2: Identifying, measuring, and valuing costs and benefits of each alternative

Benefits are all of the effects of the project or program, not only on the users of the project, but also on society within the project area. For example, if a new highway was proposed the benefits would likely include reduced travel time, accidents, emissions, and vehicle operating costs. Other benefits or costs (negative benefits) may also encompass induced travel, noise, construction delays, habitat and water quality impacts, and other impacts upon the community. These other effects are critical to making choices among alternatives. These benefits are measurable and have economic value.

The labor, real property, material, and other inputs that go into a project are the costs. The simplest way to determine the cost of a project is to review the budget that has been established by those proposing the project. If a budget is not available, the analyst should look for comparable projects in similar areas to get a reliable estimate of the costs. Costs are easier to measure because they are usually market goods and services for which a price is readily attainable.

Opportunity costs should be given consideration when determining the overall costs of a project. Opportunity costs are the benefits of the best alternative foregone so that the proposed project can be funded. Opportunities are limited to only those projects that could be funded with the monies allocated for the proposed project.[16,17]

Step 3: Calculating cost-benefit values

When performing a cost-benefit analysis, several types of measurements can be employed. This section reviews cost-benefit ratio, net present value, cost-effectiveness, and sensitivity analysis. Other measurements such as internal rate of return, marginal analysis, and payback period are also useful tools taught in applied public policy analysis courses.

The *cost-benefit ratio* is the total of the discounted benefits divided by the total discounted costs. Future cash flows – costs or benefits expected after the initial year of a project – are discounted to determine their present value. The rate at which future cash flows are adjusted is known as the discount rate. A project with a cost-benefit ratio of more than 1 has positive net benefits, whereas a cost-benefit ratio less than one is an inefficient project that should not be pursued. Projects with higher benefits relative to costs will have a higher cost-benefit ratio. The cost-benefit ratio is calculated as follows:

$$CBR = \frac{\sum_{i=0}^{n} B_i / (1+d)^i}{\sum_{i=0}^{n} C_i / (1+d)^i} \text{ , where}$$

n = the number of years over which benefits and costs are analyzed;
B_i = the benefits of the project in year i, $i = 0$ to n;
C_i = the costs of the project in year i, $i = 0$ to n;
d = the discount rate.

A simple example to illustrate the cost-benefit ratio will lead to a better understanding of the technique. In this example, the government of Ascension Island, a British Overseas Territory, wants to bring in an outside expert for a period of 3 years to help residents of the island market their handicrafts to visitors. The only costs the government must bear are the annual salary and transportation costs for the outside expert, as the remainder of the project is being funded by an international NGO. The outside expert will relocate to Ascension for 3 years and will be paid a salary of $50,000 in the first year, $55,000 in the second year and $60,000 in the third year of the project. The transportation costs the government must pay are $10,000 in both the first and third years. Accordingly, total annual costs over the 3-year project are $60,000, $55,000 and $70,000. The benefits, in the form of new revenues generated from the sale of handicrafts are forecasted to be $100,000 in the second year and $150,000 in the third year. As the project gets ramped up, no revenue is expected to be generated during the first year. Using a 10 percent discount rate, the calculation of the cost-benefit ratio for this example is:

$$CBR = \frac{[\$0/(1+0.10)^0] + [\$100,000/(1+0.10)^1] + [\$150,000/(1+0.10)^2]}{[\$60,000/(1+0.10)^0] + [\$55,000/(1+0.10)^1] + [\$70,000/(1+0.10)^2]} = 1.28$$

This results in a cost-benefit ratio of 1.28. Since the ratio is greater than one, this project is efficient and should be considered.

Net present value is the total discounted costs subtracted from the total discounted benefits. In rational political decision-making, only projects with positive net benefits should be considered. A project with a higher net present value is more justifiable than a project with a lower net present value. Net present value can be calculated as:

$$NPV = \sum_{i=0}^{n} B_i/(1+d)^i - \sum_{i=0}^{n} C_i/(1+d)^i$$

n = the number of years over which benefits and costs are analyzed;
B_i = the benefits of the project in year i, i = 0 to n;
C_i = the costs of the project in year i, i = 0 to n;
d = the discount rate.

The net present value can also be determined using the previous example of marketing handicrafts on Ascension Island. The calculation is:

$$NPV = \{[\$0/(1+0.10)^0] + [\$100,000/(1+0.10)^1] + [\$150,000/(1+0.10)^2]\}$$
$$-\{[\$60,000/(1+0.10)^0] + [\$55,000/(1+0.10)^1] + [\$70,000/(1+0.10)^2]\}$$
$$NPV = \$47,025$$

Since the net present value of this project is positive it should be considered. The project should also be given priority over other alternatives with a lower net present value.

Cost-effectiveness enables comparison between a given amount of money and the non-monetized benefits that can be achieved. For example, if a municipality was adding a new runway at the airport, a cost effectiveness ratio would be the cost per additional airline passenger, or the cost per additional commercial flight. This tool is useful when compared to other alternatives and can be used even if the benefits cannot be monetized. Cost effectiveness is calculated as:

$$CER = \sum_{i=0}^{n} \frac{C_i / (1+d)^i}{B} \text{, where}$$

n = the number of years over which costs are analyzed;
B = the given benefit (not necessarily expressed in monetary terms);
C_i = the costs of the project in year i;
d = the discount rate.

The Ascension Island handicrafts marketing project is expected to yield a total of 15 jobs. Calculating the cost-effectiveness ratio of this project in terms of the number of jobs is done as follows:

$$CER = \frac{[\$60,000 / (1+0.10)^0] + [\$55,000 / (1+0.10)^1] + [\$70,000 / (1+0.10)^2]}{15}$$

$$= \$11,190 / \text{job}$$

This estimate means that for each $11,190 invested in the project, one new job will be created. This number can be compared to estimates for other projects when deciding on alternatives. If the cost-effectiveness ratio for other projects in terms of jobs is higher, then this project should be pursued.

Sensitivity analysis examines how changes in inputs or assumptions affect the cost-benefit conclusions. Sensitivity analysis allows the analyst and decision-maker to determine the likely range of outcomes for various alternatives and compare risky and less risky projects. Any assumption that goes into an analysis, including timing, geographic focus, discount rate, and others, can be adjusted to determine the magnitude of these elements on the project and whether these assumptions, once changed, would affect the prioritized ranking of various projects. Below are additional tourism-related examples of queries that could be investigated using sensitivity analysis.[17]

1   Estimates of patronage on a new light rail system vary from 4,000 to 10,000 passenger-trips per weekday. Would the system be viable with the lower patronage?
2   There are two design alternatives for constructing a bridge over an ice-prone river. The cost of one is lower unless there is a very cold winter, in which case it will be considerably higher. Is it worth taking a chance with this alternative?
3   There are differences of opinion regarding the lifetime of a pavement project. Are the benefit-cost rankings of the project alternatives different for different lifetime assumptions?
4   Some in Ascension Island believe the handicrafts marketing project will cost 10 percent more and generate 10 percent less than what has been forecasted. Should the project still be pursued relative to other alternatives?

Step 4: Reporting the results

The ultimate purpose of a policy analysis is to assist in rational and responsible decision-making. To this end, the presentation of the report should be simple but informative for all interested parties, particularly the decision-maker. The report should be succinct yet provide detailed clarity on the methodology and results so that the analysis can be scrutinized in order to satiate critics. Even if the quality of the analysis is flawless, a presentation that is unclear will be useless. The report should highlight the following:[19]

- All assumptions made in the analysis.
- All value judgments embodied in the cost-benefit technique.
- Any technical choice made when performing the analysis.
- Any biases or subjective influences that may affect the analyst's outcome.
- Possible errors in analytical procedures or estimates.

Any opinions or judgment areas needed on the part of the analyst or decision-maker should be justified and any associated advantages or disadvantages should be highlighted. Anything that cannot be included in the monetized costs or benefits should be discussed so that information can be considered by the one who must make the decision on the project. Above all the analyst and the analysis must remain neutral.

Conclusion

While tourism is generally apolitical all decisions made by public officials, whether elected or appointed, are made in a political context. In order for the tourism industry to have a more powerful effect on tourism policy, and public policy in general, more support must be given to influence political decisions. As the chapter points out, two effective means of support are: 1) through financial contributions to elected officials and political action committees; and 2) by providing government officials with analysis that can be used to make choices between many policy alternatives.

About policy analysis, Fuguitt and Wilcox[20] write, "caution is urged along with appreciation of what has become a highly sophisticated analytical technique – one that can provide useful economic assessment yet is no substitute for the decision-maker's grappling with competing objectives and political interests in a complex real-world context." Regardless of its limitations, public policy analysis is critical and necessary.

Despite the growing popularity of cost-benefit analysis, its use is not widespread within the tourism community. Reasons for this are numerous including the lack of human and financial resources to carry out the analysis and a general lack of under-standing of the importance of and techniques for conducting policy analysis. This chapter is an attempt to introduce the important fundamentals of public policy analysis, applied to tourism issues, to a new generation of tourism industry practitioners.

The chapter also highlights opportunities for the tourism industry to make great strides in political contributions relative to other groups. As described throughout this chapter, political decision-makers act in ways beneficial to their own political interests. With well-planned giving, the industry can have a significant impact upon its own political power. Without advances in policy analysis and political contributions, the tourism industry will continue to lag behind other industries in terms of political influence.

CHAPTER REVIEW QUESTIONS

1. Why is tourism policy becoming increasingly important?
2. How are coalitions formed and how are they used to advance policy agendas?
3. What are some examples of tourism advocacy coalitions?
4. Describe public choice theory.
5. Why is tourism policy development sometimes taken less seriously than other policy development, such as healthcare?
6. What is the purpose of cost-benefit analysis?
7. What are the steps of cost-benefit analysis?
8. How can tourism gain more political attention?

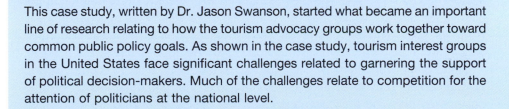

CASE STUDY 8 Influencing political decisions with financial contributions

This case study, written by Dr. Jason Swanson, started what became an important line of research relating to how the tourism advocacy groups work together toward common public policy goals. As shown in the case study, tourism interest groups in the United States face significant challenges related to garnering the support of political decision-makers. Much of the challenges relate to competition for the attention of politicians at the national level.

* * *

While progress has been made in terms of tourism's political advocacy participation in the United States, opportunities remain for continued improvement. One strategy toward this objective is to increase the political contributions made by members of the tourism industry. As laid out in the discussion on public choice theory in the chapter, political contributions are necessary in order to advance a political agenda when competing with many other industries and influences.

Elected officials are heavily influenced by special interest groups, which exist to influence specific areas of public policy. Examples of such groups include a multinational corporation taking a stance against international tariffs, an industry trade association seeking benefits for its members, trade unions for minimum wage increases, senior citizens concerned with social security benefits, and family groups focused on rating systems for video games. Within the United States tourism industry, special interest groups include the Western States Policy Council, Southeast Tourism Policy Council, American Bus Association, National Tour Association, and efforts of private-sector firms such as Marriott International. These groups influence public policy through regulatory bureaucracy, legal proceedings, or swaying the opinions of legislators. The primary method of directly affecting the actions of elected officials is through financial contributions to their campaigns, which is the focus of this case study.

Table 8.1 presents a rank order of political contributions to federal candidates and political parties in the United States given by individuals or political action committees (PACs) during 2005/06 election cycle. The numbers show how industry segments rank in total campaign giving as compared to more than 80 other industries. Specifically, the table lists the top 15 industry contributors and also the industry segments that encompass tourism. Although data presented in the table are from the last decade, significant differences in the relative contributions of the tourism lobby are minimal.

None of the industry sectors that make up tourism even break the top 25. However, if the donations of those listed in the bottom half of Table 8.1 were combined, the total of $46,079,178 would place third in 2005/06 behind those who list their occupation as retired and above members of the real estate industry – two powerful political influencers. The tourism industry segments presented in the chart may have different agendas. For example, the food and beverage sector may be interested in issues associated with meat imports that might not interest the airlines, which may be concerned more with taxes on aviation fuels. However, consolidated efforts on certain issues could help each segment accomplish their own missions while working for the good of tourism as a whole.

Based on conversations with legislators and lobbyists, tourism is often viewed as fragmented, with hotels and restaurants and airlines and other tourism-related businesses pursuing their own agendas. This dilutes what may be a common message. Among other reasons, in the United States this fragmentation is a result of the lack of a national government tourism office to coordinate such efforts. A better cooperative working relationship needs to be established.

Political action committees are a special type of interest group that is formed to raise and spend money to elect particular candidates. PACs originated in 1944, when a labor union collected voluntary contributions from workers to support the re-election of Franklin D. Roosevelt for President. This was in response to the

TABLE 8.1 Political contributions by industry segments relative to tourism sectors

Industry Segment	Rank	Total Contributions	Contributions from Individuals	Contributions from PACs
Lawyers/Law Firms	1	$68,529,030	$59,907,961	$8,621,069
Retired	2	$63,342,234	$63,342,234	$0
Real Estate	3	$40,845,073	$34,909,760	$5,935,313
Securities and Investment	4	$34,680,675	$28,081,468	$6,599,207
Health Professionals	5	$28,678,339	$18,076,074	$10,602,265
Candidate Committees	6	$25,581,260	$51,205	$25,530,055
Leadership PACs	7	$21,899,444	$388,759	$21,510,685
Insurance	8	$17,284,783	$6,635,163	$10,649,620
Commercial Banks	9	$14,599,075	$7,622,523	$6,976,552
Business Services	10	$14,274,866	$13,204,325	$1,070,541
Lobbyists	11	$13,927,601	$13,097,452	$830,149
TV/Movies/Music	12	$12,802,509	$8,644,204	$4,158,305
General Contractors	13	$10,561,001	$8,624,436	$1,936,565
Pharmaceuticals/Health Products	14	$10,432,530	$3,889,743	$6,542,787
Oil & Gas	15	$10,161,359	$6,142,602	$4,018,757
Tourism-related Sectors				
Air Transport	26	$7,115,354	$1,743,725	$5,371,629
Retail Sales	28	$6,710,258	$4,024,924	$2,685,334
Casinos/Gambling	30	$6,466,961	$2,038,252	$4,428,709
Beer, Wine, and Liquor	33	$5,599,987	$2,313,312	$3,286,675
Food & Beverage	34	$5,428,827	$3,267,959	$2,160,868
Indian Gaming	N/A	$4,355,515	$834,276	$3,521,239
Bars and Restaurants	N/A	$4,128,761	$2,470,412	$1,658,349
Lodging/Tourism	52	$3,027,839	$2,478,414	$549,425
Recreation/Live Entertainment	65	$1,649,945	$1,423,167	$226,778
Airlines	N/A	$1,341,381	$528,556	$812,825
Cruise Ships and Lines	N/A	$254,350	$119,100	$135,250

Based on data released by the Federal Election Commission on Monday, April 24, 2006.
Source: Center for Responsive Politics

Smith Connally Act of 1943, which disallowed labor unions from making political contributions to federal candidates. United States federal law has limited annual contributions by PACs to $5,000 to a candidate per election, $15,000 to a national party committee, and $5,000 to another PAC. In terms of donations received, PACs can be given up to $5,000 from any individual, PAC, or party committee contributor per year. With a ruling in a case known as *Citizens United v. Federal Election Commission* by the United States Supreme Courts in 2010, these rules were severely relaxed allowing independent political contributions by corporations and labor unions, in most cases, to be unlimited.

Back in 2005/06, twelve tourism-related PACs contributed a total of $342,425 to federal candidates in the United States, as shown Table 8.2. This classification includes hotels, motels, resorts, and travel agents.

TABLE 8.2 Lodging and tourism PAC contributions to US federal candidates

PAC Name	Total	Dems	Repubs
American Hotel & Lodging Assn	$67,200	$14,500	$52,700
American Society of Travel Agents	$47,000	$22,500	$24,500
Asian American Hotel Owners Assn	$2,000	$0	$2,000
Auto Club of Michigan	$4,125	$3,000	$1,125
Cendant Corp	$84,500	$21,500	$63,000
Conference of Natl Park Concessioners	$8,500	$1,000	$7,500
Gaylord Entertainment	$8,500	$1,000	$7,500
Holiday Inns	$29,500	$5,000	$24,500
Intl Assn Amusement Parks and Attractions	$4,100	$0	$4,100
Marriott International	$28,250	$0	$28,250
National Tour Assn	$9,500	$1,500	$8,000
Sabre Inc	$49,250	$28,750	$20,500

Based on data released by the FEC on Monday, May 29, 2006.
Source: Center for Responsive Politics

TABLE 8.3 Top 15 PAC contributions to US federal candidates

PAC Name	Total Amount	Dem Pct	Repub Pct
National Assn of Realtors	$1,768,005	49%	51%
Intl Brotherhood of Electrical Workers	$1,673,000	97%	3%
Assn of Trial Lawyers of America	$1,626,000	96%	3%
National Beer Wholesalers Assn	$1,607,500	26%	74%
AT&T Inc	$1,569,300	35%	65%
Credit Union National Assn	$1,523,899	42%	58%
United Parcel Service	$1,470,809	31%	69%
National Auto Dealers Assn	$1,353,000	31%	69%
American Bankers Assn	$1,310,374	35%	65%
Teamsters Union	$1,275,175	90%	9%
Carpenters & Joiners Union	$1,241,390	6%	34%
American Fedn of St/Cnty/Munic Employees	$1,212,171	97%	2%
Operating Engineers Union	$1,172,605	78%	21%
United Auto Workers	$1,159,500	99%	1%
National Assn of Home Builders	$1,157,000	25%	75%

For comparison purposes, the top 15 PAC contributors to federal candidates are presented in Table 8.3. When the 2005–06 lodging and tourism PAC contributions are combined, they represented only 19 percent of the largest single PAC contributor. This clearly illustrates how the tourism industries are severely lagging in political contributions. Once again, this is an opportunity as money gains the attention of the political decision-makers.

Giving is only half of the contribution equation. The other half is receiving donated funds. If monies are not donated strategically, their efficacy is diminished. There is only one sub-committee in the United States Congress that specifically mentions tourism – the Trade, Tourism, and Economic Development Sub-Committee of the Commerce, Science, and Trade Committee in the United States Senate. It therefore provides a clear target for tourism's political contributions. In addition to tourism, the committee is also responsible for the following:

Coast Guard; coastal zone management; communications; highway safety; inland waterways, except construction; interstate commerce; marine and ocean navigation, safety, and transportation, including navigational aspects of deep-water ports; marine fisheries; merchant marine and navigation; nonmilitary aeronautical and space sciences; oceans, weather, and atmospheric activities; Panama Canal and inter-oceanic canals generally, except the maintenance and operation of the Panama Canal, including administration, sanitation and government of the Canal Zone; regulation of consumer products and services, including testing related to toxic substances, other than pesticides, and except for credit, financial services, and housing, regulation of interstate common carriers, including railroads, buses, trucks, vessels, pipelines, and civil aviation; science, engineering, and technology research and development and policy; sports; standards and measurement; transportation; and transportation and commerce aspects of Outer Continental Shelf lands. Comprehensive study and review of all matters relating to science and technology, oceans policy, transportation, communications, and consumer affairs.

Tourism must compete with these other interests when trying to affect legislative decision. Table 8.4 shows total giving for the years 2000 through 2006 by

TABLE 8.4 Giving to members of the Senate Commerce, Science, and Transportation Committee

Rank	Industry	Total
1	TV/Movies/Music	$2,917,741
2	Insurance	$2,690,764
3	Oil & Gas	$1,735,047
4	Air Transport	$1,524,187
5	Telecom Services & Equipment	$1,250,854
6	Telephone Utilities	$1,234,249
7	Automotive	$1,007,461
8	Transportation Unions	$990,540
9	Sea Transport	$783,060
10	Railroads	$473,469
11	Lodging/Tourism	$440,630
12	Trucking	$361,611
13	Recreation/Live Entertainment	$233,076
14	Misc Transport	$153,502
15	Fisheries & Wildlife	$129,580

Source: Center for Responsive Politics

committee-related industries to members of the Senate Commerce, Science, and Transportation Committee for the years 2000 through 2006.

Lodging/tourism ranks number 11 in this category. This once again highlights another opportunity for tourism to increase political contributions from a strategic sense. To compete more effectively with other industries for the attention of those making the most relevant decisions to the industry, more strategic giving is required. Members of the tourism industry have an opportunity to unite in strategic and focused contributions to political campaigns. This along with providing better information will increase the political power of the industry.

Concluding critical questions

A study of political donations made by industry groups, corporations, and private citizens can raise a myriad of interesting and thought-provoking questions. One question relates to the comparisons among industry groups. Do those groups of industries that contribute more money, give more money because they have more money, or do they have more money because they give more money? Is it possible for tourism to adequately compete, in terms of political contributions, with other groups of industries?

Should political contributions be made more at the local level than at the national level? This question leads us to think about if tourism advocacy would be more effective if the focus was on influencing local government decision-makers instead of those at the national level. Another question can be raised about the differences in efficacy between two advocacy tactics of providing information through policy analysis or providing political contributions. How might that question be answered differently if the destination was a country other than the United States? Or, how might the answer differ if asked about a nation with a different form of government? Finally, how does tourism lobbying activity in the US compare to advocacy efforts of tourism interest groups in other countries?

Notes

1 Barbara, J. (2006) "Tisch to Hoteliers: Get Involved in Fed Policy." *Commercial Real Estate News and Property Resource*. Retrieved June 6, 2006 from GlobeSt.com.

2 Swanson, J.R. (2010). *The tourism policy puzzle: Pieces and precepts discovered through qualitative investigation of federal public policy preferences and advocacy activities of tourism associations in the United States*. Raleigh, NC: North Carolina State University.

3 Sabatier, P. A., & Weible, C. M. (2007). The advocacy coalition framework: Innovations and clarifications. In P. A. Sabatier (Ed.), *Theories of the policy process* (2nd ed., pp. 189–220). Boulder, CO: Westview Press.

4　Buchanan, J.M. & Tullock, G. (1962) *The Calculus of Consent*. Ann Arbor, MI: University of Michigan Press.

5　Shaw, J. (2002) "Public Choice Theory." *The Concise Encyclopedia of Economics*. Retrieved June 5, 2006 from www.econlib.org/library/Enc/PublicChoiceTheory.html.

6　Swanson, J.R. & Brothers, G.L. (2012). Tourism policy agenda setting, interest groups and legislative capture. *International Journal of Tourism Policy, 4*(3), 206–221.

7　O'Toole, R. (1988) *Reforming the Forest Service.* Washington, DC: Island Press.

8　Kline, C., Cardenas, D., Duffy, L., & Swanson, J.R. (2012). Funding sustainable paddle trail development: Paddler perspectives, willingness to pay and management implications. *Journal of Sustainable Tourism*, *20*(2), 235–256.

9　Fuguitt, D. & Wilcox, S. (1999) *Cost-Benefit Analysis for Public Decision Makers.* Westport, CT: Quorum Books, p. 10.

10　Fuguitt, D. & Wilcox, S. (1999), pp. 6–7.

11　Little, I.M. & Mirrlees, J.A. (1974) *Project Appraisal and Planning for Developing Countries*. London: Heinemann Educational Books.

12　United Nations Industrial Development Organization (1972) *Guidelines for Project Evaluation*. New York: United Nations.

13　Squire, L. & Van der Tak, H.G. (1975) *Economic Analysis of Projects*. Published for the World Bank. Baltimore, MD: Johns Hopkins University Press.

14　Carlile, W.H. (1994) "States are Closing Firms' 'Candy Store': Laws Tighten Incentives, Seek Accountability for Subsidies." *The Arizona Republic*, July 24.

15　Epstein, M.J. (1994) "Viewpoints: A Formal Plan for Environmental Costs." *New York Times*, April 3, Section 3.

16　The California Center for Innovative Transportation at the Institute of Transportation Studies, at the University of California at Berkeley.

17　Committee of the American Society of Civil Engineers.

18　Federal Highway Administration. (2002). *Status of the Nation's Highways, Bridges, and Transit: 2002 Conditions and Performance Report*. Available at fhwa.dot.gov/policy/2002/cpr/ch10.htm. Retrieved July 21, 2007.

19　Fuguitt & Wilcox (1999).

20　Fuguitt & Wilcox (1999), p. 13.

9

The international tourism policy process

Worldwide tourism has grown enormously since 1976, the year in which the global tourism policy body, the United Nations World Tourism Organization (UNWTO) came into existence. There is every reason to believe tourism will continue to increase even faster in the future. Much of the future growth in tourism will depend on local areas and national governments having good policies and strategic plans that support quality tourism development. Tourism policy links the planning function and political goals for tourism into a concrete set of guidelines to give us direction as we move ahead. Without such guidance we might find tourism's future considerably less beneficial than we had hoped. Tourism policies are needed, particularly at the international level, to reconcile private-sector concerns with the public interest. The tourism sector will require improved management of its essential functions, including planning, development, finance, human resource development, research, and evaluation. This chapter will focus on some of the conceptual tools that assist in the development of tourism policy aimed at insuring quality growth in tourism. Much of the chapter addresses tourism policy issues within a global context. Tourism policy in essence is a set of guidelines meant to facilitate achievement of a set of objectives for a government or organization. Chapter 10 will introduce strategic tourism planning and the further connection of planning with tourism policy.

Chapter 9 will also look at the symbiotic ties between the economics of international trade in tourism and the links to related non-trade issues, such as increased benefits from cultural exchanges and the promotion of mutual goodwill, and suggests that increased dialogue on tourism issues must take place at all levels. It also seeks to demonstrate that not only does international trade in tourism have an impact on the economy, foreign relations, and social fabric of most countries of the world but its growth potential for the future is so significant that it should capture the policy attention of the world's leaders.

This chapter has been deliberately kept brief and non-technical to appeal to a broader readership. The aim is to provide government policymakers (at all levels), business leaders, university professors, students, managers in tourism organizations, and the general public with an introduction and examination of important policy processes in tourism. It helps explain the role that tourism policy plays in integrating economic, political, cultural, business, and environmental benefits of tourism to improve the global quality-of-life of visitors and local citizens.

Tourism policy development

As global tourism becomes more complex and sophisticated and the competitive situation becomes more intense, it is being recognized that more effective policies need to be developed in order to address tourism's role in world economic and social development within the context of a sustainable environment. There is a need to address more clearly policy issues and policy development processes that are being utilized by the public and private-sectors of the tourism industry. Now there is greater recognition that contemporary tourism policy approaches require us to "think globally and act locally" in a responsible manner. Community involvement in the tourism development process is a necessary part of any tourism policy initiative.

As a tourism policy is developed, it should not be overly complex but rather straightforward so that it is easily understood and can be applied as practical guide-lines for resolving problem areas. It should offer up prescriptions or best practices with clearly defined steps. This applied science approach to tourism policy presents both scholars and practitioners with tools that can be readily understood within the political process.

The opportunity that tourism offers for positive economic and social benefits for tomorrow will depend on the decisions being made today. We can plan well for the development of tourism or let it happen indiscriminately and hope for the best. If we do not define clear-cut policies and plans at this juncture in the growth of tourism, there may never be another opportunity. We have a limited environment to work with and undue care must be taken to protect it for the future. Strategic planning (see Chapter 10) combined with tourism policy links the planning function and political goals for tourism into a concrete set of guidelines to give us direction as we move ahead. What this chapter and the next seek is a better understanding of the practical applications of tourism policy and planning.

The book has already mentioned that the UNWTO is the global leader in tourism policy and reference to UNWTO's policy role will be repeated numerous times more. UNWTO recognized early in its existence that without cooperation at the international level, tourism development would happen in a haphazard manner throughout the world. By working together, each nation can learn something helpful from other countries and incorporate this experience into their own national tourism policy.

Since its inception, UNWTO has had many global conventions with respect to instituting international tourism policies. In addition, many regional groups have also held tourism policy conferences to review more local tourism issues. At each such event, new tourism policy development ideas have emerged and the participating nations have gained innovative solutions for some of their problem areas. A review of a few past global policies helps us to better understand tourism policy development.

The impact of the *Helsinki Accords* on tourism policy

The *Helsinki Accords*[1] were the final act of the Conference on Security and Co-operation in Europe held in Helsinki, Finland, during July and August, 1975. Thirty-five nations, including the United States, Canada, and all European states except Albania and Andorra, signed the pact in an attempt to improve relations between the communist bloc and the West (this was a time when the "Cold War" existed between the United States and the Soviet Union, which were on opposite sides of the ideological political spectrum). While the *Helsinki Accords* were not a legally binding concord, as they did not have treaty status, they nevertheless existed in an aura implying a moral pledge to abide by the decisions taken at the conference. The *Accords* dealt with tourism provisions in the human rights section of the document.

The lengthy details of the *Helsinki Accords* covered a broad range of issues. However, peace, security, and human rights were mentioned many times in the document. The tourism section of the *Accords* acknowledged that freer tourism is essential to the development of cooperation amongst nations. With specific reference to tourism, the signatories to the *Accords*, among other points included: a) their intentions to "encourage increased tourism on both an individual and group basis;" b) the desirability of carrying out "detailed studies on tourism;" c) an agreement to "endeavor, where possible, to ensure that the development of tourism does not injure the artistic, historic and cultural heritage in their respective countries;" d) their intention "to facilitate wider travel by their citizens for personal or professional reasons;" e) an agreement to "endeavor gradually to lower, where necessary, the fees for visas and official travel documents;" f) an agreement to "increase, on the basis of appropriate agreements or arrangements, cooperation in the development of tourism, in particular, by considering bilaterally, possible ways to increase information relating to travel to other related questions of mutual interest;" and g) their intention "to promote visits to their respective countries." At the time, this agreement was considered a revolutionary move to support tourism exchanges among the signatory countries. The *Helsinki Accords* helped move forward the universal recognition and need for tourism policies whether nationally, bilaterally, or multilaterally. Future tourism policy documents would most often contain some of the *Accords* provisions.

Bilateral tourism agreements

The *Helsinki Accords* mention the opportunity for countries of the word to enter into bilateral tourism arrangements or agreements to assist in moving visitors across borders or in providing tourism information or in other forms of cooperation to improve bilateral political relations and to increase tourism between two countries. The point is that tourism has been used globally to break down numerous types of barriers between countries. While the concept behind a tourism agreement is the promotion of trade in tourism, bilateral agreements also serve additional national policy objectives, such as encouraging international understanding, friendly relations, and goodwill. There was also a movement by many countries to recognize that tourism activities of a national tourism office constitute a legitimate diplomatic and consular function within the meaning of Article 3 of the Vienna Convention of Diplomatic Relations.[2] Such recognition gives stature to international tourism promotion and puts it on a more equal footing with other governmental functions.

Usually bilateral tourism agreements begin with a preamble or policy statement indicating the reason for negotiation a tourism arrangement. This would then be follow by specific articles of the agreement. Following are a few selected principles taken directly from a number of different bilateral tourism agreements:

- Aim to increase two-way tourism
- Support efforts by the national tourism organization's travel-promotion office
- Improve tourism facilitation
- Encourage investments in each other's tourism industry
- Promote the sharing of research, statistics, and information
- Recognize the importance of the safety and security of tourists
- Suggest mutual cooperation on policy issues in international tourism
- Provide for regular consultations on tourism matters
- Acknowledge benefits from education and training in tourism
- Enhance mutual understanding and goodwill

Many bilateral tourism agreements are very brief, simply expressing a need for a better understanding of tourism exchanges between the two countries. In some cases, specific provisions are written into the agreement to allow, for example, tourism personnel of one country located in their international tourism office in the other country, to be provided with diplomatic privileges. Other interests might include support for permitting greater air and sea access. Also, the agreement might have a provision to make it easier for cultural groups from one country to enter another country without having to have a visa. It was noted in one agreement that two countries agreed to cooperate in the joint marketing of tourism. There is no lack of creativeness in what a bilateral tourism agreement might contain. Once such an agreement was negotiated and signed, it was usually effective for five years with an opportunity to renew or extend the arrangement, or to amend it in one form or another.

Manila Declaration on World Tourism

One of the early international tourism policy conferences of the UNWTO took place in Manila, Philippines, September 27–October 10, 1980. This was a particularly important gathering as it was the first comprehensive meeting on global tourism policy since UNWTO was established in 1976. Many of the delegates from the member states of UNWTO were just beginning to better understand the need for global tourism policies.

The popular and often-cited document that emanated from this conference became known as the *Manila Declaration on World Tourism*.[3] It is useful to highlight some of the important measures that were discussed and included in the declaration. As was true in the *Helsinki Accords*, likewise with the *Manila Declaration*, the words "peace" and "security" were mentioned on the first page. Peace through tourism is a recurring theme in international tourism policies and for that reason is included in some useful context in almost every chapter of this book. Security is also highlighted in both documents as most tourism policy documents and bilateral and multilateral agreements address this important issue.

The next couple of paragraphs quote extensively from the *Manila Declaration* because it clearly enunciates some important tourism policy considerations:

> *Considering* that world tourism can develop in a climate of peace and security which can be achieved through the joint effort of all States in promoting the reduction of international tension and in developing international cooperation in a spirit of friendship, respect for human rights, . . . *Convinced* that world tourism can be a vital force for world peace and can provide the moral and intellectual basis for international understanding and interdependence, . . . *Convinced* further that world tourism can contribute to the establishment of a new international economic order that will help to eliminate the widening economic gap between developed and developing countries and ensure the steady acceleration of economic and social development and progress, in particular of the developing countries, . . . *Aware* that world tourism can only flourish if based on equity, sovereign equality, non-interference in internal affairs and cooperation among all States, irrespective of their economic and social systems, and if its ultimate aim is the improvement of the quality-of-life and the creation of better living conditions for all peoples, worthy of human dignity.

If the document had closed with this last statement, it would still have been one of the great tourism policy documents. However, the document continued in a vein with best practices for implementing such policies.

For example, in Step 1 of the *Manila Declaration*, it is declared that:

> Tourism is considered an activity essential to the life of nations because of its direct effects on the social, cultural, educational and economic sectors of national societies and their international relations. Its development is linked to the social and economic development of nations and can only be possible if man has access to creative rest and holidays and enjoys the freedom to travel within the framework of free time and leisure whose profoundly human character it underlies. Its very existence and development depend entirely on the existence of a state of lasting peace, to which tourism itself is required to contribute.

The *Manila Declaration* is also important because it set the stage for later documents to build on the peace through tourism principle. One such document, for example, is *The Columbia Charter* (1988), which discusses "world peace through tourism" (discussed later in this chapter). Item number 13 of the *Manila Declaration* has this to say: "With respect to international relations and the search for peace, based on justice and respect of individual and national aspirations, tourism stands out as a positive and ever-present factor in promoting mutual knowledge and understanding and as a basis for reaching a greater level of respect and confidence among all the peoples of the world."

Item 18 of the *Manila Declaration* set the stage for a discussion of sustainable tourism many years before the Brundtland Report was issued, or the United Nations Conference on Environment and Development (*Agenda 21*) took place (see Chapter 6). This element of the document states:

> Tourism resources available in the various countries consist at the same time of space, facilities and values. These are resources whose use cannot be left uncontrolled without running the risk of their deterioration, or even their destruction. The satisfaction of tourism requirements must not be prejudicial to the social and economic interests of the population in tourist areas, to the environment or, above all, to natural resources, which are the fundamental attraction of tourism, and historical and cultural sites. All tourism resources are part of the heritage of mankind. National communities and the entire international community must take the necessary steps to ensure their preservation. The conservation of historical, cultural and religious sites represents at all times, and notably in time of conflict, one of the fundamental responsibilities of States.

UNWTO as the leader in global tourism policy is grounded in the *Manila Declaration* and enunciated in Items 19 and 25 as follows: "International cooperation in the field of tourism is an endeavor in which the characteristics of peoples and basic interests of individual States must be respected. In this field, the central and decisive role of the World Tourism Organization [UNWTO] as a conceptualizing and harmonizing body is obvious," and in the last point of the document, "The Conference urges the World Tourism Organization [UNWTO] to take all necessary measures, through its own internal, intergovernmental and non-governmental bodies, so as to permit the global implementation of the principles, concepts and guidelines contained in this final document."

The *Manila Declaration* is fundamental to understanding international tourism policy and not including it in a book on tourism policy and planning would leave a major knowledge gap in the understanding of the international tourism policy process. It also demonstrates that, while many of us who work in the trenches of tourism policy think our contemporary tourism policy ideas are new, we may find them contained somewhere in the *Manila Declaration*.

FIGURE 9.1 The state has preserved the historic Peter and Paul Fortress in St. Petersburg, Russia
(Photo: Jason R. Swanson)

Tourism Bill of Rights and Tourist Code

Another important tourism policy document is the *Tourism Bill of Rights and Tourist Code*.[4] Co-author of this book Edgell was an early advocate of delineating the rights and responsibilities of both tourists and travel-related businesses. After several years of consultations, discussions, and negotiations, the *Tourism Bill of Rights and Tourist Code* was adopted by the Sixth General Assembly of the UNWTO in Sofia, Bulgaria, in September 1985. The document was broken down in two parts: *Tourism Bill of Rights* (*Bill*) and *Tourist Code* (*Code*).

Most of the nations wanted to foster tourism growth and development, but in a balanced way to avoid potential negative impacts from tourism. This interest was partially addressed in Article III of the *Bill* by "a) encourage the orderly and harmonious growth of both domestic and international tourism; b) integrate their [national] tourism policies with their overall development policies at all levels – local, regional, national and international – and broaden tourism cooperation within both a bilateral and multilateral framework, including that of the [United Nations] World Tourism Organization." Interest in developing model local and national tourism policies are addressed later in this chapter.

While the present benchmark for concerns with respect to terrorism is most often cited as September 11, 2001, terrorism was a major problem in the 1980s with airplane hijackings and hostage-takings taking place. The *Bill* in Article IV (c) addressed this policy concern, saying nations must "ensure the safety of visitors and the security of their belongings through preventive and protective measures." The issue of safety and security is discussed in more detail in Chapter 12 of this book.

Even though the *Manila Declaration* addressed socio-cultural and environmental policy issues, many nations felt it should be reinforced. Article VI of the *Bill* stated that tourists had responsibilities to the host community in these words: "They [host communities] are also entitled to expect from tourists understanding and respect for their customs, religions and other elements of their cultures which are part of the human heritage." At the same time, tourists had the right to expect (included in Article VII) that "The population constituting the host communities in place of transit and sojourn are invited to receive tourists with the greatest possible hospitality, courtesy and respect necessary for the development of harmonious human and social relations."

There was also a concern that visitors often did not respect the destination they were visiting. The *Code* was aimed at rights and responsibilities of the tourist. Article X states: "Tourists should, by their behavior, foster understanding and friendly relations among peoples, at both the national and international levels, and thus contribute to lasting peace." This issue was addressed in more detail in some of the additional articles. In brief, the *Tourism Bill of Rights and Tourist Code* added important practical tourism policy guidelines.

FIGURE 9.2 Local residents, seen by visitors in a Kenyan marketplace, perpetuate and create culture
(Photo: Junghee 'Michelle' Han)

The Hague Declaration on Tourism

In April 1989, possibly inspired by the global progress made in tourism policy through the *Manila Declaration* and the *Tourism Bill of Rights and Tourist Code*, the Inter-Parliamentary Union (IPU) – a worldwide organization of 112 national parliaments founded in 1889 – and the UNWTO organized a global conference on tourism which took place in The Hague, Netherlands. This convocation, by far, developed the most comprehensive set of global tourism policy prescriptions yet assembled and delineated. *The Hague Declaration on Tourism*[5] is much too long to summarize but it is worth noting some selected sections of the "principles" that evolved from the conference in the next few paragraphs. To do justice to tourism policy analysis, the preamble, introduction, principles, and Part I (of four parts) of *The Hague Declaration on Tourism* are included in their entirety as Case Study 9 at the end of this chapter. These particular sections of the document were included in the case study as they best fit the intent of this chapter. However, a few special provisions of *The Hague Declaration* are highlighted below to demonstrate just how important this document is to the international tourism policy process.

In Principle I of *The Hague Declaration* it is useful to observe, "All Governments should work for national, regional, and international peace and security which are essential to the development of domestic and international tourism." The word "peace" shows up often in world meetings on tourism. Just prior to The Hague conference, the International Institute For Peace Through Tourism convened "The First Global Conference: Tourism – A Vital Force For Peace" in Vancouver, British Columbia, Canada in 1988. This conference was totally devoted to "world peace as it relates to tourism" and is sometimes referred to as *The Columbia Charter*, covered later in this chapter.

Principle II of the *Hague Declaration* is an effort to encourage countries to develop a strategic plan for tourism to balance its socio-economic growth (strategic tourism planning is discussed in detail in Chapter 10 of this book). It then leads to a discussion of tourism and the environment. Principle III is extremely important in that it sets the stage for many of the current views on sustainable tourism. The principle of sustainable tourism is summarized in this section as: "An unspoilt natural, cultural and human environment is a fundamental condition for the development of tourism. Moreover, rational management of tourism may contribute significantly to the protection and development of the physical environment and the cultural heritage, as well as to improving the quality-of-life." This principle is in essence the foundation for sustainable tourism as discussed in Chapter 6 of this book.

Principle IV discusses characteristics of the international visitor and Principle V advocates the universal need to allow everyone an opportunity for a vacation. Principle VI introduces the topic of tourism facilitation to ease the restrictions and barriers to international travel. Principle VII fits current concerns for the "safety, security and protection of tourists and respect for their dignity." Principle VIII takes up the issue of terrorism. It contains a fairly strong statement to that effect: "Terrorism constitutes a real threat for tourism . . . Terrorists must be treated like any other criminals and should be pursued and punished without statutory limitation, no country thus being a safe haven for terrorists." Additional principles are discussed and the document closes with 95 conclusive remarks and recommendations aimed at improving the overall quality of international tourism through effective tourism policies.

The Columbia Charter

This book has mentioned many times the recurring tourism policy themes of "peace" and "security." While these two issues have a long history in tourism, certainly as far back as the beginning of the Olympics in Greece in 776 BCE, they remain very much contemporary interests within international tourism policy circles and beyond. The prior section noted reference to *The Columbia Charter* as a conference devoted to the issue of peace through tourism. This conference was titled "The First Global Conference: Tourism – A Vital Force For Peace" and was convened in Vancouver, British Columbia, Canada, October 23–27, 1988. It was the first major event of the

International Institute for Peace Through Tourism (IIPT, founded in 1986) taking place during the "United Nations International Year of Peace." The convocation was partly aimed at the concern of the tourism industry with respect to major terrorism events that took place in 1985 and1986. The year 1986 was the peak year for terrorism and from that point forward, traveler safety and security were major issues and dealt with in many different forums and with many types of international agreements. IIPT held two additional global conferences in Montreal, Canada (1994), and Glasgow, Scotland (1999). These three conferences and other meetings and activities provided the information and impetus for the "First Global Summit on Peace through Tourism" held in Amman, Jordan (2000). IIPT has also worked toward mobilizing the travel and tourism industry as a leading force for poverty reduction.

The Columbia Charter built on the philosophies and principles expressed in the 1980 *Manila Declaration* and other documents related to peace and tourism. It expressed "the urgent reality that peace is an essential precondition for tourism . . . promotes tourism which is in harmony with the world's natural and cultural resources . . . advocates the development of educational systems both in institutions and in the community, in which everyone from industry leaders and government, to individual tourists, can learn the possibilities and the value of tourism as a force for peace." While the charter is generally thought of as a "peace through tourism" document, it also addressed other important tourism concerns:

- promotes mutual understanding, trust and goodwill;
- reduces economic inequities;
- develops in an integrated manner with the full participation of local host communities;
- improves the quality-of-life;
- protects and preserves the environment, both built and natural, and other local resources;
- contributes to the world conservation strategy of sustainable development.

These same elements are major topics in the current discussion of tourism policy issues.

Model tourism policies

Following the *Manila Declaration on World Tourism* and the *Tourism Bill of Rights and Tourist Code*, the interest in tourism policy became even stronger. Questions were raised as to whether there was a need for a tourism policy at the national level only or if local tourism policies were also useful. UNWTO recognized the strong interest in tourism policy and through the offices of Purdue University, requested that Dr. Edgell address some of the key issues regarding tourism policy. After some study and research he produced, *International Tourism Policy, Selected Readings* (1991).[6]

Following are examples of three model tourism policy documents (in order of preparation): a Model State Tourism Policy (January 1990); a Model National Tourism Policy (June 1990); and a Model Municipal Tourism Policy (December 1990). There have been many changes in tourism policy thinking since 1990, however, some precepts advocated in the 1990s are still relevant today.

Model State Tourism Policy

The first model, the Model State Tourism Policy (January 1990) evolved from visits by Dr. Edgell to many of the US states. While the word "state" is included in the title, it means a US unit of government as opposed to a sovereign national power. One could substitute "province" in the place of "state," or some other government unit larger than a municipality but smaller than a national government. Section I of the Model State Tourism Policy contains a preamble that speaks to the importance of tourism and then moves to Section II with examples of elements that should be included in a state tourism policy, "encourage the orderly growth of tourism . . . expand off-season tourism . . . establish tax incentives to attract investment . . . awareness of the State's cultural contributions," etc. These concerns continue to be important within current discussions of tourism policy. Section III "Duties and Responsibilities of the Governor," suggests the head of the state government, the governor of the state, operating through a state tourism office, should outline the broad state tourism goals and objectives to be implemented by the state tourism director. This section also delineates what other departments of state government should accomplish to contribute to increased tourism to and within the state. Section IV explains how to formulate a state Tourism Policy Council and the responsibilities for that council. Finally, in Section V it suggests that the governor of the state appoint a Tourism Advisory Board that represents various components of the tourism industry within the state.

Model National Tourism Policy

The second model, the Model National Tourism Policy (June 1990) was partially patterned after the US National Tourism Policy Act of 1981. That Act is included in its entirety as a case study in Chapter 2 of this book. While that Act is no longer active – due to a political *faux pas*, which has left the United States without a national tourism policy – it continues to be a good example of what should be included in a national tourism policy. A current illustration of a positive national tourism policy is that of Canada. Chapter 10 of this book mentions some aspects of Canada's tourism policy (conduct an internet search of "Canada tourism policy" for the latest changes).

The Model National Tourism Policy infers that the tourism policy would be legislated within the body politic of the country in question through whatever the legislative process may be for a nation to endorse such a policy. An alternative method, not advocated herein, is to proclaim a national tourism policy through a "head of nation" (president, prime minister, etc.) edict or executive order of one type or another. Most often, a tourism policy begins with a preamble that suggests the reasons for the action elements appearing in the document. Next, broad policy goals explaining the various aspects of what are needed in a country's tourism program are enunciated. The document will usually contain the responsibilities of the country's head of state for implementing the policy either directly or through a designated minister(s), or another identified official. The tourism policy document will usually suggest that a national tourism policy council be established. Such a council would include various ministers or officials within the government having some responsibility related to tourism policy (transportation, environment, trade, etc.). In addition, the policy document should include the establishment of a tourism advisory board, representing the various components of the country's tourism industry sectors, both the private and public sectors. The advisory board would provide advice on tourism policies, strategic planning, marketing objectives, funding mechanisms and other matters essential to implementing the national tourism policy.

Model Municipal Tourism Policy

The last model described in the *Selected Readings in International Tourism Policy* was an effort to include a Model Municipal Tourism Policy. This model was added as an illustration of what could be accomplished at the local level with respect to tourism policy. Often, municipalities are omitted from the tourism policy approach, yet few tourism policies can be truly effective unless acted upon by the local community. It is an open question as to what level of a local community should be involved in the tourism policy process. This will vary from country to country. It may be a city or an area encompassing more than one community. The key is if a local district is interested in developing or expanding its tourism program, it should have a tourism policy to guide them in their tourism planning. The principles of the tourism policy for a municipality are similar to those at the state or national levels but depend on the local governmental structure. Assuming the local community is part of a state or regional body, the policies at the local level will need to be coordinated to support tourism policies at the next level and ultimately, to the degree possible, add to the tourism policies at the national level. It should be reiterated that the above models were developed for illustrative purposes only in order to help governmental entities better understand the tourism policy process.

Projections, implications, and policy perspectives

In the tourism policy process, an area often overlooked is the need for forecasting jobs and forecasting tourism, especially arrivals and receipts. To formulate tourism policies having long-term perspectives for a destination, it is helpful to forecast or project tourism demand. A key question is what type of methodology to use in making the forecasts. This section of the chapter includes a few approaches to forecasting tourism demand that the co-author Edgell has been involved with over the past 35 years.

On a global basis, the UNWTO and the World Travel and Tourism Council (WTTC) have been making world tourism projections for many years. For example, the WTTC projects that global jobs in tourism will increase from 255 million in 2012 to 303 million in 2020 and that economic activity in tourism will increase from $6 trillion to $11.15 trillion in the same period. UNWTO forecasts that international tourists arrivals will increase from about one billion (2012 estimate) to 1.6 billion in 2020. These are important predictions and demonstrate the fast growth pace of the travel and tourism industry. Determining outlooks for the tourism industry along with the implications of such prognostications are important for planning and policy decision-making. Over the years, the methodologies for making tourism forecasts have become very sophisticated and within an acceptable margin of error, fairly accurate. It is useful to reflect on a few of the changes that have improved the forecasting techniques.

In the early 1970s, co-author Edgell, as a member of a special forecasting team at the Massachusetts Institute of Technology, was involved in an attempt to develop an econometric forecasting model (not originally designed for tourism projections) to forecast the US economy. If it were successful, the thought was that it could also be applied to forecasting individual industry sectors as, for example, tourism projections. However, for reasons beyond the understanding of the forecasting team, their track record was not very good. As a result, the project was abandoned. In retrospect it is probable that too many variables were included in the makeup of the forecasting formula or possibly the team relied too heavily on survey data that was not very accurate.

Later in the 1970s many new forecasting models for tourism were being developed. One of the reasonably successful approaches, based on reviewing the trends of the basic factors that support the tourism industry, was published in an article titled "International Tourism Development: Forecasts to 1985."[7] This effort stimulated others to take up the challenge.

Edgell, principally relying on trend analysis method and simple regression, projected with moderate success tourism demand from 1977 to 2000. These forecasts by Edgell, which were included in his lectures, were included as part of his participation in "The International Telephone and Telegraph Corporation Key Issues Lecture Series" at the University of Texas. The lectures were given by experts in various business fields and were published in the book *International Business Prospects 1977–1999*.[8]

In 1978, Edgell and two colleagues made a presentation titled "Use of Modified Scenario Research in Forecasting of Tourism in the United States" at the Joint National Meeting of the Operation Research Society of America and the Institute of Management Sciences. This approach met with a degree of success and added a new dimension to tourism forecasting. A partial version of the presentation was published in the *Travel Research Journal* in 1979.[9] In 1980, Edgell, Seely, and Iglarsh utilized a simple time-series approach to forecasting international tourism to the US and found the technique highly useful.[10]

Another forecasting technique was the use of the Delphi method. The military, seeking to improve their ability to forecast, began to use the Delphi method developed by Project RAND during the 1950s and 1960s. By the 1970s the Delphi method was being used successfully in business forecasting. Edgell and several colleagues began to experiment with using a modified Delphi method for forecasting tourism demand. It seemed to work well and the results were published in an article in the 1980 *Travel Research Journal*, titled "Utilizing the Delphi Technique at International Conferences: An Important Method for Forecasting International Tourism Conditions." They conducted further tests of this concept and included it in an article "Forecasts of International Tourism to the USA" published in 1980 by the *International Journal of Tourism Management*.

In the 1990s, after reviewing theoretical models and intuitive methods for forecasting tourism, Edgell mixed, modified, and further revised his approaches to forecasting tourism demand. He began to make various assumptions and included certain basic factors organized through utilizing a modified Delphi method. Using mostly a simple trend analysis, limited multiple regressions, and the Delphi method, Edgell used 1960 as a base year and forecasted tourism through the year 2000. The predictions were published in 1990 in Edgell's book *International Tourism Policy* in which he included a chapter titled "Projections, Implications, and Policy Perspectives of International Tourism Through 2000." The results were gratifying and fairly accurate.[11]

With the advent of computer-based forecasting models, today's tourism technician has many options for making forecasts. Edgell, with a long career in the tourism industry is convinced that statistical analysis combined with a modified Delphi method works as well as any other approach. Edgell would subscribe to the following: "For estimating tourism demand, then, *a combination of various mathematical statistical methods and the Delphi method* is believed to produce the most reliable demand estimates in any given situation."[12] In summary the Executive Judgment (Delphi) Method or a modification of the method, is just as important as the use of statistical and mathematical tools in forecasting tourism demand.

CHAPTER REVIEW QUESTIONS

1. Why should tourism policy be straightforward?
2. Why is the *Manila Declaration on World Tourism* so important to tourism policy?
3. What does the *Tourism Bill of Rights* do?
4. What is the *Tourist Code*?
5. What are the principles of the *Hague Declaration*?
6. *The Columbia Charter* is principally concerned with what tourism issue?
7. What was unique about the Model Municipal Tourism Policy?
8. Which forecasting method has been found to be effective in collecting consensus among groups of experts?

CASE STUDY 9 The Hague Declaration on Tourism

The Inter-Parliamentary Conference on Tourism,

Organized at The Hague (Netherlands) from 10 to 14 April 1989 jointly by the Inter-Parliamentary Union (IPU) and the World Tourism Organization (WTO), at the invitation of the Netherlands Inter-Parliamentary Group,

Considering that it is in the interest of all countries to facilitate both individual and group tourist travel, visits and stays which, contributing as they do to economic, social and cultural development, foster the creation of a climate of confidence and mutual understanding between the States members of the international community, the development of international co-operation and, hence, lasting peace in the world,

Considering that, in so doing, account should also be taken of the special problems of the developing countries in the field of tourism,

Recalling the Universal Declaration of Human Rights adopted by the General Assembly of the United Nations on 10 December 1948, and in particular its Article 24, which states: "Everyone has the right to rest and leisure, including reasonable limitation of working hours and periodic holidays with pay", as well as Article 7 of the International Covenant on Economic, Social and Cultural Rights, adopted by the General Assembly of the United Nations on 16 December 1966, by which States undertake to ensure, for everyone, with pay, as well as remuneration for public holidays", and Article 12 of the International Covenant on Civil and Political Rights, also adopted on 16 December 1966 by the General Assembly of the United Nations, which states: "Everyone shall be free to leave any country, including his own."

Considering the resolution and recommendations adopted by the United Nations Conference on International Travel and Tourism (Rome, September 1963) and, in particular, those concerning the promotion of tourism development in the various countries of the world and the simplification of governmental formalities for international travel,

Inspired by the principles set forth in the Manila Declaration on World Tourism, and the Acapulco Document, the Tourist Code and Tourism Bill of Rights, underscoring the human dimension of tourism, recognizing the new role of tourism as an instrument for improving the quality-of-life of all peoples and as a vital force for peace and international understanding, and defining the responsibilities of the State in its development, particularly with respect to promoting awareness about the importance of tourism among the peoples of the world and protecting and enhancing tourism resources as part of the heritage of mankind, with a view to contributing to the establishment of a more just and equitable new international economic order,

Recalling the "central and decisive role" of the World Tourism Organization (WTO) in the development of tourism as recognized by the General Assembly of the United Nations, with a view "to contributing to economic development, international understanding, peace, prosperity and universal respect for, and observance of, human rights and fundamental freedoms for all without distinction as to race, sex, language or religion",

Aware that an important contribution to the harmonious development of tourism can be made by the work of numerous inter-governmental and non-governmental organizations, such as the International Labour Organisation (ILO), the World Health Organization (WHO), the United Nations Educational, Scientific and Cultural Organization (UNESCO), the International Maritime Organization (IMO), the International Civil Aviation Organization (ICAO), the United Nations Environment Programme (UNEP), the International Criminal Police Organization (ICPO-INTERPOL), and the Organisation for Economic Co-operation and Development (OECD), and *stressing* the importance of close co-operation between those organizations and WTO,

Solemnly affirming, as a natural consequence of the right to work, the fundamental right, already consecrated in the Universal Declaration of Human Rights, the Covenants on Human Rights of the United Nations and in other universal and regional legal instruments, of everyone to rest, leisure and periodic leave with pay, and the right to use such time for the purposes of holidays, to travel freely for education of pleasure and to enjoy the benefits of tourism, both with his country of residence and abroad,

Recalling that it was at The Hague that the First International Congress of Official Tourist Traffic Associations met in 1925 and founded the International Union of Official Travel Organizations, which in 1975 was transformed into the World Tourism Organization,

Pronounces The Hague Declaration on Tourism as an instrument of inter-national co-operation, rapprochement between peoples and as a factor of individual and collective development,

Urges Parliaments, Governments, public and private authorities, organizations, associations and institutions responsible for tourism activities, tourism professionals, as well as tourists themselves, to consider carefully and draw constant inspiration from its principles, as set forth below:

PRINCIPLE I

1. Tourism has become a phenomenon of every-day life for hundreds of millions of people today:

a) It encompasses all free movements of persons away from their places of residence and work, as well as the service industries created to satisfy the needs resulting from these movements;

b) It constitutes an activity essential to the lives of human beings and modern societies, having become an important form of using the free time of individuals and the main vehicle for interpersonal relations and political, economic and cultural contact made necessary by the internationalization of all sectors of the life of nations,

c) It should be the concern of everyone. It is both a consequence and a decisive factor of the quality-of-life in contemporary society. Therefore, Parliaments and Governments should accord increasingly sustained attention to tourism with a view to ensuring its development in harmony with the other fundamental needs and activities of societies.

2. All Governments should work for national, regional and international peace and security which are essential to the development of domestic and international tourism.

PRINCIPLE II

1. Tourism can be an effective instrument for socio-economic growth for all countries, if at the same time the necessary measures are taken to tackle the more urgent national priorities and to allow the national economy to reach an acceptable level of self-sufficiency in which the country does not have to spend in excess of what it can hope to earn from tourism.

2. Consequently, the following measures should in particular be taken, if necessary with the help of the various forms of bilateral and multilateral technical co-operation, to ensure:

a) That a sound infrastructure is built up and the basic facilities are provided;

b) That training institutes are set up to meet the personnel needs of the tourism industry at different levels;

c) That tourism forms part of an integrated plan for development of the country in which agriculture, industrial development, medical care, social welfare, education, etc. are priority sectors;

d) That the development of domestic tourism be equally encouraged with the promotion of international tourism. A strong base of domestic tourism will be a big asset for the development of international tourism in the country;

e) That even in planning for domestic tourism, the Master Plan approach on an area basis is developed to bring about a balanced and integrated growth for the benefit of the community; and

f) That the overall capacity of the natural, physical and cultural environment of destinations to receive tourism (carrying capacity) be always carefully taken into consideration.

PRINCIPLE III

1. An unspoilt natural, cultural and human environment is a fundamental condition for the development of tourism. Moreover, rational management of tourism may contribute significantly to the protection and development of the physical environment and the cultural heritage, as well as to improving the quality-of-life.

2. In view of this intrinsic inter-relationship between tourism and environment, effective measures should be taken to:

a) Inform and educate tourists, both domestic and international, to preserve, conserve and respect the natural, cultural and human environment in places they visit;

b) Promote the integrated planning of tourism development on the basis of the concept of "sustainable development" which was set forth in the Report of the World Commission of Environment and Development (Brundtland Report) and in the report "The Environment Perspective to the Year 2000 and Beyond" of the United Nations Environment Programme (UNEP), both of which documents have been approved by the UN General Assembly;

c) Determine and ensure respect for carrying-capacity levels of sites visited by tourist even if this implies restricting access to such sites at certain periods or seasons;

d) Continue to compile an inventory of man-made and/or natural tourist sites of recreational, sporting, historical, archaeological, artistic, cultural, religious, scientific, social or technical interest and ensure that tourism development plans take special account of aspects related with environmental protection and the need to promote awareness among tourists, the tourism industry and the public at large of the importance of safeguarding the natural and cultural environment;

e) Encourage development of alternative forms of tourism which favour closer contact and understanding between tourists and receiving populations, preserve cultural identity and offer distinctive and original tourist products and facilities;

f) Ensure the necessary co-operation between the public and private-sector to this end both at national and international levels.

PRINCIPLE IV

1. In view of the eminently human character of tourism, consideration should always be given to the specific problems of tourists themselves, whether they be domestic or international. An international tourist is any person:

a) Who intends to travel, and/or travels, to a country other than that in which he or she has his or her usual place of residence, and

b) Whose main purpose of travel is a visit or stay not exceeding three months, unless a stay longer than three months is authorized or the three months authorization is renewed, and

c) Who will not exercise, whether or not he or she is called upon to exercise, any activity remunerated in the country visited, and

d) Who, at the end of the said visit or stay, will obligatorily leave the country visited, either to return to the country where he or she has his or her usual place of residence or to travel to another country.

2. It logically follows that a person cannot be considered an international tourist if he or she does not fulfill all the conditions enumerated in paragraph 1 and, in particular, if, after entering the country as a tourist for tourist visit or stay, he or she seeks to prolong his or her length of visit or stay so as to establish residence and/or to exercise a remunerated activity there.

PRINCIPLE V

1. The right of everyone to rest and leisure, including reasonable limitation of working hours and periodic holidays with pay, and the right to travel freely, subject to reasonable restrictions which are explicitly provided for by law and which do not call into question the principle of the freedom of movement itself, must be universally recognized.

2. In order for these fundamental rights of every man and woman to be fully ensured, it is necessary to:

a) Formulate and apply policies to promote harmonious development of domestic and international tourism and leisure activities for the benefit of all those who participate in them;

b) Give due consideration to the principles set forth in the Manila Declaration on World tourism, the Acapulco Document and the Tourism Bill of Rights and Tourist Code, particularly when States formulate or apply tourism development policies, plans and programmes in accordance with their national priorities.

PRINCIPLE VI

The promotion of tourism requires facilitation of travel. Effective measures should therefore be taken by the public and private-sectors to:

a) Facilitate tourist travel, visits and stays, both on an individual and collective basis, irrespective of the mode of transport used;

b) Contributing effectively to the expansion of tourist travel, visits and stays by taking appropriate facilitation measures with respect to passports, visas, health and exchange controls and the status of tourism representations abroad;

c) Foster, to this end, the adoption and implementation of the Budapest Convention to Facilitate Tourist Travel, Visits and Stays, thereby permitting the liberalization of the legal provisions applicable to tourists and the harmonization of technical standards concerning the operation of tourism enterprises, travel agencies and other bodies serving tourists.

PRINCIPLE VII

The safety, security and protection of tourists and respect for their dignity are a precondition to develop tourism. Therefore, it is indispensable;

a) That the measures to facilitate tourist travel, visit and stays be accompanied by measures to ensure the safety, security and protection of tourists and tourist facilities and the dignity of tourists;

b) That an effective policy concerning the safety, security and protection of tourists and tourist facilities and respect for the dignity of tourists be established for this purpose;

c) To identify precisely the tourist goods, facilities and equipment which, because of their use by tourists, require special attention;

d) To prepare and make available appropriate documentation and information in cases of threats to tourist facilities and/or tourist sites;

e) To implement, in accordance with the procedures specific to the systems of law of each country, legal provisions in the field of tourist protection, including in particular the ability for tourists to seek effective legal remedy from the national courts in the event of acts harmful to their persons, or property, and in particular the most grievous acts, such a terrorism;

f) That States co-operate within WTO to prepare a catalogue or recommended measures governing the safety, security and protection of tourists.

PRINCIPLE VIII

Terrorism constitutes a real threat for tourism and tourist movements. Terrorists must be treated like any other criminals and should be pursued and punished without statutory limitation, no country thus being a safe haven for terrorists.

PRINCIPLE IX

1. The quality of tourism as a person-to-person business depends on the quality of the personal service provided. Therefore appropriate education for the general public starting at the school level, education and training of tourism professionals and the preparation of new entrants in the profession are essential for the tourist industry and the development of tourism.

2. To this end, effective measures should be taken to:

a) Prepare individuals for travel and tourism, in particular by including tourism in school and university curricula;

b) Enhance the status of tourist professions and encourage young people in particular to embark upon a career in tourism;

c) Establish a network of institutions capable of providing not only training but also education in tourism on the basis of an internationally standardized curriculum which would also facilitate mutual recognition of qualifications and exchanges of tourism personnel;

d) Promote, in accordance with the recommendations of UNESCO in this field, training of trainers, permanent education and refresher courses for all tourism personnel or teachers regardless of level;

e) Recognize the vital role of the mass media in developing tourism.

PRINCIPLE X

1. Tourism should be planned on an integrated and coherent basis by public authorities, and between them and industry, taking into consideration all aspects of this complex phenomenon.

2. Whereas tourism has in the life of nations industrial importance at least equal to that of other economic and social activities, and whereas the role of tourism will expand in step with a scientific and technical progress and increases in free time, it appears necessary to strengthen, in all countries, the powers and responsibilities of the national tourism administrations, according them the same rank as administration responsible for other major economic sectors.

3. The need for a global approach to the problems raised by tourism requires the establishment of a genuine national tourism policy, in whose formulation Parliaments, when properly equipped, can play a special role so as to be in position to adopt specific legislation on tourism and, if required, an authentic Tourism Code.

4. Recognizing the international dimensions of tourism, worldwide as well as regional, international co-operation is essential for its harmonious development thorough direct inter-State co-operation and through the channel of international organizations, such as WTO, and between the different component of the private-sector tourism through non-governmental and professional organizations.

The Inter Parliamentary Conference on Tourism,

Also approves the Specific Conclusions and Recommendations contained in the Annex.

SPECIFIC CONCLUSIONS AND RECOMMENDATIONS

The Inter-Parliamentary Conference on Tourism,

Having set out the principles contained in the Hague Declaration on Tourism,

Adopts the following specific Conclusions and Recommendations.

I. THE PLACE OF TOURISM IN ECONOMIC AND SOCIAL DEVELOPMENT

Conclusions

1. The present importance of tourism and its economic future potential are indicated by the following statistics (referring to 1988):

- Total expenditure on domestic and international tourism (including air fares) is estimated to represent 12 per cent of total world GNP.
- Some 1.5 billion domestic and international tourist trips were made involving one-third of the world's population.
- International tourism accounted for 6 percent of total world exports and 25–30 percent of world trade in services.
- International tourism is forecast to increase at an annual rate of approximately 4 percent up to the year 2000, by which time it will be the world's largest export industry.

2. The potential impact of this dramatic growth on the economy, environment and people is of such magnitude that it may be referred to as the "Tourism Revolution."

3. Tourism is the way in which the individual can savour the unknown, acquire understanding and experience the world in its fullness; it is a revolution which enables all citizens of the world to travel, and one in which they can be wholeheartedly proud to participate.

4. Tourism stands out as a positive and ever-present factor in promoting mutual knowledge and understanding, and therefore peace and détente; conversely, tourism is strongly hampered by tension and conflicts and always fostered by peace.

5. Adequate leisure is a social necessity, but can become a burden if not put to proper use; among the many possibilities of spending spare time, not one (with the possible exception of television) has achieved such importance as tourism.

6. The economic potential for tourism development is almost unlimited; however,

7. Tourism expenditures, in addition to producing direct revenues, percolate down through many levels of the economy, creating not only direct buy also indirect employment, foreign exchange earnings, State revenue, patronage of craftsmen

and artists and development of regions with no other commercial or industrial base.

8. At present, the share of developing countries in worldwide tourism revenues is comparatively small; however, the developing countries are in a position to reap more benefits from international tourism, but should never lose sight of the fact that the benefits should not be sought at any cost.

9. Domestic tourism trips and expenditure, and therefore their contribution to economic wealth and employment at national, regional and local levels, are already a very large proportion of total worldwide tourism. Furthermore, the development and facilitation of domestic tourism is an important contributor to the enhancement of social contacts and understanding between people.

10. The development of domestic tourism also creates a basic tourist infrastructure and manpower skills which will assist countries in developing and harmoniously integrating an international tourism industry.

11. Tourism is a smokeless industry and is not necessarily accompanied by the devastating consequences that often come with industrialization; there are however potential dangers to both the physical and cultural environments which require the attention of States.

12. Well-preserved monuments, vital living traditions and a pristine natural environment will attract tourists and encourage them to return again; the expenditures of these tourists will in turn provide an economic motivation for the preservation of a nation's culture and environment. On the other hand, if such monuments are not well preserved, tourists will no longer be attracted and the economic benefits of tourism will diminish.

13. If uncontrolled and unplanned, tourism growth can lead to negative social, cultural and economic friction between tourist visitors and the local population, and to a uniform type of tourist behavior and requirements which in the long term could have an adverse impact on the cultural diversity and identity of local populations in the receiving countries.

14. The present pattern of worldwide tourism demand is very seasonal and highly concentrated in certain months of the year. This is not only due to climatic and motivational factors on the part of tourists, but is also caused by current industrial practices and national legislation governing annual factory closures and paid annual leave for employees, coupled with the calendar of school holiday dates.

15. The tourism industry has failed to present the real image of tourism and, at least until now, has not been successful in developing effective support for tourism particularly from parliamentarians.

16. The national tourism industries in most destination countries are highly fragmented, consisting of small-scale, individually operated and under-capitalized

tourism enterprises. While this can satisfy the diverse and individualistic needs of tourists, there is a growing imbalance between these and the increasingly concentrated nature of international tourism supply (international tour operators, airlines and hoteliers).

17. Due to international competition, the costs of promoting tourism industries are increasing, both in developing countries and "mature" economies (where tourism is increasingly seen as one of the solutions to regional development). There is also a need to measure the effectiveness of national, regional and local tourism promotion policies.

18. It is essential for public authorities at all levels in all countries, especially Parliaments, to take an active role in creating favourable conditions for tourism, and, in particular, to provide the financial and other means for comprehensive information programmes about tourism.

19. The present and future development of tourism demands more active Government support for information and promotion of tourism as well as provision of infrastructure; new markets need to be developed and steps should be taken to ensure co-operation in all spheres – public and private – in the best interest of stimulating the tourist sector.

Recommendations

20. Tourism should be planned on an integral basis taking into account all aspects of legislation relating to other sectors such as transport, employment, health, agriculture, communications, etc.

21. The overall role of parliamentarians, through legislation, should be to analyse, co-ordinate, facilitate and regulate both domestic and international tourism development within the context of their national development priorities.

22. Countries should determine their national priorities and tourism's role in the "hierarchy" of these priorities as well as the optimum tourism strategy, within these priorities. This strategy should define, among others, the balance to be sought between international and domestic tourism, and take into account the carrying capacity of destinations and the roles of state, regional and local organizations.

23. Within the overall national tourism strategy, priority attention should be given to selective and controlled development of tourist infrastructure, facilities, demand, and overall tourist capacity, in order to protect the environment, and local population, so as to avoid any negative impacts which unplanned tourism might produce. In tourism planning and area development it is essential for States to strike a harmonious balance between economic and ecological considerations.

24. National and transnational corporations should be required by law to take adequate preventive measures to avoid damage to the environment and tourist

sites; these corporations should be properly called to account in the event of their causing damage as well as obliged to take all measures to reduce the consequences and repair such damage.

25. Dangerous industrial practices, particularly the transport, treatment and storage of toxic and radioactive substances and waste, should be subject to strict legal controls, and the dumping of such waste made illegal, so as to avoid damage to the natural and human environment. National and transnational corporations that are the source of such damage should be obliged to assume responsibility for it and to repair it.

26. Research and back-up are essential to develop a country's tourism potential effectively and with maximum benefits; this requires parallel enhancement of the status of the tourism administrations of each State – which does not imply that the State need exercise an interventionist role in tourism – rather it should ensure that the tourism industry has the maximum opportunity to exercise its functions.

27. As tourism infrastructure is created, it is absolutely essential that general tourism education for the population as a whole, particularly in schools, as well as specialized training for tourism professionals, be developed at the national level; major goals should be the establishment of tourism as a respected profession and tourism consciousness on the part of the population.

28. All tourist-generating countries should more effectively stagger their industrial and school holidays in order to reduce the harmful effects of the over-seasonal nature of tourism demand (over-crowding and delays at airports, frontier crossings, etc.) and the associated negative effects these have on tourist employment, tourist facilitation and security (health, exploitation).

29. Governments should provide the basic infrastructure for tourism development and take special support measures for "infant" tourism industries, especially small enterprises and in development regions. This support may take the form of direct investment, financial incentives to private investment, and expenditure on promotion.

30. In a country which is not self-sufficient in many areas and which does not have a tourist infrastructure already in place, it is vital for costs to be weighed against prospective earnings from tourism, and the entire equation then viewed in the light of national priorities. All efforts should be made to ensure that destination countries receive the maximum share of receipts from tourist activities. This implies that countries should optimize tourism development strategies in order to make the greatest possible use of local facilities and resources.

31. Special assistance, which need not be financial, should be given by developed countries to developing countries, this could well take the form of encouraging their citizens to take their holidays in the developing countries.

32. Governments, national tourist organizations and private industry should make every effort to work together in providing the financing to bring tourism to its full fruition and enable all people to reap its benefits.

33. Great stress must be place on the promotion of tourism by industry, with the support of Governments, in terms of both financing and encouragement. Such support can contribute to economic development and increased employment, while likewise ensuring a good infrastructure and protecting the environment as well as the cultural assets of each country. Therefore, all Governments together with the tourism industry should carry out active tourist policies to the benefit of their countries now and in the future.

34. States should assume the responsibility for devising ways of using tourism to develop new forms of patronage – thus enabling traditional cultural forms to retain their integrity, vigour and quality.

35. In a developing country just at the beginning of its tourism activity, it is essential that planning and implementation be co-ordinated at national level and all efforts should be made through international co-operation to benefit from the positive experiences and avoid the mistakes of other more developed tourist countries.

36. There are limits to the degree of decentralization that is possible in the tourism sector; at the very least, it implies the need for national machinery to ensure co-ordination of tourism policy between the national and the regional level of the State.

37. States should encourage the development of domestic tourism which is based on the right of the individual to holidays, offers each citizen the opportunity to get to know his or her own environment, to reaffirm national identity and to forge links of solidarity with compatriots, and helps each country to develop a basic tourism infrastructure.

38. Tourism legislature should be framed with three goals in view: (a) to protect the tourist, (b) to protect each country from the potential problems caused by tourism, particularly as regards environmental impact and cultural identity and (c) to promote tourism. In this respect, there is a need for close co-operation between the tourism industry and its specialists and the scientific bodies responsible for maintaining natural, man-made and cultural resources.

Concluding critical questions

International tourism agreements are designed to facilitate the movement of people across borders for leisure travel experiences by providing information, security, and facilities amenable to visitors. The ultimate goal of a tourism agreement is to improve bilateral political relations while enhancing tourism demand among the countries involved. *The Hague Declaration on Tourism*, along with other agreements mentioned in the chapter, is a good illustration of the complexities involved in creating the tourism agreements among nations. The inherent complexities in such documents lead to questions that can create a rich discourse among students of tourism policy. For example, does tourism produce only minimal environmental impacts? This is implied in Conclusion 11, which states tourism is "a smokeless industry."

As stated in the Hague document, and throughout this book, tourism cooperation can be a vehicle for creating peace. However, is the opposite true? Does the lack of a multilateral tourism agreement contribute to international unrest? Another point to debate relates to viewing tourism as a necessity versus a luxury. For example, if the right to leisure time is a fundamental human right, is travel during leisure time a right as well? On a different note, how effective have international tourism agreements been? How could one evaluate the effectiveness of tourism agreements? What complications might arise in developing and implementing an international agreement?

Conclusion 15 is about the difficulties in getting support for tourism from the government. Why is this common among most nations? How important is tourism relative to other industry sectors and other public policy issues. For example, should school and industrial holidays be staggered in order to reduce seasonality, as mentioned in Recommendation 28? Can tourism advocates have a strong influence on education policy and other industry sectors? What other questions arise from reading the Hague document that can stimulate discussions about tourism agreements?

Notes

1 *Helsinki Accords*. Conference on Security and Co-operation in Europe, Helsinki, Finland, July–August 1975.

2 *Vienna Convention on Diplomatic Relations*, Vienna, Austria, April 18, 1961.

3 *Manila Declaration on World Tourism*, United Nations World Tourism Organization, September 27–October 10, 1980.

4 *Tourism Bill of Rights and Tourist Code*, United Nations World Tourism Organization, Sofia, Bulgaria, September 17–26, 1985.

5 *The Hague Declaration on Tourism*, Inter-Parliamentary Union and the United Nations World Tourism Organization, The Hague, Netherlands, April 10–14, 1989.

6 Edgell, Sr., David L. & Edgell, Jr., David L. (1991) *International Tourism Policy, Selected Readings*. West Lafayette, IN: Purdue University.

7   Edwards, Anthony D. (1976) "International Tourism Development: Forecasts to 1985." Special Report No. 33. London: The Economist Intelligence Unit Ltd.

8   Edgell, David L. (1978) "International Tourism and Travel." In Howard F. Van Zandt (ed.) *International Business Prospects 1977–1999.* Indianapolis, IN: The Bobbs-Merrill Company, Inc.

9   Edgell, David L., Tesar, George, & Seely, Richard L. (1979) "Use of Modified Scenario Research in Forecasting of Tourism in the United States," *Travel Research Journal*, Edition 1979/1.

10 Edgell, David L., Seely, Richard L., & Iglarsh, Harvey J. (1980) "Forecasts of International Tourism to the USA," *International Journal of Tourism Research*, June.

11 Edgell Sr., David L. (1990) *International Tourism Policy*. New York: Van Nostrand Reinhold.

12 Goeldner, Charles R., & Ritchie, J.R. Brent (2012) *Tourism: Principles, Practices, Philosophies*, 12th edn. Hoboken, NJ: John Wiley & Sons, Inc., p. 295.

Strategic tourism planning

Just as a traveler must strategically plan his trip through information and education about the chosen destination to obtain the optimum value from his travel, so must a nation, community, or destination plan well for the future success of their tourism programs. Strategic tourism planning in its simplest definition is envisioning a desired future for a destination, tourism organization, or other entity and then organizing and implementing the steps to get there. Alternatively, think of strategic planning as a "roadmap" to lead tourism related organizations or destinations from their present level of tourism development to where they would like to be in the next five years or at some other future date. This chapter presents some of the practical steps in the strategic tourism planning process.

Strategic tourism planning is not a mysterious difficult theory left only to experts to develop, prepare, and implement. It is simply a process or tool aimed to optimize the benefits of tourism so that the result is a balance of the appropriate quality and quantity of supply with the proper level of demand. The strategic planning process should take into account economic, environmental, and socio-cultural factors within the area and their relationship to the overall sustainability for future needs of the organization. In effect, strategic tourism planning is a framework designed to provide direction for a tourism organization or destination.

Tourism planning takes place at all levels of organizations. Writing in *National and Regional Tourism Planning*, Edward Inskeep cites as an advantage of tourism planning, "Establishing the overall tourism development objectives and policies – what is tourism aiming to accomplish and how these aims can be achieved."[1] There are many different approaches to strategic tourism planning depending on the desired end goals the organization seeks to accomplish. In the past what is generally referred to as a *strategic plan* today was often called a *master plan*. Master plans sometimes conjure up an image of being static whereas strategic planning is dynamic and future-oriented. However, many master plans do include a section or chapter on, for instance, a strategic vision, or key strategic challenges and constraints, or other sections that meet the same pragmatic aims as a strategic plan. Other groups sometimes prepare a strategic plan, then develop a brand, produce a business plan, generate a marketing scenario, and determine a budget for the organization. The strategic plan presents a broad picture of what the organization desires to accomplish and provides the identifiable paths to follow to achieve that end. As opposed to a business plan with lots of numbers, the strategic plan usually consists of words explaining the key decisions that an organization will need to make in future years. It looks at where the organization has been, where it wants to go, how it will get there, what resources will be needed, and when the process will begin.

Strategic tourism planning is a collaborative management tool that can be used to help determine a destination's vision, mission, goals, objectives, strategies, and tactics. It also lays the groundwork for a destination to develop a brand identity as it moves forward in preparing a marketing plan. It drives the organization to produce fundamental decisions and actions for the future. The process is strategic because it gives the organization a rational approach in directing the use of resources and in communicating the interests of the stakeholders and community leaders emphasizing quality, efficiency, and effectiveness.

FIGURE 10.1 Stakeholders at a farmer's market in Seoul, South Korea are an important part of the local tourism planning experience (Photo: Junghee 'Michelle' Han)

Depending on the circumstances and the needs of the destination, strategic tourism planning may be either a simple straightforward decision-making process or in some cases a complex set of multiple decision directions each of which has a bearing on the ultimate plan. It helps to assure the destination management organization (DMO) to be responsive to the needs of the community and the stakeholders and contributes to organizational stability and growth. Strategic planning seeks to obtain an overall consensus of the members of the community as a foundation for long-term planning and goal-setting. Pictured in Figure 10.1 is a farmer's market, which are becoming more popular with tourists looking to experience authentic cultural aspects of their destination. Community stakeholders in such a farmer's market include not only retail merchants, but also farmers that supply the produce, the landlords from which the merchants rent space, and also the customers.

The strategic tourism planning process

A strategic tourism plan is not an activity of and by itself, but rather it takes place within an overall tourism policy and development program for a destination or organization. "Good policy and sound planning must be conducted to ensure that a destination will be both competitive and sustainable."[2] From a broader perspective, effective strategic tourism planning today seeks to integrate stakeholders' concerns, effective management, efficient development and innovative marketing, and community interests within the overall goals of the destination. More and more, DMOs are seeking to conduct long-range strategic planning based on an agreed upon vision and mission, often highlighted and promoted based on the development of a brand that explains what the organization wishes to accomplish in the future. This chapter will assume that for most purposes the future or long-range is considered to be the next five years.

The process of strategic tourism planning takes into account that a destination must be able to adjust to new trends, changing markets and a competitive market environment. Destinations that have planned well for tourism usually have a competitive edge in the marketplace. A planning effort focused on the sustainability of the tourism destination will assure consistent quality of the tourism product(s) and yield the most benefits. In addition, good planning will override short-term goals aimed solely at profit motivations and emphasize many of the important future attributes that are more positive for the entire community.

Strategic planning to better manage sustainable tourism, is receiving increased attention. In *Managing Sustainable Tourism: A Legacy for the Future*, Edgell explains the importance of planning and management in developing sustainable tourism goals and objectives: "In general, most studies have found that a well-researched, well-planned, and well-managed tourism program that takes into account the natural and cultural environment has a good chance of improving the local economy and enhancing the quality-of-life of residents."[3] In brief, tourism planning is essential to the sustainability of the destination in the future and must foster the conservation of the resources that tourism is dependent on as well as improve the quality-of-life for local residents.

Tourism planning in the past did not receive the same kind of interest by the DMO in managing the destination as is true today. The history of the travel, tourism, and hospitality industries is replete with examples of tourism areas and destinations that deteriorated or failed as a result of the lack of planning or because of poor planning. Much of this decadence can be traced to haphazard planning and development that has motivated modern tourism managers to insist on more careful planning.

Good tourism planning gives a destination many advantages, six of which are mentioned below:

1. There is a close relationship between policy and planning; strategic tourism planning strengthens an area's or organization's tourism policies.
2. Strategic tourism planning is a highly organized effort of rational thinking and, like tourism policy, is future-oriented.
3. Strategic tourism planning contains many steps that begins with inventorying an area's tourism product and ends with a blueprint for future development.
4. Strategic tourism planning balances economic goals with the need for conserving the environment, built and natural, and improving the quality-of-life for local residents.
5. Strategic tourism planning fosters the conservation of the resources that tourism is dependent on for future growth.
6. Strategic tourism planning emphasizes quality, efficiency and effectiveness throughout the process to improve the organization's operations and marketing success.

Tourism planning contains many steps, initiating from inventorying an area's tourism products to providing the blueprint for development. It is a highly integrative process. Tourism planning helps assure that the DMO remains relevant and responsive to the needs of the community and stakeholders, and contributes to stability and growth. The planning process answers such key questions for a destination as: what to do; when to do it; and how to do it.

Those who work in the field are accustomed to seeing myriad variations of the tourism strategic planning process. The co-authors of this book, with some considerable experience in tourism planning, have often used different approaches to strategic tourism planning depending on the circumstances, the destination, and the community. One strategic plan may focus on organizational capacity, while another aids in building the appropriate supply. A strategic tourism plan may concentrate on visitor research, or may work toward developing stakeholder involvement or may recommend ways to spend the marketing budget. A comprehensive strategic tourism plan will incorporate all of these elements and address others as well.

Strategic planning in the tourism industry is usually a policy/planning/management tool to assist the tourism entity (national tourism office, destination, local community) in organizing to accomplish its desired interests, while focusing on available resources for obtaining the greatest benefits. In effect, it is a blueprint to help shape and guide the entity in reaching its future goals. A good example of a well-organized and effective strategic tourism planning document is that of the Canadian Tourism Commission's *Corporate Plan for 2012–2016*. Canada has been producing effective tourism plans for many years.

As a practical matter a strategic tourism plan should at a minimum, include a vision, mission statement, goal(s), objective(s), strategies, and tactics in one form or another. Some plans may use different descriptive words from those above, as for example priorities, aims or targets, but the ultimate usage is the same, to improve the destination's position in the tourism marketplace. A destination's brand usually reflects its vision and should be included in a discussion of strategic tourism planning.

The process of strategic tourism planning includes several steps. If the destination is comfortable with its brand image then it simply needs to identify the brand at the beginning of the planning cycle and move forward to the next step. The brand's tagline is usually very short, just a few words as for example: *Canada, Keep Exploring*; *Virginia is for Lovers*; *Dominica, The Nature Island*; *Britain, Timeless, Dynamic and Genuine*; or *Australia, The Land That Tells A Thousand Stories*. A brand identification phrase that is easy to remember is very important. A good branding campaign will bring attention to the destination, and an effective marketing plan will help promote the brand. The brand itself is not necessarily a specific part of the strategic tourism plan, but it is a spin-off of an overall strategy of a destination.

Vision

Determining the vision is the first step of the strategic tourism planning process whereby a community, country, destination, or other entity develops a vision statement. Composed of just a few words, the vision statement will depict an image of what the destination or other entity should be like in the future. It is the image of what the destination wants to be no matter how idealistic it may seem. It may be inspirational, letting the world know how your destination wants to be known. In other words it provides a common ideal or dream that all the stakeholders can endorse.

When penning a vision, the vision author needs to have a thorough understanding and knowledge of the destination or area and the desired plans for future development and promotion of the tourism products. There are a number of different techniques that can be used in preparing a vision. It might evolve from a simple brainstorming session, where the stakeholders gather to discuss their ultimate interests in the destination. In some circumstances, it makes sense to use focus groups to share a wide range of different opinions in building the vision. This may also be a good time to utilize the services of an experienced strategic marketing/planning consultant who can help with developing the vision and branding of the destination.

A couple of examples of vision statements may shed some light on the modus operandi for developing a vision. For example, Canada's tourism vision is "Inspire the world to explore Canada." The British Virgin Islands Tourist Board "envisions the British Virgin Islands being a premier tourist destination, retaining and showcasing the values, heritage, culture and natural beauty of the British Virgin Islands." For the most part this last vision statement is too long but necessary in this case because the British Virgin Islands is not a well-known destination and therefore needs greater identification. The vision should be future-oriented as, for example, the vision for New Zealand is: "In 2015, tourism is valued as the leading contributor to a sustainable New Zealand economy." This visionary statement lets you know how important sustainability is to New Zealand. As mentioned earlier in this chapter, a strategic tourism plan should be concerned with sustainability in all its various ramifications and future orientations and a good visionary statement will help guide the destination toward this goal.

Mission statement

Usually the next step in the strategic tourism planning approach is to develop a mission statement. A mission statement is an agreed-upon statement by the organization that supports the vision and that helps to explain the pathway(s) to accomplishment. It helps chart a course of action to support the vision for the destination and it provides grounding for setting goals and objectives. Unlike the vision statement, the mission statement is generally longer in that it outlines how to get there – much like a road map. The mission statement is goal-oriented and designed to inspire people to make decisions and take actions.

Like the vision, there needs to be a wide range of people involved in preparing the mission statement. Using Canada as an example again, its mission statement is to "Harness Canada's collective voice to grow export revenues." In other words, if international visitors come to *explore Canada* they will add to Canada's foreign *export revenues*. The mission statement for the British Virgin Islands says "To foster, develop and promote a sustainable tourism industry for the British Virgin Islands." Thus, the vision and mission statement go hand-in-glove to support the desire of a tourism destination to be recognized and to be highly successful with respect to meeting what is expected of the tourism program.

Next steps in strategic tourism planning

Tourism planners do not always agree on the next steps in strategic tourism planning. Co-author Edgell, based on his long experience, suggests the representative planning headings of: goals, objectives, strategies, and tactics as an outline approach in the strategic tourism planning process. Developing goals, objectives, strategies and tactics is vital to the entire process. Figure 10.2 depicts this approach.

By using the above scenario the vision and mission statement help formulate the goals and objectives. The goal(s) are the driving force of what the strategic plan intends to achieve and, therefore, needs careful crafting to be effective. Goal setting will establish a target level for tourism development, marketing, promotion, and sustainability for the destination. For most tourism-related projects, there may be

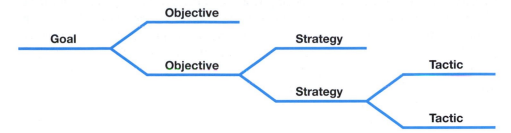

FIGURE 10.2 Tree diagram: Goal-oriented tourism planning

several goals, which represent the aim or purpose intended by stakeholders when the decision to develop the tourism project is initially visualized or an already developed destination may want to change the direction of its programs. The goal-oriented method utilized may be short-term (one to two years) or long-term (usually not more than five years before being reviewed and possibly revised). The goals should be measureable, as for example "it is expected that growth in visitation to the destination will be a certain percent each year or in a future year the organization will reach a certain number of visitors."

Objectives support the goal(s), they are stepping stones to reach the goal and are concrete, real, practical steps or intentions that define expected achievements in the strategic tourism plan. Objectives are specific-oriented targets of the destination that can be implemented and made operational in meeting the goal(s) of the plan. Generally the objectives are in priority order such that the available resources earmarked to achieve the highest priority objectives are dealt with first. The idea is to think about the overall goal(s) and seek out innovative approaches and creative guidelines (objectives) to reach or go beyond what is expected.

Strategies relate to actions and operations that are necessary to meet the objectives included in the strategic tourism plan. In some circumstances, the strategy may include the development of new products or special programs for implementing the objectives. The strategy should also identify key target audiences that are a part of the overall planning process. One strategy might be to provide the leadership necessary to accomplish the objectives or set the criteria for measuring the quality of the tourism project. Strategies also involve identification of funding needs and sources, as well as a review of existing resources related to the objectives of the plan. Furthermore, a strategy might include forming a partnership or collaborating with other interested entities or introducing new technology. The key is that the strategies are aimed towards reaching the identified goals and objectives.

The last item in the diagram is tactic(s). The tactic is the short-term action (usually less than six months) for immediate achievements related to the plan. It is, in effect, the activity for securing the objectives designated by the strategy. Tactics are the day-to-day activities and details, whether setting the agenda for the stakeholders meeting or making arrangements to support the planning process to be used to achieve the strategic planning goal.

Implementation of a strategic tourism plan

The beauty of achievement, on finalizing a strategic tourism plan, lies in the knowledge that tough decisions have been made concerning the most important issues and that the destination can now move forward proactively. Within the strategic plan there is considerable analysis that must take place. Like most other tourism planners, the co-authors of this book use many different tools within the planning process. The well-known SWOT (strengths, weaknesses, opportunities, and threats) analysis is often utilized in strategic planning. Another tool, SMART (specific, measurable, achievable, relevant, and time-bound), may be used to help set the goals. Most plans will also build into the process a situational analysis (or needs assessment), a competitive analysis, a monitoring device, an evaluation, built-in performance measures, and research to improve the process. Branding the destination can also be included in the strategic tourism planning process. The strategic tourism planning approach is dependent on the conditions existing in the destination/organization and the marketplace. Commonly, the planner or leader will hold numerous brainstorming sessions to enable all stakeholders to reach a consensus on which tools are best for the specific strategic plan in question. This supports the notion for continuously monitoring and evaluating the strategic plan, as dynamic processes may be taking place while the plan is being developed and implemented.

Advisers, planners, and consultants have many different tools they use for organizing a strategic tourism plan depending on the needs, circumstances, and size of the project. For example, Edgell and colleagues organized an action plan for a project they were working on by first developing a schematic diagram similar to Figure 10.3, which allowed them to think through the various steps to take in developing a strategic tourism plan for a specific destination. A diagram helps explain to the stakeholders the marketing framework for analyzing the destination's desire to increase sales in their target customer segments of the marketplace. Later, this marketing planning approach evolved into an article "Strategic Marketing Planning for the Tourism Industry."[4] While some of the steps utilized in this particular example are similar to a classic strategic tourism plan, the framework approach taken has many differences as well. It was not designed as an overall strategic tourism plan but was instead, at the time, a strategic tourism marketing plan effort for a specific destination and for purposes of illustration.

The diagram in Figure 10.3 is just one illustrated example of some of the steps that were involved in a practical example of one destination's strategic marketing plan. It is not intended to be a model but rather to demonstrate that each situation may call for a unique set of approaches in the planning process. In some cases it is a simple process with little need for detail and in other circumstances it is a complex mix of factors that taken together form the strategic plan.

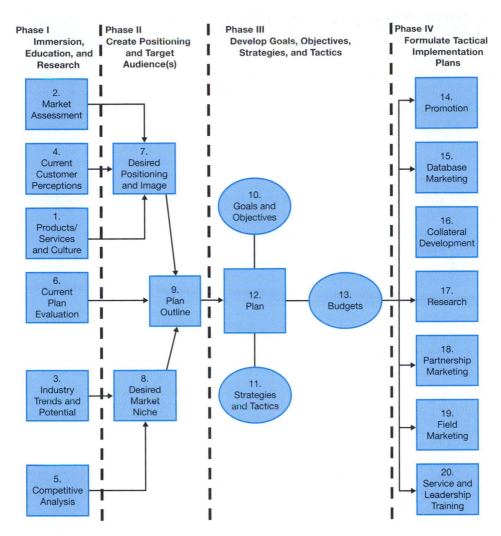

Phase I
Immersion,
Education, and
Research

Phase II
Create Positioning
and Target
Audience(s)

Phase III
Develop Goals, Objectives,
Strategies, and Tactics

Phase IV
Formulate Tactical
Implementation
Plans

2. Market Assessment

4. Current Customer Perceptions

1. Products/ Services and Culture

6. Current Plan Evaluation

3. Industry Trends and Potential

5. Competitive Analysis

7. Desired Positioning and Image

9. Plan Outline

8. Desired Market Niche

10. Goals and Objectives

12. Plan

11. Strategies and Tactics

13. Budgets

14. Promotion

15. Database Marketing

16. Collateral Development

17. Research

18. Partnership Marketing

19. Field Marketing

20. Service and Leadership Training

FIGURE 10.3 Tourism strategic development plan flowchart

Internal analysis

Internal analysis reviews the factors that characterize the destination. Characteristics may include highway demand, heritage, sports facilities, outdoor recreation activities, the natural environment, or proximity to major metropolitan areas, among many other factors that serve to drive tourism demand to the destination. Not only is it important to understand a destination's tourism product, or supply, it is equally important to identify the community's organization structures that will influence tourism development. A few steps that can be incorporated into the internal analysis of tourism strategic planning are the following:

A.　Analyze the destination's natural environment:

　　1.　Assess the area's geography to identify opportunities and threats to tourism development.

　　2.　Evaluate previous and predicted climate issues that could affect visitation to the area.

　　3.　Gauge resident's attitudes towards tourism and tourism development by enabling community members to voice their views and concerns through either a local community meeting or a web-based survey.

　　4.　Measure the general condition of service provided by the tourism industry workforce, addressing relevant training needs.

　　5.　Identify meaningful elements of the area's culture that could be incorporated into the overall tourism experience.

　　6.　Review the history of the area to maintain or revive critical characteristics important to heritage tourism.

B.　Examine the assembled elements:

　　1.　Identify current mission, goals, objectives, strategies, and tactics of key community organizations; areas of concordance, overlap, and conflict; and common and shared human financial resources related to tourism development.

　　2.　Review budgets and funding of comparable destination management organizations (DMOs) as a benchmark to identify enhanced and sustainable funding opportunities for a destination-related organization.

　　3.　Identify specific tourism-related infrastructure needs or opportunities that may not meet visitor expectations and may detract from the destination's appeal.

　　4.　Analyze the signage and transportation routes to and through the destination to ensure ease of access for visitors to attractions and other supply components.

　　5.　Assess the use of technology by destination promoters in the areas of customer relationships, packaging, booking and travel planning, demographic information, promotion, communications and revenue management, among other areas.

　　6.　Review quality, availability, and distribution of visitor information about the destination.

　　7.　Evaluate the community's existing crisis contingency plan to ensure it is proactive and can handle a wide array of incidents that could arise at any time.

C.　Conduct extensive visitor research:

　　1.　Plan visitor research study by working with destination managers to establish and understand the survey objectives.

　　2.　Design and test what type of visitor survey instrument is used to collect data from visitors.

3. Complete interviews with the general population as well as additional interviews with those who have visited the destination.
4. Prepare a summary report to include descriptive statistics of the data along with tests of the hypotheses stated in the original study design phase.
5. Identify existing and new market segments and decision patterns that will increase visitation to the region.

D. Investigate industry-operating sectors:

1. Inventory businesses in all tourism operating sectors (accommodations, meeting spaces, transportation, activities and entertainment, food services, outdoor recreation, visitor services and shopping) in order to determine quality and quantity.
2. Identify opportunities for improvement in all operating sectors.
3. Meet with selected tourism industry members, including supply operators, tourism managers and developers.
4. Conduct a web-based survey of local industry members to identify tourism development issues and concerns important to the stakeholders.
5. Gather information on new attractions and expansions that may be planned.
6. Examine the potential to repackage existing tourism products and develop new special events and niche tourism supply (convention center, heritage, military, sports, nature, trails, and agritourism and industrial activities, among others) that may bolster tourism in the shoulder and off-season months.
7. Evaluate the impacts of existing outdated facilities and inadequate supply, including the aesthetic appeal of architectural design standards, such as streetscape, gateway, signage and façade improvements.

The above are just a few additional steps that may need to be included in the strategic tourism planning mechanism, depending on the destination, organization, and accessible information.

External environmental scan

It is crucial for a destination to understand how it fits in the larger tourism industry and how various factors at all levels may have an impact on visitation at the local level. This is done by studying industry trends at the local regional, national and international levels. Competitive analysis is also a vital activity when pursuing a sound tourism development strategy.

A. Explore details of larger tourism systems:

1. Identify the 'outside' (non-destination) stakeholders and design an effective and efficient means of outreach to them. Outside organizations may include neighboring DMOs, local and national tourism entities, economic development, environmental and transportation agencies, among other groups.

2. Review current and anticipated industry trends in terms of visitation, origin of demand, revenues, supply development, consumer preferences, safety and security and other indicators at the local/national and international levels.
3. Research trends in particular activities and industries important to the destination.

B. Perform competitive analysis:

1. Examine competitive destinations in the region.
2. Determine the competitive position of the destination against similar areas in terms that may include current and historical visitation, tourism revenue, market segmentation, markets-of-origin, marketing expenditures and/or other pertinent data.

Strategic tourism planning recommendations should lead towards optimized tourism in the destination. Research should focus on determining the future of tourism in the region and how it can achieve its highest and best goal within the context of infrastructure and environmental constraints in the destination, and in accordance with the wants and needs of area visitors and community stakeholders. This disciplined process of scanning the internal and external environments and formulating tourism strategies calls for a certain order and pattern to keep it focused and productive. It should raise a sequence of questions to help planners examine the tourist's experience, test viable interpretations of certain data, incorporate information about the present, and anticipate the destination's future impact on the tourism marketplace. In effect, as mentioned earlier, the strategic tourism plan is no more, and no less, than a set of decisions about what the desires of the organization are, what it wants to accomplish, and how will it get there.

Canadian strategic planning

Canada is a diverse tourism system that includes a wide array of geographic and cultural diversity, from the European influences in the east, the Rocky Mountains in the west, the Arctic Circle to the north, and the border with the United States to the south. Efficient planning is crucial for tourism success in Canada in light of this diversity. Figure 10.4 shows just one small element of this diversity. A classic strategic tourism plan is that of *The Canadian Tourism Commission's 2009–2013 Strategy*. Canada not only produces excellent strategic tourism plans but continually updates its planning efforts. From a research or teaching perspective, the *2009–2013 Strategy* flows right into the Canadian Tourism Commission's *Corporate Plan for 2012–2016*. These two documents, inclusive with the case study at the end of this chapter, provide a wealth of information about an organization's strategic tourism planning process.

As the Canadian plan demonstrates, strategic tourism planning is a management tool meant to meet the desired purposes and directions of the organization or destination. It sets attainable goals, outlines desired achievements in a responsible

FIGURE 10.4 An image of an inukshuk statue welcomes visitors to the small village of Nain, Labrador in the polar regions of eastern Canada (Photo: Jason R. Swanson)

sustainable fashion, and responds to the competition from other destinations. It is adaptable to the changing demands of the tourism industry and seeks to introduce new tourism products. Overall, a strategic tourism plan must be clear and transparent, incorporate goals and objectives, be responsive to the available resources and adjust to the dynamic nature of the tourism industry.

Following this section is Case Study 10 titled "Canada: An effective tourism policy." It was originally written to help explain Canadian tourism policy and planning initiatives. The case study was well-received by readers of the first edition of *Tourism Policy and Planning: Yesterday, Today and Tomorrow*.[5] It is repeated in this edition with two changes. The first change is the section on the future of Canadian tourism has been dropped because the Canadian Tourism Commission (CTC) has produced two new strategy documents: *The CTC's 2009–2013 Strategy* and the *2012–2016 Corporate Strategy*. Both these documents can be found on the internet. The second change involves not including a copy of the Canadian Tourism Commission Act, which followed as an addendum to the case study, because of changes to the legislation. The latest version of the Act in 2012 can be found at http://laws-lois.justice.gc.ca/eng/acts/C-23.3/index.html or by contacting the Canadian Tourism Commission, which provides this website.

Strategic tourism planning is, in summary, a practical, intensive, idea-packed approach to improving a destination's opportunities for sustainability of its tourism programs over a long period. It is a thought-out system that aims to stretch the available resources through careful planning, monitoring, and evaluation. It is an action-oriented plan to benchmark and counter competitors' strategies with built-in performance measures. Strategic tourism planning proposes to develop a coherent strategy to build upon destinations' strengths and to learn from the past while correcting for the future in order to increase tourism's positive impacts upon the organization and community. The overall goal is to match tourism supply and demand – to provide adequate and appropriate facilities, amenities, services and events (supply) after identifying what visitors want and need (demand) in consideration of what is wanted and needed within the community. Successful implementation of good tourism development strategies will result in the creation of new jobs, additional visitor expenditures and increased incomes. Tourism development, if planned carefully, can improve an area's quality-of-life, which will be appealing to new residents, companies, and entrepreneurs.

CHAPTER REVIEW QUESTIONS

1. What are some of the advantages of good tourism planning?
2. Why can a brand be an important part of a tourism destination strategy?
3. Why is the vision statement an important first step of the planning process?
4. How does the mission statement compare to the vision statement? Give examples of each.
5. Explain the tree diagram of goal-oriented tourism planning.
6. What kind of tools can be used to analyze situations for tourism planning?
7. What is the overall goal of strategic tourism planning?

CASE STUDY 10 Canada: An effective tourism policy

This case study was written by Scott M. Meis, Stephen L.J. Smith, and David L. Edgell, Sr. Two of the three co-authors – Meis and Smith – had already written extensively about some of the developments in Canada's tourism program. Their information became the base of this case study. David Edgell reviewed the earlier documents and included what he thought best met the intentions of this chapter. Tom Penney – who at the time of the writing of the case study was CTC's vice-president for planning and evaluation, product development, and emerging markets – provided numerous helpful documents. The case study is an illustration of the makeup of a good tourism policy and planning initiative. Certainly, some of the information and references in the document are dated, but it continues to provide a valuable history of Canada's push to have one of the best tourism agencies and planning efforts in the world. It is an example of the development of a positive national tourism policy strategy.

* * *

The Canadian Tourism Commission (CTC) report *Options for a Long-Term Funding Solution for the Canadian Tourism Commission* (31 August 2005) says that, in 1995, CTC was established as a "special operation agency" within the federal government department of Industry Canada. The report further states that in January 2001, the CTC became a Crown corporation, allowing it more independence from federal government departmental financial and administrative controls. The mandate of the CTC is to:

- Sustain a vibrant and profitable Canadian tourism industry;
- Market Canada as a desirable tourist destination;
- Support a cooperative relationship between the private-sector and government; and,
- Provide information about Canadian tourism to the private-sector and to the governments.

The report further states:

Since its inception, the CTC has operated on a public/private-sector partnership basis with core funding coming from the Federal Government and matching or greater contributions coming from other industry partners. In response to both the opportunities and challenges presented by the current global tourism environment, the CTC believes it is crucial that it increase its marketing and research investments as part of ongoing efforts to protect and grow Canada's global tourism market share, and to increase associate economic returns to both the public and private-sectors.

Background

Government tourism policy in Canada has an interesting history. It formally began during the Great Depression in 1932 with the establishment of the Canadian Bureau of Tourism (CBT). The mandate of the CBT was to promote Canada as a hunting and fishing destination to Americans with the intent of generating new jobs and income. Tourism promotion continued as a minor federal activity until 1967, Canada's Centennial Anniversary. One of the key events of that year was the World's Fair, Expo '67, in Montreal. The phenomenally popular and critical success of Expo '67 put Canada on the world map as a tourist destination. Recognizing the potential of more aggressively competing in the global tourism market, the federal government created the Canadian Government Office of Tourism (CGOT) and expanded its role to include tourism research, planning, policy, product development as well as marketing. The CGOT became Tourism Canada in 1985. While the responsibilities of the federal government in tourism waxed and waned over the years, one constant has always been marketing. Another constant has been the complaints by industry that whatever agency was responsible for tourism marketing, it was: (1) underfunded; and (2) not responsive to the market.

In response to industry discontent, a series of governmental and industry task forces and reports explored alternative structures and the future of tourism in Canada. This began with the 1985 "Statement of Principles of Tourism," prepared at the 1985 Federal-Provincial-Territorial Conference of Ministers of Tourism. As the title suggests, this report focused on the respective responsibilities of the various senior governments in tourism marketing, research, policy, planning, and development. One outcome of the agreement was that Tourism Canada would no longer conduct domestic marketing, leaving that function to the individual provinces and territories (a decision reversed with the creation of the CTC a decade later).

Between 1985 and 1995, there were numerous discussions, meetings, and conferences, which took place in an effort to establish an effective tourism policy. One of the important discussion documents was the report submitted by the Tourism Industry Association of Canada (TIAC), *Prosperity Through Tourism* (1995). This report reviewed the state of the industry and recommended changes in legislation, product development priorities, promotion strategies and human resource development. One of the most significant recommendations was to replace Tourism Canada with a national tourism authority jointly funded by the government and private-sector but whose decisions would be industry-driven. The Prime Minister and his cabinet accepted the advice and established the CTC on February 1, 1995. In October of the preceding year, the federal government already had approved and published the federal overall micro-economic policy of Canada, *Agenda: Jobs and Growth, Building a More Innovative Economy* (1994). This recognized for the first time the significance of tourism in contributing to the economic wellbeing of Canadians as an essential element of national economic policy and specifying the role and focus of the federal government's involvement in tourism and its relation to overall government microeconomic policy objectives of promoting innovation and employment. Later on October 20, 2000, the federal government's policy commitment to tourism was further formalized in legislation with the passing of Bill C25, the Canadian Tourism Commission Act establishing the commission as an independent government Crown corporation. In relation to government tourism organizations throughout the world at that time, this new partnership arrangement was truly revolutionary. Today, this model continues to be studied by many countries.

Organizational structure

The CTC is a true hybrid of the public- and private-sectors, industry-led, with a board of directors dominated by the private-sector and a minority of board members from federal, provincial, and territorial governments. Purchasing and contract procedures and the terms and conditions of employment are governed by federal regulations for government corporations with the salaries of employees paid by the CTC from the annual allocations to the commission for the approved programs, supporting organization, and associated human resources.

Marketing and program policies, organizational planning, and strategic management are established and directed by six marketing and two industry development committees. The marketing committees include Canada, US Leisure, Business, Europe, Asia/Pacific and Aboriginal Tourism. Industry development committees are Industry Enhancement and Research. A Performance Measurement Committee provides guidance on the development of evaluation criteria or performance indicators for each program. Committee membership comes from both the private and public-sectors, with one or more designated full-time professionals providing logistical support.

A private-sector representative, working with an executive sub-committee, serves as a director on the board of directors, which oversees the management of the affairs and business of the commission. These committees consult with industry to develop sub-program activities and budgets, such as the 1999 Research Program technical paper *A Research and Development Program for Improved Tourism Industry Decision Making* (CTC, 1999).

Formulated as a three-year medium-term strategy, they must be sent to the board for approval. Once the board has voted on the overall program strategy such as the *Strategic Plan 2002–2004: Overview* (2002) for example and the proposal and resource allocations are in place, negotiations begin on tactics and implementation. Detailed annual work plans for each designated committee-led program are developed through committee consultation and brought to the board to ensure they are in line with the program and require approval in principle. The board sub-committee chairpersons are responsible for presenting the plans to the board and for overseeing the implementation of the plans, while staff program directors are responsible for managing the actual implementation of the plans. Unique to the CTC, staff persons – who may be officers, employees, agents and any technical advisers – are accountable to their respective program directors, and through them and the senior management hierarchy to the president and the industry-led board of directors.

Funding and partnerships

The budget of the CTC is drawn from federal, provincial and territorial governments as well as from the private-sector. The goal, as set by the Prime Minister, is 50 percent funding from the federal government and 50 percent from all partners (both public and private-sectors). This is an effort to have a true partnership between the government and private-sector.

The issue of partnership and matching funds is integral to the operation of the CTC. The CTC conducts a variety of marketing, product development and research projects to achieve its goals, virtually all of which are conducted with one or more partners. The CTC does not function as a granting agency; thereby, an organization only approaches the CTC with a proposal expected to make a significant contribution to its implementation.

Partnership is an increasingly common term in many nations' tourism industries; however, it often lacks operational definition. Because the CTC requires that the federal contribution be matched by an equal partnership contribution, it became necessary to operationally define partnership and associated business process and appropriate practices. For example, does an organization actually have to transfer cash to the CTC to be a partner? Could they not, instead, contribute to covering program costs? What about contributing in-kind, such as providing air tickets or lodging for persons traveling on CTC business? What about expenses incurred for programs managed independently of the CTC but are consistent and operated in parallel with CTC program initiatives?

To resolve this, the CTC defines partnership as "a commitment to share resources on common objectives to achieve mutually beneficial results." Allocation of resources including in-kind contributions by partners involving an explicit commitment to work towards common objectives that achieve desired mutual results counted as a partnership contribution. In-kind resources are valued at current retail price for purpose of measuring a partner's contribution.

Results

The initial creation of the CTC and the associated integration of tourism into the national microeconomic policy led to an initial threefold increase in national federal funding for the national initiatives. Subsequent partnership funding from other levels of government and the private-sector led to a further doubling of overall contributions to the organization's budget and program. In addition, the newly developed strategic and annual operational planning processes led for the first time to a full coordinated public and private-sector approach to national tourism marketing, research, and industry development. The new planning, coordination, and partnership funding and decision-making approaches have sustained the Canadian tourism sector equally throughout the relatively positive conditions of the general business environment of the late 1980s as well as the more turbulent period experienced after September 11, 2001.

Challenges

While the structure of the Canadian national tourism organization has changed over the past 70 years, more changes are likely in the future. CTC cannot sit idly by and expect the market to grow, it must be innovative and creative in meeting the demands and trends in the tourism market. Tourism is a dynamic industry, with changes in product, market, communications, competition, and technology taking place frequently. The use of e-commerce tools in tourism is but one dynamic in our fast-changing world of technology. Tourism products are always in a state of flux as tourists change their interests. New competition enters the market every day and challenges existing products and markets. Tourism businesses without a dominant internet presence, effective website, or social media strategy will eventually face decline.

There are other challenges as well. CTC must find ways and means to get greater cooperation from small- and medium-sized firms to compete in the marketplace (another use of *coopetition* as mentioned earlier in the book). In addition, Canada's total land area of 9,976,140km^2 (3,851,809 square miles) makes it such a huge country that effective cooperation and joint marketing planning and actual marketing have potential for hindrance. In the opinion of the authors, the CTC is probably better equipped to adjust to markets faster and more efficiently than most other government programs around the globe. Stated another way, the CTC is better organized compared to many national government tourism programs and the joint government/private-sector approach is best in the current marketplace.

Concluding critical questions

Some questions as to marketing strategies have arisen from the Canadian approach to tourism planning. Is it better to use cluster marketing, geographical marketing, niche marketing, or some other form? How do you approach branding the country better? How does a national tourism office balance small, medium, and large firms in the national marketing strategies? Financing is always a discussion topic. Does the government follow the private-sector or vice versa? Which markets are most effective and need greater financial attention? Is it possible to switch the market budget to meet short- and long-term needs in the industry? Are the common complaints among tourism professionals about inadequate tourism budgets unfounded? If not, what is an optimal budget for tourism promotion and development and how can the optimal budget be determined?

The Canadian case also raises other questions. For example, what adjustments should be made relative to safety and security issues? A final important question is, why is Canada so effective at tourism policy and planning when other developed nations routinely struggle to create tourism policy and plans?

Notes

1   Inskeep, Edward (1994) *National and Regional Tourism Planning.* New York and London: Routledge.

2   Goeldner, Charles R., & Ritchie, J. R. Brent (2012). *Tourism: Principles, Practices, Philosophies*, 12th edn. Hoboken, NJ: John Wiley & Sons, Inc.

3   Edgell, Sr., David L. (2006). *Managing Sustainable Tourism: A Legacy for the Future.* New York: The Haworth Hospitality Press.

4   Edgell, Sr., David L., Ruf, Kurtis M., & Agarwal, Alpa (1999) "Strategic Marketing Planning for the Tourism Industry." *Journal of Travel & Tourism Marketing*, 8(3).

5   Edgell, Sr., David L., Swanson, Jason R., Smith, Ginger, & DelMastro Allen, Maria (2008) *Tourism Policy and Planning: Yesterday, Today and Tomorrow.* London: Elsevier Inc.

CHAPTER 11

Transformative leadership, poverty alleviation and tourism policies

Turbulence, strife, poverty, conflicts, and unrest aptly describe much of today's world. Nearly 80 percent of the world's population is in poverty, 70 percent is illiterate and more than 50 percent suffer from hunger and malnutrition. Issues relating to a world economic crisis, misdistribution of wealth, belligerency, global warming, disaster relief, impoverishment, sickness, and ineffectiveness of governments to find solutions to problem areas are demanding creative leadership and policy attention by individuals and organizations.

Poverty exists throughout the world – in some countries more than others – and representing differing degrees of being poor. Many areas lack food, shelter, clothing, healthcare, education, and the physical means of improving one's life. The concern is not a new one but what has changed is the transformation of leadership interests in the problem of poverty, and, as this short chapter will explain, the impact role that tourism policy plays in poverty alleviation.

Politicians, philosophers, and religionists, like, for example, the late Mahatma Gandhi, Mother Teresa, and others have pleaded the case for poverty alleviation for a long time. Social and religious groups, charity organizations, and specialized agencies continue to conduct special country missions to provide medical assistance and other support to help the world's poor people. What appears to be a fairly recent trend is the increased transformation by some of the world's business leaders in utilizing their immense wealth to support societal wellbeing programs. For example, Microsoft mega-billionaire Bill Gates initiated a $600 billion challenge (to include many additional philanthropists) to fund global social change. In addition, entities such as the Bill & Melinda Gates Foundation conduct projects aimed at reducing poverty through, for instance, sustainable agricultural productivity in developing countries. Furthermore, individual country programs and global organizations have also stepped forward to utilize their expertise and financial resources toward reducing and eradicating poverty in specific locations.

A question for this chapter is "what can global tourism policy accomplish in such a chaotic world?" Where does tourism fit with respect to poverty reduction? How does the world's tourism leadership transform tourism policy in a way to respond to such world challenges? Who in the tourism industry will initiate innovative and creative solutions to these problems?

The United Nations poverty alleviation challenge to the tourism industry

The United Nations (UN) has accepted the world's leadership role in advocating equality, equity, human rights, peace, sustainability, and programs for the general wellbeing of the world. At the Millennium Summit in 2000[1] (at the time of this meeting, it was the largest gathering of world leaders in history), the UN identified world poverty alleviation as one of the most important and challenging issues. The 189 member states supported the UN in setting as one of its goals "to free humanity from extreme poverty, hunger, illiteracy and disease by 2015." At the September 2010 Millennium Development Goals Summit,[2] world leaders discussed the progress made toward accomplishing the "2015 goal."

In 2011, the United Nations issued *The Millennium Development Goals Report*,[3] which informed the world the progress that had been made toward the 2015 goal of reducing extreme poverty. The report was mostly positive, citing that millions of people had been lifted from severe poverty conditions. Despite real progress, however, the document noted that the most vulnerable cases of poverty were still in dire need of help. Some of the severe disadvantaged, living in remote rural areas, where about three-quarters of the two billion people under extreme poverty conditions are located, are simply hard to reach. This reality has left disparities in progress made toward poverty reduction between urban and rural areas. In addition, those poor who were living in zones where conflicts were taking place had the increased likelihood of becoming even more distressed. The UN called upon all of its organizational units to help with programs aimed to reduce poverty, including the UN's specialized agency, the United Nations World Tourism Organization (UNWTO).

The UNWTO and poverty alleviation

One key component of the UN in addressing world poverty is the UNWTO, which is the tourism policy agency accountable for the promotion of responsible, sustainable, and universally accessible tourism. The UNWTO fully endorsed the idea of using tourism as a mechanism for poverty reduction, principally through economic development in small- and medium-size enterprises in poverty-stricken countries. UNWTO's membership includes 155 countries, seven territories and more than 400 affiliate members representing governments, the private-sector, educational institutions, tourism associations, and local tourism authorities. This organization, as the global body for tourism policy, has a major focus on economic development, international understanding, peace, prosperity, sustainability, and universal respect for human rights and fundamental freedoms through world tourism policies.

The UNWTO responded to the UN goal with recommendations for action in its "Tourism and Poverty Alleviation" report.[4] The initiative cited in the report suggests that one approach toward poverty alleviation should take place through the provision of assistance in sustainable tourism development projects. The UNWTO has in its definition of sustainable tourism in Part 3 to "Ensure viable, long-term economic operations, providing socioeconomic benefits to all stakeholders that are fairly distributed, including stable employment and income-earning opportunities and social services to host communities, and contributing to *poverty alleviation*."

The UNWTO recognized the transformation powers and fundamental roles that tourism can play in addressing global poverty issues. Over the years, UNWTO has made a mark in utilizing tourism development as an opportunity to increase the welfare of peoples throughout the world. Because tourism is forecast to grow substantially in developing countries, where much of the poverty exists, there is considerable interest in utilizing tourism as a tool for poverty reduction.

While most of the economic advantages of tourism in the world take place in the developed nations, the growth of tourism in the least developed countries (LDCs) is increasingly being recognized for its economic potential to contribute to the reduction of poverty. Many LDCs have a comparative advantage in tourism over developed countries as they often have not yet desecrated their scenic beauty, natural landscapes, wildlife, cultural heritage, and other sustainable tourism related attributes to the same extent as some developed nations. Because tourism is so diverse and creates jobs and income more quickly than is true of most other industries, it can provide LDCs with much-needed foreign exchange. Tourism is generally labor intensive, offering employment opportunities for both skilled and unskilled persons, especially with respect to women and young people in LDCs. Tourism is an industry largely composed of small businesses and the start-up costs and barriers to entry are usually lesser than is true in the manufacturing sector. Tourism development, if properly planned for and supported, can provide an economic opportunity for LDCs and help alleviate unemployment and the resulting poverty.[5]

The UNWTO has recognized for some time the ability of the world's tourism industry to create jobs and increase income to the poorer nations of the world. Its leadership has fostered many different programs aimed toward improving the welfare of those countries in the most need of help. UNWTO understands that it takes considerable cooperation and coordination at the global level with many different organizations and agencies to make even small inroads of progress toward poverty elimination. In addition to UNWTO, specific country international development agencies – as for example the US Agency for International Development, United Kingdom Department of International Development, and others – know of tourism's potential for poverty alleviation and have sponsored tourism programs aimed in that direction.

United Nations Environmental Program and poverty alleviation

Another UN agency, the United Nations Environmental Program (UNEP) produced a report "Tourism: Investing in Energy and Resource Efficiency" in 2008 that also addressed the issue of tourism and poverty as well as environmental programs related to tourism.[6] UNEP, in partnership with UNWTO, elaborated in the report the important economic impact that sustainable tourism can have on small- and medium-sized businesses. The report also stated:

> In greening the tourism sector, therefore, increasing the involvement of local communities, especially the poor, in the tourism value chain can contribute to the development of local economy and poverty reduction . . . There is increasing evidence that more sustainable tourism in rural areas can lead to more positive poverty-reducing effects . . . Governments and international organizations can facilitate the financial flow . . . with an emphasis on contributions to the local economy and poverty reduction.

UNEP basically has three principles to be followed in the definition of sustainable tourism. "Thus, sustainable tourism should:

1. Make optimal use of environmental resources that constitute a key element in tourism development, maintaining essential ecological processes and helping to conserve natural heritage and biodiversity.
2. Respect the socio-cultural authenticity of host communities, conserve their built and living cultural heritage and traditional values, and contribute to inter-cultural understanding and tolerance.
3. Ensure viable, long-term economic operations, providing socio-economic benefits to all stakeholders that are fairly distributed, including stable employment and income-earning opportunities and social services to host communities, and contributing to poverty alleviation."

UNEP also fosters guidelines to support ecotourism programs keeping in mind the importance of including the social-cultural aspects of tourism development. In addition, the organization calls for strong political leadership aimed toward bringing together diverse stakeholders so that sustainable tourism development will be endorsed by the entire community. The ultimate goal is to maintain a high level of visitor satisfaction through a superior sustainable tourism product that will increase the number of repeat visitors as well as promote sustainability to a larger world market. This can best be accomplished by strong local involvement, support by the government, developing private-sector partnerships and utilizing help from organizations such as UNEP and UNWTO.

The growth in tourism helps visitors to better understand social issues

Poverty alleviation through tourism or by other efforts contributes to the overall wellbeing of the human race. It is not just an issue of jobs and income but of improving global literacy, creating a healthier population, and ensuring better environmental conditions. Tourism is and has been a world growth industry. By organizations working together, it is possible for more of the activity of tourism growth to be aimed toward improved living conditions and helping those in need to move from the ranks of poverty to becoming productive world citizens. Poverty alleviation through tourism is a major policy issue and an area that needs greater attention at the local and global levels.

Changing society to better respond to world social responsibilities is complicated. To create a global environment where the majority of the people can grow, thrive, and live in peace and prosperity has been a challenge since the beginning of time. Equity, social justice, and quality-of-life values in a milieu of harmony with nature and sustainability for future generations sounds idealistic and improbable in today's world. But just because it is difficult does not mean that society should give up striving for a better world. The travel and tourism industry should share in the global leadership role in helping to improve the social and economic wellbeing of the world's population. No matter how one views this concern, it is necessary to reduce world poverty in order to transform global policies to improve opportunities for universal peace and provide the economic means for more people to travel. As more people travel, economic conditions improve; international understanding leads to greater freedoms; and people become more aware of the advantages of sustainability.

Many of the leaders in the tourism industry, as in other industries, are engrossed in expanding the business of travel and tourism and are unable or unwilling to address world needs. Policymakers are focused on improvements in their respective countries and may not have a vision of how they too, can improve on world economic and social conditions. Occasionally, an unusual leader such as Mahatma Gandhi, steps forward on the world platform to address principles of social justice, but there are not yet many such champions of causes for the marginalized populations of the world from within the tourism sector. There are some exceptions but most of the leadership role from a tourism policy perspective takes place through global organizations.

Global peace through tourism helps alleviate poverty

As already discussed many times in this book, today's world, like that of yesteryear, continues to be negatively impacted by disharmony, civil strife and conflicts. We do not live in a very peaceful world. A recurrent theme in this book has been the need for peace to support the orderly growth of tourism. A peaceful world also makes it easier for utilizing tourism as an economic development tool in the poorer nations of the world. Thus, the more peaceful the world, the greater are the opportunities for helping to reduce poverty. Areas of the world where conflicts are taking place tend to exacerbate the problems of the poor.

The interests in the contribution of tourism to a more peaceful society have been expressed in many different ways in chapters of this book and alluded to in various documents. Co-author Edgell's first interest in tourism policy and peace evolved after reading the report on *International Travel* mentioned in Chapter 2. Reiterating the introduction of a letter in the report addressed to US President Dwight D. Eisenhower (April 17, 1958), Presidential Assistant Clarence B. Randall stated that: "I hold the strong conviction that tourism has deep significance for the peoples of the modern world, and that the benefits of travel can contribute to the cause of peace through improvement not only in terms of economic advancement but with respect to our political, cultural, and social relationships as well." For Edgell, that statement set the stage for his interest in investigating the impact that peace issues have on tourism policy.

As previously noted, since the organizations founding in 1976, the UNWTO has made many references related to peace through tourism. Other documents mentioned in earlier chapters also make mention of peace and tourism. One such reference was to the International Institute for Peace through Tourism (IIPT) which is not only concerned with the goal of peace through tourism, but also a better understanding of other cultures, environmental matters, poverty reduction and sustainable tourism. IIPT has held many worldwide conferences advocating tourism policies aimed toward a more peaceful world.

In Edgell's book *International Tourism Policy*[7] he wrote on the first page:

> International tourism in the twenty-first century will be a major vehicle for fulfilling people's aspirations for a higher quality-of-life, . . . laying the groundwork for a peaceful society through global touristic contacts. International tourism also has the potential to be one of the most important stimulants for global improvement in the social, cultural, economic, political, and ecological dimensions of future lifestyles . . . tourism will be a principal factor for creating greater international understanding and goodwill and a primary ingredient for peace on earth. This supports the author's view that the highest purpose of tourism policy is to integrate the economic, political, cultural, intellectual, and environmental benefits of tourism cohesively with people, destinations, and countries in order to improve the global quality-of-life and provide a foundation for peace and prosperity.

Tourism support for the general welfare of mankind

In addition to governmental programs to support efforts for the general welfare of mankind, there are many not-for-profit organizations and volunteer agencies that have the same goal of helping the citizens of the world have a higher quality-of-life through the avenue of travel and tourism. A few brief comments about "volunteer travel" might help to explain some of the general principles of such activities. Interest in such programs has grown significantly in recent years.

Volunteerism travel is world travel that includes people traveling and volunteering their time, and in some cases money, for charitable causes to help improve local communities. Many people on a vacation or mission are willing to devote time to helping on projects in developing countries ranging from providing medical aid or building a school to cleaning up areas so they are more sustainable. In many cases it is young people, like those in universities, looking for a special international opportunity that includes devoting time and effort aimed at helping to develop projects in poorer nations of the world. Another group, the so-called "baby boomers," those individuals who may have retired early and have the money and time to volunteer and have professional experiences they can transfer to others toward improving conditions in the world, often travel to destinations where they can support local development projects. While some volunteers have a specific reason for donating their time to special projects, others see helping needy people as a morally rewarding experience.[8] There are too many such volunteer travel organizations to mention in this section. Many are doing an excellent job, but there may be others that are less than ethical in their activities. However, overall, most such travel volunteer groups provide a service that helps toward the wellbeing of the citizens of the locale or the country involved.

Rural tourism and poverty

Possibly the most overlooked tourism policy question is that of tourism's impact in rural areas of the world. While most of the world's population lived in rural environments during the nineteenth century, as the Industrial Revolution evolved there was a gradual movement of people into urban areas in the twentieth century. By the twenty-first century, the greater portion of the world's population now lives in metropolitan communities. As a result, from an economic and tourism development perspective, little attention is being paid to poor rural communities in most parts of the world. It tends to be more difficult to find leaders in rural areas that have the interest or ability to recognize the great potential of tourism as an economic development tool. And yet, it is the rural areas of the world that suffer the most from poverty.

In *International Tourism Policy*,[9] Edgell noted that "Rural environments have vast expanses of land and water and wide diverse topographies (mountains, plains, forests, grasslands, and deserts) that provide outstanding settings for tourism." Later in *Tourism Policy: The Next Millennium*,[10] Edgell, mentioned that "Almost every local community in the world has some resource, attraction, activity, event or special interest or adventure opportunity that can motivate a traveler." That was followed by co-author Edgell's *Best Practices Guidebook for International Tourism Development for Rural Communities*,[11] where he stated that "Rural travel destinations still offer the most diversity in beauty, experience, culture, heritage and service." More recently in 2011, in "Investigating Best Practices for Rural Tourism Development" in the *Journal of Hospitality & Tourism*,[12] Edgell noted in the Abstract:

> [T]he research suggests that the ideas expressed in the paper are useful for both developed and lesser developed countries throughout the world. It presents research, concepts, philosophies, principles, and practices for investigating rural tourism. The paper argues that the utilization of the concepts of "coopetition", "clustering", and "sustainability (sustainable tourism)" offer the best opportunities for success in rural tourism development . . . The article advocates a need for additional research to bolster best practices applications in developing rural tourism destinations on a global basis.

As mentioned in many reports, rural areas throughout the world have a disproportionate amount of poverty in comparison to urban areas. Economic development through rural tourism has the potential to provide jobs, increased income and other economic benefits to poor communities, and improve the quality-of-life of the local citizens.

Many rural areas are turning to ecotourism development in an effort to improve their economies. While ecotourism has already been introduced in this book, very little has been said about its potential to alleviate poverty. In the case study at the end of this chapter, a discussion takes place with respect to ecotourism and its impact on a rural area in the Commonwealth of Dominica.

Conclusion

Transformative leadership in the context of this chapter related to the ability of tourism organizations to cope effectively and creatively to seek to provide a positive impact on world socio-economic conditions through the medium of tourism policy. The results of such leadership should aim toward an overall improvement of the world's social structure and add to the quality-of-life of citizens locally and globally. The thesis in this section is that tourism policies can have an ameliorating effect on some socio-economic issues with a result of overall improvement in the general welfare of mankind. The notion that tourism can contribute to alleviating poverty has attracted considerable interest by agencies for international development and donors alike. For tourism to have a significant impact on poverty reduction in the future, and to make global improvements in the welfare of society, the world's tourism leadership will need to make major policy shifts and plan new programs specifically aimed toward the support of the world's poorer nations.

This brief chapter concentrated on "transformation," that is, utilizing tourism as a transforming agent to alleviate poverty, to provide for a more tranquil environment, to improve economic conditions, especially in rural communities, and to seek a more peaceful world. Case Study 11 highlights ecotourism and its potential impact on the community of the Carib Indian Territory in the Commonwealth of Dominica. It is a good fit for the discussion that took place in this chapter. Utilizing ecotourism as the transforming tool to alleviate conditions of poverty that exists within the territory is a good experimental initiative to reflect on many of the concepts in the chapter. It touches on local realities in terms of potential poverty reduction by utilizing the principles of ecotourism.

Concentrating on ecotourism takes advantage of the fact that more than a third of travelers prefer an environmentally-friending tourism experience. Ecotourism, nature, heritage, cultural and "soft adventure" tourism are taking the lead in expected strong growth over the next two decades. It is estimated that global spending on ecotourism is increasing about six times the industry-wide rate of growth and hopefully the territory can share in such an opportunity.

CHAPTER REVIEW QUESTIONS

1. How would you describe today's world?
2. What is the United Nations' goal with respect to poverty reduction?
3. Does the UNWTO have a role in poverty reduction?
4. What role does the UNEP play in poverty alleviation?
5. How would you describe "volunteer travel"?
6. Does a peaceful world lead to more tourism and poverty reduction?
7. How does tourism help improve the wellbeing of society?
8. Are rural areas more susceptible to being poorer than urban areas?

CASE STUDY 11 Developing ecotourism in the Commonwealth of Dominica

This case study was written by David L. Edgell, Sr. Some information for the case study is based on Dr. Edgell's trips as a knowledgeable volunteer on ecotourism and rural tourism oriented toward the needs of the Carib Indian Territory in Dominica. During his visits, he had an opportunity for both formal and informal conversations, community meetings, and discussions with the Minister for Tourism and Legal Affairs; Minister of Environment, Natural Resources, Physical Planning and Fisheries; Minister of Information, Telecommunications and Constituency Empowerment; CEO/director of tourism; and Dominica's Carib Chief and other interested parties. The principal reason for Edgell's January 2012 trip to Dominica was to provide advice on the feasibility and direction of an ecotourism project within the 3,700-acre Carib Indian Territory located on Dominica's east coast.

This unique case study discusses some of the background information for the project which is ultimately aimed toward utilizing ecotourism to contribute to the socio-economic wellbeing of the Carib Indian society in Dominica. In the long-term it may be the springboard for other such initiatives in the territory, which eventually could have a positive impact on the overall sustainability of the area.

* * *

The Commonwealth of Dominica is a uniquely beautiful "nature island" or, as some might say, the lost "Garden of Eden". It is in the tranquil Caribbean Sea between the two lovely French islands of Guadeloupe and Martinique. As noted from the map in Figure 11.1, it is not a very large island. Yet it contains majestic mountains, serene coastlines, clear fresh-flowing rivers, geothermal springs, unbelievable greenery throughout the island, lush forests, and magnificent waterfalls. Mother Nature certainly left the island with bountiful amounts of different kinds of birds and butterflies, flowers of every variety, fruit and nut trees everywhere and a soil rich in nutrients conducive to good agriculture production, the mainstay industry of the island. In addition to the wide varieties of fruits, nuts, and vegetables the waters along the coastline are teeming with fish, the other main sector of the economy.

A little-known destination, Dominica, has preserved more national forests, marine reserves, and parks, per capita, than possibly anywhere else on the planet. The 72,800 inhabitants of Dominica present a distinct culture through the mix of the indigenous Caribs, and English, French, and African heritages that can be found in the food, music, dance, language, and traditions of the people. The people are very friendly, helpful and polite which makes the visit to Dominica such an enjoyable experience.

The Commonwealth of Dominica as one of "the world's best islands"

In Chapter 6 of this book, a discussion took place regarding criteria used by the *National Geographic* Center for Sustainable Destinations. These criteria were: 1) environmental conditions; 2) social/cultural integrity; 3) condition of historic structures; 4) aesthetics; 5) tourism management; and 6) outlook. A panel of 522 experts in sustainable tourism and destination stewardship donated time to review conditions in 111 selected islands and archipelagos. The experts' report containing the ratings on the sustainability of the islands appeared in the November/December 2007 issue of the *National Geographic Traveler* magazine.

The categories listed in *National Geographic Traveler* were "Best-Rated Islands," "Islands Doing Well," and "Islands in the Balance and Islands in Trouble." The "Best-Related Islands" were described as "In excellent shape, relatively unspoiled, and likely to remain so." Dominica's rating fell into the "Best-Rated Islands," with

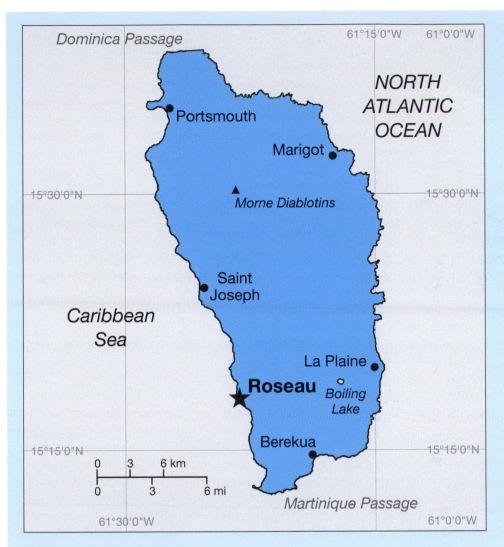

FIGURE 11.1 Map of Dominica and its major cities (Image: CIA)

comments from the experts who made the ratings: "Rugged, green, friendly . . . offers an authentic, unspoiled experience, with natural and cultural amenities." The only other Caribbean island with this high a rating was the Grenadines.

Tourism statistics for the Commonwealth of Dominica

A question that comes immediately to mind is why such a beautiful island as Dominica with such a high rating in sustainable tourism receives, relatively speaking, such a limited number of tourists? The Caribbean Tourism Organization (CTO), which Dominica and most of the Caribbean countries are members of, produces most of the accepted tourism statistics. In CTO's 2012 report on tourism statistics for the year 2011, it lists tourist arrivals to Dominica at 75,546. Comparable island numbers would include Anguilla with 65,783 and St. Vincent and the Grenadines with 73,866 and possibly Grenada's 116,398 visitors.

The CTO statistical report provides only brief insights with respect to where the visitor arrivals originate. Initially, one might think that the principal markets for Dominica would be mainland United States, Canada, and Europe. However, those three markets only accounted for a little over 40 percent of the total visitors in 2011. Much of the current visitation to Dominica is from within the Caribbean region.

In a review of the CTO's reports on "Tourist (stop-over) Arrivals and Cruise Passenger Visits in 2011," Dominica shows some 341,503 cruise passenger visits. Those numbers are higher than the 309,574 passengers for Grenada and a little less than the 347,914 such passengers for the Dominican Republic. The problem with cruise passengers is their visits are short and they do not usually spend very much money. However, the hope is that if such passengers have pleasant experiences during their visit, they may become good candidates for overnight stays in Dominica in the future.

So what is the reason for the relatively low numbers of visitors to Dominica from the three potentially large markets of the United States, Canada, and Europe? This is an important question and the answers are many and varied. Certainly a small island with a limited population is not likely to be able to compete, from a marketing standpoint, with some of the larger Caribbean islands because its tourism program is not as fully developed and the marketing budget is small. While Dominica's tourism office is well organized and managed, it does not have very many resources or an opportunity to partner with many businesses. There are no large hotel chains to rely on to market to a broad international audience. Much of the marketing must depend on participating in trade shows, producing and distributing tourism brochures and through the internet. In addition, while Dominica is a beautiful place for adventure and nature travel, it is not considered a beach destination, lacking the miles of white sand beaches advertised by its competitor Caribbean islands. Possibly the best current marketing tool for Dominica is word-of-mouth advertising by satisfied visitors.

From a development and marketing perspective, Dominica must contend with heavy competition from the other Caribbean islands. For example, in 2011 over a million Canadians flocked to Cuba for their vacations. US vacationers tend to visit destinations within their own islands of Hawaii, Puerto Rico and the US Virgin Islands as well as to nearby islands like Bermuda and the Bahamas. Europeans tend to favor Cuba, the Dominican Republic, the British Virgin Islands, the Dutch islands of Aruba, Bonaire, and Curacao, and the French islands of St. Martin, Martinique, and Guadeloupe.

Another difficulty for Dominica is the number and size of airplanes traveling to the island. While there are two airports, the major airlines do not fly their large airplanes to Dominica. For the airlines to increase the size of the aircraft or the number of flights is usually based on the simple question of demand. Currently Dominica does not yet have a large enough market to warrant an expansion in air service.

Commonwealth of Dominica as an ecotourism destination

Dominica is an excellent island for ecotourism development. Generally speaking, an ecotourism destination is described as being connected to the natural environment and local culture and implies that visitors should have an opportunity for a pleasant experience but in such a way that the destination is sustained for future generations to also enjoy. Ecotourism is a growing market for those destinations with the right qualities and which are willing to follow sustainable tourism management. The International Ecotourism Society (TIES) defines ecotourism as "Responsible travel to natural areas that conserves the environment and improves the well-being of local people."[13] TIES has developed specific Principles of Ecotourism: "Ecotourism is about uniting conservation, communities, and sustainable travel. This means that those who implement and participate in ecotourism activities should utilize the following ecotourism principles:

- Minimize impact.
- Build environmental and cultural awareness and respect.
- Provide positive experiences for both visitors and hosts.
- Provide direct financial benefits for conservation.
- Provide financial benefits and empowerment for local people.
- Raise sensitivity to host countries' political, environmental, and social climate."

Dominica is a good example of the attempt to implement these principles. It is one of the finest ecotourism destinations available anywhere in the world, with exciting adventure travel, hiking, bicycling, trekking, kayaking, fishing, diving, river tubing, aerial tram riding, horseback riding, snorkeling sailing, whale watching, and a visit to the Caribbean's only natural World Heritage Site, the magnificent Morne Trois Pitons National Park. The tourism opportunities epitomize the best in terms of sustainable tourism products, outdoor recreation, and leisure activities. Posted comments from visitors who have experienced Dominica readily extoll its many virtues as an unspoiled destination.

The government of Dominica both welcomes the opportunity to expand its tourism market but at the same time wants to protect its natural environment and its history, heritage, and culture. *Sustainable tourism* is the watchword for this beautiful island. Currently the best option to increase those visitors interested in sustainability and nature and adventure tourism is through ecotourism. Dominica is currently experiencing positive results from ecotourism development.

The Caribs and ecotourism development

The Caribs (English name for the Kalinago peoples), indigenous people of Dominica, have a fascinating history, some of which is encompassed in legend and other historical segments based on written accounts that have been studied over many years. Dominica apparently was first settled in about 500 BCE by a group of Amerindians, the Arawaks, who traveled by sea from the Orinoco River region of what is now Venezuela and landed on Dominica. They lived peacefully for almost 1,000 years until they were conquered by the Carib Indians.

The first European contact came on Sunday, November 3, 1493 during the second voyage of Columbus. It is not clear whether his boat actually landed in Dominica or simply passed close to the island. Columbus called the island Dominica; Domingo being the Latin word for Sunday and the name stuck with the Europeans who later dominated the island. The Carib name for the island was Waitikubuli or "tall is her body."

The Spanish first attempted to subjugate the Caribs but later learned it was easier and more convenient to simply trade with the natives, mainly for foodstuffs. The Spanish searched the island for gold and then left when they could not find any. Without a Spanish colony on the island, it was easy for France in 1635 to claim Dominica (along with several other Caribbean islands).

Initially France did not attempt to colonize the island. However, in 1715 France sent colonists to the island, which added another dimension to the island's culture. However, in 1763 the British, in a war they won against France, made Dominica a British colony.

Later, the French attempted to retake the island but, after that failed, the British fully settled the island bringing with them British customs and language. The British brought African slaves to the island and this resulted in an African heritage on the island. After many years of British ownership, on November 3, 1978, the Commonwealth of Dominica was granted independence by the United Kingdom.

Dominica is one of only a couple of islands in the Caribbean that still has populations of the pre-Columbian Carib Indians. Many of the Caribs in Dominica live on a 3,700-acre designated "territory" on Dominica's east coast that was set aside for them in 1903 by the British. The approximately 3,400 Dominica Caribs that live in the territory elect their own Chief who serves in that position for four years.

Thus far, the Caribs, as a group have been only a small part of the tourism industry of Dominica. Visitors can watch Carib artisans at work and purchase craft items from roadside stands. Their handicraft production, which include uniquely weaved baskets, has been handed down for many generations prior to the time of Columbus's visit to the island. Each one is different, in effect an original work of art, making such an item far more special than a simple souvenir of the island. This unique product begs a more practical marketing strategy.

Recently the Caribs have sought greater involvement in Dominica's economic structure, which includes tourism development. For the first time in Dominica's history, the Carib Indians have been awarded the separate cabinet position of a full minister. In addition the newly-elected Carib Chief has also expressed a desire for greater involvement by the Caribs in Dominica's economy. These political moves bode well for future possibilities of greater involvement of the Caribs in Dominica's tourism.

The ecotourism project in the Carib territory

A local Carib entrepreneur is currently working in the Carib territory, developing an ecotourism type project. He has three buildings under construction and hopes to have them completed before the end of 2012. Since one of the goals of ecotourism development in the Carib territory is to preserve and protect the Kalinago way of life through integrated sustainable economic development, he has used the Kalinago word "Aywasi" Echo Lodges as the name for his project.

There are many questions that still need to be answered for the Aywasi project, but the construction on site in the territory has been started. He has the support of the Carib Chief, and encouragement from other local Caribs of the territory, to move ahead on the project. The long-term hope of the community is that ecotourism projects in the Carib territory will eventually provide an economic stream within the territory and an incentive to preserve the best features of the area. Ultimately, if the initial ecotourism project is successful, then tourism can be counted on to help increase economic development, add additional income, create jobs, spawn new small businesses, and contribute to overall economic integration while enriching and improving the quality-of-life of the local Caribs and others in Dominica.

Dominica's tourism minister (political) and tourism director (operating officer) are fully supportive of an ecotourism strategy for the Carib territory as are other governmental leaders. If ecotourism in the territory expands beyond the initial project, it will need to be marketed as a very special experience within the overall marketing mix of Dominica's tourism products. Fortunately, Dominica already has considerable experience with ecotourism projects so there is a wealth of information to draw from at this stage. What may be helpful for the future development of ecotourism in Dominica, and particularly in the Carib territory, is to apply the concept of *coopetition* which has been fully explained earlier in the book. There would appear to be a greater need for an association of ecotourism sites in Dominica for the sharing of information.

Feasibility of the project

One question considered in the development of an ecotourism project in the Carib territory is whether there is a precedent elsewhere for this kind of a project. A very limited review of the literature on ecotourism-type projects on native lands suggests that in general "sustainable tourism" type destinations (includes ecotourism projects) are becoming more popular. The indication is that cultural heritage and nature visitors are increasing and are willing to spend more money and stay longer in their travels to cultural related destinations than is true for the average visitor to a tourism destination.

There are not many models to draw from that lend examples appropriate to the unique landscape of Dominica. One possible example is that of the Kuna Indians of the San Blas Islands of the Republic of Panama. This society has been reasonably successful in presenting to visitors their unique culture, language, customs, and locally-made products without undue corruption of their heritage and lifestyle.

Another reasonably successful example, also from Panama, is the sustainable ecotourism development project of the Embera indigenous communities that live within the Chagres National Park in Panama. The natives worked together to form a not-for-profit sustainable tourism organization and a community development tourism plan. The tribe feels that through sustainable tourism they can preserve their traditional way-of-life, protect the Chagres National Park, and improve their economic status. It has met with limited success.

Though certainly not a Caribbean destination, and not a part of a native tribe, The Denali Education Center in Alaska is worthy of consideration. It is a not-for-profit organization that partners with the National Park System. The center offers education-based packages to their visitors that present information on the unique flora and fauna of Alaska. Given the exceptional natural environment and Carib culture of Dominica, using non-traditional innovative ideas may be the key to a successful project.

Already mentioned in this book is the highly successful Maho Bay ecotourism resort in St. John, US Virgin Islands. Again, it is not connected to a native tribe but does provide an example of what can be accomplished through ecotourism if it is developed in the right way. This ecotourism destination has been around since the 1970s and provides helpful information for almost any location interested in ecotourism development. It provides a convenient ecotourism destination to visit and learn about the reasons it has been so successful.

To reiterate the original question of whether an ecotourism type project may be feasible and successful for the Carib territory in Dominica will not be known in the short-term. As the first project moves ahead, it will be helpful to carefully monitor the progress. While this initial project has been started, there remain many developmental questions to be answered. However, if successful, ecotourism in the Carib territory might just be the transforming initiative to help stimulate the economy, alleviate poverty in some parts of the territory and bring greater prosperity and quality-of-life to the local population.

Concluding critical questions

The leadership of Dominica, as is true for the leaders of other communities, has faced some tough decisions regarding tourism development. Questions that may have been raised in the past by those making development decisions can lead to a fervent discussion among students about the challenges and opportunities faced by a community looking for transformation. An initial question could be: Should a small island with limited natural and physical resources approach tourism development with an initial focus on supply or demand? In other words, should planners think about increasing marketing to the island or should they first consider ways to increase access to the island along with tourism activities and facilities? Much of this will depend on what already exists within the destination's infrastructure. However, Dominica has been gaining international recognition as a pristine environment that is worth visiting, which may lead to new visitors. How closely should the public-sector monitor or be involved with the private-sector developers looking to capitalize on opportunities in an untapped market? How does a community determine the optimal mix of new eco-tourism supply and new eco-tourism demand so that development does not tip toward being unsustainable and lead to a negative transformation?

Notes

1   United Nations (2000) *Millennial Declaration.* New York, September 6–8.

2   United Nations (2010) *Millennial Development Goals.* New York, September 20–22.

3   United Nations (2011) *The Millennium Development Goals Report.* New York.

4   Yunis, Eugenio (2004) "Tourism and Poverty Alleviation." Madrid, Spain: United Nations World Tourism Organization.

5   UNWTO (2011) "Report to the United Nations . . . Global Review of the Program of Action for the Least Developed Countries for the Decade 2001–2010." April 6.

6   United Nations Environmental Program (2008) "Tourism: Investing in Energy and Resource Efficiency." New York: United Nations.

7   Edgell, Sr., David L. (1990) *International Tourism Policy.* New York: Van Nostrand Reinhold.

8   Swanson, J.R. & Kline, C. (2013). SAVE Tourism in the Polar Regions: A Research Exploration (Chapter 7). In *From Talk to Action: How Tourism is Changing the Polar Regions.* Lemelin, H., Maher, P., & Liggett, D. (eds.). Thunder Bay, Canada: Centre for Northern Studies Press.

9   Ibid.

10   Edgell, Sr., David L. (1999) *Tourism Policy: The Next Millennium.* Urbana, IL: Sagamore.

11   Edgell, Sr., David L. (2002) *Best Practices Guidebook for International Tourism Development for Rural Communities.* Provo, UT: Brigham Young University.

12   Edgell, Sr., David L. (2011) "Investigating Best Practices for Rural Tourism Development." *Journal of Hospitality & Tourism*, 9(2).

13   TIES (1990) www.ecotourism.org.

CHAPTER 12

Future world tourism policy issues

According to most global forecasts, and information from leaders in the tourism industry, the future of the tourism industry will be one of change, vibrancy and growth. Travelers are demanding high-quality tourism experiences, variety, and flexibility in their tourism products along with a clean and healthy environment. Tourism policy and strategic planning will be crucial to economic prosperity, sustainable management and quality-of-life opportunities for most communities, destinations and countries of the world. A key to the prospective growth of tourism will be to ensure that careful planning and effective policies are in place. This chapter will introduce selected major tourism issues advocated by the co-authors that are important to an enduring tourism industry for the future. Each section identifies and briefly discusses an overarching tourism issue of important concern to the future.

The impact of the world's economy on tourism

What is happening with respect to the world economic situation has a major impact on the future of global travel. The global economic recession that took place for many countries in 2009 put a heavy strain on travel and for the first time in many years (since the terrorist attacks in 2001, which had a negative impact on world tourism) international tourist arrivals declined. In 2010 and 2011, while the world economy was still in jeopardy, global tourism increased slightly. However, some world economic reports suggest that final data for 2012 may indicate the economy is beginning to move slowly in a positive direction. The years 2013 and 2014 should show a slight increase in the world economy and by 2015 a full recovery should be underway.

The prospects for increased world tourism are very much dependent on a sound and balanced global economy. Many potential international travelers have faced economies in their respective countries that included high unemployment rates, increases in fuel prices, lower wages, stagnant product markets, and ineffective individual country economic and political policies.

Even though the world economy remains in a state of economic stress, there are a few countries whose economies and travel markets look promising. Two large populated countries, China and India, accounting for about one-third of the world's population, have had, over recent years, and continue to have, robust economies. Both these countries are generating substantial amounts of outbound travel. Some additional developing countries like Brazil are also showing improvement in their economic outlook. The economic situation in Europe remains sluggish and the United States' economy appears to be improving.

In spite of the recent economic setbacks, the global tourism market anticipates slight increases in travel in 2012–14. Looking back in the annals of the history of travel, in 1975 international tourist arrivals were 214 million and international tourism receipts were $40.7 billion. In 2011, international tourist arrivals increased to 983 million and receipts amounted to over $1.2 trillion. The United Nations World Tourism Organization (UNWTO) is predicting that "international tourist arrivals are set to hit a record one billion this year [2012]." This landmark number is indeed encouraging and possibly a good sign for the future growth of the dynamic travel market. Taken together, domestic and international tourism reached $6.4 trillion in 2011 accounting for 9.1 percent of global Gross Development Product. In addition, in 2011, the total contribution of travel and tourism to employment was almost 255 million jobs or 8.7 percent of total world employment. The World Travel and Tourism Council (WTTC) estimated that employment would be over 260 million jobs in 2012 and reach 328 million by 2022. While these numbers are impressive, if the global economy declines, and fuel prices increase, travel and tourism may not grow as fast as it has during the recent past. Obviously, a vibrant world economy means more people will travel.

Also related to the impact on world travel is population growth. The population of the world in 2012 was estimated at about 7.5 billion. The five most populous countries – China, India, United States, Indonesia, and Brazil – account for about half the world's population. If the economies of these five countries alone expand, global tourism will continue to grow. However, the world today is a global village and often what happens in one region of the world can have repercussions for other regions. Other than the world economy, population growth and fuel prices, there are many additional elements that impact on tourism growth. Factors such as a peaceful world versus wars and civil strife, the cost of passports and visas, airline and other transportation costs, government regulations, political relationships within the country and in conjunction with other countries, climate change, poverty alleviation, issues of congestion at some destinations, special events such as the Olympics, World Cup, and World Fairs, and the impact of world disasters all contribute to the growth (or decline) in tourism. But, in the long-run without improvements in the world economy, the global travel market will stagnate.

The chapters of this book strongly suggest that tourism growth is dependent on a country having good tourism policies and plans aimed at improving the opportunities for tourism development. It is clear that positive national and local leadership in tourism policy helps a country improve its tourism marketing capabilities, which eventually result in increased tourism. Strong policy action is required to adjust political divides over how to tackle economic and other problem areas currently taking place in much of the world. Since the world economies are deeply intertwined, world policymakers will need to work together to avoid a downward spiral in the world economy which ultimately would have a negative impact on travel and tourism.

Safety and security in tourism

Concern for the safety and security of world travelers remains an extremely important issue for the travel and tourism industry. Providing safety and security in the travel industry will continue to be a major challenge for tourism policy and planning. In brief, safety and security are vital elements in the provision of quality tourism. A tourism destination that is not considered to be safe and secure is not going to survive very long.

A first item on many security agendas is the universal issue of the relationship of tourism to terrorism; a factor in both safety and security. Over the years there has been considerable discussion about safety and security with respect to terrorism. While terrorism has existed throughout history, the terrorist attacks in the United States on September 11, 2001, became a rallying cry in terms of a need for national and international tourism policies to counteract the impact of terrorism on the tourism industry. The aftermath of this tragic event seemed to galvanize many nations to act together to design policies to thwart the actions of potential terrorists. Even though the 2001 event was many years ago, for the older traveler going through the onerous inspection systems at airports, it is a continued reminder of just how important safety and security is for the travel and tourism industry. The process of travel has become increasingly more complicated whether it is traveling by air, obtaining a passport or visa, or knowing which destinations are safe. It is important that we have good tourism policies that protect the traveler but at the same time are not so overbearingly restrictive and time-consuming to deter travel.

Chapter 11 mentioned turbulence, strife, and unrest as a matter of concern for the travel and tourism industry. Over the last few years the world has been troubled with many different global political problems, wars, and other kinds of turmoil that detract travel. But terrorism continues to be the most important single issue when it comes to safety and security. It was the concern for potential terrorist attacks, for example, that caused the British Government to spend large amounts of money, to amplify its security systems and to position 25,000 military personnel in London to ensure the 2012 Olympics were safe and secure for visitors and athletes. At many world events today there is heightened awareness of the vulnerability of the global hospitality and tourism industry to the challenges from crime and civil disorder to terrorism. Data and research on safety and security in the tourism industry clearly support the old adage, "When peace prevails, tourism flourishes;" but unfortunately the present state of the world is not very "peaceful."

Measures to support security, once seen as an encumbrance to travel (and for many travelers, particularly business travelers, it remains an irritant) are now endured, if not welcomed and demanded by many tourists. Accordingly, safety and security is now not only a requirement for transporting travelers, but also part of a destination's responsibility to assure the visitor of a safe and sound vacation experience. While the issue of terrorism permeates the agenda for security, perceived crime at a destination is also of concern for many visitors as well.

General crimes against tourists such as robbery, kidnapping, and murder are important issues for destination planners to combat in one form or another. In many places, statistics regarding a victim's status as a resident or visitor are not regularly reported or collected by local police departments. Nevertheless, when crimes against tourists are featured in global media stories and reports, the result is often detrimental to the overall image of the destination, despite the fact that the destination may be a low level of risk area and that the number of actual offences is minimal. A destination today may very well market their attractions as not only a wonderful place to visit but also a safe and secure experience. Increasingly questions from potential visitors to a destination often include: Is it safe to go out at night? Is it safe to wear jewelry in public? What areas should I avoid during my visit?

Global travel has increased despite the efforts of terrorists and criminals to disrupt the visitor experience. While the potential for attacks creates threats to the sustainability of any destination, safety and security issues may cause destination planners to implement positive strategies to mitigate future threats that would disrupt travel to the area. Many destinations, hotels and recreation areas have now developed readily accessible crisis management plans to ameliorate a highly volatile dangerous situation requiring immediate remedial action. Such emergencies may be due to climatic conditions (hurricanes, tsunamis, floods, etc.), fires, crime, terrorism, or some other situation. Destinations able to counteract such emergencies effectively and efficiently will earn a reputation as a safe and secure place to visit. They may brand themselves as a safe destination resulting in increased tourism. Most progressive tourism policies and plans have carefully designed measures to counteract the problems that might occur with respect to safety and security. Safety and security in the tourism industry will remain a major issue for tourism policies to resolve now and in the future.

Managing sustainable tourism responsibly

Sustainable tourism is part of an overall shift that recognizes that orderly economic growth, combined with concerns for the environment and quality-of-life social values, will be the driving force for long-term progress in tourism development and policies. We have a limited environment to work with, and much of the environment is already under siege from the many different industrial, technological, and unplanned tourism developments under way. To preserve these environmental resources, to impact positively on the social values of the community, and to add to the quality-of-life of local citizens worldwide and at the same time elicit favorable economic benefits for tourism is indeed a challenge. Sustainable tourism policy, planning, and management support social goals important to tourism and provide guidelines to give us direction as we move ahead. Without such guidance we might find tourism's future considerably less beneficial than we had hoped.

While Chapter 6 discussed many of the issues in sustainable tourism and included a case study with respect to climate change, there are many additional sustainable tourism issues to contemplate for the future growth of tourism. Better measures to educate tourism enterprises, small communities, and the traveling population about sustainable tourism must be continued as world populations and international travel increase. Respect for a destination's social, cultural, historical, natural and built resources today will be our legacy for future generations to sustain. More destinations will include sustainable tourism principles in their strategic plans. New policies on sustainable tourism will emerge as more and more host communities and travelers see the advantage of saving pristine destinations so that their children and grandchildren will be able to enjoy the same places as they did.

Research and education with respect to sustainable tourism is increasing quite rapidly. In the last five years there have been more books, research, and articles produced related to sustainable tourism than were available in the previous 25 years. There are more university courses and graduate programs in sustainable tourism today than was true over the past 25 years. While European, and a few non-European, universities have had programs on sustainable tourism education for many years, it is still a relatively new topic in many countries. For example, the first Master of Science Degree in Sustainable Tourism in the United States was started in 2010 at East Carolina University. Shortly thereafter, many additional programs have become available. This phenomenon is also true worldwide in many nations, as their tourism educational programs include a component on sustainable tourism. In addition, there are large numbers of conferences and general assemblies taking place each year with sustainable tourism on their agendas. Meeting and event planners are now frequently asking about sustainable practices at a potential conference site. TripAdvisor found in its recent survey on eco-friendly travel choices that 71 percent of travelers plan on making greener travel choices in the future. Furthermore, the number of tourism businesses implementing green practices is also growing.

While this book has given considerable importance to sustainable tourism, the significance of managing the cultural, natural, and social impacts of tourism cannot be overemphasized. Enhancing an understanding among nations and in promoting a culture of peace will result in improved sustainable tourism development.

In addition, an issue of interest in sustainable tourism that we are just beginning to better understand is the impact of climate change on tourism. So far there has not been enough attention in the travel industry to mitigation plans for responding to climate change. It will require collaboration and coordination from many world groups and organizations acting in unison to help solve some of the sustainable tourism problems resulting from climate change.

Progress in the field of sustainable tourism has made enormous progress and more is on the horizon. As tourism grows, so does the need for tourism policy and planning to help guide the development of sustainable destinations. The building of new airports, roads, ports, and sewage and water treatment plants improve the lives of the local people when they are designed with sustainability in mind. In short, the concept of sustainable tourism development has become better understood as an important outcome of good policy and planning.

In sum, the tourism industry can ill afford to go backwards and create additional problems for the natural and built environment. We now know that sustainable destination management within the tourism industry can augment global society's outlook and contribute to protection of tourism resources for future generations. We have also realized that science, education, and business practices are critical partners in the management of long-term sustainability. The world is also recognizing the contribution of sustainable tourism to alleviating poverty throughout the world. The future for a more sustainable planet is indeed promising.

Utilizing electronic commerce tools in tourism

Utilizing electronic commerce (e-commerce) tools in tourism is at the threshold in terms of its impact on the tourism industry. The increase of travelers using the internet in planning their travel and vacations has grown dramatically over the past five years. Many people now use smart phones for checking weather, destinations, directions, and other information during trips. A destination without a website is unheard of in today's tourism marketplace. True, some websites are much better than others but there is no longer an excuse for a poor website even for small properties and destinations. Today, "copy, copy, and copy" is the protocol for website design. Find a good website and use those pieces that best fit your destination or property. Websites have put large and small players on equal footing in many cases. For example, a bed and breakfast property with a good website can compete with the chain hotels such as Marriott or Hilton.

As internet access continues to increase in many nations, so will online travel revenues. The number of internet users around the world was estimated to be nearly 2.27 billion in 2011; a 528 percent growth rate from the 361 million in 2000. The bulk of this growth has come from the East Asia-Pacific region. There is every reason to believe that the use of the internet will continue to grow by large percentages in the future.

Although the interactions between business and consumer, or destination and visitor, are becoming less personal, tourism still exists in what might be called the relationship economy. While the internet gives the power to the consumer, strategic advantages will be gained by those organizations who can effectively utilize technology to create and nurture relationships. As slow-movers catch up to fast-movers, new technological advances must be constantly pursued in order for any advantage to be maintained. The future will include increased use of content customization based on visitor research. A proactive e-commerce strategy is crucial for tourism businesses to enjoy sustained success.

It is obvious that the use of e-commerce tools for tourism use will continue to grow and occupy a high-level placement in tourism policy, planning, and marketing discussions now and in the future. Several current e-commerce tools equip tourism well for what surely will be a high-tech future for the tourism industry. Information is a critical marketing tool for tourism destinations, and providing it to the traveler most effectively provides a strategic advantage. Tourism is an experience – a combination of products and services – the multimedia attributes of e-commerce can be effectively applied to tourism in cutting-edge ways to increase destination attractiveness.

Since a large part of tourism is marketing, tourism promoters who are technically savvy in interactive marketing will outpace their less skilled competitors. E-commerce tools not only connect consumers with suppliers but also create bridges among consumers and provide avenues for information exchange. Arguably, word-of-mouth travel accounts may be the best form of advertising for tourism businesses (if the experience of the traveler has been positive); however, today, through technology, there are many more ways to get the word-of-mouth experience to more people. Included in some of the tools being utilized for marketing are weblogs, podcasts, smart phones, internet, Global Positioning System, Travelytics, Facebook, Twitter, Pinterest, and many more. While tourism is still an industry where people-to-people contacts are extremely important – such as the pleasant person at the check-in counter or the concierge providing valuable information about a good restaurant – like in other industries, technology is replacing some of the people jobs. We have just begun to open the pages of the book on technology applications with respect to tourism that will emerge in the future.

Tourism policy and strategic planning

In Chapter 1 of this book, tourism policy was defined as "a progressive course of actions, guidelines, directives, principles, and procedures set in an ethical framework that is issues-focused and best represents the intent of a community (or nation) to effectively meet its planning, development, product, service, marketing, and sustainability goals and objectives for the future growth of tourism." Tourism policy and strategic planning should usually start at the local level so that the community where tourism is taking place or the location of the destination involved and the stakeholders all have an opportunity to express their views. However, in some situations it is better to enunciate a national tourism policy so that guidelines are available to follow at all levels of government and industry. The point is that tourism policy and planning may take different avenues of approach in ultimately providing improvement in the quality-of-life of the local citizenry. Many writings on tourism policy and planning get lost in an overabundance of research, or too many theories, and not enough practical advice, for non-academic individuals or communities to understand or be interested. Most of the chapters of this book have attempted to provide the basic research needed or practical examples that can lead an interested constituent directly to actions and applied solutions in formulating tourism policies and plans at many different levels.

The global tourism industry will face many differing kinds of issues over the coming years, and quite certainly, tourism policy and strategic planning will drive many of the dynamics of tourism well into the future. We can expect to see a greater global focus on the tourism industry's potential for quality growth. In tandem, sustainable benefits of tourism for local communities will continue to grow in priority and importance. There will be greater efforts towards partnerships of the private and public sectors in facilitating tourism in combination with poverty alleviation, developing policies to combat negative impacts on tourism and supporting the economic, socio-cultural and environmental contributions of tourism for the benefit of world citizens.

There are many global tourism issues on the horizon today and there will be more for tomorrow that will require innovative policies and creative planning. For example, how does the tourism industry respond to the global economic slowdown? Are there new approaches to making destinations more safe and secure? What can the tourism industry do to improve global socio-economic conditions? Will the ups and downs of fuel prices continue to disrupt the transportation of visitors? What can the industry do to maintain and improve sustainable tourism progress? Will we have available crisis management plans to deal with natural and man-made disasters? Where is the new technology going to take us? Which countries will be the newly emerging tourism destinations? What are we going to do about climate change? Where is the leadership for global, national, and local tourism polices going to come from in the future? These are just a few of the world tourism questions we must find answers to if tourism is to grow quantitatively and qualitatively in the future.

Developing new tourism projects, maintaining present destinations, and improving travel-related facilities and services require comprehensive policies and detailed plans that combine local needs, market competitiveness, and tourism sustainability. Those destinations, localities, and nations that prepare good policies and implement detailed strategic plans will reap the benefits for sustaining their tourism products in the future. When the policies and plans are multi-focused to include all aspects of tourism, the opportunities for future success will be greatly enhanced. Tourism policy for the future must link the planning function and political goals for tourism into a concrete set of guidelines to give us direction as we move ahead.

Tourism education and training

New education and training programs are emerging rapidly in response to the growth of the tourism industry. In the ultimate analysis, the success of the travel and tourism industry in the global environment will depend on the professionalism of its workforce. If a more professional workforce is to surface, tourism education and training programs will need to be strengthened. Industry-wide improvements are being made in the areas of quality service and customer satisfaction in most cases (the airlines being an exception). Recognition of travel and tourism career patterns, and of the training and higher education policies and programs necessary to support them, has taken a longer time to evolve. Much more progress needs to be made in fostering policies and plans to improve tourism education and training, but the prognosis now is better than ever.

Most university programs at the undergraduate level perform a credible job in teaching the basic tourism principles and practices. What is lacking is advanced courses at the undergraduate level or at the graduate level that teach leadership, especially with respect to the transformative impact of tourism on global socio-economic progress (see next section of this chapter). We need to search the research and information available to find what we believe to be the most basic and valuable principles and relationships in the tourism industry that serve the public good and ensure that our education programs include such in their curriculums. In that respect, effective leadership is an essential ingredient of positive social change for the tourism industry. Organizations such as the International Academy for the Study of Tourism and the Travel and Tourism Research Association provide some information on tourism leadership but it has not been a primary focus of such organizations. Earlier this book mentioned the University of Hawaii's Executive Development Institute for Tourism as a positive source of advanced training for executives and managers who, for the most part, have already demonstrated leadership qualities. Yet, it remains a challenge for the academic community to produce more research and possibly an advanced textbook that engages higher education in leadership principles and practices toward social change in the field of travel, tourism and hospitality.

Often travel, tourism, and hospitality students have very little exposure to world tourism issues unless they are fortunate enough to have a professor or required textbook that presents a global outlook. In many of our hospitality and tourism programs we teach the traditional required courses but may not discuss what it takes to become an effective leader in the tourism industry. While some professors may incorporate team-building in their classes, usually there is only limited emphasis on directions needed to develop transformative leaders who will be able to devise more effective solutions to present and future concerns in the global tourism industry.

Notwithstanding what has just been stated, considerable progress has been made in educating students and training employees to provide the quality services needed in the tourism industry. There are excellent basic training programs provided by institutions and businesses that prepare many of the millions of tourism workers to be better and more effective employees. There are also many innovative programs at some of our universities that provide courses steeped in the needs for managing tourism and hospitality programs. What we sometimes forget is that "education" is a lifelong pursuit and we need refresher courses along the way to keep us abreast of the new trends in tourism.

One area of tourism education and training that has seen many recent innovations is the application of online education and training in the global travel and tourism industry. In a new article (2013): "Online Education & Workforce Development: Ten Strategies to Meet Current and Emerging Workforce Needs in Global Travel and Tourism" online education expert Dr. Kristen Betts and Dr. David L. Edgell, Sr. address education policy as it relates to tourism education and training in the travel and tourism industry. It notes that institutions of Higher Education are primed to develop curricula that align with the current and emerging needs of today's workforce in the tourism industry.[1]

Transformative impact of tourism on global socio-economic progress

Until recently there has not been a concerted focus by the travel and tourism industry on socio-economic issues. Business people in the tourism industry, like most other industries, seek, as their major goal, to obtain an economic gain by developing and marketing their tourism products. Sometimes, in doing so, there may be little interest by some businesses in the impact their efforts may have on conserving the environment or improving the quality-of-life of the local citizens. The good news is that it appears that more and more businesses today are becoming interested in sustainable tourism and in concerns for the social-economic concerns of the local population.

Interest in sustainable tourism development by many in the tourism industry is having a positive impact for humanity and for the natural and built environments. It has become a collaborative activity at all levels, with the UNWTO leading at the global policy level and individual countries and destinations changing policies and plans to reflect the need for sustainability at the local level. In addition, regional organizations such as the Organisation for Economic Co-operation and Development, the Organization of American States, the Asia-Pacific Economic Council, the Caribbean Tourism Organization, and many others have also come a long way in supporting and emphasizing the positive attributes of sustainable tourism development.

Chapter 11 discussed many of the issues related to socio-economic progress resulting from tourism development, especially with respect to the lesser developed countries (LDCs). It included a discussion of the issue of poverty alleviation, a principal goal of the United Nations (UN). The UN recognized early on that the tourism industry could play a major role in helping to reduce poverty, especially in the LDCs. The UN challenged its specialized agency, the UNWTO, to take up the cause of poverty alleviation. While the LDCs have less than 3 percent of world tourism market share, their growth is taking place at a much higher rate than that for the developed countries. Part of the reason goes back to the discussion of comparative advantage in Chapter 4 of this book. Much of the underdeveloped parts of the world offer beautiful natural assets, unique and interesting culture, large quantities of flora and fauna, and enormous opportunities for adventure travel.

In addition, tourism is a very diverse industry. It has the potential for supporting additional jobs and providing economic benefits through the demand for tourism. A brief example may suffice to better explain this aspect of tourism. Over a period of years, tourism to beautiful Ambergris Caye Island in the country of Belize has been increasing as more and more visitors have come to appreciate the special opportunities offered by the barrier reef off the coast of the island (the second largest barrier reef after that of the Great Barrier Reef in Australia). As a result, new construction of accommodations has taken place, providing jobs for hundreds of low skilled young males who were otherwise unemployed. In addition, to accommodate the increased tourism, a new beautiful airport was built on the island, adding even more jobs. This has spawned an increase in other goods and services and provided an increase of opportunities for more female workers on the island. At the same time, Belize has launched a major sustainable tourism project throughout the country. As a result of the sustainable tourism initiative and the growth of tourism on Ambergris Caye Island, Belize is realizing the impact that tourism can have on improving economic conditions in the country and conserving the environment.

One of the case studies in this book discussed the potential opportunity that ecotourism may provide for the Carib Indian Territory in Dominica. If that project is successful and other natives in the territory take advantage of the opportunity that ecotourism development can have on their economy, a major step in helping the disadvantaged peoples of the territory may take place. The project has the potential to create additional small tourism-related businesses and provide new opportunities for agricultural and fish markets that are critical to the economic growth in the territory.

The impact of health issues, natural disasters, and climate change on tourism

Global health issues, natural disasters and climate change are extremely critical and worrisome issues with respect to their potential impact on tourism. Visitors to destinations around the world have become interested in knowing as much as they can about such issues before they travel. Fortunately, there is a substantive and growing body of literature by numerous experts on these topics such that our discussions here serve only as signposts to the future.

Health issues and tourism

With respect to health concerns, most travelers avoid areas that have high health risks. In addition, the likelihood that travelers can spread epidemics of certain diseases is a constant concern. Policymakers across the globe are concerned about the potential disastrous effects that, for example, avian flu could produce. It is well documented that diseases spread more rapidly due to travel, especially through international aviation.

Fear of disease reduces travel demand. For example, a few years ago SARS (severe acute respiratory syndrome) spread rapidly throughout Asia and Canada, causing a scare across the travel community. Another example is that of foot and mouth disease that moved from the United Kingdom to continental Europe, alarming many international travelers and local populations. Fortunately, the World Health Organization (WHO) follows closely such potential transfers of diseases by tourists and if needed, will issue travel advisories for those who do plan to travel to areas that have been affected by contagious diseases. Policymakers now need to address health crises in their own countries as well as to formulate strategies to react and provide support to the WHO.

Effects of natural disasters on tourism

The United Nations reported in 2011 disasters were the costliest ever recorded with costs approaching $380 billion. Earthquakes, tsunamis, floods, hurricanes, storms, mudslides, and other disasters will continue into the future and will impact heavily on tourism. Such disasters not only pose great problems for destinations, but may also cause airline disruptions and many other types of problems. Policymakers and governments alike are instituting early warning systems and preparedness measures in an effort to reduce the impact of such disasters. Potential visitors avoid areas that have been impacted by disasters, which in turn means tourism as an economic development tool is negated. As the tourism industry evolves and grows, new public policy tools and best practices need to be developed that respond to natural disasters. Policy formulation will need to be three-pronged to address: 1) the immediate needs of the industry and guests; 2) long-term recovery and rebuilding; and 3), prevention and/or impact minimization.

Climate change and tourism

Another rapidly emerging trend of international importance for tourism policy is climate change and its impact on tourism. This issue has become so large and controversial that its treatment is beyond what can be discussed in this section. A few of the concerns with respect to climate change were briefly discussed in the case study in Chapter 6. One aspect of policy is clear, tourism administrators must undertake a paradigm shift away from overuse of natural resources toward more interest in environmental stewardship. It is hoped that the lessons learned, and best practices developed and implemented by knowledgeable tourism industry professionals today – through sustainable tourism polices and strategic destination planning – will help improve management processes in place and make a positive difference for the future.

Quality tourism products and experiences

Today, tourists are demanding greater variety, flexibility, and quality in their tourism products. Quality tourism experiences are, and will continue to be, an important tourism issue for the future. Tourists are somewhat fickle, in that their demands for tourism products are constantly changing, although quality in their tourism experiences is always high on the list.

One segment of the travel industry that receives frequent complaints is the quality of air travel. Air travel remains a contentious travel issue as far as quality is concerned. Mature travelers experienced much higher quality airline services in the 1980s and 1990s and are not generally very happy with air travel today. Many airlines have dropped the important service ingredients of "flexibility" and "quality," making the worse part of a vacation the travel by air to the destination. The customer has very little recourse but to use the sub-par quality of many of today's airlines. However, to be fair, there are some exceptions and a few airlines still consider quality service as important.

There are many new tourism products coming on the market based on tourists' interests in a variety of experiences. Possibly some of the television programs, such as *Survivor* or *Amazing Race*, or other reality shows and travel and nature television channels are partially driving some of the interest in adventure travel or in exotic international travel.

One of the most interesting relatively new tourism experiences is that of space tourism. On April 12, 1961, the Russian cosmonaut Yuri Gagarin became the first space traveler. Up until that time the dream fantasy of traveling in space was just that, an impossible dream. While Gagarin's flight lasted only 108 minutes, it set the world on a completely new course of possibilities for space tourism. The stunning news of Yuri's accomplishment resonated across the globe and people were mesmerized by the magnitude of such a happening. If not for Yuri's space venture, US astronauts Neil Armstrong and Edwin "Buzz" Aldrin may not have walked on the lunar surface in 1969, creating another wave of hysteria for the world to comprehend. Again, while the thought of space tourism was on many people's mind in the past, it may be a reality in the future.

As the space programs in Russia and the US took off in the 1960s, the reality of space tourism, that is travel for recreational, leisure, or business, became a possibility in the late 1990s. The US never developed a space tourism policy but fortunately Russia did come up with a policy that basically said that if a potential space tourist had the physical capabilities, was willing to train for space travel, and had the money to pay for it, an arrangement to travel into space and visit the International Space Station could be arranged. From 2001 when the first space tourist Dennis Tito paid $20 million for eight days in space until 2009 when the last of seven space tourists, Guy Laliberté paid $40 million for 11 days in space, it was Russia's Space Agency that provided the training and the space craft necessary for the trip into space. Russia halted their space tourism program in 2011 but may revive the program in 2013.

The US retired its space shuttle and currently the only way to get to the Space Station is by a Russian spacecraft. In 2004, Microsoft co-founder Paul Allen and aerospace pioneer Burt Rutan teamed up to send the first privately financed, manned spacecraft called SpaceShipOne into sub-orbital space. In the meantime Sir Richard Branson's Virgin Galactic licensed the technology and is developing SpaceShipTwo. Richard Branson has announced that he and his children will go into space in 2013. There are a large number of people who have signed up to become space tourists, hoping that flights will become available soon. Tourism for many people, whether it is their first trip abroad, or traveling to a favorite destination, or desiring to travel in space, fulfills some of life's most cherished dreams. The future of tourism will only foster programs for those dreams to become reality.

Conclusion

This book has emphasized that it is tourism policies and plans that will best lead to resolving the issues on the horizon for the tourism sector. Stakeholders in tourism development should safeguard the natural and built environment and cultural heritage with a view to achieving sustainable economic growth that meets the needs and aspirations of present and future generations. The book has advocated that local populations where tourism takes place should share in the economic, social, and cultural benefits generated by visitors. The book has recognized the role that international institutions play in developing tourism policies, particularly that of UNWTO. It has also brought to light lessons learned from meaningful conferences such as those included in the *Manila Declaration on World Tourism* or *The Hague Declaration on Tourism*. In short, tourism policy and planning is essential for the future quality growth of tourism.

It is our hope that the understanding gained from yesterday's and today's tourism policy and planning will set the stage for future world tourism policy. The world is increasingly characterized by complex interdependence and, as such, needs to be cognizant of both the differences and similarities of peoples and cultures as we plan for the future of tourism. Explaining policies that include beneficial results to foster greater peace and prosperity to the world leading to a higher quality-of-life for communities and visitors alike has been a key purpose of this book. Tourism is not a panacea for resolving socio-economic and socio-cultural problems of the world but through well-developed tourism policies and plans the tourism industry can help establish a foundation for the future growth of quality tourism experiences for the next generations to enjoy.

CASE STUDY 12 Ten important world tourism issues for 2013

This case study is simply based on a note from the "News & Research information" section of the 4th Edition 2012 Official Publication of the Travel & Tourism Research Association (TTRA) which reproduced the "Ten Important World Tourism issues for 2013" as authored by David L. Edgell, Sr. TTRA according to Goeldner and Ritchie in their book *Tourism* (twelfth edition) "… is an international organization of travel research and marketing professionals devoted to improving the quality, value, scope, and acceptability of travel research and marketing information. The association is the world's largest travel research organization, and its members represent all aspects of the travel industry…" Reprinted from TTRA's newsletter, here are the issues for 2013.

Ten important world tourism issues for 2013

Submitted by: David L. Edgell, Sr., PhD
(Professor of Tourism, East Carolina University, School of Hospitality Leadership and Research Scholar, Center for Sustainable Tourism, Charter Member, International Academy for the Study of Tourism, Fellow, Center of Economic Excellence in Tourism and Economic Development)

1. Repercussions on the travel and tourism industry resulting from the global economic slowdown
2. Concern for safety and security remains an important issue for the travel and tourism industry
3. The transformative impact that travel and tourism has on global socio-economic progress
4. Negative impact of the travel and tourism industry of increases in fuel prices and airline fees
5. Importance of maintaining a destination's social, cultural, natural and built resources
6. Effect on travel and tourism from natural and manmade disasters and world political disruptions
7. Influence of increased use of electronic and other technologies on the travel and tourism industry
8. Changes in tourism demand resulting from increased travel by emerging nations
9. Greater interest in potential long term consequences of climate change on tourism
10. Need for increased national/local leadership in tourism policy and strategic planning

(Sources of information: university discussions; conferences and seminars; tourism documents; survey information; industry data; books, articles, and publications; utilization of a modified Delphi approach to gather certain research information and comments from interested colleagues, students, and others)

Note

1   Betts, K., & Edgell, D. (in press). Online education & workforce development: Ten strategies to meet current & emerging workforce needs in global travel and tourism. *Journal of Tourism & Hospitality*, Omnics Publishing Group.

Index

Note: page numbers in *italics* refer to figures; page number in **bold** refer to tables.

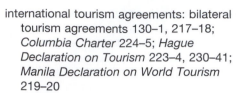